GLOBALIZATION AND RACE

TRANSFORMATIONS IN

THE CULTURAL PRODUCTION

OF BLACKNESS

Duke University Press   Durham and London   2006

GLOBALIZATION

Edited by **KAMARI MAXINE CLARKE** *and* **DEBORAH A. THOMAS**

AND RACE

© 2006 DUKE UNIVERSITY PRESS   All rights reserved

Printed in the United States of America on acid-free paper ∞

Designed by Amy Ruth Buchanan

Typeset in Minion by Keystone Typesetting, Inc.

Library of Congress Cataloging-in-Publication Data

appear on the last printed page of this book.

Duke University Press gratefully acknowledges the support

of the Frederick W. Hilles Publication Fund at Yale

University, which provided funds toward the

production of the book.

CONTENTS

ACKNOWLEDGMENTS

Academic books, like all books, represent journeys, and all the contributors to this volume have embarked on a four-year journey with us as we contemplated the analytic and practical relationships among processes of globalization, racial formation, and the cultural production of blackness in various localities. Accordingly, this book is truly the result of a collaborative effort. The idea for the volume first emerged as a result of a double session called "2001 Black Odyssey: The Cultural Politics of Race and Nation at the Dawn of the New Millennium" at the American Anthropological Association meeting in 2001. Organized by Deborah Thomas, Kamari Clarke, and John Jackson and co-sponsored by the Association of Black Anthropologists and the Association for Africanist Anthropology, this session was designed to interrogate the relationships between globalization and race in a range of ethnographic and historical settings. Most of the authors in this book participated in that panel, and our discussants—Maureen Mahon, Faye Harrison, Randy Matory, and Charlie Piot—contributed dynamically to our deliberations and we are grateful to them for their input, participation, and feedback.

The addition of several other essays here was intended to build on the ideas presented in that AAA session, and we extend our gratitude to the following presses for their permission to reproduce versions of copyrighted material:

University of Wisconsin Press, for Lee D. Baker, "Missionary Positions." A version of this essay was previously published as "Research, Reform, and

Racial Uplift: The Mission of the Hampton Folklore Society 1893–1899," in *Excluded Ancestors, Inventible Traditions: Essays Toward a More Inclusive History of Anthropology, Volume 9*, ed. Richard Handler, pp. 42–80, University of Wisconsin, 2002. Reprinted by permission of The University of Wisconsin Press.

The American Anthropological Association, for Jacqueline Nassy Brown, "Diaspora and Desire: Gendering Black America in Black Liverpool." An extended version of this essay previously appeared as "Black Liverpool, Black America, and the Gendering of Diasporic Space," *Cultural Anthropology* 13 (3): 291–325. All rights reserved. Copyright 1998, American Anthropological Association. Used by permission.

University of Michigan Press, for Tina M. Campt, "Diaspora Space, Ethnographic Space: Writing History Between the Lines." An extended version of this essay appears in *Other Germans: Black Germans and the Politics of Race, Gender, and Memory in the Third Reich*, University of Michigan Press, 2004.

Duke University Press, for Kamari Maxine Clarke, "Mapping Transnationality: Roots Tourism and the Institutionalization of Ethnic Heritage." A version of this essay appears in *Mapping Yoruba Networks: Power and Agency in the Making of Transnational Communities*, Duke University Press, 2004.

Isar P. Godreau, "Folkloric Others: Blanqueamiento and the Celebration of Blackness as an Exception in Puerto Rico." A version of this essay was previously published as "Changing Space, Making Race: Distance, Nostalgia, and the Folklorization of Blackness in Puerto Rico" in *Identities* 9 (3): 281–304 (2002). Reproduced by permission of Taylor & Francis, Inc., http://www.taylorandfrancis.com.

Indiana University Press, for Deborah A. Thomas, "Modern Blackness: Progress, America, and the Politics of Popular Culture in Jamaica." An extended version of this essay previously appeared as "Modern Blackness: What We Are and What We Hope to Be," *small axe* 6 (2): 25–48 (2002).

We would like to thank the Duke and Yale University departments of Anthropology and the Yale department of African American Studies for their support of this project and the Center for African Studies, including Robert Harms, Lora Le Mosy, and Feyi Adunbi, for their tireless efforts. Generous funding for the follow-up round table around which the ideas for this volume were debated and finalized came from the Yale Center for International and Area Studies (YCIAS) and we are grateful. Also, special thanks go to the discussants, Alondra Nelson, Michael Veal, and Patricia Pessar for their critical engagement.

Finally, we also wish to extend special gratitude to the various anonymous reviewers of this manuscript for their incisive yet supportive critiques and to Ken Wissoker and the rest of the editorial staff at Duke University Press for their ideas and hard work with us through the various iterations of this project.

INTRODUCTION

Globalization and the Transformations of Race

DEBORAH A. THOMAS AND KAMARI MAXINE CLARKE

It has become commonplace to speak of the contemporary intensification of processes of globalization and the ways in which they are continually reconfiguring the structures of everyday life. Late capitalist processes of production, circulation, and consumption have altered interactions among economic, political, social, cultural, and legal spheres and have generated complex deterritorialized practices. While scholarly analyses of globalization have proliferated, and while there have been recent attempts within the social sciences to consider the articulations among ethnicity, gender, and sexuality within a global frame of analysis (Verdery 1996; Povinelli and Chauncey 1999; Schein 2000), race and processes of racialization are not usually considered central issues in academic discussions of global economic and political transformations. Yet, because globalization today is facilitated by the transmission and reproduction of deeply embedded social prejudices rooted in a past characterized by territorial concepts of belonging that both generated and were generated by racial inequalities, the contemporary redistribution of wealth has exacerbated historically entrenched racial hierarchies. These are hierarchies that also articulate with ideas about ethnic, gendered, and cultural difference.

If we know that racial formations dynamically reflect and shape global processes and are not merely effects of them, why, then, have contemporary accounts of globalization tended to render insignificant a macroanalytics of racialization? In part, this appears to be the result of the anti-essentialist impulse in much of the progressive scholarship on race and racial identity, which though moving us away from biological notions of difference has also mitigated against generalized formulations of racial processes across time and space. The assumption here is that to make assertions about race in relation to globalization is to essentialize it because once we have "gone global" race cannot hold local epistemological purchase, except insofar as individual instantiations of race in specific locations can be exposed as fictions when bumped up against other iterations of race and racial difference. Therefore, invoking race in a global context seems to conjure up Western experiences of difference or generalized concepts such as white racial supremacy, concepts that reek of a kind of ontological approach to whiteness and blackness—an absolute truth about racial difference everywhere—that the constructionist approach disavows. The disconnect between our de-essentialization of race and our fetishization of the global, therefore, seems rooted in the difficulty of making an argument that gives race explanatory power once it has been established that race operates differently in different contexts.[1] Moreover, the analytic shift toward transnationalism as an interpretive framework in the social sciences and humanities, while providing a broader sense of peoples' networks across territorial boundaries and the ways these networks are both constituted by and constitutive of a changing global political economy, has tended to obscure the role of racial categorizations and racisms in contemporary social fields. This has been the case even though the transnational analytic has generated critical insights into the ways racial meanings circulate and how transnational political action has undergirded important social movements.

Yet the complexity of contemporary global processes can never be fully grasped without a deep understanding of the historically specific and dynamic ways race has both constituted and been constituted by global transformations. This volume intervenes in the debates between those interested in the political economy of contemporary global transformations and those who take a more culturalist approach to racial processes in the twenty-first century by foregrounding the ways that histories, institutional sites, and popular cultural imaginations are racialized. By compiling a volume that details the various ways that people traditionally classified as "black" or of "African descent" are actively transforming racial meanings, we have sought to develop an apparatus for thinking through the ways and extent to which contemporary global transformations are producing new forms of subjectivity, cultural practice, and political action that also move us beyond racism. Our goal is to build upon recent historical and ethnographic theorizations of transnationalism, diaspora, and globalization that chart contemporary processes not merely from the top down but also from the inside out in relation to historically complex and uneven regional formations.

Rethinking Race through the Geopolitics of Globality

How might we recuperate the power of race as a central category of social analysis without either falling into essentialisms or forestalling the possibility of developing a critical analysis that overarches the specificities of location? Of late, ethnographic approaches to globalization have made significant contributions to understanding how new developments at local, regional, national, and transterritorial levels have generated shifts in ideas about and experiences of citizenship, belonging, and racial difference. Scholars who use ethnographic methods—such as anthropologists, sociologists, oral historians, and cultural studies theorists—are in a unique position to bring to light such processes because long-term field research can enable complex insights into global-local interrelationships. As Leith Mullings has argued, "with its emphasis on underlying social relations and the informal workings of structures, networks, and interactions that produce and reproduce inequality, anthropology has a set of theoretical perspectives and a methodological tool kit that lends itself to the interrogation of new forms of structural racism and to unmasking the hidden transcripts of the process through which difference is transformed into inequality" (2005).

Furthermore, the more recent turn to multisited ethnographic research has reflected a growing insistence that these interrelationships must always be contextualized within wider webs of power and change over time (K. Clarke 2004; Clifford 1997; Gupta and Ferguson 1997; Marcus 1995; Matory 1994). Increasingly, therefore, anthropological accounts of global processes have offered a simultaneous focus on the specificities of particular locations (and hierarchies of locations)—whether these locations be villages, invented communities, nation-states, networks, or imaginative processes—and on the particular institutional and ideological matrices that exist at national, regional, and global levels, influencing and being influenced by local developments. By using terms like racial formation (Brodkin 2000; Omi and Winant 1986; Winant 2001) and racialization (Small 1994) to talk about processes that are having similar effects across a wide range of locations, without intimating that these processes are enacted everywhere in the same way, various scholars have demonstrated that "race" is neither fiction nor fixed. Instead, they theorize the ways people understand, perform, or subvert racial identities by mobilizing knowledges gleaned both from the particularities of their local circumstances and from the range of ideas and practices that circulate within their public spheres, showing that racial subjectivities are always "coalitional, contingent, and performative" (Visweswaran 1998: 77).

What we seek to do in this volume is to highlight contemporary work on the changing meanings and politics of blackness and in doing so to give readers a sense not only of how one dimension of racial politics in the twenty-first century is changing but also of how new theoretical approaches to contemporary processes of globalization are both shaping and being shaped by these changes. Many questions confront us: What are the qualitative shifts in forms of socioracial identification and subject formation that have been generated by new global circulations? How have modern conceptions of racial biology been replaced by new attachments of social value by which other measurements of human differentiation prevail? How has a changing global political economy generated dynamic ideas about belonging, "progress," "tradition," and "modernity"? Where do visions and invocations of "Africa" as an index of black origins stand in relation to the contemporary cultural politics of race? What constitutes blackness in the twenty-first century, and to what extent are American black hegemonies restructuring everyday practices in a range of global sites? What is the role of popular media and popular culture in generating and disseminating new conceptualizations of citizenship or community among people of African descent in the diaspora? What are the competing visions of community promoted within popular cultural forms? How do these articulate with those promoted by other social institutions and organizations, and how have they changed?

Combined, the essays identify some of the contemporary ways blackness is being reconceptualized, a reconceptualization that requires new forms of interdependence and autonomy and that is grounded in new ideologies, practices, and modes of communication. By examining both the particularities of global movements and the ways that these flows are mediated by historical processes, legal and scientific knowledges, and various forms of mass media and popular culture, we can learn much more about the complex ways individuals both adapt to and contest the hegemony of the nation. We can also examine the complexities of globalization in relation to locally specific processes of racial formation that in turn shape national and global public spheres. We present this work in order to begin to generate more accurate vocabularies to describe differences, to develop new analytics for understanding the globalizing forces of capital, labor, and technologies, and to situate current hierarchies in the making within histories of racial ordering. In doing so, we hope to demonstrate the ongoing power of blackness while still debunking racial essentialisms.

What Do We Mean by Globalization?

Social scientists, cultural critics, and historians have been engaged in heated debates concerning how to define the characteristics of globalization today and whether these characteristics actually signal the dawn of a new era (F. Cooper 2001; J. Friedman 1994; Hardt and Negri 2000; Maurer 2000; Tsing 2000). Though processes of racialization are not central to these analyses, they inspire us to think about ongoing transformations in the relationships among racial ideologies, trade networks, capital mobility, and governance. They call us to consider how the new ideas and practices that confront us are deeply grounded in centuries of movements—of capital, people, products, and ideas. They also demonstrate the ways the unevenness of these transnational movements has served the related processes of modern state formation and capitalist development and has reflected ongoing (re)organizations of social divisions and (re)classifications of human value in relation to changing social conditions. In other words, analyses of globalization that are grounded in a certain skepticism about its newness compel us to consider both continuity and change over time. Nevertheless, a substantial and growing contemporary literature has charted the diverse ways global transformations in the late twentieth century, and particularly after the cold war, have been different from earlier periods, particularly in the ways they have influenced—and been influenced by—racial, gendered, and class practices at national and local levels.[2]

Over the past three decades, the massive decentralization of capital accumulation worldwide has resulted in the growth of new centers of economic expansion, while older imperial centers and sites of power have declined. Simultaneously, rapid advances in information and transportation technology, as well as the circulation of new technologies of knowledge and communication, have changed the ways in which notions of space and place are both conceptualized and experienced. Moreover, the postcolonial and post–cold war decline of particular models of empire, and the subsequent remobilization of ethnic and national groups, has fundamentally reorganized global political spaces and economic configurations. The intensified mobility of postcolonial subjects has been spurred by a process whereby notions of racial and ethnic belonging have become increasingly dislodged from place, and once neocolonial subjects are "speaking back" to empire in complex ways.

Within the fields of anthropology and cultural studies, much of the early research on these processes tended to celebrate globalization as a postmodern liberation from the prisons of nationalism and other territorially rooted structures of domination. These scholars focused more on "flows" of people, culture, and capital within and between states and less on parsing the ways in which these flows were actually quite differentiated depending on one's point of reference. As a result, some early accounts offered unbounded elaborations of imaginative and circulatory processes generated by increasingly nomadic and cosmopolitan subjects, implying that everyone could equally avail themselves of the opportunities of (and for) mobility (e.g., Appadurai 1990, 1996, 2001; Featherstone 1990; Hannerz 1996). Other scholars have critiqued this model, calling for a more moderate detailing of the limits and possibilities in which these flows circulate. In other words, they have parsed how the mobility of some has been contingent upon the immobility or homelessness of others (e.g., de la Fuente 2001; Ferguson 1999; J. Friedman 1994; García Canclini 1999; Glick Schiller and Fouron 2001; Ong 1999; Trouillot 2003). These scholars have been intent to challenge universalist and celebratory analyses of globalization, paying specific attention to the sites where linkages are *not* being forged, where mobility is being restricted, and where forms of racism are intensifying.

More recently, scholars have also critically reflected upon the structural effects of neoliberalism, both within and between nations. They have demonstrated how worldwide deindustrialization and the rise of the service and informal economic sectors, the proliferation of information technologies, and (throughout the Third World) the implementation of structural adjustment policies have widened the gaps between rich and poor, developed and underdeveloped, north and south. What these processes have generated has not been, as several more triumphalist accounts of globalization would have it, an integration of the world economy (Fukuyama 1992) but rather a "fragmented globality" (Trouillot 2001: 129). In other words, the processes associated with globalization have been profoundly uneven and contradictory, and the result has been an intensified polarization of capital, labor, and consumer markets between and within countries.

While capital has become increasingly flexible, this flexibility has primarily benefited the new regional centers of the global economy—North America, Asia, and western Europe (Trouillot 2001; Ferguson 2002). Workers have not enjoyed globally standardized wage measures and integrated labor markets but instead have become increasingly differentiated across sectors and across national boundaries. The new transnational political economy, therefore, has worked through the persistence of an old racial order organized through socially entrenched divisions of labor in which a global working class not only remains in place (as compared to capital, which moves) but also remains segmented along racial, gender, ethnic, and national lines. And finally, though there has been an expansion of consumer markets throughout the world, this expansion has been facilitated by the economic, political, and military hegemony of the United States and has therefore privileged American styles and tastes (Jameson 1998; Lomnitz 1994; Trouillot 2001). For many scholars, then, the "planetary integration" of global consumer markets, especially among youth, has exacerbated tensions within and between nations due to the "limited means available to satisfy those new desires, and the always-specific discrepancies between global models and local ones" (Trouillot 2001: 129).

These transformations have generated an increased concern among scholars and policy-makers about the power and will of states to meet citizens' needs, especially postcolonial states throughout the global South. However, states have not become irrelevant and we are not living in a postnationalist era (K. Clarke 2004; Comaroff and Comaroff 2001; Glick Schiller and Fouron 2001; Sassen 1994, 2000b; Trouillot 2001). National governments continue to intervene in economic processes and state power is being redeployed in a range of sometimes unexpected sites, such as nongovernmental organizations, supranational agencies, and community-based institutions. In other words, as states have attempted to respond "to the challenges of transnationality" (Ong 1999: 7), some more successfully than others, the nation-state "continues to define, discipline, control, and regulate all kinds of populations, whether in movement or in residence" (15).

While the privatization drives associated with current processes of globalization have often had debilitating effects on communities at various levels, and while consumerism and individualism have "gone global" with U.S. markets, styles, and tastes saturating aesthetic and political preferences worldwide, it is also true that recent reconfigurations of capitalism have allowed some individuals to enter global circuits in new, and sometimes lucrative, ways. This is, in part, the point of researchers who have examined emergent transnational forms of family formation, economic advancement, political organization and mobilization, and cultural practice within the rubric of transnational migration.[3] Several scholars have also begun to explore the ways contradictions within processes of globalization have, in some cases, given rise to cross-race and cross-national projects, feminist movements, anticolonial and antiglobalization struggles, and other politicized cultural practices.[4] In these accounts, attention is often directed to the important links that are sometimes forged between such differentiated movements.

Generally, this body of scholarship tends to emphasize the ways individuals and communities negotiate, revise, and sometimes subvert the hegemony of the global political-economic and cultural marketplace, thereby playing an active role in defining global processes for themselves. In doing so, it also demonstrates that just as globalization has not rendered states irrelevant, global processes have not led to a worldwide cultural homogenization. Instead, contemporary capitalism has been shown to operate through difference, negotiating, integrating, and reflecting particularities while "stage-managing" the independence of nations it seeks to incorporate (S. Hall 1997 [1991]: 28). Moreover, while there has been a decline in the hegemony of (Western) modernist narratives that were previously framed as universal, the celebration of a kind of contemporary cosmopolitanism has emerged simultaneous to the intensification of narrowly defined nationalisms, fundamentalisms, racism, and xenophobia (S. Hall 1997 [1991]; J. Friedman 1994, 2003). In other words, as individuals, families, and communities attempt to create new boundaries for their own subjectivities in the contemporary era, older parameters through which difference has been measured have sometimes become reactivated and reenergized, ultimately resulting in a resurgence of racial and ethnic hierarchies. This is because global political, economic, and cultural processes and local experiences have constituted each other within the contexts of particular histories and hierarchies of power and knowledge. These hierarchies change over time but are always influenced by the legacies of earlier periods.

What is clearly critical to a more complete understanding of contemporary global processes is an integrated analysis of the historical precedents of current circulations, of how imperialism and racial ordering have shaped global movements, and of the ways conceptualizations of belonging, membership, and citizenship have been both imagined and institutionalized in racial terms. The relative absence of detailed analyses of the particularities of contemporary racialized circulations—who travels, what travels, and how transnational alliances are tied to particular knowledge economies—points to the need for historically grounded, multileveled ethnographic and critical research. It also requires the development of an analytic that makes central the relationships between institutional practices and racial ideologies, ideologies that are also simultaneously ethnicized, gendered, and sexualized in particular ways. In other words, blackness does not just index race; it also indexes gender, class, ethnicity, sexuality, religion, labor, nationality, transnationality, and politics. These dynamic relationships create social meanings specific to local, national, and regional contexts.

Recuperating a Racial Analytic for Contemporary Processes

The contributors to this volume explore how global political and economic restructuring over the past two decades has shaped and reshaped the ways that people experience, represent, and mobilize around racial, class, national, generational, and gender identities. Throughout, they insist that contemporary transformations in the production of blackness are as relevant to the globalization of late capitalism as deployments of "race-thinking" (Silverblatt 2004) were to earlier periods of imperialism, state formation, and nationalism. This is because the spheres of power that order micro- and macro-governance continue to be fueled by ideologies which emerged with the development and reformulations of our social worlds. From various perspectives and vantage points, authors explore the articulations between the forces of capital and cultural production known as globalization and the processes of subject articulation known as racialization. They examine how these two processes constitute each other over time, both materially and ideologically, and how they are part of a divergent set of changes that are producing new forms, concepts, practices, and patterns. They also theorize how experiences of racial, sexual, and generational identities that are often labeled "transnational" are still constituted in relation to very specific histories, cultures, and societies. Balancing macrolevel explanations—both material and ideological—for racial inequality and racial ambition with analyses of local responses, translations, and innovations, the authors explore the ways intensified globalization has both reproduced essentialist and racialized structures of citizenship and community and provided new technologies through which these structures are potentially transcended and/or subverted. They also investigate how the geopolitics of blackness are structured through complex relationships of dominance at various levels of interaction.

Their analyses, in turn, help to generate an analytic vocabulary for measuring the interplay between historical categories of racial differentiation and other linked social distinctions (class, gender, sexuality, religion, nationality, ethnicity) and the ways historically embedded patterns of racialization play out in contemporary transformations of daily practice.

The Scope of the Volume

We have identified three areas through which to focus our discussion of the transformations of race and globalization: (1) diasporic movements, missions, and modernities; (2) geographies of racial belonging; and (3) popular blacknesses, "authenticity," and new measures of legitimacy. Each of these areas captures particular dimensions of the political-economic and sociocultural shifts we have been parsing. In the first section, contributors explore how notions of community articulate particular understandings of blackness. That is, they examine the ways processes of racialization have been integral to the elaboration of ideas about humanity (or the lack thereof) and community, as well as how these ideas have changed or are being mobilized in alternative ways by different actors. The authors in the second section investigate how deployments of politics have both informed and transformed blackness. In other words, they show how processes of racialization have been imbricated with political mobilization at various levels and how these relationships have changed in the contemporary period. Finally, the essays in the third section consider how practices of consumption have empowered blacknesses, exploring how contemporary racial formations articulate with circulations of popular cultures. Of course, the dynamic dimensions of our subject matter overlap, a fact that has frustrated our attempts to create boundaries between sections. For us, the essays speak critically with one another, engaging similar thematic inquiries within vastly different historical and ethnographic contexts, both within and across sections. By grouping them in this way, we hope to emphasize particular aspects of globalization and racial formation while at the same time recognizing that the boundaries between sections are permeable.

Diasporic Movements, Missions, and Modernities

The contributors in part I of the volume seek to ground contemporary discussions about globalization's effects in relation to the trajectories of earlier moments. They demonstrate that the ideological fields in which people of African descent throughout the diaspora currently constitute subjectivities and political identities have not been limited to those generated by the contemporary period of neoliberal, capitalist globalization. Instead, these fields also always recall or revise earlier models of subject formation because current processes of globalization evoke—indeed build upon—those of earlier periods. The essays in this section explore the complexities of popular relationships to modernist projects, seeing modernity, in Donald Donham's formulation, as "the discursive space in which an argument takes place, one in which certain positions continually get constructed and reconstructed" (2002: 245).[5]

The idea of race and the hierarchical institutionalization of racial difference emerged dialectically in relation to sixteenth-century economic transformations that ultimately created what we now know as "the modern West" (Holt 2000; Silverblatt 2004; Trouillot 1995). While notions of difference operated prior to this period, the expulsion of Muslims from Europe, the initial European voyages of exploration and discovery, and the development of mercantile trade generated a novel situation whereby, for the first time, racialized labor became "crucial to the mobilization of productive forces on a world scale" (Holt 2000: 32). At the same time that the associations between nation building and imperialism and between racial slavery and the development of export-oriented mass agricultural production became more tightly integrated, new ideologies began to circulate in Europe about the nature of mankind. Within religious, philosophical, scientific, and political discourses, hierarchies of human value were mapped onto gendered, racial, and civilizational difference (Trouillot 1995). In this way, early state formation and mercantile capitalism inaugurated material and ideological processes that indelibly linked the "New World" and the "Old" in a common project of defining modern subjectivity in racial terms. In other words, Western modernity's roots are tangled up with the projects of imperial conquest, plantation slavery, and racial domination (Carnegie 2002; Gilroy 1993; Mintz 1996; Palmié 2002; Trouillot 2002; Winant 2001; Wolf 1982). Here, we use the term modernity not only to refer to the disciplining of a racialized labor force and the innovation of rationalized production and consumption on a mass scale that was made possible by the Atlantic slave trade (Du Bois 1935; Mintz 1977; Trouillot 1992; Carnegie 2002; Palmié 2002). We also mean to invoke what the anthropologist Stephan Palmié has referred to as the "sense of the displacement, rupture, heterogeneity, instability, flux, and incompleteness that characterizes virtually all social projects enacted in the region's troubled past and contradiction-ridden postcolonial present" (Palmié 2002: 42; see also Ortiz 1995; Stoler 1995). Because these racialized processes also remade Europe itself (Coronil 1996; Dussel 1998; Mignolo 2000; Mintz 1985; Wolf 1982), this formulation of modernity conceptualizes the Atlantic Ocean as an integrated geohistorical unit, an "area" in social scientific terms, where the structural transformations associated with early European expansion westward created what ultimately became a triangular web of political, economic, and sociocultural relations joining individuals, communities, and classes on three continents in a single sphere of interaction.

European capitalist expansion via imperialism and slavery was therefore crucial to the establishment of the first truly global markets of exchange (of both bodies and commodities—or more accurately, of the African body as one among several commodities), as well as the infrastructures these markets required (E. Williams 1993 [1944]). The nexus of capitalism, imperialism, state formation, and modernity also generated an approximation of political and economic spheres of interaction within both the Caribbean colonies and their European metropoles, and within the emergent United States. This early moment of globalization engendered a common language not only for an accepted wisdom regarding scales of humanity but also for related notions of personal freedoms and political revolutions (Holt 2000; C. L. R. James 1989 [1963]).

From various vantage points, therefore, the contributors in part I historically and ethnographically introduce themes that will animate the rest of this volume by asking several questions. What does it mean to be "modern"? What is the place of people of African descent in the "modern" world given their cultural heritage (or purported lack thereof)? How have people defined progress and development while simultaneously critiquing the rational logic of universal truths? And how do we, as scholars, locate and interpret these definitions? The authors not only attempt to define the changing relationships between North American, Caribbean, and European blacks and modernity (variously conceived as civilization, freedom, progress, and community building), but in doing so they also reveal the political concerns that have been current during various moments of social reevaluation. In turn, these emphases allow them to raise questions about the assumptions that have shaped the elaboration of political and cultural communities.

This work moves away from earlier formulations of diaspora that tended to rely upon the idea of an initial dispersal or migration from an originary homeland. Instead, the contributors here view diaspora as process, a process that generates subjects through negotiations arising from particular structural and historical conditions that change over time (Axel 2002; J. Brown 1998; Campt 2004; K. Clarke 2004; B. Edwards 2001). We are interested in "examining how historically-positioned subjects identify both the relevant events in transnational community formation and the geographies implicated in that process" (J. Brown 1998: 293). This is an intervention begun in earnest by Paul Gilroy, who argued that black communities were linked transnationally not through a perceived connection to an actual or mythical "Africa" but by the mutual perception of a shared racial oppression (Gilroy 1987). Borrowing from Robert Farris Thompson's development of diasporic black unity, Gilroy uses the term "Black Atlantic" (1993) to designate a different kind of community, one that simultaneously defied racial essentialism, nationalist narratives of belonging, and ethnic absolutism, foregrounding instead the ongoing generation of "a relational network" (Gilroy 2000: 123) in ways that would transcend territorial boundaries and epistemological frameworks.

Gilroy's intervention also redirected a scholarly emphasis on migration and displacement through his demonstration of how black communities worldwide were actively made and remade via the circulation and adaptation of cultural and political resources among them. By highlighting the ways twentieth-century black communities in England appropriated black American "raw materials" in the production of popular meanings of blackness, Gilroy began a focus on understanding how power works through the construction of diasporic belonging. Subsequent studies built on his insights, further unpacking the contextual complexities implicated within these circulations. In her analysis of Gilroy's work, Jacqueline Nassy Brown has argued that "diaspora may very well constitute an identity of passions, but these passions, and the means of pursuing them, may not be identical within particular communities" (1998: 298). Here, she suggests that we must recognize that the relational networks among different black communities, and between differently gendered or classed people within particular black communities, are also structured by the same dynamics of power and hegemony that constituted the diaspora itself (see also Campt 2004). On one hand, this means that we must pay close attention to the ways the geopolitical dominance of the United States has shaped the relationship of African Americans to people of African descent elsewhere. On the other, it forces us to examine the diasporic "communities" not as unitary but as divided by issues related to class, gender, sexuality, and generation.

We are interested, therefore, in highlighting not only the potential solidarities that might be generated by the invocation of either "diaspora" or "Black Atlantic" but also the misunderstandings, differences, and arguments that arise because these solidarities are always contextualized within power relations that are locationally and temporally specific. Where Gilroy prefers the term "diaspora" as an alternative to the "totalizing immodesty and ambition of the word 'global,'" (2000: 123), we choose a critical, historical, and place-specific approach to globalization in order to foreground an analysis of the circulations and hierarchies contextualizing black communities at particular times in particular locations and in particular relations of power vis-à-vis one another. We also use globalization rather than Black Atlantic as our analytic rubric here in order to move beyond the spatial and geopolitical dynamics of the Atlantic cartography to consider other circulations as equally critical in the unveiling of counterhistories and the constitution of community.

Lee D. Baker, a historian of anthropology, starts us off by tracing the connections among American Protestant missionaries' civilizing projects, U.S. imperialism, and the political uses of folklore in order to make two important points. First, he demonstrates that initiatives that perhaps look like diasporic cultural projects with political implications—such as redeeming the cultural value of "Africa" for people of African descent in the "New World"—might instead be socially conservative schemes linked to imperial missions. In the case he examines, members of the folklore society formed by educators at the Hampton Normal and Agricultural Institute used the late nineteenth-century collection of African American folktales as part of their attempt to foster a Christian civilization among its graduates by identifying and then rooting out (rather than celebrating, as would be the case later during the Harlem Renaissance) American cultural patterns thought to be West African in derivation. In doing so, leaders in the industrial education movement emphasized a politics of racial accommodation and cultural assimilation. Second, Baker links this difference in the political purchase of African American cultural forms to more general civilizing missions among America's newly colonial "natives" during the late nineteenth century throughout the South Pacific, and later among Native American populations. In directing our attention to how religion has been a critical institution that mediates and shapes ideas about Africa and African cultural heritages that circulate within a global public sphere at different times, this essay clarifies how missionaries defined modernity, progress, and ultimately citizenship among communities of people (African Americans, Pacific Islanders, and Native Americans) who were thought to be related.

While Baker's essay focuses on how religious practice was linked to processes of colonial state formation and cultural reform in the late nineteenth century and the early twentieth, Robert Adams directs our attention to the dynamism of popular religion and its articulation of alternative modernist projects during the same period. His investigation into the conditions surrounding the rise, fall, and legacy of Olivorio (Liborio) Mateo, a messianic leader in the Dominican Republic's San Juan Valley at the beginning of the twentieth century, gives us insight into the ways *campesinos* came to define modernity dialectically in relation to visions of progress elaborated both by elite Dominicans and by U.S. Americans. For Adams, Dominican Vodú is best understood not as a simple African "survival," but as a living and growing practice, one that addresses the changing economic, political, and social realities facing San Juaneros. Again, Adams's essay shows how local expressive cultural practices have emerged from particular relations of power and circulations of labor—in this case, a history of Spanish colonialism and rising American imperialism, Haitian economic and political dominance, economic liberalization, technological innovation, and the move toward establishing a centralized modern Dominican nation-state. Yet here he emphasizes how people mobilized alternative definitions of community (diasporic, intercultural, anti-imperialist) and progress (collective land use, charismatic religious authority). Aligning himself with other recent scholarship on the kinds of religious expressions and spectacles that have accompanied twentieth-century integration into global capitalist markets (Comaroff and Comaroff 1993, 1997, 2001; Piot 1999), Adams argues that scholars need to take seriously these kinds of alternative formulations during earlier periods as well, seeing them as part and parcel of what modernity is—fantastical, fetishized, magic— and understanding them as innovative interventions people make in order to shape modernity for themselves.

Both Baker's and Adams's contributions address the articulations between growing U.S. hegemony throughout the twentieth century and the visions of "Africa" and "African cultural heritages" that were being mobilized toward divergent ends within a global public sphere. The three remaining essays in this section elaborate these themes, concerning themselves not only with the place of "Africa" in diasporic imaginations and political formations but also with the place of "African America" and its relationship to black communities outside the United States at specific historical moments during the long

American century. Jacqueline Nassy Brown investigates the formative influ-ences "black America" has had on racial identity and politics at critical junctures in Liverpool, England. In her essay, she charts the changing con-nections between black Liverpool and black America in the immediate after-math of World War II and during the era defined by U.S. civil rights and black power movements. She focuses on the circulations of African, Afro-Caribbean, and native black Liverpudlian men who were employed as sea-men by Liverpool's shipping companies; of black Liverpudlian women who emigrated to "black America," often as the result of alliances with black American men; and of black American cultural productions that circulated with American GIs. Nassy Brown's historical and ethnographic exegesis here is designed to ground processes of globalization and racial formation in localities rather than through displacement and in terms of difference rather than similarity in order to challenge notions of the Black Atlantic as a soli-dary community.

Tina Campt builds on Brown's arguments to show how lateral connections between communities of black people throughout the world can unravel as quickly as they are forged, even in dialogical encounters between individuals. Like Brown, Campt is interested in thinking through the limits and tensions of diasporic solidarity. To do so she parses when and how moments of connection and disconnection occurred between herself as a researcher and the black German individuals she interviewed as part of her broader project about Afro-German histories of racism, resistance, and struggle; the pro-cesses of racialization during the Third Reich; and the politics of race, gender, and sexuality in early-twentieth-century Germany. Campt's agenda is to clar-ify what is distinctive about the experiences of Afro-Germans, thereby chal-lenging the tendency to privilege similarity and commonality in discussions of the relations among black communities transnationally. She also questions the centrality of narratives of home, belonging, and community within Black Atlantic populations by demonstrating that black Germans have had to mo-bilize a vision of diaspora that, because of their specific histories, is not rooted in a memory of an experienced commonality but is conceptualized as a "space in which the relations, definitions, and identifications within and between communities come to materialize and to matter as 'real' in ways that are strategically useful" (p. 110).

Naomi Pabst continues this line of inquiry by investigating what is at stake in negotiating the geopolitical axis of black subjectivity. Pabst argues that black Canadians are doubly marginalized. On one hand, they are cast out of

Canadianness through the official discourse of multiculturalism, a discourse that disavows racism by positioning citizens as cultural, rather than racial, others. On the other hand, she maintains that black Canadians are also cast out of hegemonic definitions of blackness. This is because blackness is seen as American, and Canadian nationalist ideology is rooted in "a collective sense of self as *un*-American" (p. 118). This dual displacement persists, Pabst notes, despite the documentation of a black presence in Canada since the early 1600s, despite visions of Canada as a prospective (if often symbolic) home-land for antebellum African Americans following the underground railroad, and despite the fact that Canada hosted the inaugural meeting of W. E. B. Du Bois's Niagara Movement, the movement which would later become the NAACP. For Pabst, blackness is always already transnational. Throughout her essay, she thinks through the early transnational subjectivities forged across the border between the United States and Canada and the ways they were formed in relation to geopolitical and transhistorical manifestations of global processes. Like Brown and Campt, she argues that "if diaspora gestures to simultaneous difference and sameness among a transnational circuitry of subjects partially descended from Africa, it is also about geopolitical power differentials" (p. 116).

Geographies of Racial Belonging

While the essays in part I provided windows into specific instantiations of the cultural dynamics of globalization, parsing the particular histories of politi-cal, economic, and racial circulations that both shaped and were shaped by local experiences, those in part II move us toward an engagement with how these dynamics have been mobilized by scholars, policy-makers, and activists over time. The key issues to clarify in the mapping of diasporic circulations of belonging have to do with the kinds of relations that emerge in various local fields of engagement where race has been fundamental to membership and where the production of knowledge, as it moves in space, has been firmly tied to the production of racial difference.

Imperialism, slavery, and colonial exploitation created enduring global linkages that were sustained through the postemancipation period of the mid-nineteenth century and into the twentieth century. As science eclipsed religion as the dominant discourse of empire, advocates for slavery and colonial expansion helped to institutionalize the new science of anthropol-ogy, in part to counter abolitionists' claims based on morality and biblical tenets. As the discipline developed during the late nineteenth century, human difference was parsed along a color-coded hierarchy from savage to civilized—from black to white (Baker 1998). The fact that some researchers documented customs and behaviors while others measured brains and bodies did not change this hierarchy because human diversity and cultural differences were blurred and racially mapped in a way that privileged biology as the basis for human difference.

Though in the United States some anthropologists effectively challenged the basis of eugenics research, the institutionalization of anthropological science had the effect of solidifying earlier hierarchical classifications of racial groups. During the early twentieth century, these classifications were further concretized through village studies that conceptualized the distinctiveness of various "peoples" and "cultures" in relation to territorially based conceptualizations of belonging. Yet because racial biology—as the science of empire—was fundamental to the founding of the circumatlantic world, these territorially rooted distinctions continued to be mapped racially. Despite Franz Boas's early argument for an analytic (and political) distinction between race and culture, traditional debates within the anthropology of the African Diaspora—and among various activist communities—have often employed nineteenth-century biological notions of race as the predominant basis for connection and continuity.

However, other changes were afoot in the early twentieth century as altered relationships between production and consumption also transformed racial meanings, which now circulated with the movement of both laborers and intellectuals between the United States, Europe, and Africa (Gilroy 1993; B. Edwards 2003). The emergence of race-conscious movements such as pan-Africanism, Garveyism, and the Niagara Movement reflected some of these transformations while further reinforcing a cultural politics of racial belonging and membership. While pre-Fordist socioeconomic and political arrangements in the United States required that racialized labor forces remain fixed within the particular (material and ideological) places to which they were transported, by the middle of the twentieth century Fordist models of production and consumption instead relied upon a massive movement of these same labor forces out of their place, "from South to North in the United States, from colony to metropole in the British and French West Indies, from country to city in southern and western Africa" (Holt 2000: 70). This movement, facilitated by the liberalization of U.S. immigration laws in 1965, generated a transnational wave of cultural practices from homelands (in particular, the Caribbean, Latin America, and Asia) to new lands (the United States, and to a lesser degree, Europe and Canada).

By the mid-twentieth century, these changes spurred the transformation of locally particular notions of difference into discourses of ethnic and national descent and belonging. And as Kamari Clarke's essay will demonstrate, this reordering of human subjectivity increasingly in terms of ethnic heritage—such as African American, black British, black Canadian,[6] and Indo-Chilean—follows structurally related shifts in the language of contemporary American racial organization particular to the post-1965 period. During this period, the intensification of civil rights discourses against discrimination generated new ideologies about racial belonging and racial difference. These changes, combined with the earlier establishment of African American transnational political and cultural institutions, set the stage for the formation of a post–civil rights heritage movement and the development of closely connected corporate interests willing to exploit lucrative markets (see also Hernandez-Reguant 1999; K. Clarke 2004). The cultural formation of a new *commercial* politics of linkage between people in the Americas and those in related "homelands" set the stage for the establishment of a heritage category through which linkages to origins were used to supplement national identity and citizenship. In the social sphere, this emphasis on diasporic interconnection redefined prevalent notions of biological race to that of cultural race, here shaped by conceptions of ethnicity, or ancestral heritage. Though it manifested in deterritorialized contexts, this notion of heritage was actually deeply territorial but reflected a historical rather than an ontological or biological notion of race.

This is not a trend that has been limited to the United States, but is one that manifests differently within different contexts. Recognizing that diasporic connections are made and remade, undermined and transformed means that we must recognize that they are neither universally constituted nor static. Placing change and innovation at the center of examining the making and circulation of meanings has significant implications for how we approach the category of race in the twenty-first century. It makes it critical to understand the historical and geopolitical processes through which transnational formations are reconceptualized through regional networks and, therefore, the need for studies of racial process to be more attuned to the ways changing relations of power globally have generated innovative alliances.

The essays in this part frame the ways in which racial categories invented in Europe were imported and developed in the Americas and have set particular standards of racial value by which social hierarchies were established in the building of the West. They ask how the events of slavery and later dispersals, as well as the invocations of spatial geographies, constitute the resultant inequalities being redressed. How do these experiences generate a transnational language through which to interrogate the making, excluding, and legitimization of alliances? And how does attention to the salience of difference and disjuncture undermine this project? The arguments presented underline how critical a recognition of the historical particularities that shape black enslavement and the workings of transnational capital in the production of new capitalist markets are to an understanding of what is new about the workings of claims to racial belonging today. At the same time, the contributors in this section are investigating the conditions of possibility undergirding contemporary racial formations and forms of economic mobilization in which geopolitical approaches to racial difference in the contemporary present are negotiated in complexly historical forms.

Building on conceptions that speak to a postbiological race context in which people are struggling to talk about and live notions of racial difference in a range of ways, Kamari Clarke explores a U.S.-based historical example of the ways that racial categories are being reconfigured institutionally via a broad-based diasporic reformulation of race and citizenship in terms that have more to do with culture and heritage. This reformulation also provided a terrain for the constitution of racial distinctions that would reflect a quest for rights—for protesting for better working and social conditions, access to employment, gender equity, and overall equality for dispossessed people. By demonstrating how the development of particular popular cultural conceptions of black identity enabled African American cultural brokers—such as public intellectuals, religious leaders, cultural workers, and government officials—to create new kinship narratives of the black past, Clarke traces a genealogy of black popular activism over the late nineteenth century through the twentieth in order to track the emergent forms of institutional racial consciousness that took shape in the late twentieth century. However, as she argues, these new conceptions of race based on heritage and a rights-endowed subject have not supplanted biological conceptions. Instead, the politics of rights and the shifts in market technologies worked alongside economic and political institutions to produce a new language for classifying race institutionally. What Clarke is suggesting here is that while the materiality of biological concepts of race, such as phenotype, still operate to enforce hierarchies of racial aesthetics and value, within the U.S. context of the mid- to late-twentieth-century biological race as a cultural and institutional unit of classification has in some cases been replaced and in many cases supplanted by cultural heritage classifications. The trend toward cultural heritage has also had significant implications for notions of political belonging. Biological race, which, through modern science authorized the terms of U.S. citizenship, has subsumed a redefinition of ancestral heritage that was propelled by the rights movement, transnational migration, and the flexibility of economic markets.

Kesha Fikes continues our exploration of how the geopolitical has generated innovations in identity classification. Her essay is an attempt to examine how the Portuguese colonial state utilized voluntary and forced labor migrations in a fashion that mapped ideals of racial progress and social degeneracy within Cape Verde. By examining the ways that identity patterning can be traced through the histories of migrant plantation laborers and the creation of contemporary forms of globalization (i.e., transnational labor migrations), she documents how people engage the global labor market to transform their political identities via their places of settlement. In the same way that Clarke examines how narratives of slavery and nobility are used by some middle-class black Americans to draw linkages to Africa, Fikes questions how American representations of Cape Verdean raciality—as nonbinary—emerge as resources that 1) confirm U.S. models of racial identification, which are associated with appropriate ideals of racial consciousness and struggle, while 2) eliding the fact that Cape Verdean raciality was a colonial production that serviced Portuguese labor interests across nations and empires. In short, Fikes questions how the collaborative consequences of these two processes service diverse transnational interests; they each position the Cape Verdean subject as a dehistoricized and/or demoralized entity. Her objective, thus, is to consider how Cape Verdeans' use of the Portuguese passport—and thus Portuguese nationality and/or citizenship—became a means of guaranteeing one's participation in labor activities that were voluntary and not regulated by the Portuguese. Fikes observes how such efforts, which necessarily required transformations in one's racial status, are made possible through forms of legal belonging that emerge through transnational movement.

Like Fikes and Clarke, Isar Godreau highlights another social mapping of space—that of the intentional geographical mapping of state-organized neighborhoods. Her essay begins with an exegesis of the discursive terms through which blackness was folklorized and celebrated institutionally as part of the nation in Puerto Rico. Godreau examines a government-sponsored housing project that was revitalized as a historic black site. In an attempt to document the controversy that emerged from this initiative, she elaborates the government's approach to racial discourses that represent blackness as a vanishing and distant component of Puerto Rico. Arguing that this simultaneous inclusion, celebration, and marginalization complements ideologies of *blanqueamiento* (whitening) and race-mixture that push blackness to the margins of the nation, and that it romanticizes black communities as remnants of a past era, Godreau, like Adams in part I, examines how modernizing state agendas and discourses of authenticity are also used to fuel cultural nationalisms in transnational contexts.

John Jackson's essay is an attempt to rethink globalization, race, and space by considering how Harlem, New York, was differently imagined at the beginning of the twenty-first century. Like the essays before it that map space and race in relation to restructurings of social identities, in this essay Jackson rethinks Lefebvre's distinction between quantitative and qualitative space to consider the various issues related to the gentrification of urban spaces like Harlem. Beginning with an attempt to understand the markings of new racialized spaces through particular forms of numberings, Jackson charts the political and economic changes in the New York metropolis and the ways in which race and space are being differently read in a postmodern temporal and spatial order. He concludes by arguing for a kind of racioscape, one that would span the distance between quantitative and qualitative representations of social life. Racioscapes, he argues, mark the color-culture compressions that bring various diasporic black people into greater and greater everyday contact on the streets of neighborhoods like Harlem, bringing into relief the class and national distinctions that constantly threaten to destabilize notions of racial solidarity and common community. As with the other essays in this section, the geopolitics of space is critical for understanding both the transformations of race and neighborhoods, as well as the impossibility of escaping racial inequality. By calling for a critical geography of globality, Jackson ends by highlighting the ways that articulations of racial subjectivity and spatiality are central to contemporary theorizations of globalization.

Moving away from racial spaces of globality to the economic and political relations of globality, Jayne Ifekwunigwe's essay addresses the dialectics of victimization and empowerment as exercised and experienced by trafficked Nigerian sex workers in Italy. In doing so, she seeks to understand the feminization of globalization and the ways that economic underpinnings of this ra-

cialized process are embodying an economic and political Third World marginality that is circulating globally. Like Jackie Brown, who in the first section
calls for a decentering of transatlantic slavery narratives, Ifekwunigwe also
argues against the tendency to privilege narratives of transatlantic slavery in
theorizing and periodizing the African Diaspora. Further, she displaces the
centrality of particular social and historical processes of imperialism and post-
colonialism. By focusing on the earlier circuits of trade, processes of settlement, and political economic regimes that created points of reference for African diasporic constituencies, she elaborates new epistemologies of the African
Diaspora, which in the twenty-first century are "not predicated on current
problematic distinctions between 'authentic' diasporas of transatlantic slavery
and to a certain extent . . . *faux* diasporas ("economic" migrations)" (p. 206).
These "new" African diasporic formations, she demonstrates, allow scholars
to reassess understandings of volition, agency, and victimhood. They articulate a language of movement and search for labor from West African urban
centers to western and southern European metropoles, themselves under-
going processes of economic and demographic restructuring. In an attempt to
locate these movements in relation to globalization and transnationalism,
Ifekwunigwe shows that contemporary everyday African diasporic formations are constantly being reinvented by late capitalist geopolitical processes.

To conclude part II, Grant Farred's essay further reinforces the workings
of race and globalization by examining the manifestations of racial logic in
the "New South Africa," exploring how the institutions that are reinforcing
the language of universalism and nonracialism reflect paradoxical workings
of race that are still present in global reconfigurations. Farred argues that race
and racism are fundamentally central to the new universalism. In examining
contemporary manifestations of race, he also asks what has race become? In
this case, questions about how race continues to function in relation to daily
logics are centered around an inquiry into what the struggle for racial equality has become. Into what kind of political tool has it been transformed? By
interrogating Paul Gilroy's suggestion that the body is more than an unreliable marker of racial knowledge, Farred argues that the "crisis of raciology" is
located firmly within the (black) body and is a process that destabilizes race
as a secure and reliable political category. As such, arguing against Paul
Gilroy's call to move beyond race in particular contexts, Farred calls firmly
for an inclusion of the racialized body as the ongoing object of inquiry. He
suggests that though some might argue that the black body goes in and out of
various subjectivities, it is important to recognize that if "difference cannot

be maintained, what will become of the racialized politics founded upon it, in different forms, for centuries?" (p. 227).

Popular Blacknesses, "Authenticity," and New Measures of Legitimacy

While the circulation of expressive cultural forms has been an area of interest for many contributors to this volume, the authors in part III explicitly address the ways that the mapping of race and space has also influenced, and been influenced by, the production of popular cultural forms, themselves conduits for the conceptualization of blackness globally. The relationships between performance and popular culture on the one hand, and political expression and historical consciousness on the other, have been of particular interest to scholars of the *African Diaspora* because popular culture—and especially music—has been seen as one of very few sites in which Black Atlantic populations have been able to articulate alternative political, economic, and social visions, given their historical marginalization from centers of political, economic, and social power. Fueled by a desire to understand more clearly the processes of cultural accommodation, innovation, amalgamation, and rejection that have occurred throughout the diaspora, research on performance and popular cultures has attempted to illuminate the complex relationships people of African descent have had to the dynamics of nationalism, imperialism, modernity, development, and globalization by reading these relationships through the cultural forms produced by diverse sectors of black populations.

Popular cultures, then, are sites from which we can analyze shifting expressions of subjectivity and the articulation of complementary subjectivities. They are multifaceted and multivalent fields of cultural production that have the potential both to challenge and reproduce aspects of dominant systems and meanings. Moreover, popular cultural forms are created and re-created within the context of changing transnational circuits of ideas, opportunities, and constraints, a point that again returns us to a discussion of the relationships among migration, contemporary processes of globalization, and cultural production.

Global economic restructuring has resulted in the immiseration and displacement of huge numbers of people from Africa and the Caribbean who, in search of some degree of economic stability, have concentrated within the formerly imperial European centers and the currently dominant United

States, especially in urban areas. Many scholars have ethnographically considered the (sometimes unexpected) links between migration, racial formation, processes of ethnic identification, the development of political consciousness, and cultural production. More recent research on migration has also examined the ways changing conceptualizations of the relationships between ethnicity, race, culture, and citizenship in the United States and Europe have been critical in terms of shaping migrants' public presence and political life in the countries to which they migrate. Central to these processes have been the circulation and innovation of popular cultural forms among and within groups.

Migration, however, is not the exclusive institutional domain through which popular cultural forms currently travel. The proliferation of new technologies, as well as greater access to older technologies, has also resulted in an intensified circulation of popular cultural forms worldwide. For many, this has seemed like little more than cultural imperialism, and in particular American cultural imperialism, and has been decried as such. For others, however, the circulation of American popular cultural forms and media technologies has heralded new openings, new kinds of collaborations among marginalized groups (McAlister 2002), and new opportunities for the elaboration of different ideas about the relationships between progress and the development of racial, national, class, gender, and generational identities (D. Thomas 2004; Wilk 2002). The critical question that emerges here has to do, again, with the positioning of African American (and to some degree, Jamaican) popular cultural forms within these circulations, and the implications of this positioning for narratives of black solidarity.

For example, while many activist struggles throughout the *Black Atlantic* have drawn from the language and tactics of the civil rights and black power movements in the United States, and while many black communities worldwide have borrowed from African American musical and fashion tastes, for black people outside the United States, African Americans stand in for both halves of their dual monikers. That is, while they may represent the Africa of political progressivism or the black chic of youth style, they also represent the hegemony of America, and particularly of the American dollar, which are ambivalently admired and only tentatively trusted by those who would draw the boundaries of global black solidarity to exclude those in the "belly of the beast." This was a point made by several contributors in the first part of this volume. In this part, authors also explore the ways the boundaries between black folk are often as blurry as they are policed. While hip-hop could be seen as the current globally hegemonic black popular cultural form, picked up as the language of protest and expression by communities around the globe as diverse as Japan, Australia, and Mexico just as reggae was during the 1980s, it is worth noting that many of hip-hop's early and contemporary "stars" were the sons and daughters of black West Indian migrants to New York City. There has also been a proliferation of collaborations among African American hip-hop artists and Jamaican reggae and dancehall DJs, with the result being re-remixed musical forms that also constitute revised and revamped racial formations, now broadcast to a transnational listening audience within a global public sphere. The liminal spaces of African American and Afro-Caribbean identity formation, therefore, provide fertile ground for examining emergent tensions in global-local interrelationships.

But it is not just the fact that American blackness holds a place of privilege within the cultural production of race that is notable. What is even more salient about the contemporary post–cold war era is that the process of subject formation more generally is occurring primarily through consumption. Indeed, the contributors to part III demonstrate how racial, gender, sexual, and national identities are not only commodified but are made real—individually and collectively—through consumption. The emergent emphasis on consumption and, alongside it, individualism has destabilized totalizing narratives of revolution and has generated intense debate among sectors of both popular and academic communities. While consumption has become "a privileged site for the fabrication of self and society, of culture and identity" (Comaroff and Comaroff 2001: 9), and as the culture of neoliberalism "re-visions persons not as producers from a particular community, but as consumers in a planetary marketplace" (13), the extent to which different consumers are able to access or influence this market remains clearly uneven. This has led many scholars to approach the tight links between consumerism and identity formation skeptically. Generated by processes of globalization that exacerbate old social polarizations and create new ones, the ideology of consumerism, for these scholars, seems to have eliminated the potential for collectively mobilized, transformative political action (see, for example, Gilroy 2000). However, if we reorient our vision of politics in a way that decenters totalizing revolutionary narratives and pays special attention to very locally grounded negotiations, incorporations, and rejections, we can more clearly see new attempts to confront and revise both structural and ideological systems of power and domination through an engagement with popular culture. In this part of the volume generation becomes a key analytic tool because it provides a way to mark the significantly changed relationships to political structures and economic mobility that characterize contemporary youth experiences.

Through their analyses, contributors in part III argue against a view of globalized blackness that assumes a homogenization of transnational black (American) identities. Rather, they show that identities remain bounded by local experiences, experiences that are rooted within very particular historical and contemporary political economies. They demonstrate that globalization opens up the possibility for the rearticulation of racial, sexual, and national identities within transnational interpretive communities, but this does not mean that identities are themselves transnational. Instead, participation in transnational networks of popular culture and a referencing of events and images that are situated beyond the immediate territorial surroundings contribute to the reformulation of experience by providing new elements of similarity and contrast. However, despite the heightened circulation of media icons and mass culture across borders, the reconfiguration of state sovereignties, and the increasing interconnections between metropoles, this participation is not equally available to all. As a result, the raced, sexed, and gendered subjectivities fostered by the practices of borrowing and resignification are positional, contingent, and historical.

Ariana Hernandez-Reguant's essay begins part III by examining particular movements of popular meaning. She emphasizes the ways contemporary reformulations of racial, gendered, and sexual identities are tied to material transformations that offer few avenues for socioeconomic survival and mobility for people who are on the margins of global networks of power yet who are integral to their operation. However, in this case the essay involves an examination of how, in the process of challenging the very basis of revolutionary governance and its social hierarchy, the public spectacularization of black masculinity mobilizes the power of an "interpretive community" of audiences, musicians, dancers, media personalities, recording staff, and label executives. The focus is on how, as the revolutionary government was forced to implement capitalist reforms in the 1990s, Cubans began participating in global consumer cultural production in order to confront the crisis caused by the disappearance of socialist trading partners. Thus, Hernandez-Reguant focuses on the political economy of race, sexuality, and nation embodied in the performance, representations, and labor practices of *timba*, a hard-edged form of salsa that came to be known in Cuba simply as "the Cuban music." Here, she highlights how young Afro-Cuban men involved in the popularization of timba crafted an ethos of black machismo and a narrative of male hypersexuality which paralleled the advent of mass foreign tourism during Cuba's "Special Period." Within this context, she argues that the possession of male sexual prowess became an important key to the empowerment of young Afro-Cuban men whose participation in an underground transnational economy could lead not only to financial gain and upward mobility but also to emigration through marriage. The result? New and old identifications emerged, and race reappeared as both a form of social segmentation and an idiom of positive difference. In this landscape of transnational tourism, Afro-Cubans engaged in new discourses of black pride through popular timba music. As such, timba articulated a counternarrative of race that had the effect of undermining the myth of the *mestizo* and the state rhetoric of color blindedness. It emphasized Afro-Cuban heritage through tropes of blackness, difference, and inequality by turning negative stereotypes about black men into positive features.

Oneka LaBennett's essay provides a counterpoint to those scholarly and popular critics who view youth, and particularly black female youth, as lacking the ability to consume critically. LaBennett explores how first- and second-generation West Indian adolescent girls develop racial, ethnic, and gendered subjectivities—in part through their consumption of the protagonist of the American television program *Buffy the Vampire Slayer (Buffy)*— that differ significantly from their parents, who migrated from the West Indies. LaBennett demonstrates that while *Buffy* supports the dominant racial ideology by representing blacks as peripheral (and at times primitive), female West Indian adolescent viewers identify with its white protagonist without denying their blackness. She argues that this is the case in part because as consumers of this program, these teenagers came to understand what it means to be black and female in the United States, negotiating their own relationships to both West Indian and American racial formations. For them, she argues, "a primary method of either distancing themselves from, or allying themselves with African Americans was through selective consumption of products coded as white, African American, West Indian, or West Indian *and* African American" (p. 287). These teens identified with Buffy precisely because her identity as both a student and a vampire slayer made her just like them, *not* regular teenagers. By clarifying why second-generation West Indian adolescents identified with Buffy, LaBennett also positions them as critical spectators with the ability to question those representations that undermined their identities and to extract from popular culture what they could utilize positively. In this space, *Buffy* becomes simultaneously a source of pleasure and a moral lesson about racial formation in the United States, and the popularity of the show provides insight into the ways first- and second-generation West Indian migrants use cultural products to forge transnational identities.

While LaBennett focuses on the ways African Americans and West Indians in the United States negotiate racially marked popular cultural forms, Raymond Codrington investigates the effects of the circulation of black American popular culture within England. In doing so, he interrogates the currency of "place" and "authenticity" in relation to popular cultural forms and raises questions about what translates when popular cultural forms travel. Codrington is particularly interested in how American rap music, and the wider hip-hop culture in which it is embedded, is incorporated into the cultural production of localities in London. More broadly, his essay considers the ways blacks in London represent themselves through the manipulation of popular diasporic icons. By ethnographically grounding the indigenization of rap music in London, Codrington discusses how the current generation of black Britons negotiates British, West African, West Indian, and African American influences as they strive to represent what is simultaneously black and British. He also examines how, within this multicultural milieu, popular culture can be a space through which people form and practice new identities that can sometimes obscure racial differences among working-class populations. What Codrington demonstrates is that British hip-hop not only provides a way for the contemporary generation of black Britons to publicly critique the inequalities obscured by the discourse of multiculturalism that has emerged as one of the state's responses to processes of globalization. It also establishes the ongoing ground upon which various actors—working together in sometimes unexpected ways—reformulate blackness in London.

With Lena Sawyer's essay, we move away from a focus on popular cultural circulations from black America, returning to an analysis of the place of "Africa" within the production and consumption of expressive culture. Here, we are confronted with how Africa is strategically mythologized in Swedish spaces of African dance to meet different needs and to negotiate different power imbalances. For Sawyer, African dance classes provide a window into what she calls the "micropolitics of globalization" (p. 316), sites where both white Swedish women and migrant West African men negotiate conceptualizations of belonging and authenticity that are raced, classed, and gendered. Sawyer mobilizes her ethnographic data to demonstrate how the geographical space of Africa is used both to reproduce and to challenge embodied notions of power and hierarchy within so-called leisure settings. The essay raises the issue of the "translatability" of Africa in Sweden, and it stands as an example of how older parameters of difference are being reactivated and reenergized in the commodification and consumption of African dance. Ultimately, Sawyer argues that "African dance was not only an economic niche for black African men living in the periphery of the Swedish economy, and a cultural one for stressed out white Swedish women to, through an encounter with an imagined Africa, meet their natural womanly selves. It was also a space where people *performed* 'Africa' to debate and negotiate racialized, gendered, and sexualized understandings of belonging and community in Stockholm" (p. 332). With this case study, Sawyer shows us how globalization, while still structured by old colonial racial hierarchies and taxonomies, creates a situation in which mobility, liberation, and consumption embody different meanings, create different limitations for claims to belonging and authenticity, and impose different restrictions for people who occupy distinct conceptual and geographical locations within global hierarchies of power and value.

The final essay in part III brings us back to our earlier concerns with connections and translatability, and with the importance of historicizing assessments of the place of "Africa" and "America" in relation to different moments of globalization. Yet Deborah Thomas's essay also moves us into the contemporary period, discussing transformations in blackness in relation to the changing relationship between what she calls the "respectable state" and popular culture (p. 353). In doing so, Thomas ultimately challenges the assumption that popular cultural production must necessarily be countercultural to be counterhegemonic resistance. In analyzing the ways progress has been defined by Afro-Jamaicans, and the ways these definitions have changed over time in conjunction with other material and ideological transformations, Thomas examines a shift in the public power of the ideologies, practices, and aesthetics of lower-class black Jamaicans from the end of the nineteenth century to the end of the twentieth. In doing so, she positions Afro-Jamaican popular culture and popular consciousness as complexly derived formulations that defy easy categorization in relation to political struggle. Here, she makes explicit the argument that has been implicit within many contributions to this volume—we must render binary formations such as modernity and tradition, global and local, sacred and secular, state and nation, and hegemony and resistance relationally, that is, as "mutually constituting conceptual tools rather than oppositional categorizational poles" (p. 350).

Conclusion: New Institutions, New Networks, New Approaches

In order to understand the diverse ways people participate in producing new forms of practice—and thus, new forms of meaning—within the contemporary context of globalization, social theory must render more clearly how culture becomes dislodged from place, even as the ideological politics of state governance continue to reference territorial terrain (regions, villages, nations) as the basis for particular ancestral and, therefore, originary orders. On one hand, as scholars we have asserted that culture is not naturally linked to any given territory. On the other hand, cultural production continues to be inscribed within the particularities of historically contingent zones of exchange, resulting in a complex, yet uneven, reterritorialization. As the essays in this volume have argued, we need to understand not just how these relations and meanings circulate, are transformed, and gain legitimacy, but also how they are deeply embedded in particular historical formations. These are formations, after all, that have shaped the ways people mobilize particular conceptualizations of their regions, ethnic and racial groups, and nations in order to constitute subjectivities in the present, while also moving beyond these conceptualizations.

So, what can the convergence between globalization and race tell us about the decentering of modern biological categories and the emergence of new categories of belonging? About people's various endeavors to reformulate their relationships to communities, regions, and states? How has the contemporary moment reconfigured notions of racial difference and of belonging to racial communities, communities that are also gendered, classed, and nationalized? The authors here show that in the current period, civil rights discourse is on the wane because states are less powerful in some locations, and in others, less willing in others to hold "equality" as a value. At the same time, the postcolonial context is one in which migration, movement, and media—though unevenly experienced—have created a situation in which "the nation-based dimensions of racial solidarity have atrophied" (Winant 2000: 180). The transformation of global race relations and the entrenchment of American exceptionalism have meant that claims to pan-Africanity have become increasingly fraught with dismissals of racial fraternity and fissured by the distinctions between the West and the rest. Yet, migration and technological shifts have also meant that notions of blackness and diaspora are more instantaneously debated across space and time, particularly in the realm of popular culture, which is now, to a degree (because of U.S. mass media domination) shared. As a result, a new common language has emerged, and this is a language that is differently political—not the civil and political rights discourses of the mid-twentieth century, but something else that is rooted in changed notions of racial community. Belonging is being recognized as contingent and incomplete, and commonalities are being rethought in relation not only to historical specificities that position black people who are differently national, classed, and sexualized in complex relationships to each other, but also to contemporary processes that seem to solidify particular kinds of hierarchy within diaspora.

Ultimately, as the authors in this volume point out, contemporary transformations command us to think about racial formation as a process—and as a process that articulates with other processes—rather than as a stable (and knowable) category. As these essays indicate, examining locality alongside globality, charting the circulation of concepts and their transformation, and examining the transformation of cultural norms force us to revisit older patterns of social hierarchy. To understand contemporary processes of racial formation, it is critical to clarify the relationships between older imperial relationships and current configurations of power, to identify the ramifications of these two projects' motivations for classifying populations, and to clarify their visions of the future. In other words, context is everything, and historical specificity is crucial. The discussion in which we are engaged is not just about a silence around racial formation in theoretical exegeses of globalization, but is also about the spread of particular Americanized categories of understanding race both outside and in relation to the United States.

We need also to recognize how contemporary processes of globalization and racialization are drawing new and further exasperating preexisting forms of disenfranchisement, thereby generating new forms of dispossession. We are confronting a world in which larger and larger percentages of national populations are illiterate, where the avenues for self-advancement have become increasingly limited, where remittances constitute ever greater percentages of developing countries' GNPs, where sexual tourism and sex trafficking are on the rise, where the availability of critical social services is on the decline, where a commitment to social equality becomes framed as anticapitalist, and where an assertive call for peace is seen as suspiciously unpatriotic. The shift in the United States from a politics of consensus to one of coercion on the world stage (Harvey 2003) parallels another shift. While the "color line" was central to struggles throughout the Americas during the twentieth century, it is the poverty line—or, as Manning Marable has put it, the "problem of global apartheid" (Marable 2004)—that will be central in the twenty-first century.

When W. E. B. Du Bois was writing, race was mapped easily in terms of slavery, then still a visceral memory for many African Americans. While various white Americans towed the ontological line about race as scientific truth, various black Americans struggled against this in order to enter the national body politic. Currently, the color line has a different geometry. Class, enfranchisement, and nationality no longer graph so easily onto a black/white axis, and racial power is more difficult to locate but is equally insidious. In the present, with the exception of extremist communities, the public discourse about blackness within the dominant public sphere is nearly nonexistent. Indeed, in the United States today race seems to be invoked most often either ahistorically in relation to debates regarding affirmative action, or apolitically in relation to popular culture. We will soon see whether the horror of Americans and others over the delayed federal response to the 2005 devastation visited upon mainly poor black New Orleanians by hurricane Katrina, and the mainstream media's indictment of racialized poverty in the United States, can be sustained and translated into real change over the long haul. In the meantime, and despite public erasures of the ways citizenship is still racialized, African Americans and other diasporic blacks are struggling to maintain a sense of racial community and racial political mobilization in the face of persistent prejudice and discrimination. For scholars, this affects how we must think of the political significance of race and racial difference, and it puts us in the complicated position of debunking black racial essentialisms even as we parse how the color line really still does divide. It also requires us to move beyond facile understandings of what constitutes "politics" or "counterculture" to seriously consider how emergent practices might more successfully confront a changed context and to map how these innovative practices continue to be in dialogue with those developed in earlier periods. It is our hope that this volume contributes to this kind of anthropological endeavor.

Notes

1. We thank John L. Jackson Jr. and Ronald Wayne Crooks for helping us to clarify these points.

2. Though many scholars have provided insights into the various transformations in the global political economy since the 1970s, our understanding has been shaped by the following works: Appadurai 1990, 1996; Jean and John Comaroff 2001; J. Friedman 1993, 1994, 2003; Ferguson 1999, 2002; Graeber 2002; Gupta and Ferguson 1992; S. Hall 1997 [1991]; Harvey 1989; Petras 1990; Sassen 1994, 2000b; and Trouillot 2001. Several scholars have also focused explicitly on the ways global processes are gendered in the discourse about globalization (Freeman 2001), in the ways people experience contemporary transformations, and in the ways they mobilize to transform their situations. See, for example, Aymer 1997; Bolles 1983, 1996; Colen 1989; Colen and Sanjek 1990; Deere, Antrobus, and Bolles 1990; Enloe 1990; Fernandez-Kelly 1983; Harrison 1991; Kempadoo 1999; McAfee 1991; Mies 1982, 1986; Mohanty 1997; Nash and Fernandez-Kelly 1983; Ong 1987; Parreñas 2001; Safa 1981, 1995; Sen and Grown 1987; Ward 1990.

3. For examples of some of the path-breaking scholarship on transnational migration, see Basch, Glick Schiller, and Szanton-Blanc 1994; Chamberlain 1997; Glick Schiller, Basch, and Szanton-Blanc 1992; Glick Schiller and Fouron 2001; W. James 1998, James and Harris 1993; Kasinitz 1992; Kearney 1991; Rouse 1995; Smith and Guarnizo 1998; Sutton and Chaney 1987.

4. See, for example, Grewal and Kaplan 1994; Gleeson and Low 2001; Hardt and Negri 2004; Kingsnorth 2003; Lowe and Lloyd 1997; Mohanty 1991; Nielsen 2003; Striffler 2003.

5. Donham's formulation here is part of a growing body of literature that has been concerned to theorize "the modernities that are produced out of the articulations, productions, and struggles between capitalist forces and local communities in different parts of the world" (Ong and Nonini 1997: 15; see also Comaroff and Comaroff 1993, 1997; Donham 1999; Ferguson 1999; Gaonkar 2001; Hanchard 2001; Knauft 2002; Miller 1994; Ong 1999; Piot 1999; Pred and Watts 1993; Robotham 1997; Rofel 1999a; Tsing 1993). The study of alternative, multiple, or critical modernities has been part of a more general attempt among anthropologists to particularize concepts that have been presented as universal, such as democracy (Paley 1999) and development (Ferguson 1990; Escobar 1995; Deere, Antrobus, Bolles 1990).

6. Black British and black Canadian came to be ethnic terms within the context of multiculturalism in the United Kingdom and Canada.

PART I

DIASPORIC MOVEMENTS,

MISSIONS, AND

MODERNITIES

MISSIONARY POSITIONS

LEE D. BAKER

As I was exploring the ways in which Franz Boas's *Journal of American Folk-Lore* articulated ideas about Africa during the Harlem Renaissance of the 1920s, the threads of evidence led me to the Dakotas and Hawaii and to the early missions on the Sandwich Islands during the 1840s—west across the Pacific, not east across the Atlantic.[1] These civilizing missions form a discursive diaspora of colonial desires that are as much a part of (and have forged) global processes as the political and economic dimensions so often referenced. Indeed, missionaries and reformers deployed folklore in complex ways to contribute to a project of racial uplift that linked Hawaiians, American Indians, and African Americans together during the late nineteenth century. During this earlier period of globalization, the macronarrative of Christianity worked hand in glove with the reproduction of racial ideologies to discipline peoples whose customs and behaviors did not conform to the puritanical (and tyrannical) desires of colonial administrators and church leaders. In this essay, I demonstrate that in forging networks across diverse populations, reformers engaged in projects whose civilizing missions transcended the specific racial and colonial contexts that confronted them, ultimately leading to the formulation of a universal model of industrial education.

Uplift and the Uses of Folklore

Documenting, conserving, and reifying African cultural practices in the Americas was not initiated by Melville and Frances Herskovits in the 1920s, as Sally and Richard Price have contended (Price and Price 2003). In the United States, these processes started right after the Civil War when missionaries and military personnel began documenting the languages and customs of indigenous peoples in North America and the South Pacific, and of African Americans during reconstruction. In order to "convert the heathen," the colonial logic went, they first had to understand and document their languages, behaviors, and customs. Although the term culture (as we know it today) was not employed, missionaries, scholars, and educators confidently described and documented aboriginal practices that were "a real hindrance and obstacle in the way of civilization" (Eastman 1896: 93). This obsession with eradicating traditional African, Indian, and Hawaiian practices and beliefs motivated people like Merrill E. Gates, president of the influential reform group The Lake Mohonk Friends of the Indian, to confidently declare: "We are for a vanishing policy" (M. Gates 1900: 12). By the 1880s, anthropologists joined this group and eventually took over the colonial project of documenting disappearing cultures in the wake of "Christian civilization."

By calibrating culture as the index with which to measure civilization, missionaries, reformers, educators, and ethnologists sutured culture to race, helping to fuel the exploitation of imperial and colonial regimes. The goal of these maneuvers was racial uplift, a pedagogical project that emphasized individual savings and thrift, back-breaking and exploitative labor, temperance and sobriety, fidelity and monogamy, and Christian salvation in the disciplining of countless "savages" from South Africa to South Dakota, Montego Bay to Maui, Perth to Pohnpei (Gaines 1996; Hoxie 1984; Brumble 1988). Reformers and missionaries involved in these projects shared a putatively progressive Lamarckian vision that social and racial traits were acquired and then transmitted to the next generation. In the United States (inclusive of its territories and protectorates) and the Caribbean, the racial uplift discourse made a particularly deep impress, so deep that even the venerable Frederick Douglass played this race-as-indexed-by-culture card in his influential speech on Colored American Day at the 1893 World Columbian Exposition in Chicago. He juxtaposed American Negroes with the extended Fon family from present-day Benin who resided at the fair in a living ethnological exhibition called the Dahomey Village. Pushing the racial uplift metaphor to its limits, Douglass implored his rapt audience to "look at the progress the Negro has made in thirty years! We have come up out of Dahomey unto this. Measure the Negro. But not by the standard of the splendid civilization of the Caucasian. Bend down and measure him—measure him from the depths out of which he has risen" (Douglass 2000 [1893]: 194).

There is little epistemological difference between Douglass's call to "bend down and measure him" and reformers' vanishing policies. Both articulated a theory of racial progress predicated upon the eradication of putatively indigenous customs and beliefs. This was the same gospel of racial uplift that flowed around the world during the 1890s as American Protestant missionaries began to dominate the foreign mission movement and the United States slowly, but never surely, blazed its way through the Wounded Knee massacre, Chinese exclusion, the Spanish-American War, acquisition of island territories, Jim Crow segregation, and the Progressive Era (Hutchison 1987: 62–124).

In 1922, Elsie Clews Parson published "Playing Dead Twice in the Road" in the *Journal of American Folk-Lore*. This was a short folktale from Elizabeth City County, Virginia, that articulated the distinctive pan-African trickster motif. This was not unusual. During the 1920s and early 1930s, Boas's *Journal of American Folk-Lore* published a half-dozen issues dedicated exclusively to African and African American folklore. Affectionately known as the "Negro Numbers," these issues became standard fare for "New Negroes" as they documented and celebrated African cultural patterns in the Americas. What made this one tale from 1922 unique was the fact that a member of the Hampton Folk-Lore Society had originally recorded it in 1893. The educators and graduates of the Hampton Normal and Agricultural Institute had formed the society to record cultural practices of rural blacks in order to demonstrate that industrial education had succeeded in fostering the so-called Christian civilization of its graduates, in part by identifying how much African heritage remained to be rooted out. "Playing Dead Twice in the Road" was one of hundreds of tales, jokes, and conundrums Alice M. Bacon, founder of the Hampton Folk-Lore Society, organized into many notebooks of fieldwork during the last decade of the nineteenth century. During the Harlem Renaissance, therefore, African Americans interested in celebrating their rich African heritage were actually drawing from folklore that had been collected with the intention of eradicating it.

To begin to understand the complicated racial project articulated at Hampton during the 1890s, we must turn to the founder of the Hampton Institute, General Samuel Chapman Armstrong, and his father, Dr. Richard

Armstrong. In 1831 after graduating from Princeton Theological Seminary and marrying Clarissa Chapman, a teacher at the Pestalozzian Infant School in Brooklyn, Richard Armstrong became a missionary in the South Pacific. The newlyweds were initially placed on the island of Maui, where they stayed for seven years until Dr. Armstrong was appointed to the First Native Church in Honolulu. During his years on Maui, Armstrong observed that the natives were in need of "steady industrial occupation." Thus, as he ministered to the health of the populace, he also convinced the Hawaiians to build schools, churches, sugar plantations, and saw mills.[2]

Armstrong rose through the ranks of the missionary and government agencies and soon became the island's minister of education and a close advisor (both on spiritual and policy matters) to King Kamehameha III (Lindsey 1995: 1–2; Talbot 1969 [1904]: 3–37; S. Armstrong 1909: 1–4; "Death of Rev. Richard Armstrong" 1860: 76–77). He was perhaps best known for his creation and administration of the many missionary and government schools bearing his distinct philosophy of moral and industrial education, which above all aimed to civilize the natives. Armstrong outlined this philosophy in a letter to King Kamehameha III in which he accepted the position as minister of public education in 1847:

> No sphere of labor sir, would be more congenial to my feelings, than the department of public instruction, and I may add, no branch of the government, seems to me of more vital importance to the welfare, of the Hawaiian race than this. Education, intellectual, moral, and physical, is the great lever by which philanthropists of every land, are seeking to redeem and elevate the mass of people. *Here* it is of peculiar importance, where the glory and safety of the nation must depend in so great a degree upon the proper training of the young. If depopulation here is to be arrested; if the vices which are consuming the natives are to be eradicated; if an indolent and thriftless people are to become industrious and thrifty: if Christian institutions are to be perpetuated, the work must be accomplished [sic] mainly where it has been so prosperously begun, *in the education of the young.* (Quoted in M. Armstrong 1887: 29–30)

Writing to his daughter on October 6, 1844, he explained why the "inhabitants" were in need of this type of education: "Had they skill and industry they might abound in every good thing. . . . But, poor creatures, they will not very soon shake off the low wretched habits of their former state. Their government, until recently, was one of the worst forms of despotism . . . and in those days *a character* was formed which will not soon be entirely re-formed. When I look over this valley, I think what a little Yankee skill would do here" (S. Armstrong, Letters: RA/CA). Armstrong even complained in a letter of February 18, 1844 that the "king himself is as near to being an animal as man can well be & most of the high chiefs are ignorant, lazy, and stupid." His remedy to help advance what he called "Christian civilization" among these near-animal heathens was to improve "the heart, the head & the body at once." As he surmised, "this is a lazy people & if they are ever to be made industrious the work must begin with the young. So I am making strenuous efforts to have some sort of manual labor connected with every school. . . . Without industry they cannot be moral" (R. Armstrong: RA/RCA).

Dr. Armstrong's intimate knowledge of the traditional language, customs, and folklore of his charges was the key to his success as an educator, missionary, and confidant to the king. Using his genuine respect of Hawaiian language and culture, he was an important facilitator of the so-called great awakening when thousands of Hawaiians converted to Christianity by the mid-nineteenth century.[3] Armstrong often used folklore or other cultural markers to demonstrate how far the Hawaiians had come, suggesting, for example, that the natives "have better clothes than they used to have" and explaining, "we rarely see a native now unclad or even wearing native kapa." But he also used such markers to show how much civilizing work remained to be done, lamenting that the natives "still live in small and filthy grass huts, destitute of every comfort, and herding together often a dozen sleeping on mats in one small house without even a partition" (M. Armstrong 1887: 63).

During the Armstrongs' final year on Maui in 1839, Mrs. Armstrong gave birth to Samuel Chapman Armstrong, the sixth of their ten children. Samuel grew up close to his father and would later explain that his father's philosophy of education shaped that of Hampton. Comparing the Lahaina-luna Seminary, which taught Greek and Latin, to the Hilo Boarding and Manual Labor School, Samuel Armstrong explained, "As a rule the former turned out more brilliant, the latter less advanced but more solid men. In making the plan of the Hampton Institute that of the Hilo School seemed the best to follow. . . . Hence came our policy of teaching only English and the system of industrial training at Hampton. Its graduates are not only to be good teachers but skilled workers, able to build homes and earn a living for themselves and encourage others to do the same" (S. Armstrong 1909: 4–5).

In 1860 Samuel Armstrong left Hawaii to attend Williams College, and as the Civil War erupted, he accepted a commission as captain, recruiting and training Company D of the 125th Regiment of New York. Promoted to major and then to colonel, Armstrong was put in command of the 9th Regiment of U.S. Colored Troops. In March of 1865 Abraham Lincoln made the 26-year-old Hawaiian citizen a brevet brigadier general.

As the war ended, he searched for a mission in life, both personal and Christian. As a commander of Negro troops, he had been impressed by "their quick response to good treatment and to discipline" and he was convinced that African Americans yearned for education because he witnessed how his soldiers were "often studying their spelling books under fire" (S. Armstrong 1909: 6). Immediately after the war, the commissioner of the Freedmen's Bureau, General Oliver Otis Howard, appointed Armstrong as the superintendent for the tidewater area of Virginia; its headquarters was the small town of Hampton. General Armstrong's jurisdiction was populated with a large number of formerly enslaved people, and his area quickly became a bellwether for radical reconstruction experiments as missionaries, bureau agents, and the new freedmen and women negotiated competing agendas, policies, and plans.

After the war, the American Missionary Association took the lead in establishing schools for African Americans in the South. Armstrong used his access to both government and missionary resources to establish a co-ed industrial and normal school that would train African American elementary school teachers. This school opened in 1868 with two teachers and fifteen pupils, but it grew quickly and soon became independent of both the missionary association and the government. Armstrong often touted his brand of industrial and moral education, known as the Hampton idea, as "the only way to make them good Christians" (S. Armstrong 1909: 12). The Hampton idea found powerful support among philanthropists, missionaries, and the nation's political and industrial leaders. Although interest was generated by Hampton's civilizing mission, white backers were also attracted to its political and economic components which, as they saw it, would foster regional stability by discouraging students from participating in party politics while encouraging the efficient exploitation of their labor (Spivey 1978: 22). The majority of black colleges followed Hampton's model, and when Hampton's own graduate, Booker T. Washington, reproduced Armstrong's model at Tuskegee Institute in the late nineteenth century, it became *the* most influential model for black schools (Fredrickson 1971: 216).

Not only did Armstrong create the blueprint for Washington's popular industrial education with its concomitant policies of racial accommodation and cultural assimilation, he also helped to shape the federal government's policies regarding Native American assimilation through education. From 1878 through 1893, Hampton "experimented" with Indian education, again employing the notion that industrial education helped to civilize the savages (Lindsey 1995; Robinson 1977; D. Adams 1995: 28–59). In 1878, Captain R. H. Pratt, who after the Civil War had commanded black troops and Indian scouts on the Great Plains, searched without success for a school to continue the education of a group of Indians under his control. General Armstrong welcomed the opportunity to extend Hampton's civilizing mission to American Indians and invited Pratt to bring them to Hampton. The experiment was seemingly so successful that President Rutherford B. Hayes announced in his State of the Union address the following year that the Department of Interior would reproduce Armstrong's Hampton idea for Native Americans, extolling the virtues of "the experiment of sending a number of Indian children of both sexes to the Hampton Normal and Agricultural Institute, in Virginia, to receive an elementary English education and practical instruction in farming and other useful industries" (Hayes 1966 [1879]: 1390). And that year, 1879, Captain Pratt, along with some American Indian students from Hampton, started the influential Carlisle Indian Industrial School. Like Tuskegee and Hampton for Negroes, the Carlisle School became a defining institution for the education policy to assimilate Indians.[4]

Armstrong's gospel of industrial education was even spread to Africa. With close ties to the American Missionary Association, Hampton provided many recruits for the association's work of converting and educating West Africans (A. White 1878: 54; also see Sharps 1991: 121). General Armstrong deployed a transnational and transracial discourse about Christian civilization, assimilation, and industrial education to build an institution that defined dominant approaches to the education of African Americans, American Indians, Hawaiians, and even Africans. And, like his father, General Armstrong realized that understanding the folklore and cultural practices of these peoples would facilitate the mission.

Bedeviling Christian Civilization

Armstrong explained the role "comparative ethnology" played within the process of "civilization" in his introduction to a series of 1878 reports for Hampton's *Southern Workman* that explored Negroes' "firm belief in witchcraft and conjuration." He compared the way Negroes and Sandwich Islanders practiced the "tangle of superstition, demonology, and fetish worship," which he described as "a combination of Salem and Central Africa." After discussing the parallels between the Hawaiian " 'kahuna' or native witch-doctor" and the Negro conjure doctor, he concluded that both groups had "the same love of the supernatural, and dense ignorance of the laws of living," and that the Negroes thus possessed the "elements which form the soil for a growth of superstition as rank and as fatal as that which is helping to depopulate Hawaii" (S. Armstrong 1878: 26).

The reports on conjure doctors were intended "to throw light upon the mental condition of the masses of this people, and the kind of work that must be done among them if they are to be raised to civilization or even saved from extinction" (S. Armstrong 1878: 30). The reports spawned a flurry of published responses. Orra Langhorne, a regular contributor to the *Southern Workman*, reminded readers that conjure doctors were "evidently a legacy handed down to [American Negroes] from their savage ancestors." As if to illustrate Langhorne's contentions, a member of Hampton's junior class offered compelling examples of the good and ill work of conjure doctors and closed his letter to the editor "by saying that I believe in the conjure Drs. and all this that I have written I can vouch for my self" (31). Armstrong's faith in the civilizing mission of the Hampton Institute prompted him to comment, "Two years more in the school will change his ideas, it is to be hoped" (30).

W. I. Louis, a Hampton alumnus teaching in Spartanburg, South Carolina, took a different tack. Upset with the reports, he wrote, "I fail to see what is gained by your repeating this dark legend of a by-gone day." He wanted the *Southern Workman* to report "facts that are elevating, facts that will inspire even the humblest." He concluded by noting that "our days of childhood are (if not, they should be) fast taking their flight, and the advent of manhood is at hand" (quoted in S. Armstrong 1878: 35).[5] This letter provoked perhaps the most spirited response from the good general, and he candidly and confidently described why the *Southern Workman* frequently published missionary accounts and folklore from around the world:

> It is time for every man who loves his people to lay aside sensitive feeling and go to work with all the aid he can get. And the first step of all is to make known the true state of the case. When a general begins a campaign, the first point is to get a true map of the country, and spy out all the enemy's forces and know the strength of every battery. It is not the beauty of his banners and his martial music that will win the victory, but knowledge of the work before him, and hard fighting. . . . Let us not be afraid to

face our own faults and follies, to drag them into the light where they will show for what they really are. (ibid.)

Combining espionage with exorcism, folklore and ethnology not only became a way of demonstrating how Hampton succeeded at civilizing students, but also of demonstrating the need for continual financial support. More importantly, the *Southern Workman* reports of the cultural practices of Native Americans, Hawaiians, and African Americans were used in the service of a complicated racial project that articulated a putatively progressive discourse about an individual's ability to rise to a state of civilization during a period when many scholars argued that every member of these groups was doomed to eternal savagery.

The graduates and educators of Hampton, Fisk, Howard, and other black schools explicitly used the terms of this discourse in their programs of racial uplift. These self-described Negro elites most often framed their pejorative descriptions of their less civilized neighbors in terms of class, but the Hampton Folk-Lore Society did so in terms of culture (see Gaines 1996). Virtue, chastity, and cleanliness were the key signifiers of civilization that black elites embraced while chastising vice and sensuality. Uncivilized blacks were the ones who believed in conjure doctors, told animal stories, sang work songs, and gyrated their bodies in the ring shouts and jook joints. They were also the field hands, manual laborers, domestics, and washer women who never had the opportunity to attend one of the normal schools in which strict discipline and obsession with proper behavior convinced students they had become civilized. It was these uneducated and less refined souls who were held responsible for the vice, promiscuity, and debauchery associated with all black Americans. Moreover, the notion that African culture underpinned the behavior of uncouth black people was so routine that it provided useful shorthand for one Hampton graduate who complained about the rural school district of his first teaching job. Displeased with all of the "drinking, swearing and fighting," he reported, "when I came here I thought that there was as much Africa here as I cared to witness" ("Dear Teacher" 1876: 46; see also Hunter 1997: 175).

During the 1870s and 1880s the boosters of the civilizing project combined ideas from many sources. They employed referents from the Bible that resonated with the ideas of Adam Smith, Herbert Spencer, Jean Baptiste Lamarck, and Lewis Henry Morgan to foster the idea that an individual could work hard and attain civilization while unloading the cultural baggage of African savagery. As General Armstrong explained, however, in order to civilize the Negroes, reformers had first to "spy out" those Africanisms that bedeviled the civilizing project and debilitated the health and welfare of the poor. This approach animated the efforts of Alice Mabel Bacon and, through her, became the mission of the Hampton Folk-Lore Society.

Theory and Practice of the Hampton Folk-Lore Society

Alice Bacon, born in 1858, was the youngest daughter of Leonard Bacon, an influential abolitionist, professor at Yale Divinity School, and long-standing pastor of the First Church of New Haven. Her brother Francis was a professor of surgery at Yale and married Georgeanna Woolsey, who was the cousin of Yale's president, Theodore Dwight Woolsey. Georgeanna was the sister of Jane Stuart Woolsey, who supervised nurses during the Civil War and established training schools for nurses in New York City and New Haven. Jane was stationed in Virginia during the final campaigns of the Civil War, and General Armstrong persuaded her to come to the Hampton Institute in 1868 to direct the Girls Industrial Department, where she stayed until 1872. Jane's sister-in-law, Rebecca Bacon, also made the trip to Virginia's tidewater and became Armstrong's assistant principal (D. Waters 1983: 5).

In 1870, just two years after Hampton was underway, Rebecca Bacon brought her youngest sister, Alice Mabel Bacon, to Hampton for only a year. But in 1882, when her mother passed away, Alice immediately applied for a post at Hampton, where she taught for five years. At the invitation of her childhood friend Countess Oyama, she then left Hampton to spend a year in Japan, where she worked to help westernize the schools for elite Japanese women (D. Waters 1983: 6; Sharps 1991: 32). Returning to Hampton in 1889, she worked to establish Hampton's Dixie Hospital to provide health care to the needy in the area and nursing training for students at Hampton Institute. Bacon conducted case studies in communities in the surrounding Elizabeth City County to assess the need for the hospital, and in an effort to raise funds for the hospital, she wrote an essay for the *Southern Workman* that included graphic descriptions based on her investigations. Her essay opened by describing "the poorest and most ignorant of the colored people" who lived "in the little slab cabins with their mud chimneys, where father, mother, children of both sexes, and frequently adult lodgers of either sex, are thrown together at all times under all circumstances." She surmised that this "life must be more the life of the savage than that of civilization":

That the Negroes are by degrees moving upward, that every year more and more of them lift themselves a little above the merely animal life of the roughest plantation hand, is a fact that none but the most pessimistic can doubt, but to those who are working among them the question often arises, what can we do that will help to relieve, on some measure, those who from years or by reason of infirmities can never lift themselves out of the squalor and misery about them? (Bacon 1890: 124)

All they needed, she proposed, was basic medical attention and the "healing gift of Christian civilization."

Bacon soon discovered that one of the major obstacles to delivering medical care and Christian civilization to those she euphemistically called the cabin people was their tenacious belief in conjuring and superstitions. Thus, in her view, sociological and anthropological research ought to be used as an aid in missionary and health work (D. Waters 1983: 36). By 1893, Bacon's efforts were joined by those of some Hampton alumni, students, and faculty who began to see the need to salvage the songs, stories, and African survivals that made up Negro folklore. Combining Armstrong's commitment to espionage and exorcism with a desire for historical preservation, Bacon published a call to form the Hampton Folk-Lore Society in the form of a circular letter, reprinted in the December 1893 issue of *Southern Workman:*

Dear Friends: The American Negroes are rising so rapidly from the condition of ignorance and poverty in which slavery left them, to a position among the cultivated and civilized people of the earth, that the time seems not far distant when they shall have cast off their past entirely, and stand as an anomaly among civilized races, as a people having no distinct traditions, beliefs or ideas from which a history of their growth may be traced. If within the next few years care is not taken to collect and preserve all traditions and customs peculiar to the Negroes, there will be little to reward the search of the future historian who would trace the History of the African continent through the years of slavery to the position which they will hold a few generations hence. Even now the children are growing up with little knowledge of what their ancestors have thought, or felt, or suffered. The common school system with its teachings is eradicating the old and planting the seeds of the new, and the transition period is likely to be a short one. The old people, however, still have their thoughts on the past, and believe and think and do much as they have for generations. From them and from the younger ones whose thoughts have been moulded by them in regions where the school is, as yet, imperfectly established, much may be gathered that will, when put together and printed, be of great value as material for history and ethnology.

But, if this material is to be obtained, it must be gathered soon and by many intelligent observers stationed in different places. It must be done by observers who enter into the homes and lives of the more ignorant colored people and who see in their beliefs and customs no occasion for scorn, or contempt, or laughter, but only the showing of the first child-like, but still reasoning, philosophy of a race. . . . To such observers, every custom, belief or superstition, foolish and empty to others, will be of value and will be worth careful preservation. The work cannot be done by white people, much as many of them would enjoy the opportunity of doing it, but must be done by the intelligent and educated colored people who are at work all through the South among the more ignorant of their own race, teaching, preaching, practicing medicine, carrying on business of any kind that brings them into close contact with the simple, old time ways of their own people. (Bacon 1893: 180–81)

Bacon's initial rationale for continued research on the so-called cabin people was to make missionaries more efficient health-care providers, and she effectively articulated this rationale in her later work (Bacon and Herron 1896). But the emphasis on cultural preservation so evident in her 1893 statement spoke to another, perhaps less obvious motivation: the urgency with which Bacon enjoined the graduates to go out and salvage disappearing Negro lore stemmed from the educators' need to demonstrate the success of the Hampton idea. One of the most effective publicity and fundraising tools of both the Hampton Institute and the Carlisle School were before and after photographs of Indian students. Native Americans were routinely photographed fully adorned in their religious regalia as they enrolled in school and then later in a formal suit and tie or frilly dress in order to demonstrate the schools' success at civilizing their charges (D. Adams 1995: 45). In her 1893 call, Bacon seems to suggest that her proposed folklore society might be the last opportunity of Hampton educators to record the "ignorant people" before the impact of common schools eclipsed the remaining folk culture. Armed with a record of African American folklore that was no longer practiced, the educators at Hampton would be able to reproduce the popular before and after images used to raise money for their Indian program.

Bacon's call for the formation of the Hampton Folk-Lore Society was greeted with great enthusiasm. Letters of support came in from all corners of the intellectual community, yet African American supporters of the society held nuanced views of its promise. For example, the missionary, educator, and early pan-Africanist Alexander Crummell strongly supported the formation of the society, but he warned that its members must offer a positive interpretation of their African heritage and not a negative one. "The truth," he explained, has been "the dinning of the 'colonization' cause into the ears of the colored people—the iteration of the idle dogma that Africa is THE home of the black race in this land; has served to prejudice the race against the very name of Africa. And this is a double folly:—the folly of the colonizationists and the folly of the black man" (Crummell 1894: 5). Another activist, educator, and author, Anna Julia Cooper, also commented on the philosophical foundation of the organization:

> What you say is true. The black man is readily assimilated to his surroundings and the original simple and distinct type is in danger of being lost or outgrown. To my mind, the worst possibility yet is that the so-called educated Negro, under the shadow of this overpowering Anglo-Saxon civilization, may become ashamed of his own distinctive features and aspire only to be an imitator of that which can not but impress him as the climax of human greatness, and so all originality, all sincerity, all *self*-assertion would be lost to him. What he needs is the inspiration of knowing that his racial inheritance is of interest to others and that when they come to seek his homely songs and sayings and doings, it is not to scoff and sneer, but to study reverently, as an original type of the Creator's handiwork. (A. Cooper 1894: 5)

The comments by both Crummell and Cooper suggest that even with the formation of the first black folklore society, some African Americans understood that folklore could provide a positive interpretation of their African heritage or a scientific basis to identify and preserve their distinctive culture. Still, they did little to influence the twenty or so Hampton students, teachers, and alumni who made up the society. Most Hampton graduates did not question their desire to ascend to a civilized state, and even more perhaps loathed any association with Africa. However, other students departed from this trend. Robert R. Moton, for example, one of the society's elected leaders, used the folklore and the society to challenge the "contempt and derision" of the minstrelsy industry that transformed black folksongs, stories, and sayings into laughing-stock buffoonery, which crystallized stereotypes for all African Americans (Lott 1993).

One could argue that the Hampton Folk-Lore Society's approach amounted to a form of "applied folklore" (Sharps 1991: 65). The core of the society was a group of young men and women who graduated from Hampton and went on to work in business, education, or medicine. By better understanding the practices and lore of their clients, patients, and students, these young professionals believed they could contribute to racial uplift by developing more efficient ways to sell, heal, and teach. More generally, the society's work, as published in Hampton's *Southern Workman*, formed part of a missionary discourse integrated into a complex racial project whose proponents engaged in a racial politics of culture that shaped communities from Hawaii to Hampton.

Although missionary efforts to civilize people of color made little distinction with regard to the savage state of Indians, Hawaiians, and Negroes, their methods and rhetoric served remarkably well at making distinctions between individuals within each group who had supposedly reached a state of civilization. Specifically, the putatively civilized people of color in the late nineteenth century used the discourse that homogenized difference between groups to mark the heterogeneity within their group—describing and inscribing a distinction between themselves, the civilized, and those others, the uncivilized. Moreover, the American Folk-Lore Society, founded by William Wells Newell in 1888, participated in and scientifically validated this racial project by supporting and collaborating with the Hampton Folk-Lore Society.

By 1893, Newell had distinguished himself as a skilled administrator and editor within the closely knit anthropological circles, but he also wanted to distinguish himself as a folklorist and folklore as its own discipline, not as an adjunct to anthropology (Darnell 1973: 28; Bell 1973: 11–13). When Alice Bacon organized the Hampton society, Newell saw an opportunity to develop the Negro department of the journal, and thus to pursue a topic that few anthropologists were then exploring. He was "a personal friend" of one of Hampton's trustees, and there was considerable overlap between the founders of the American Folk-Lore Society from the Boston area and supporters of the Hampton idea, well before the Hampton Folk-Lore Society was even formed (Newell 1983 [1894]: 187).

Newell wasted no time incorporating the members of the HFLS into the AFLS. On May 25, 1894 he traveled to Hampton to deliver the keynote address for Hampton's first folklore conference, which followed the spring commencement exercises. Speaking to "trustees, teachers, officers and graduates of the school," he gave a talk entitled "The Importance and Utility of the Collection of Negro Folk-Lore," which struck a note that resonated with General Armstrong's notion of civilization. He began by explaining, "I came from Cambridge, in the hope of forwarding an undertaking which appears to me most meritorious, and of promoting the work of the Negro Folk-Lore societies, a movement which is significant in regard to the present intelligence and rapid progress of Southern Negroes" (Newell 1983 [1894]: 186).

Alice Bacon became an integral member of the AFLS and eventually was elected to its council. Bacon and delegates from the HFLS participated in the meetings of the AFLS, and she and her colleagues published several collections in the *Journal of American Folk-Lore* (Banks 1894, 1895; Bacon 1898; Bacon and Herron 1896). When Alice Bacon left Hampton in 1899 to return to Japan to administer a school for young women, the Hampton Folk-Lore Society was not sustained. She died in 1918, but the notebooks of folklore she collected to articulate one racial project were republished in 1922 under her name, although they were used to articulate a very different project.

Lifting as We Climb

The Hampton Folk-Lore Society was operational as the so-called Progressive Era waxed and the Gilded Age waned. During that period, the tidewater region of Virginia was marked by increased lynchings and restrictions on black male suffrage, and the routinization and legalization of Jim Crow segregation. Under the leadership of Bacon, the work of the society sewed a tapestry of thrift, self-reliance, morality, and Christian faith. The society does not, however, fit neatly within the discursive practices of Progressive Era reformers, the black women's club movement, or the black men's self-help leagues. Although the society's members grappled with identical issues and emulated many of these other groups' practices, they are distinguished from the others by the particular attention they paid to ideas about culture, as well as class, to articulate the ideology of racial uplift. The former students of Hampton who made up the bulk of the membership of the society were part of a Negro elite who shared faith in Jesus and a moral obligation to uplift the race. Shouldering the responsibility of what would have amounted to a talented 2 percent, these "college-bred" Negroes (Du Bois and Dill 1968 [1910]) of the late nineteenth century promulgated a complex ideology of racial uplift inflected with gender and class distinctions. Black ministers, educators, journalists, doctors, and social workers used rhetoric, research, and writing to combat egregious and dehumanizing claims that African Americans were inherently inferior and incapable of assuming the rights and responsibilities of citizenship or civilization.

Imbued with the optimism and progressive spirit of the age, these black leaders enlisted the support of white political and business leaders to foster racial progress, primarily through a trickle-down theory of education. College graduates would fan out throughout the South, teaching students in small schools the Victorian and Yankee ideals learned from the missionaries, ideals thought to improve the material conditions of blacks and demonstrate that they were capable of citizenship, civilization, and respect—indeed humanity. The efforts to show racial progress, however, were largely predicated upon identifying distinctions between those blacks who rose to a civilized state and those not quite there, and such distinctions often turned on status or class distinctions. Although proponents of uplift did not advance unified themes about racial progress, the idea that the race would progress toward a civilized citizenry served as a unifying theme as people searched for various ways to create an authentic and positive black middle-class subjectivity.

The Hampton Folk-Lore Society was also articulating a racial uplift ideology. Its members, too, were propounding the notion that "we are here." But this was not the temporally static "we are here, right here." It was a "we are (up) here, not (down) there." Knowingly or not, society members used an anthropologically inflected folklore to plot the perceived temporal distance between the college-bred Negroes and the cabin people in the same way Frederick Douglass did when he plotted his graph "out of Dahomey." Although this folklore helped to demonstrate how far they had come in their racial progress, it was ultimately deployed to document how quickly they were closing the gap and to measure the success of lifting as they climbed. The society provided an additional dimension to the idea of racial uplift by inserting notions about stages of culture. By explicitly distinguishing the low and savage African culture from the high and civilized Christian culture, they appropriated the comparative method of evolutionary anthropology to exploit the politics of culture to advance the status of specific individuals as citizens. Instead of coding culture in racial terms, they coded race in cultural or performative terms and set no limits on their access to the civilized citizenry. Challenging the prevailing science articulated by scholars such as Daniel G. Brinton, who envisioned civilization in the strict terms of a racial hierarchy where "the European or white race stands at the head of this list, the African or negro at its foot" (Brinton 1890: 48), members of the society believed civilization was about how one behaved and what one believed. Access to it, therefore, was contingent upon the head and heart, not the brain and body.

Conclusion

The overwhelming success of Protestant missionary schools in the Pacific, Hampton, Tuskegee, and the Carlisle School demonstrates how U.S. nation building and empire building were mutually defining (Kaplan 1993). Although it might be a slippery and dangerous slope to make an argument about a common heritage that turns on a shared experience of colonialism, racism, and religion, one cannot ignore the fact that for several influential generations at the turn of the twentieth century, industrial school education, in Natal, Perth, Carlisle, Hampton, Kingston, Cape Coast, and Hilo, looked virtually identical. Each one of these poles reinforced and solidified a shared philosophy of racial uplift that transcended the particularities of community and history. These schools and their respective institutions (clubs, fraternities, churches, settlement houses, and so forth) played an increasingly important role in mandating and dictating very similar roles for the educated people of color during the very years that white supremacy became synonymous with civilization, the industrial revolution craved foreign markets, colonialism seemed like a success, and the United States tried its hand at empire.

Notes

1. I thank Kamari Clarke and Deborah Thomas for their leadership in putting this volume together. It is an honor and privilege to be asked to contribute. The special collections librarians at Williams College were very helpful as I tracked down some of these sources. As well, the editorial and research assistance given to me by David Rease and Bayo Holsey was instrumental. Charlie Piot and Randy Matory gave useful comments as I began to think how I could use my "narrow research" to contribute to larger discussions about race and globalization. However, it was Deborah who really pushed me to use my history of anthropology to explore global issues—thanks. As always, thanks to my lovely wife Sabrina L. Thomas and my daughter Yaa Asentewaa Baker for their help and inspiration.

2. He succeeded in having the indigenous Hawaiians build much of the island's infrastructure, despite the fact they probably engaged in various forms of resistance,

or as Mrs. Armstrong recalls: "The natives were awkward and very destructive, breaking their tools and ox-carts and always relying upon their 'kumu' to repair them" (M. Armstrong 1887: 21).

3. Even King Kamehameha IV, who detested the influence of the missionaries, noted that Armstrong "was an eloquent preacher in the Hawaiian language" and commented on "his accurate knowledge of the Hawaiian language, and the facility with which he wielded the pen of a translator" ("Death of Rev. Richard Armstrong" 1860: 76; see also M. Armstrong 1887: 57–58).

4. For an interesting discussion on the relationship and parallels between Hampton, the Carlisle School, and the Indian boarding school movement, see D. Adams 1995. For information about the number of Native American students, graduation rates, gender balance, and so forth, see Hampton Normal and Agricultural Institute 1893. For an analysis of the Native American experience in the boarding schools, focusing explicitly on Hampton, see Makofsky 1989 and Robinson 1977.

5. As with many of the letters to the editor in the *Southern Workman*, some are signed, others are anonymous, and others only include initials. For these letters addressing the papers on conjuring, I note them all under the editorship of Armstrong because he clearly chose which submissions to print and which to respond to. In addition, when an article or an entry in the *Southern Workman* was difficult to cite, because it was anonymous or a letter within an article or editorial, I simply note the date, volume, and page number.

HISTORY AT THE CROSSROADS

Vodú and the Modernization of the Dominican Borderlands

ROBERT L. ADAMS JR.

To articulate the past historically does not mean recognizing it "the way it really was" (Ranke). It means appropriating a memory as it flashes up in a moment of danger. Historical materialism wishes to hold fast that image of the past which unexpectedly appears to the historical subject in a moment of danger. The danger threatens both the content of the tradition and those who inherit it. For both, it is one and the same thing: the danger of becoming a tool of the ruling classes. Every age must strive anew to wrest tradition away from the conformism that is working to overpower it. The Messiah comes not only as the redeemer; he comes as the victor over the Antichrist. The only historian capable of fanning the spark of hope in the past is the one who is firmly convinced that *even the dead* will not be safe from the enemy if he is victorious. And this enemy has never ceased to be victorious.

—Walter Benjamin, "On the Concept of History"

In his last known writings, Walter Benjamin argued that forgetting the "later course of history" was the key to discovering the past. Historical events offer multiple interpretations if the hegemonic present does not blind us to them.[1] We have to question the authoritative story, master narratives that naturalize elite perspectives and control as the inevitable outcome of history. Benjamin encouraged critical historians to "brush history against the grain," subjecting it to alternative readings that question master narratives. The goal of critical interpretation is to break free of the "whore called 'once upon a time'" in order to "blast open the continuum of history" (Benjamin 2003b [1940]: 391–92, 396).

Sharing Benjamin's suspicion of master narratives, Eric Wolf's *Europe and the People without History* (1982) suggested that anthropologists reintroduce history into the discipline as a means of reinvigorating it. The discipline, Wolf argued, was trapped into reifying the "West" and its supposed correlates: Christianity, democracy, reason, industrialization, and so forth. The "Western civilization" discourse overemphasized difference and downplayed how local cultures were shaped globally. The misplaced focus on purity and isolation obscured the dialogic production of culture, ignoring hybridity and the development of networks. Thus, Wolf criticized anthropological studies for reducing "dynamic, interconnected phenomena into static, disconnected things," mainly by failing to highlight how global processes shaped specific cultures, places, and people (Wolf 1982: 4–5). He imagined that critical history could be the way out of this quagmire.

Wolf conceptualized history neither as a straight chronological account, nor as a Greek myth (i.e., an allegorical tale of civilization, superiority, and conquest). Instead, Wolf's history reflected the relentless search to momentarily capture the faint, multivocal echoes of the past. His anthropology recognized the multiple authorship of history because "common people were as much agents as they were victims and silent witnesses" (Wolf 1982: x). Wolf places us firmly on Walter Benjamin's ground, sifting through the trash of history—those neglected, discarded, or suppressed people, events, ideas, and objects from the past—in order to uncover the multivocal history of modernity. Paying close attention to contested historical interpretations illuminates the dialogic nature of culture, complicating the false dichotomies that two-dimensional anthropology rests upon. It also forces us to place contemporary instantiations of global processes within a broader historical context that also considers how late-nineteenth-century nationalist modernization campaigns, for example, reflected anxieties about the racial, religious, and economic circulations that were occurring across the territorial and cultural boundaries elites were trying so assiduously to fix.

In the pages that follow, I examine these issues within the context of the Dominican Republic at the beginning of the twentieth century. Many aspects of Dominican culture remain obscured and ignored as a result of the consolidation of Dominican nationalism, *Dominicanidad*. While Afro-Dominicans comprise the largest racial population in the country, and black cultural practices—such as Dominican Vodú—are important components of national culture, these practices are not recognized within official versions of Dominican uniqueness that affirm the nationalist myth that Dominican culture is exclusively white, Spanish, and Catholic. Yet despite its unofficial status, Vodú remains an important repository of popular Dominican history.

Dominican Vodú is a web of Afro-Dominican religious institutions—secret societies, carnival groups, Catholic brotherhoods, and healing cults. Each historical period has left its mark on Dominican Vodú, which has incorporated new materials, ideologies, and spirits. Taíno culture and history, slavery, *marronage*, the Haitian Revolution, and military occupations are all reflected in Vodú rituals and spirits. Vodú spirits—*loas* in Haitian Kreyol and *luases* in Dominican Spanish—Sämi Ludwig points out, are more than spiritual beings, they are signs of history. "Like Bakhtin's 'language,'" he writes, "the loas are fundamentally rooted in history; they represent the 'socio-ideological' points of view of ancestral tradition" (Ludwig 1994: 328). As such, the spirits and practices of Vodú can be read as what James Scott would call a "hidden transcript": "If subordinate discourse in the presence of the dominant is a public transcript, I shall use the term *hidden transcript* to characterize discourse that takes place "offstage," beyond direct observation by the power holders. The hidden transcript is thus derivative in the sense that it consists of those offstage speeches, gestures, and practices that confirm, contradict, or inflect what appears in the public transcript" (J. Scott 1990: 4–5).

As a hidden transcript, Vodú constitutes an alternative public sphere where its adherents address their past, present, and future. Therefore, the religion provides an excellent text to chart the march of the "people without history" through Dominican history.

In this essay, I consider the reaction of Afro-Dominican peasants in the San Juan Valley to the Dominican modernization campaign initiated by local elites in the latter half of the nineteenth century. The elite hoped that modern reforms would stamp out the national habits they considered "primitive," blocking the promise of "civilization." Peasants in the San Juan Valley did not simply resist these reforms, they used Vodú to articulate an alternative vision of the "modern" future. In 1908, nearly forty years after the start of the modernization campaign, a messianic leader named Olivorio Mateo (often called Liborio) emerged in the San Juan Valley. His emergence and the new rituals generated by his appearance (*Liborismo*) represented the creation of fresh spirits to capture the "socio-ideological" experiences of the people. My essay begins with an examination of the modernization campaign, exploring the racial and geographic desires embodied in the campaign, and then moves on to an account of Liborio's appearance and the significance of Liborismo as an alternative vision of Dominican modernity. I conclude by highlighting the legacy of the *Liborista* movement and its struggle to guide Dominican futures through the contemporary global moment.

Dominican Modernism

Modernity, Trouillot contends, is an ambiguous term. A universal modernism does not exist; instead, there are countless modernities, even in supposed premodern places (Trouillot 2002: 220–22; Comaroff and Comaroff 1993; Geschiere 1997; Mbembe 2001a). When contemplating modernity, we are really engaging with a sign, a nearly empty, fluid signifier that reflects meaning in relation to specific and particular places, cultures, politics, histories, and economies. All these relations rest on a foundation of desire, the dreams of a better tomorrow. But as we know, one person's dreams are another's nightmares. Modernity, therefore, should be considered not so much a condition as a project, the mobilization of particular desires as the means to achieve a contingent "progress." The project consists of two parts: modernization and modernity. Modernization seeks to materially change the physical world, signaling the realization of desire: "To speak of modernization," Trouillot writes, "is to put the accent on the material and organizational features of world capitalism in specific locales. It is to speak of that geography of management, of these aspects of the development of world capitalism that reorganize space for explicitly political and economic purposes" (2002: 223).

The modernist project combines modernization, a material change, with modernity, an idealist transformation. Modernity is a geography of the imagination, a "map" of collective desires, dreams, and hopes defined against the backdrop of places in time (past, present, and future) and space (here and elsewhere). It is imagined dialogically, in relation to people, events, and places with which particular groups do not want to identify (224–25). It is the combination of the material and the ideological that comprise the topography of Dominican modernism.

At the end of the nineteenth century, Dominican political and economic elites began to imagine a different future, a tomorrow based in modernism. Dominican modernist desire grew out of the broader Hispanic modernism that had fueled independence movements throughout Latin America in the first half of the nineteenth century. Employing the language of social Darwinism (e.g., development, progress, and order), Hispanic American modernism promised an egalitarian and prosperous future for all who followed its doctrine (Zavala 1992: 9). The Dominican dreamscape emphasized national autonomy in the face of dwindling Spanish colonialism, continuing Haitian economic and political dominance, and rising American imperialism. Autonomy, the elite reasoned, could only be achieved by establishing a modern nation-state defined by stable boundaries and a distinctive Dominican identity coupled with economic liberalization and technological innovation (2–4).

The establishment of modern sugar plantations across the country, financed by Cuban and American capitalists in the 1870s, launched Dominican modernization in earnest. Sugar became the engine of Dominican modernism, pushing the country into the new technological age. While the cultivation of sugar on the island began in the fifteenth century, the nineteenth-century sugar plantation and its *central* (mill) marked a new stage of its evolution, characterized by its massive scale, steam power, scientific planning, time schedules, and advanced agricultural methods (Moya Pons 1981: 218). The signs of modernism spread from the plantation into the surrounding landscape. The newly expanded urban centers surrounding the plantations (e.g., San Pedro de Marcoris) became de facto expositions of modernity with their opulent displays of trains, electricity, parks, and grand houses, all heralding the world to come (Baud 1987: 140–45). Before long, sugar fostered societal changes in regions outside the southern and eastern plantation belt, even in areas like the San Juan Valley.

Located in the central southwest region of the country bordering Haiti, the San Juan Valley had long been characterized by porous borders, subsistence agriculture, political and economic isolation, and fluid bicultural identities. Although the area was marginal due to its relative isolation, the emerging Dominican state assigned a central, symbolic role to the frontier. Everything about the frontier, the elites despaired, demonstrated the weakness of the Dominican state. The bilingualism of the region, the population's economic orientation to the then more prestigious Haiti, its political autonomy, and the large Haitian (read Afro-Dominican) population challenged elite dreams of the future. Not surprisingly, the area became a test of Dominican modernism's power to impose firm borders, a modern plantation economy, political and economic subordination to a centralized state, and a stable national identity (a "we" diametrically opposed to "them"). Therefore, the valley became an important battleground of Dominican modernism, and many intentional and unintentional changes were wrought on the borderlands (Baud 1993: 51).

Before the onset of the modernization campaign, and for some time after, cattle ranching was the principle economic activity of the San Juan Valley. National elites considered cattle ranching an obstacle to modernization because the cattle economy was based on freely roaming animals, unfenced communal lands, and transnational grazing spaces ("Dominican" animals were kept on both sides of the border). The valley's small-scale ranchers—most of whom placed their products (hides, meats, and so forth) into global circulation through Haiti, which denied export duties to the Dominican state—were pitted against the modern ideals of "mechanized" production (e.g., the steam-driven sugar plantation), private property, and firm national boundaries. Under the modernization campaign, however, sugar began to assert its hegemonic power in the San Juan Valley, remaking the economy.

The rapid development of sugar plantations in the eastern and southern parts of the country created a related displacement of cattle ranching in the San Juan Valley. As southern towns such as Azua and Barahona abandoned production of staple food crops (manioc, rice, beans, plantains, and potatoes) in favor of the more profitable sugar, cultivation of these staple products shifted north into the San Juan Valley, challenging the cattle economy. These economic shifts prompted other changes, including the privatization of communal lands and the fencing of the valley (Lundahl and Lundius 1990: 219). A culture based on communal access to land for subsistence crops and the right to hunt wild cattle came to an end with the privileging of individual-oriented models of property ownership. As a result, dispossessed *campesinos* were forced into wage labor on the sugar plantations outside of the San Juan Valley.

Yet the modernization campaign did more than change labor and production in the valley; it also reoriented valley trade away from its traditional markets. Dominicans in the borderlands had maintained important trading relationships with their more prosperous neighbor in the west since the creation of the French colony of Saint Domingue in the sixteenth century. Contraband valley trade circumvented the state circuit by exporting untaxed cattle into Haiti while importing consumer goods into the domestic markets without increasing the state coffers. The untaxed flow of goods represented a grave threat to Dominican national consolidation because the government was desperate for funds to repay the costly loans used to finance its modernization campaign. To ensure the repayment of the loans, American banks took control of the country's customhouses, applying the collected duties to the repayment of the debt. By 1905, the U.S. government had intervened directly, taking control of the Dominican customhouses from the banking interests, in order to guarantee the repayment of the international loans (Moya Pons 1995: 281–91). The contraband trade also stymied the Dominican government's efforts to reorient the economic center of the valley away from Port-au-Prince and back toward Santo Domingo. Thus, the evolving Dominican state considered the trade a serious financial and political threat. The elimination of unregulated trade became one of the important goals of Dominican modernism.

Despite resistance, the modernization project forged ahead. There would be no return to communal lands, untaxed trade, or wild cattle. Under the cover of Dominican sovereignty, American control deepened as the Dominican government took out more loans to advance its dreams. The more capital American financial institutions risked in the Dominican Republic, the less they were willing to trust Dominican politicians to safeguard their economic interests. In 1916, the U.S. government, using political unrest as a cover, invaded the country, occupying it for the next eight years. The more extensive American military occupation accelerated the modernization project and the formalization of the border (Lundahl and Lundius 1990: 215). While the occupation ended in 1924, the U.S. government only relinquished control of Dominican customs in 1940.

Dominican modernism complicates simplistic claims of "progress" and "development." Nationally, sugar provided the engine for decades of change that reshaped every region of the country. In the Dominican borderlands, the new economic, political, and social realities produced different results in the San Juan Valley. There were no shiny new trains, no advanced sugar plantations, no tremendous displays of conspicuous wealth. Yet, the physical signs of change were evident. The shift from a wild cattle economy to staple crop production, the transformation of communal lands into privatized domains, the development of the "stateless" borderlands into the state-defended border, and the transfer of power from the "local" elites to transnational political formations (e.g., the American borderland officials and their Dominican military forces) marked Dominican modernization in the valley. But this new physical environment was not enough for the Dominican elite; they also wanted to shape a new national imagination of Dominican modernity.

Racial and Regional Geographies of Dominican Modernity

Dominican modernism was more than a sum of new economic practices, shifting forms of consumption, and increasing scales of production. It was an ideology, a discourse of desire that sought to transform colonial society and its citizens (Zavala 1992: 4). The desire to become modern meant completing the transition into the future by breaking completely with a past of colonial subjectivity and reshaping national "habits" into modern practices that signaled progress and order. The elites hoped that a thorough reordering of the national imagination would bridge the gap between modernization and modernity, and the national image that they sought to foster reflected their anxieties about class, gender, racial, and regional differences and inequalities.

Dominican elites coupled their optimism—fanned by vibrant economic growth—with liberal ideas from the political and social revolutions of Europe and the United States:

> Heavily influenced by European positivism, such Dominican liberals as Américo Lugo argued that due to the "deficiency" of the Dominican racial mixture and low level of mass literacy, the "people" were not prepared for self-governing democracy as in the United States. In this view, the state must be accorded the role both of educator of civic values and of agent of nationhood. The state, lead by the "cultured" aristocracy, must be a civilizing force exercised through "tutelary law," a force that both collectivized the nation as it separated individuals. (Derby 1994: 501)

The elite targeted the Dominican social habits that were considered uncivilized, low class, or unproductive for reform. New state laws would impose, they adamantly believed, bourgeois habits on the population, fostering greater economic growth, social harmony, and individual happiness. State-financed modernization projects (e.g., schools, parks, and sanitation schemes) supplemented the laws. These projects occurred alongside transformations in Dominican racial ideology. Prior to 1870, elites perceived Afro-Dominicans as immoral (e.g., shameless and lazy) and primitive. The onset of the modernist campaign caused elites to view black Dominicans as a biological threat, capable of derailing the modernist project through miscegenation. A newspaper article written in 1914 warned Dominicans of the relationship between racial makeup and development potential: "The degree of civilization and general culture among the Ibero-American people can be measured by the size of the African population they lodge" (*Listín Diario* quoted in Lundius and Lundahl 2000: 573). The large population of blacks and mulattoes became the explanation for the major problems (e.g., political instability, economic crisis, and underdevelopment) facing the country. Blackness thus became a stain on the balance sheet of modernity.

Dominican modernists sought to privilege an ideal somatic type (white European), preferred regions (Cibao and the Southeast), dominant gender (male), and supreme status (property owner)—standards that would define the modern Dominican citizen. Regions and national subjects that diverged from these standards were deemed threatening and would have to be transformed. San Juan and *Sanjuaneros* were targeted for change:

> However, the border has concurrently been seen by *capitaleño* elites as the primordial sign and site of barbarism, of a hybrid space of racial and international admixture, and of the dangers of caudillo, or strongman, rule. Inherited from Spain, this imaginary spatial map delimits those included and excluded from the nation and has justified conquest by the Creole elite from the cosmopolitan capital, in which civilization resides, of the savage and uncontrolled backlands, which represent barbarism. . . . The border or skin of the body politic was perceived to be transgressive because it mixed social taxonomies, was a threat to the nation in its very liminality, and was an area as yet undomesticated by the state. (Derby 1994: 491)

The San Juan Valley, imagined as black, was therefore seen as a threat to the economic, geographic, and racial desires of the modernist project.

In the new order, the San Juan Valley was clearly part of the past. The elite dreamed of rescuing the valley from its isolation and autonomy. In order to achieve its goal, the valley's purportedly backward tendencies had to be changed, by force if necessary. Elites hoped that an emphasis on privately owned (rather than communally held) property, building fences, the development of vagrancy laws, and a heavily defended border would force Sanjuaneros into the nation-state. In turn, these geographically focused efforts would also allow the state to challenge the racially "inferior" types who resided in these regions. Afro-Dominicans had to be broken of their "natural" inclination toward vice and idleness that impeded the advancement of the entire country. Elites declared an open war on the Sanjuaneros, only to be met with an aggressive countervision of Dominican modernism, Liborismo.

Liborismo

The sugar economy created tremendous new wealth for the Dominican elite. Nevertheless, modernity was at best bittersweet for the Dominican majority; economically marginal areas like the San Juan Valley bore the brunt of the changes. Landless and persecuted by new vagrancy laws, male Sanjuaneros left the valley in search of employment on the sugar plantations of the east and south, leaving their families to fend for themselves. Even those fortunate enough to find employment found it hard to cope with the rampant inflation caused by economic speculation. While elites assumed that Afro-Dominican religious practices would naturally die out as a result of modern economic transformations, pervasive unemployment, poverty, and social upheaval made Vodú even more vibrant, ultimately giving birth to Liborismo (Baud 1987: 147). The popular classes in the San Juan Valley, rather than acquiescing to the elite versions of modernity, challenged the elite-imposed program by offering alternative visions of the future. Their popular modernism embraced the need for "progress" but rejected any indiscriminate discarding of the "past." Instead, the past itself would provide the road map to the future. Liborismo was one embodiment of this vision.

Olivorio (Liborio) Mateo was a fifty-year-old Afro-Dominican campesino from the valley who, long before his elevation into a Vodú prophet, had developed a reputation as a credible clairvoyant. Prior to 1908, Liborio had been a "soldier" of elite modernism. Working for a local political strongman in the valley, Liborio served as a field hand helping to fence off the newly privatized lands (Lundius 1995: 41–45; Baud 1993: 59). Popular history maintains that Liborio unexpectedly disappeared during a tremendous storm in 1908. Relatives and friends presumed that he had died during the storm. On the ninth and final day of the memorial services being held in his honor, he reappeared and recounted the story of his disappearance to those present: he had traveled far away, he told them, carried to heaven by an angel on a white horse. While in the spiritual realm, God recruited Liborio to be his servant to spread His word, cure illness, and save the world. Like Jesus's life, Liborio's mission was to last for a total of thirty-three years (Esteban Deive 1978: 187). Liborio revitalized a religion in need of renewal and a society in need of healing: "The blind, the maimed, the crippled, and the tuberculoid sought something more than a remedy for their chronic ailments. The ill appearance of these unfortunates was the symbol of an ailment more serious and general: the [affliction] of a whole society suffering in a situation of crisis" (194). As a novel materialization of divine power, he quickly attracted a faithful band of followers. The sick visited him from all corners of the republic in search of healing. Local newspaper articles reported in 1909 that over twenty-five hundred people arrived weekly to see the messianic leader (Lundius 1995: 51).

In the process of healing the sick, Liborismo articulated a popular vision of modernity. The sugar modernism defined by the elites advocated paid labor (rather than reciprocal labor), cash crops, privatized land, unfair distributions of profits, dependency, state law, and the related persecution of "primitive" culture. Liborio, in contrast, established his camp, Ciudad Santa (Holy City), based on shared volunteer labor (*convite*), equitable distribution of resources, subsistence agriculture, communal lands, self-sufficiency, spiritual law, and the celebration of Afro-Dominican culture. He also refused to charge for his services: "Curaba pero no cobraba" [He cured but did not charge]. Moreover, he and his followers welcomed visitors to Ciudad Santa regardless of their class or background. Elite visitors mixed easily with contraband smugglers, fugitives from justice, and the poor in Liborio's camp (Lundius 1995: 63–74).

The elite quickly recognized the threat posed by Liborio to their form of modernism. In 1909, a prominent medical doctor in San Juan accused the peasant healer of illegally practicing medicine. The doctor disapproved of Liborio curing the sick with Vodú methods: herbs, rocks, charms, dreams, the laying of hands, crosses, rum, water, and prayers (Esteban Deive 1978: 195). Other critics questioned his skills and honesty because of his class. For example, *La Voz del Sur*, a newspaper from San Cristobal in the South, referred to Liborio as a "dirty vagrant, completely unable to take a headache from anybody" (*La Voz* quoted in Lundahl and Lundius 1990: 201; Lundius 1995: 51–52).

The valley bourgeoisie also objected to the religious ceremonies occurring in Ciudad Santa, considering them indecent. Their disgust increased as the national press wrote sensationalist accounts of Liborio's activities. The newspaper accounts depicted the ceremonies as shameful acts, pageants of provocative dancing, nudity, foul language, and sexual orgies. To demonstrate their commitment to elite modernism, the bourgeoisie and its agents stepped up the persecution of Liborio and his followers (Lundius 1995: 63–68). The harassment only made Liborio more popular, especially as supernatural wonders, natural disasters, and political upheaval (the appearance of Haley's Comet in 1910, the earthquake of 1911, and the civil war of 1912) pointed toward the imminent end of the world (Lundius and Lundahl 1989: 10–16). His growing popularity did little to change the elites' view of Liborio; they continued to regard the messianic leader as a moral threat to the burgeoning Dominican future.

The Liboristas, followers of Liborio, constituted more than a moral threat; they were considered a security threat as well. Liborio and his followers possessed firearms acquired during their service in the civil war of 1912. The arms provided a measure of protection from the continuous harassment from government troops. When the Americans invaded the Dominican Republic in 1916, the armed Liboristas resisted the U.S. project of consolidating Dominican state authority and power. Moreover, the armed valley residents aided the Haitian nationalists (*Cacos*) who were fighting a guerilla campaign against American forces across the valley border following the 1915 U.S. invasion of Haiti. Because of labor, trade, and political alliances, as well as familial connections, Haitians and Dominicans who lived along the border also developed a shared sense of struggle and resistance. Many of the Haitian guerillas had participated in the Dominican civil war of 1912 just as many of the Liboristas had taken part in the Haitian civil war of 1914. The later war brought the Haitian borderland *caudillo*, Oreste Zamora, to the presidency of Haiti for a brief period. The *Caco* leader, Charlemagne Péralte, was believed to be one of Liborio's numerous Haitian adepts. The persistent Haitian resistance campaign occurring right across the border made subjugating the San Juan Valley a central goal of American military strategy (Lundius 1995: 226–27).

Liborio and his followers quickly came to the attention of the American authorities following the U.S. occupation of the Dominican Republic in 1916, and the troops forced the Liboristas to surrender their weapons in early 1917. However, the disarmament did not ease the distrust or harassment of the Liboristas. Tensions continued to rise as members of the valley elite, seeking to ingratiate themselves with the U.S. authorities, fabricated stories of pending attacks by the Liboristas. A force of U.S. marines set out in search of Liborio's mobile Ciudad Santa in the spring of 1917. On April 7, the occupation forces engaged hundreds of Liboristas in a battle that lasted several hours. Nine of Liborio's followers were killed in the attack. In the battle's aftermath, the messianic leader reduced his group to only twenty loyal men and women, and they sought refuge in the mountainous forests of the San Juan Valley (Lundius 1995: 91–97).

Liborio and his small band eluded the authorities for most of 1917 and 1918, despite the numerous traps set up to capture them. The group moved continuously throughout the Haitian-Dominican borderlands, healing the sick, tending to garden plots hidden deep in the mountains, and smuggling goods to and from Haiti. By 1918, Liborio's group had joined Haitian nationalists in their fight against the American occupation of Haiti. The Liboristas fought against the U.S. troops in Haiti and provided sanctuaries and supplies for Haitian rebels in Dominican territory. Liborista participation in the Haitian resistance intensified the desire of the elites for occupation forces in both countries to destroy Liborio and his movement (Lundius 1995: 97–115).

The U.S. led Dominican National Guard (GND) aggressively pursued Liborio, destroyed his known camps, confiscated his food stores and cattle, and persecuted suspected adherents. Even after the death of Péralte in 1919, Liborio still managed to elude authorities for another three years. The GND finally caught up with Liborio in 1922, killing him in an early morning ambush. The soldiers dragged Liborio's corpse into the central plaza of San Juan de la Maguana on a litter, where they displayed it prominently as a demonstration of their power. The authorities even photographed his dead corpse, creating a trophy of their success (Lundius 1995: 111–23).

Liborio's corporal death only increased his power and popularity; his assassination transformed him from a fleshy saint into a more potent spiritual one. For Liborio's followers, the photo failed to provide proof of his death, and so the authorities unwittingly created another Liborista charm. The photo of Liborio's corpse remains an essential icon for Afro-Dominican Vodú practice in the San Juan Valley today. It is prominently displayed in altar rooms as well as in living rooms throughout the Dominican borderlands. Containers can be destroyed, but the essences, ideas, and spirits they reflect often transform, multiply, and relocate despite the best-laid "progressive" plans.

The Liborista Legacy and the *Palma Sola* Movement

They will never be able to kill us, and if they somehow did, no one would believe them. Because others would dream they were us."
—Paco Ignacio Taibo II, *Four Hands*

What I have is not mine, it belongs to everyone. It is mine and it is not mine. I cannot say I am Olivorio, but like me he came in order to carry out the force of the Spirit. . . . There is only one grace, and it is for everyone, but [the force] comes forth with the help of particular persons who have to show it to others. His name is Olivorio, mine is Enrique, those are only names. Two names, but the same grace.
—Enrique Figueroa, quoted in *The Great Power of God in San Juan Valley* by Jan Lundius

While other healers emerged to take Liborio's place, healing the social ills of modernism, proponents of elite modernism continued to wage war against Liborismo and Dominican Vodú, even after the end of the U.S. occupation in 1924. Upon assuming the presidency in 1930, Rafael Leonidas Trujillo increased his consolidation of power, begun during the occupation. Suppressing popular religion and assassinating regional power figures comprised a central part of his plan for eliminating threats to his power. In 1930, Trujillo's agents killed the most important Liborista leader of the day, José Popa, and also assassinated the aging frontier caudillo Desiderio Arias in 1931. Additionally, Trujillo outlawed the practice of Vodú, threatening adherents with imprisonment (Lundius and Lundahl 1989: 47; Baud 1993: 55–56). Trujillo's reign marked a new phase of elite modernism in the valley as well.

While the privatization of communal lands increased, the changes were now largely benefiting the personal economic interests of the dictator. Unlike the southern and northern economies of the Dominican Republic, there were few foreign interests in the San Juan Valley; and so Trujillo could claim it for himself (Baud 1987: 49). Trujillo pursued his goals in the valley by monopolizing distribution of the crops produced by commercial agriculture (e.g., rice), dislocating campesinos "squatting" on communal lands, and distributing land to peasants who were willing to follow the dictates of the state. The killing of thousands of Afro-Dominican small landholders during the 1937 "Haitian" massacre freed vast amounts of land on the frontier. By 1961, the year Trujillo was assassinated, his family owned more land in the San Juan Valley than in any other part of the country (Turits 1998: 294–96, 316–17; Martinez 1991: 100). Many valley peasants were forced into exile or voluntarily left in the face of religious persecution, state-sponsored genocide, land privatization, and political repression. Ultimately, *Trujillista* modernism, despite its extensive coercion and violence, failed to destroy, or even suppress, Afro-Dominican religious practice. Liborismo continued to thrive in the San Juan Valley in the shadow of the Trujillo dictatorship.

The disintegration of the Trujillo dictatorship in the late 1950s sparked renewed activity in the Liborista communities of the valley. Around 1960, Leon and Plinio Ventura Rodríguez, Los "Mellizos" (the "Twins") of Palma Sola, emerged to extend the Liborista legacy to form the *Palma Sola* movement. The "Twins" came from a family that spanned both sides of the Dominican-Haitian border and had been active participants in the various peasant struggles that marked the modernity campaign. Their paternal grandfather, Nicolas Cuevas, served as Liborio's trusted lieutenant and was also a renowned healer (Lundius 1995: 106). The extensive U.S. manhunt for Nicolas, the destruction of his house, the persecution of his family, and his ultimate assassination by occupation forces reflects his importance in the Liborista movement (Martinez 1991: 80). The departure of the Americans in 1924 did not relieve the persecution of the Ventura Rodríguez family. The harassment increased under the Trujillo dictatorship, especially in the 1930s, when Trujillo actively consolidated his power. Perceiving the family as a threat to his growing power in the valley, Trujillo persecuted them. In 1935, the dictator assassinated the "Twin's" maternal uncle, Manuel Ventura, another important Liborista. Prompted by the assassination, some family members, including the "Mellizos," fled into exile in neighboring Haiti, staying with extended family there (Martinez 1991: 126–31).

Like Liborismo, the Palma Sola movement developed from Vodú's dialogue with the changing political and economic environment (i.e., the terror and chaos of the Trujillo dictatorship and the post-Trujillo period). In 1960, the Holy Spirit commanded the "Twins" to establish a sacred site to await the world to come. Trujillo, the Holy Spirit informed them, would soon die and the Old World would die with him. Campesinos left their fields in the different districts of the valley to converge in Palma Sola, the reincarnation of the earlier Liborio's Ciudad Santa (Martinez 1991: 133). Leon and Plinio marked the presence of the Holy Spirit by constructing a church, a calvary (a group of three crosses representing the Holy Trinity), and two large wooden crosses, all enclosed in a sacred corral (151). Soon, thousands of pilgrims traveled to meet the "Mellizos" in search of healing. The "Twins" mobilized the usual tools and techniques from the visible and invisible realms of Vodú—the dead, rocks, springs, possession, dreams, herbs, prayers, the forest, Liborio, and the Holy Trinity (150). The brothers reenergized Vodú by introducing two new personal charms into Vodú—the sacred site of Palma Sola and the "Twins" themselves. The *Palmasolistas* articulated a populist vision of the post-Trujillo future. "The *Mellizos* worked to obtain the sanctity of the campesinos, eliminate the evils of the earth, and achieve the equality and unity of their followers" (133).

Elite protests against the Palmasolistas began almost immediately. The objections started locally as valley professionals, businesses, and churches of all faiths began to alert national authorities to the threat posed by the "Twins" (Martinez 1991: 34). The national press soon joined in the defense of elite modernism; a 1961 editorial in *El Caribe*, a newspaper founded by Trujillo, deemed the Palmasolistas "a painful anachronism in the middle of the twentieth century" (Ferreras 1983: 317–18). The war of words assumed the form of a moral outrage. However, the autonomous organization and articulation of the peasant agency concerned the elite. It reflected the modernist campaign's failure to maintain elite subjugation of the valley's campesinos (San Miguel 1994: 86).

While the local concern was with peasant agency, the significance of the Palma Sola movement changed as it gained national attention. Outside the valley, many observers read the Palma Sola movement against the disconcerting backdrop of the post-Trujillo political scene. As various factions of the elite engaged in a bitter fight to control the spoils of the post-Trujillo state, rumors that the Palma Sola movement was a plot to create public disorder were spread by the sensationalist press. The Palmasolistas were, the gossip maintained, Trujillista agents of suspect nationality trying to return Trujillo's family to power, despite the long history of the Ventura Rodríguez family's opposition to Trujillo. Ironically, Liborismo emerged from the shadows of the Trujillo dictatorship only to be confronted by the heirs of the elite modernism professing their newly found opposition to Trujillismo. Like the earlier campaign against Liborio, the elite responded to the threat of Palma Sola with state violence, sending out the national armed forces to subjugate the rebellious citizens. The confrontation came to a head in 1962 as the Dominican army massacred eight hundred Palmasolistas and arrested seven hundred more followers (Martinez 1991: 233–43). The show of state violence could not rid the valley of its new charms and alternative texts of modernity. Like Liborio's sacred sites, Palma Sola continues to function as a sacred Vodú site of power and practice. Today, in spite of the latest phase of Dominican modernism—neoliberalism—popular religion persists in the San Juan Valley, and the struggle to control the outcome of modernism continues.

Conclusion

There is neither a first nor a last word and there are no limits to the dialogic context (it extends into the boundless past and the boundless future). Even *past* meanings, that is, those born in the dialogue of past centuries, can never be stable (finalized, ended once and for all)—they will always change (be renewed) in the process of subsequent, future development of the dialogue. At any moment in the development of the dialogue there are immense, boundless masses of forgotten contextual meanings, but at certain moments of the dialogue's subsequent development along the way they are recalled and invigorated in renewed form (in a new context). Nothing is absolutely dead; every meaning will have its homecoming festival.
—M. M. Bakhtin, "Toward a Methodology for the Human Sciences"

"History," the old adage goes, "is written by the victors." While the "official" record may reflect the victor's version of history, popular history is never entirely displaced. The "people without history" keep their own books. Their "hidden transcripts" masquerade in plain view, disputing "official" accounts while waiting for their homecoming. Popular history brashly challenges anthropology, daring the discipline to look beyond the "official" records, and inviting us into the folds of history conveniently left out of the books. By embracing the dialogue of history—that is, competing hidden and public narratives—critical anthropology questions the ideological concepts that create the illusion of elite order and control (Benjamin 2003a [1939]: 164). The dialogic approach to history emphasizes the idea that "human beings participate in history both as actors and narrators" (Trouillot 1995: 2). Yet the trick is to discover the forms, media, and places in which the nonelite narrators and actors have elaborated their memories and histories. In the San Juan Valley, Vodú is one of the stages on which popular interpretations of the local, regional, and national past have been performed.

The Dominican elite dreamed of progress and civilization for more than a century. It is the particulars, the specificities of time and space, which challenge the universality of modernism. No individual, group, or community can lay exclusive claim to modernism. We can only "make sense" of modernism, a fluid sign, through dialogue with other signs (Appadurai 1996: 2; Comaroff and Comaroff 1993: xii). Accepting modernism as a sign engaged in semiosis, instead of an objective condition or ending point, we can better understand modernism as a sign of desire utilized to create belonging and order in a changing world (M. Berman 1988: 6). Dominican modernism, as imagined by the country's elite, was not the U.S. modernism of skyscrapers and regional imperialism. Instead, Dominican modernism focused on economic growth, scientific agriculture, the proliferation of technology, and the expansion of urban centers. Despite the differences between the two modernities, the two projects were related because the transformation of the Dominican landscape occurred hand in hand with the development of an increasingly globalized American financial market and an increasingly militarized U.S. foreign policy agenda. With the merging of economic and political interests, political decisions in the Dominican Republic depended on politicians in Washington as much as those in Santo Domingo. The modernist dream in the Dominican Republic was simultaneously local and global.

Dominican elites' vision of the future was built on the foundation of forgetting a past characterized by economic dependency, political disorder, and cultural hybridity, all considered obstacles to the glorious future that was waiting right around the corner. Shedding the past required more than collective amnesia: it compelled the elite to wage a legal, social, political, and economic war against the fleshy remnants of the "disappeared" past. The elites' determination to become modern heralded a genocidal campaign, yet Dominican popular classes survived the long period of oppression, refusing to yield entirely to elite desires. Yearning for change, they offered their own version of modernism. Beyond the simplistic narrative of resistance, Afro-Dominicans participated as active agents of change in the transformation of the Dominican Republic. The new Dominican economy of the late nineteenth century demanded new spirits, rituals, and priests to activate the healing powers of Vodú, curing the social dis-ease resulting from the economic and political upheaval. The emergence of Liborio and Liborismo demonstrates the dynamic nature of Dominican popular religion, which is constantly engaged in a process of renewal, shedding "inactive" saints and adding new and more potent spirits to the pantheon. Through popular religion, the peasants of the San Juan Valley advocated for their own dynamic version of modernity. They mobilized the past as a guide and kept Liborio and Afro-Dominican culture alive, nurturing a flash of the spirit that could be openly read by all who believed.

Notes

1. This essay is dedicated to the late Doña A. for her motherly love and infectious spirit, Ache! I gratefully acknowledge the friendship and guidance provided by *mis panas* in the San Juan Valley, Mimi and Elaine, and to all the other *Sanjuaneros* who helped me during my fieldwork in the San Juan Valley.

DIASPORA AND DESIRE

Gendering "Black America" in Black Liverpool

JACQUELINE NASSY BROWN

"Black Liverpool" and "black America," no less than the "African Diaspora," refer to racialized geographies of the imagination.[1] The mapping of racial signifiers onto geographical ones lends such terms the illusion of referring to physical rather than social locations. That there is no actual space that one could call the African Diaspora, despite how commonly it is mapped onto particular locales, points attention to the ways that social spaces are constructed in tandem with processes of racial formation.

In 1991, I set out to study race and nation in Liverpool, England. Set in a city with one of the longest-settled black populations in the United Kingdom, my research investigated why and how black identity is constituted as the mutual opposite of English and British identities. Yet in pursuing these themes, I became increasingly amazed at how frequently my informants made discursive forays into "black America." Nested at key moments in their narratives were references to the formative influence that black America, in many forms, has had on racial identity and politics in their city. The experiences they narrated were varied, and the narratives themselves were rich, poignant, and deeply gendered. Black Liverpudlians told of their relations with the black American servicemen (or GIS) who were stationed outside their city for some twenty-five years beginning in World War II. Men and women also spoke about the travels of their own African, Afro-Caribbean, and black Liverpudlian fathers who were employed as seamen by Liverpool shipping companies. The global wanderings of the city's black men often brought them to black environs around the Atlantic world, including in the United States. Narratives of black Liverpudlians' diasporic encounters also referred to the migration of local women to the mythical place called "black America." Finally, and crucially, men and women told of how and why they have accessed the many black American cultural productions that have, for decades, circulated around the social space of black Liverpool.

This essay focuses on the politically, culturally, and sexually intimate relationships that unfolded between black Liverpool and black America over two historical moments: the postwar period on the one hand, and the era defined by the U.S. civil rights and black power movements on the other. Examining one of countless forerunners to what is today dubbed globalization, I show how a nascent American hegemony actually facilitated the development of radical blackness in Liverpool. Yet this is not to treat the local as an inert receptacle of global flows of black American culture. Nor is it to reduce the local to a trope for ethnographic specificity, as so frequently happens in the anthropology of globalization. The local, I suggest, is an ideological construct and as such merits scrutiny in its own right; in Liverpool it forms a racial and spatial basis of identity that forcefully mediates and sanctions appropriations of black America.

"Diaspora" has become one of the buzzwords of globalization discourse—a discourse which, for all its currency and cachet, relies largely on the classical definition of the term. Most scholarship defines it as any population living outside of its original homeland. That approach generally takes an initial moment of dispersal—or "scattering," as per the Greek etymology of the word diaspora—to be the starting point of analysis, while also defining displacement from and longing for ancestral homelands as paradigmatic of the so-called diasporic condition. As an alternative to that approach, I examine the way historically positioned actors identify the processes involved and the geographies implicated in the formation of diasporic subjectivities and communities.[2]

Paul Gilroy has reinvigorated diaspora studies by suggesting that black communities across the Atlantic are linked both by the mutual perception of a shared, wholly racialized condition and by the cultural-cum-political resources they make available for overcoming the racial oppression that grips them all, albeit in different ways (1987). Through such practices, Gilroy further argues, differently located blacks transcend national boundaries, creating a mutually accessible, translatable, and inspirational political culture that invites universal black participation (Gilroy 1993). His hopeful vision elides the contentious politics that serve to differentially apportion the privileges of membership in the diasporic community.[3] I show that power differentials across black communities mediate power relations within them and likewise that power asymmetries within individual black communities shape members' participation in—and production of—the transnational space of diaspora. Ultimately, I argue that gendered ideologies about locality have effectively produced black Liverpool and black America as social spaces to be differently occupied, experienced, bridged, and traversed.

Becoming Local, Becoming Black

Liverpool owes its birth and growth as a city to its role as an international seaport, trafficking first in enslaved Africans and later in goods from around the globe, including from Britain's colonies worldwide. Beginning in the mid-nineteenth century and extending well into the twentieth, African (and to a lesser extent Afro-Caribbean) men were hired as seamen by Liverpool shippers. Up until the industry's death in the late 1970s, shipping was the primary source of male employment in Liverpool. And despite the industry's obsolescence, the shipping life still served in the 1990s as the keystone of Liverpudlian identity. For example, the origin story that blacks most commonly rehearse centers on African sailors, who are celebrated as the founding fathers of what has become black Liverpool. The generations-long participation of black men in global seafaring forms a very gendered basis of local tradition, identity, and community, while also contributing profoundly to the construction of travel as a male activity.

African sailors, as well as their seagoing male children, have provided the larger community access to local identity. Africans are also noted for setting into motion both the institution of interracial marriage and its one-way gendering. African men commonly docked in Liverpool's port, formed romantic relationships with white English and Irish women, and settled in the city—so the origin story goes. It continues by noting the dearth of marriageable black women in the early years of the African presence. When black women's numbers did begin to rise, their male counterparts did not consider them potential spouses. Black men I knew reported that they had grown up with these same women, clustered as they all were in a tiny neighborhood in south Liverpool. Black men explained that the kinship they felt toward black women precluded the formation of any sexual desire for them. Others described the contemporary prevalence of interracial partnering as an exercise in "freedom of choice."

Although African seamen are credited with giving birth to the black community, many of their adult children describe them as having been obstacles to the formation of black identity itself. Historically, the children of interracial unions were regarded, both by their parents and society at large, as "half-castes." They also considered themselves as such. Their struggle to recognize and overcome the stigma of that inscription is an absolutely crucial theme in black Liverpudlian accounts of the way they became black. American influences dating back to the 1940s feature centrally in those narratives.

World War II was a formative moment in Liverpool. The city was heavily bombed, many of its men were killed on the high seas, and its economic situation was dire—as in the rest of Britain. Yet, by many people's account, blacks had an active social life, some of which centered on the rituals that celebrated seamen's comings and goings. Alluding to the repression that also characterized life in the city for blacks in this era, Scott, a black man in his sixties, recalled, "When someone's uncle or father would come home from sea, you couldn't go to the pubs, so they'd arrange a party that would be mainly of an African style. There'd be yams and there'd be fruit." The global travels of African seamen gave the local community access to foodstuffs unavailable in the rest of Britain. Yet it was not only food that the seamen brought into Liverpool, but music. The World War II generation was able to enjoy recordings by Billie Holiday and Lena Horne because, as Scott relayed, "In some instances, fathers and uncles had been over to America as seamen and had brought records back. So within the black community of Liverpool, we've always grown up with a type of traditional black music. If it wasn't African, it would be American—it wouldn't be so much West Indian, Caribbean music around at that time."

Into the impoverished yet lively wartime environs entered American servicemen, black and white, who were stationed at bases across Britain; Liverpool was sandwiched between two of them, Sealand and Burtonwood. Scott described the social scene in the mid-1950s created by the presence of these men, whom my informants commonly referred to as either "the Yanks" or "the GIS":

By that time, we had our own community centers as well as nightclubs. But the actual nightclub scene was fantastic. The black American GIs—'cause *that's* what they were called—would come in with their big cars. Some of them were regular servicemen . . . [but] some, in comparison to British servicemen or to the black population, were quite rich. So they could afford to have their cars shipped over from the States. And they would drive into Liverpool with these American Cadillacs. Some of them would be in their uniforms, and some of them would be in their American-style, civilian clothes. And they'd come into the nightclubs. . . . You'd have a bit of a dance floor, and everybody would come in and enjoy themselves. . . . It was the first time that you'd hear the likes of the Platters, and a lot of the old black groups that are dying out now.

An important site in the cultural geography of race in the city was a place called the Rialto, which consisted of a ballroom, where white musicians performed black American jazz for exclusively white patrons, and a cinema that did admit blacks. With the arrival of the GIs in the 1940s, white musicians were displaced and the black section of Liverpool began to draw the attention of neighboring areas for its booming musical life.

While the nostalgia of some of the city's black men, across generations, revealed a distinct reverence of black America for its musical contributions to black Liverpool, many men also expressed concern about the Yanks' apparent wealth and the monied image they struck. Scott's recollection was vivid: "The high-ranking ones drove big Pontiacs. It was the first time I had seen these cars apart from seeing them in American films. And you'd see one of the GIs walking down Upper Parliament Street with conked hair, and he'd be flashing his wallet and sweet-talking the women." Some black men of the city joined white British men in commenting on this politic of location, saying that "there's nothing wrong with the GIs except that they're overpaid, oversexed, and over here." Black women had a different opinion. Invariably, they spoke of "the Yanks" and their appeal in terms of the good times the GIs gave them. What follows is the description that Claire, a woman in her fifties, provided of the postwar dating scene:

We always looked forward to the weekend because Friday to Sunday, around the Rialto area, it was packed with men with either blue uniforms or brown uniforms. At Burtonwood Club they all had the brown uniforms on. And at the Sealand Club, they were Air Force, so they all had the blue uniforms on. So there was this color of brown uniforms and blue uniforms, and we would be looking for stripes. If they had no stripes, they wouldn't get a looking. One stripe, you didn't get a looking. You had to have two stripes and over before we would entertain them.

At this point I asked Claire what the black men of Liverpool had to say about all this, and here is her response:

> Well, there was a fight! The black men said that the Americans—"the Yanks" is what they said—the Yanks were taking away our women. So there was a fight. They beat each other up! They beat each other up terrible. But the women stayed firm and said, "We don't want home-grown." When the Rialto was a cinema, they'd come and pick us up and sometimes they'd have a car. . . . Well! And it'd be an American car. And if you got one—an American man who had a car—oh, you were a star! And they'd take you to the Rialto. Or, if they didn't have a car, just to be seen walking up the road and going into the Rialto with this man, in this uniform, was something you knew that people were looking [at] and nudging one another, and we just thought it was wonderful! When you go up the stairs to the Rialto, they would put their hand on your elbow and help you up, and we just thought that was marvelous! Now we did not get that attention from the blacks in Liverpool. So after we had experienced these wonderful manners, this is what we wanted. We wanted to be treated like we were queens. And we were getting that treatment from the Yanks. And that's why we didn't want anything to do with the men of the area.

Here Claire gives evidence that supports the view that black Liverpudlian men commonly articulated. That is, she intimates that Liverpool's black women were attracted to the Americans for their glamour and for what they could offer. Yet Claire also notes, importantly, that women were not getting that kind of attention from "homegrown" black men.

Two sisters of the World War II generation, Caroline and Jean, were in their absolute glory reminiscing about those days. Caroline showed me her photo album, crammed with pictures of herself, Jean, and their various American beaus. At one point in this interview, Caroline nudged her sister, asking with a gleam in her eye, "We had some good times, didn't we [Jean]?" Her sister responded with equal enthusiasm: "Oh, honest to *God!*" Their private, though telling, little exchange suggested that they were calling up some rather racy memories indeed. In the memories they did verbalize, the GIS' presence was represented as key to the making of Liverpool, even if these men were a tad unsophisticated. As Caroline commented, "Liverpool used to be a smashing place! All the smart ones got out. The GIS used to come in from Sealand and Burtonwood. Most of them were into partying here and partying there. But they were nice, you know?! They spoke nice. You know, they had the accent! They were good company—that is, every now and again you'd get one that you *could* converse with!"

Caroline and Jean are the daughters of a white Irish mother and a Nigerian father—"a Yoruba man," as Caroline would proudly phrase it. Her photo album was crammed with pictures of him, too. Caroline enjoyed pointing out his dignified poses and how he was dressed: in stunning English attire. Part of what she loved about him—and, indeed, the generation of African seamen to which he belonged—was the way he traversed two cultural worlds with seeming ease. He would dress fashionably English, expressing no sense of contradiction, yet also took pride in teaching his English-born children to cook Nigerian food. The sisters' representations of their father and his compatriots contrasted dramatically with those of younger black Liverpudlians whose relations with their own African fathers, as we shall see later, were fraught with tension. In speaking about their father's identity, these women added another plotline to the unfolding drama of 1950s Liverpool, for here they had occasion to condemn the black Americans for speaking so disparagingly of Africans. Caroline recalled, "One of them asked me—now I'm going back a long way—he asked me where my father was from and I said, 'My dad's African.' And do you know what that man said? 'Oh, one of them jungle men.' I said [to him], 'You don't know what you are! You're only government issue!'" She and Jean added that when they would go to the cinema with the Americans, these men would make racist comments about the Africans depicted occasionally on the screen. The sisters explained the Americans' unsavory behavior in sociological terms, through reference to their class positions. Caroline supposed that in comparison to her own father, who was a chief chef on board a ship, most of the GIS came from poor backgrounds. She speculated that it was only through their employment in the services that they came to have "a few dollars in their pockets," as she put it.

Just as black American men would descend upon the Rialto area on weekends, so too would black women travel to the American bases on Liverpool's outskirts to attend dances and meet men. Kathleen, in her fifties, explained:

The two American bases were within commuting distance; it would take an hour and a half to get there on the bus. And the buses would be at Lime Street Station and they'd pick up the girls and go to these dances, which is how a lot of the romances got started, including my own. Black men in Britain—and these were the homegrown ones—were not into us "half-castes," as we were called in those days. They were only interested in the white girls. The Americans came in and they were interested in anyone in skirts, basically.

Interracial relationships in Liverpool have been composed most visibly of black men with white women. Many black women I interviewed expressed intense emotion when talking about the practice of interracial dating. Although they often struggled to find some charitable explanation for black men's behavior toward them, inevitably they would talk about the pain of their perceived rejection. As another woman, Crystal, put it: "If you talk to black ladies in Liverpool, they'll say to you, 'the black men in Liverpool never seem to want to date us.' I know a lot of black men in this community, and they do not date black women. And that's why when the men from America—the black men—came from the base, it was like, 'Hey, thank you!' And we are so proud to be asked out by a black man." Like Crystal, many black Liverpudlian women married Americans and migrated to the United States, giving rise to a now institutionalized debate of the classic chicken-and-egg variety. Black women said they were perpetually overlooked by black men, while the latter commonly recited the refrain that "the Yanks stole our women." Men of the 1950s generation say that they did not have fancy cars, that they were poor and skinny from having lived off of rations for years, and that they could not offer black women what "the Yanks" were offering. There grew, then, some animosity between black American men and Liverpool's black men that would extend into the next generation.

As the postwar years gave way to the period marked by the U.S. civil rights movement, new black American iconography was ushered into Liverpool. These images contrasted sharply with the image that the "Yanks" had hitherto embodied. Caroline and Jean bluntly described the transformation that took place across generations. Caroline said, "When all this American civil rights happened in the 1960s, the GIs changed their tune. They all wanted to be 'black African' and that kind of thing. It's like today some of these people are wearing African things and it's all like a fashion to them, you see." Jean added, "They haven't got a clue about Africans and the different tribes, and that. After the civil rights started . . . they all wanted to be dressed in the caftan or whatever, with the big Afros." Like Jean and Caroline, black people commonly and proudly represented Liverpool as a distinctly "African" city, a place where African food and music color everyday life, and where many blacks know their ancestors' exact origins on the continent. The 1970s generation had much to say about the positioning of the black Americans vis-à-vis "Africa."

Civil Rights and Black Power in an "African" City

In the late 1960s and early 1970s, the imaginations of young blacks were captured by the resistance practices they commonly associated with black America. They seized and appropriated the wealth of black American resources available to them, imbuing all manner of iconography and cultural productions emanating from the United States with a racial meaning and significance that could be productively utilized in Liverpool. Black youth fashioned these materials, in all their variety, into a distinctly—and distinctly gendered—black Liverpudlian politic. For example, this generation of black men adopted the strategies of the Black Panthers in defying the young fascist groups that sought to restrict them from traveling into exclusively white areas of the city. One black man I knew spoke of such practices in an interview that took place just outside of Liverpool 8, which is, strictly speaking, a postal designation, but which takes on its cultural significance as the section of the city where blacks are perceived to live in the largest numbers:

> You wouldn't want to be in this area in them days because you'd be at risk. At my age—then I was in my teens—you were at risk of being beaten up by the police or the skinheads. And where I was was the heart of it, where these guys lived and hung out. This was their homeland, not mine. It's funny—up by Lodge Lane there's a pub called The Boundary. And it actually *was* the boundary for black people as far as I was concerned. You actually couldn't go down there and down by Wavertree Road; it was like South Africa. Cops would actually say, "What are you doing going out of your area?" We didn't like it, but. . . . The black community was [in] Liverpool 8, Granby Street, Carter Street. To go into town meant hand-to-hand combat. And also around then—you're talking about the late 1960s and early 1970s—you were not only being around black people and a black family, but also the Black Panthers. . . . We were reflecting what was going

on in the States. I mean we weren't actually—some of the older people were politically motivated. But we just—we couldn't see why we couldn't go here, there, and the other place. So we organized.

Others spoke of similar contributions black America made to their racial sensibilities. Joseph, another black informant in his thirties, recalled that black American music during the civil rights era was always "reverberating around the house." Joseph said that he gained a perspective on racism by studying the lyrics of the Temptations, which he described as "pure philosophy," and by reading the backs of their album covers. He added that as a child he had idolized Muhammad Ali for the pride he showed in black people and for his rejection of what Joseph described as "mainstream, white-dominated, American values." With that, Joseph said that if whites in his neighborhood were calling him a "nigger," he was proud to be that because, as he put it, "There are some powerful niggers in the world. Look at Muhammad Ali."

Unlike blacks of the previous generation, younger ones often perceived their African fathers as cultural gatekeepers due to these men's steadfast refusal to share any aspects of African culture as they knew it. As embodied in their relationships with their fathers, these blacks' experiences of "Africa" were tinged with the pain of exclusion. Greg, a black man in his thirties, said that his father "wanted to keep bits of his self and not necessarily share them with English people—which we were really perceived as. I mean English mixed-race Nigerian-British people." Ronni, who is Greg's age and is also of mixed parentage, said she wanted to learn Yoruba but claimed that her father "seemed to want to put her off it." She movingly offered her understanding of her father's position:

> To be honest, I don't know if he was a bit prejudiced against his own daughters because of our color. I think he was a bit disappointed because, like, three of us were very light (not me, I was one of the darker ones), and they seemed to get a lot of pressure. . . . He was a funny man, mentally. His mentality was different, like. Sometimes he'd go on, "Oh you don't know what them white people done to my father," and all this. And he'd take it out on us. These African men—these old ones what come from back home—they have some heavy mentality that is very difficult to understand. You don't know if they love you or they hate you. Your own flesh and blood.

Black Liverpudlians' pained relation to "Africa" coexisted with their pride in how "African" their city is. Yet Greg and Ronni are not expressing desires and longings for Africa as a generalized and idealized ancestral homeland; rather, they give voice to a profound sense of displacement from their African fathers. In this context, "black America" became the object of diasporic longing, for it answered these and other problematics—however partially and contentiously.

Black American iconography and ideologies traveling into Liverpool helped some black youth grapple with issues of both racial identity in the face of white British racism and nationalism and cultural identity in the face of what they perceived as their African fathers' distancing postures. In what follows, Greg suggests that through the gripping, and mutually class-based and masculine image these men embodied, black Americans effectively re-routed the previously fruitless search for an African identity among people of his generation. He does so by describing the way the GIS, with their trappings of glamour and wealth, ever so visibly occupied Granby Street—the symbolic heart of black Liverpool.

The American bases would accommodate a particular type of American black culture. They would accommodate it in style and fashion and big cars. The thing about poverty in Liverpool—you didn't see big cars. You see them now, but [then] you didn't see big cars and flashy clothes. And although you didn't fully understand what was going on, you actually did get a vibe from it: a serious uplifting feeling from seeing someone with black skin in a huge car driving down Granby Street! And that opened up other areas, like the crème de la crème of the whole dancing culture within black people. So you picked up on that level as well. There wasn't a lot of connection to Africa other than via America. There wasn't that direct connection. There is that massive connection within the large West African settlement in Liverpool, [but] at that time it really wasn't an *African* agenda; it was an *American* agenda and you got your information on Africa via America.

The GIS, and "black America" more generally, were increasingly gaining authority in Liverpool, for the resources they provided proved eminently useful and translatable in local struggles around race. As Greg recalled,

Because I'm from a mixed background . . . you had separate answers to questions anyway. My dad deals with colonialism in Nigeria and his thinking was that "they're all crazy, they're all mad, they're white—they're all crazy" . . . so his answer was just to ignore it. . . . Going toward me mum . . . She'd say, "Well you say this and you say that." But it still left the questions. It was all coming out of me not being the same as the majority in the school. I'm aware that the majority of the school is British and Liverpudlian on a white basis and aware that I definitely wasn't in that area. I wasn't quite sure of the area I was in. I wasn't fully positioned in any position.

By the time I went to secondary school I was definitely seeing myself as black; there was a political context to how I was looking at myself. That was informed by international things: Afros and style and fashion, my sisters' contact with the American air base, and things like that. It brought politics on a wider scale than just immediately in Liverpool 8. Yeah, it informed things! It was in an international context that I was starting to get feedback on things. Youth in the area were taking on things. Growing Afros, wearing arm bands, wearing one black glove to a certain extent. I was brought out of this sort of West African upbringing where they put you in a bubble. I could set my own agenda. It opened up things and my identity was, like, being informed by wider things rather than just being informed by the family.

The particular character of diasporic identification now in formation can be thrown into relief by examining the shift in black Liverpudlians' class status across generations. It will be remembered that Caroline, speaking from the World War II generation, linked the GIS' lower-class status to their lack of African identity; they denigrated Africans, she said, because they were too poor to know any better. A similar, though inverted, set of class relations between American and Liverpudlian blacks may be operating in Greg's generation. It may be conjectured that the rising rate of black unemployment that accompanied the decline of Liverpool's shipping industry in the 1970s lent the GIS and their apparent wealth even more prestige among Greg's peers than Caroline's. In her generation, as Scott relayed in his own narrative about the 1950s, cars signified America's affluence relative to Britain; in Greg's 1970s version, these same flashy accoutrements were reconstituted as signifiers of black possibility. The black American men who would drive these spectacles down the impoverished streets of Liverpool became entrusted with an unprecedented authority on Africa. And in contrast to Caroline and Jean, who remarked upon the hollowness of the GIS' African identification in the civil rights and black power eras ("They haven't a clue about Africans and the different tribes. . . . It's all like a fashion to them"), Greg drew on the GIS as a valuable resource ("You got your information of Africa via America"). In expressing their awe of the GIS, people of his generation commonly catalogued which images associated with black America left indelible impressions on them—images like the Afro, which people commonly assigned an "African" significance. Displaced by their African fathers, young black Liverpudlians accepted the invitation to universal belonging being issued from black American quarters. But mutually imbricated ideologies of gender and locality—ideologies profoundly mediated by changes in black Liverpudlians' class positioning—were also being transformed in the process, giving rise to a set of sanctions that would sharply circumscribe the ways blacks could appropriate "black America."

Despite the fact that young black Liverpudlian men and women have shared the same pained relation to "Africa," as embodied in their relations to their fathers, their common retreat to black America has actually resulted in the fracturing of local identity along distinctly gendered lines. Note the role Greg attributes to black women in the fallout between the black Liverpudlian and American men of the late 1960s and early 1970s: "There was definitely a thing that, it's hard to generalize it too much, but Liverpool black women were definitely interested in American men more so than Liverpool black men, really. Now the knock-on effect was that Liverpool black men resented that, obviously, and tended not to mix so much with the American black men, really. That didn't stop the information coming through on a cultural basis about black identity. That wasn't hindering that." A similarly gendered view and experience of black America was articulated by other men of Greg's generation who tended to trivialize women's attraction to the GIS, projecting onto women what seemed to be their own attraction to the Yanks' manifest blackness. Another man put it this way: "All the GIS were coming into the funk clubs. They had long coats and double-knit jumpers [sweaters] that you couldn't buy in England at the time, big Afro combs, and things like *Jet Magazine* and Afro Sheen. And local girls wouldn't go out with local black guys 'cause we were just scum. And their idea was [that] if they married a GI, they'd get back to the States where it was all happening."

Women's representations of their attraction to the GIS differed considerably. Karen, who married a GI, moved to the United States, and eventually moved back to Liverpool, described in quite different terms why black America appealed to her in that era. Karen made some of the same references to black American culture and thwarted African identity as did the men previously quoted. But she draws on black America to position her racial identity within a feminist framework that challenges oppressive African and "homegrown" black narratives concerning local black womanhood. Unlike Joseph and Greg, Karen constructs black identity with scant reference to white domination:

> My consciousness . . . came from the black movement in the States. At the Olympic Games, when those guys put their hands up in the air, it was a source of pride for me as a black person. And because of the problems with Africans and what they termed us as, "half-caste" [the products of mixed marriages], I affiliated black Americans as being more kin to me than Africa. I joined the black women's liberation group and I joined the Angela Davis march in this country and was very political in my sense as a black person. Anything that emanated from there—from music to culture—was part of *my culture!*

In one forceful sweep, Karen critiques the pathologized category "half-caste" and chooses black America as her culture—and indeed, her "kin"—over the ancestral Africa with its problematic premises regarding racial birth. But the betrayal does not stop there; it is also the cherished seafaring history that she scorns. She spoke of the gendering of local blackness in equally forceful terms:

> A woman like me was marginalized because I was seen as a feminist. A couple of black men were good on the issue, but very few. So you would get that sort of commentary like, "Oh, they're all chasing after the American dream" and "They didn't want to know us." Black men in the city said it was a *historic* thing about white women; they say it was since the days when sailors came into town, and they actually had relationships with white women because there were no black women here. What happened when there *were* black women here?! They *still* didn't want to know black women. The hurtful things that actually happened to black women here meant you could go after "the American dream" thing and feel some respect for yourself as a black woman.

Karen critiques local black men for invoking the proud seafaring narrative—the basis of Liverpudlian identity itself—to condone a contentious aspect of racialized sexual politics in the present day. She suggests that the manufacture of seafaring as an invented tradition has compelled black Liverpudlian women to access black America as a counterhegemonic diasporic resource, one that they can draw upon to feel some respect for themselves—as black women. Black Liverpudlian men's idealized constructions of black America notwithstanding, the American dream for Karen did not have much to do with flash and glamour, or class mobility. For Karen and other women who indicted Liverpool's racial-sexual politics, black America represented a resource for attaining a form of self-respect that was unavailable locally. In this context, it bears remembering Crystal's observation about what she and other black Liverpudlian women gained from the black American presence in Liverpool. "We are so proud to be asked out by a black man," she said. Yet and still, it was not only as women that Crystal and Karen appropriated black America, for they also spoke to black America's contributions to the broader causes of antiracism and black empowerment. Crystal's narrative, quoted earlier, followed her (unquoted) discussion of the advances black Americans have made in the struggle for affirmative action in the United States. Likewise, Karen lauded the two black American athletes who, at the 1968 Olympics, put their gloved fists in the air in support of the struggle for black liberation. Crystal's and Karen's specific references to "pride" and "self-respect" went even further, revealing the gendered and sexualized nature of the radical blackness they fashioned out of black American raw materials.

Diasporic subjectivity among black Liverpudlians was produced in the context of gendered antagonisms that, at once, mutually implicated Africa, black America, and black Liverpool while also rendering each a highly contested resource for racial identity formation. Moreover, racialized politics of desire have informed the construction of different categories of men: African, "homegrown," and American. Hence, the ethnographic material and analyses presented here directly challenge contemporary theory, first, by complicating the place of "longing" in the formation of diasporas, and second, by problematizing the assumption that migration and "displacement" are the necessary hallmarks of diasporic community and subjectivity. That is, in this case, migration did not result in diasporic longings; diasporic longings resulted in migration. A typical insight about the cultural politics of diaspora, here articulated by Arjun Appadurai, can now be reframed—but only if we dare to allow the ancestral tropes he implicitly invokes to refer us not to Africa, but to Liverpool: "The politics of desire and imagination are always in contest with the politics of heritage and nostalgia" (Appadurai 1989: iii). In their appropriations of black America, black Liverpudlian women effectively contested both the hegemony of Liverpool as homeland and the rigidly racialized forms of desire that some say constitute its black heritage.

Black Liverpudlian narratives on community formation, both local and diasporic, articulate an inextricable tie between time and space. Again, these narratives challenge some of the foundational and unquestioned premises of contemporary diaspora theory. Black seamen's decidedly fluid orientation in space is commonly heralded as a triumphant history; seamen are credited with essentially giving birth to the black community. Liverpool was created as a diasporic space through local black seamen's actual engagements with multiple geographies. Like the black seamen, the GIs brought another world into Liverpool 8 by "opening things up," as Greg put it. The city was further transformed through the appropriation of black American strategies of racial empowerment by the young blacks who pushed back the boundaries of where local blackness could be lived. Speaking from an earlier generation, Caroline also recalled the presence of black America joyfully: "Liverpool used to be a smashing place." These nostalgic reminiscences offer occasion to rethink the ways that time and space should figure in theories of diasporic subjectivity, for in Liverpool it seems that "the past" is not a trope for Africa; on the contrary, it signifies the glory days of black Liverpool. But gendered antagonisms profoundly shaped the production of another form of diasporic space, the one mapped by black Liverpudlian women's transatlantic travel.

Setting Sail

Black women's travels, like those of black Liverpool's men, were born of rigidly gendered historical circumstance: the GIs were men. This fact alone enables inquiry into how men and women, as travelers, are differently valued as producers of diasporic space. Just as the African seamen "created" black Liverpool, black women's migration to the United States expanded the space within which black Liverpool presently exists. I scarcely knew a black Liverpudlian who did not have at least one female relative in the United States. Despite men's rather neutral stance on their own sisters' migrations, when black men commented upon the general phenomenon of black women moving to the United States their remarks were drenched in disapproval. Men's narratives on the exclusively male migrations from Africa to Britain were completely devoid of critique, unlike the views they expressed about black Liverpudlian women as migrants. In contrast to black women's representation of their mass exodus, black men said things like "America is like a dream, a carrot. America is seen as an escape. It's seen as a place of prosperity."

The gendering of travel can be analyzed further by comparing the meanings attached to the return of black seamen and black women migrants to Liverpool. As Scott said earlier, black seafarers' return to Liverpool's shores was an event marked by parties "of an African style." In contrast, the tendency among women to drop their anchors back in the city's port is narrated with criticism—by men. On the matter of black women's return, one man chided women for having pursued an American avenue of opportunity in the first place, deriding women's return as a failed defection. He remarked, "And then there were the ones who got married, went to the States, couldn't handle it, and came back. The story's out now: it's not milk and honey, the grass is not any greener." In a more generous vein, black men spoke of black women as naive, suggesting that they were taken in by the apparent wealth of the Yanks, as it was rather deceptively manifested in Liverpool, and by their big talk about having huge homes back in the States. Scott added another factor in their return: "They couldn't handle the racism in the southern states."

Kathleen was one of four black women I knew who had married GIs, moved to the United States, and subsequently returned to Liverpool. She felt acutely the criticism leveled against black women for leaving and the stigma attached to their return. Her father, an African, absolutely loathed the idea of her marrying an American and moving to the United States. She left despite his wishes. Kathleen recalled that her father bid her good-bye thus: "It's not like you're leaving; it's like you're dying." Kathleen's marriage dissolved not long after she settled in Pittsburgh. She considered returning to Liverpool but changed her mind after receiving a letter from her father in which he mentioned that the daughter of a friend of his who had "gone to the States and married an American, and look at what happened to her! She's back in England now with her three babies, living off her father." She delayed visiting Liverpool for years, so that she could save enough money to go back in style and escape the criticism for having left. On that first visit back she observed, "It felt as depressed as it was when I left, and in fact it felt even more depressed because now I had seen something different. So I made the conscious decision to remain in the U.S. because I felt I had more opportunities." In stark contrast to most black Liverpudlian women I knew, those who went to the United States and later returned to Liverpool are now successful professionals. Kathleen said specifically that the survival skills she honed in the United States "made me the woman I am today."

Indeed, these women's difficulties in adjusting to life in that mythical land called "black America" began with their complete isolation. The demographic spread of these women's relocation, across the geographic expanse that is the United States, made it unlikely that they would be able to form a community with other black women from Liverpool. In their singularity, these women were absolute novelties, the charm of which wore thin rather quickly. And after two generations of black American hegemony in Liverpool, these women were understandably shocked that black Americans were so completely ignorant about the black presence in England. Two women, independently of each other, said that when they told black Americans that they were from Liverpool, they were met with the question "Liverpool? What part of Africa is that?"

Conclusion

The black Liverpudlians in this analysis have given voice to the fractured subjectivities formed and transformed along axes of nation, gender, class, and sexuality—all mediated through "race" as constructed locally and through locality. Their accounts suggest the benefit of an ethnographic approach to the study of diasporic identity formation and its cultural politics. Produced in the crucible of multiply inflected and spatially organized relations of power, transnational formations of community are best understood by studying the processes through which certain geographies rather than others attain a hegemonic position at the center of a group's diasporic consciousness. Even though diasporas are formed through processes that are themselves global in scope, these processes and their effects are not everywhere localized, gendered, and racialized in the same way.

American hegemony took a decidedly black form in Liverpool, allowing black Americans to exert a class privilege that they would not have had if they had lived in the United States during the postwar, civil rights, and black power eras. Hollywood images shown at the Rialto must have been powerful shapers in the construction of the United States (and by extension the black GIS) as glamorous and wealthy. More specifically still, the myth unleashed by American hegemony was that there existed a place called "black America" that would somehow resemble its various embodiments in Liverpool—a premise embedded in statements referring to the States as "the place where it was all happening." Despite men's critique of both the Americans and the women migrants who appropriated the fabled land of "black America" as a material resource, Liverpool's black men were nonetheless able to draw on the GIS' presence, their relentless visibility, as a symbolic resource of their own—as proof that it is possible for a person with black skin to drive a big car down Granby Street, as Greg put it.

The power imbalance between black America and black Liverpool—characterized by the decidedly unidirectional transnational flow of iconography and ideas, ideologies and inspirations—is still evident everywhere. Black politicos in Liverpool were heard grumbling when, in 1992, a black youth organization invited Leonard Jeffries (the noted proponent of Afrocentrism and a professor at City College in New York) to speak in the city. "Why not invite a black British person?" they queried, wearily. When, in 1994, the city's Maritime Museum opened a permanent exhibit to document Liverpool's history as a slave port, the African American poet Maya Angelou accepted an invitation to be the keynote speaker. But locals still insisted that a black Liverpudlian also play a prominent speaking role. In the public library across the street from The Boundary (a pub cited earlier), low-budget posters promoting local black artists grace the walls, but these are overshadowed by the presence of much slicker ones featuring the African American writers Alice Walker and June Jordan. To this day, when black American sailors dock in Liverpool's port, black women flock to the city's nightclubs "looking for the Yanks!" as one twenty-something black woman excitedly told me. Except for these sailors and some scattered former GIS, American blacks do not know that this community—so profoundly affected by black America—even exists.

As alternately embodied in people, place, and culture, "black America" opened up liberating spaces for people who, for varied reasons, felt that they were not "fully positioned in any position," as Greg so nicely put it. Yet liberating spaces scarcely free everyone completely, or in the same way. The anthropology of diaspora must attend, therefore, to multiple axes of difference and the often contradictory desires they produce. These longings show, in turn, that the geographies lying at the heart of diasporic subjectivity are never fully positioned in any position.

Notes

1. The data presented here are based on research funded by the National Science Foundation (BNS #9024515), the Wenner Gren Foundation for Anthropological Research, and the Center for European Studies at Stanford University. I extend heartfelt thanks to the people of Liverpool for their participation in this research and to numerous colleagues and friends for their contribution to the ideas presented here.

2. See Julia Sudbury (2004) for an innovative analysis of space and geography in the formation of diasporic subjectivity. Her focus on the racial politics of confinement over that of movement is a critical and much-needed intervention in diaspora studies.

3. A fuller critical analysis of diaspora theory, including Gilroy's contributions, appears in J. Brown 1998 and 2005.

DIASPORA SPACE, ETHNOGRAPHIC SPACE

Writing History Between the Lines

TINA M. CAMPT

In exploring the ways black Germans were read and responded to by Germans during the first half of the twentieth century, there seems to be an insistent, underlying subtext, a nagging assumption or question that cannot be ignored. This question has to do with how to read the history of black Germans in relation to the similar histories of other black populations. Indeed, comparisons might be drawn between Afro-German histories of racism, resistance and struggle, and affirmation and identification, and those of black communities in other cultural contexts. Might there be points of similarity and commonality among different black cultures that connect their historical and cultural trajectories? Might we not view these links as parallels that offer us a deeper understanding of the social and political status of black people more generally?

This essay responds to this subtext of suggestive and provocative questions about the links and commonalities among different black communities. Examining the relations between black communities transnationally and the ways in which these connections can be utilized constructively toward important cultural, political, material, discursive, and analytic ends is at the core of a growing and complex literature on the African Diaspora. Yet scholarship theorizing black community and cultural formations often relies on a discourse of diasporic relation in which similarity and commonality are privileged. In the pages that follow, I hope to complicate and, perhaps more ambitiously, contribute to a rethinking of how the relations of the African Diaspora might be conceived more productively. This essay grows out of a desire to understand the diaspora as a formation that is not solely or even primarily about relations of unity and similarity, but is more often and quite profoundly about the dynamics of *difference*. It illuminates these dynamics by thinking about the question of translation among different black communities and how difference and translation are themselves crucially constituent elements of the African Diaspora.

Hence, this essay looks backward but also offers a very future-oriented end to this historical study of German blacks in the early twentieth century by considering how this community might refigure the politics of the African Diaspora in the twenty-first century. Linking narrative excerpts of interviews with Fasia Jansen, a black German singer and activist, to a more general discussion of diasporic differences, I explore how the ethnographic exchanges out of which these narratives emerged reflect complex tensions within the relations between black communities. At the same time, I illustrate some of the exigencies of diasporic relation that make the concept of diaspora something more than an analytic tool—indeed, for many people, it is a practical and political necessity. This essay explores these issues by way of a particularly rich set of ethnographic phenomena that characterized my exchanges with Jansen, phenomena that occurred at different times and in different forms in all of my interviews. A complex citational practice that Jansen strategically invoked throughout our exchanges, the phenomenon I refer to as "intercultural address" raises fascinating questions about the implicit notions of similarity and relation often assumed between the histories and experiences of black communities transnationally.

Intercultural address describes a series of eruptions and interruptions that I encountered repeatedly in the process of interviewing: as an African American, I often became the object of "address," directly and indirectly spoken or referred to—at times even becoming the topic of our conversation—by my Afro-German interview partners in their attempts to explain and describe their experiences as black people in German society. During these unexpected exchanges I became aware of gaps of translation and moments of interpellation between us, as well as how we actively produced black identity in our dialogues (B. Edwards 2001). My interview partners repeatedly made strategic use of black America to articulate their assumptions of our similarities and commonalities as black people while always emphatically insisting on the specificity of our culturally distinct experiences of race in our respective societies. As we will see, in Fasia Jansen's narrative, intercultural address most often took the form of crosscultural queries that challenged me to situate myself in relation to the issues of race and identity that I unintentionally attempted to impose on her through my questioning. Intercultural address illuminates important tensions of diasporic relation through the ways in which it simultaneously contests and affirms the assumptions of similarity between black communities that were negotiated discursively in our interviews. In the pages that follow, I cite quotations from interviews, place them within the original interview contexts from which they were extracted, and reread them in relation to the ethnographic settings in which they occurred.

Re-membering Diaspora

When we set the history of the black German community in relation to notions of diaspora, it is critical to reflect on the role of an undertheorized element of diasporic relation—the role of memory in processes of cultural formation. In the German context, the absence of the forms of memory so central to many models of black diasporic identity and community raises the question of what happens when a community lacks access to such memories, as has historically been the case for Afro-Germans. Until recently, few Afro-Germans had any connection to one another, for most members of this largely mixed-race population grew up as the only blacks in their surroundings. With the exception of the current generation, most black German children did not grow up with their black parents, thus hindering almost any transmission and preservation of memory in a fundamental way. Despite the fact that points of contact and relation among early black migrants to Germany did exist, the death or departure of these almost always male black parents often meant that these nascent networks of relation were rarely, if ever, sustained from one generation to the next.

Hence, what marks much of this group is the lack of shared narratives of home, belonging, and community that sustain so many other black communities and on which they draw as "resources" in numerous ways. As a result, black Germans have never regarded a sense of relation and belonging among themselves or to other black communities as self-evident. The transnational relations of diaspora have come to be negotiated only in the past two decades.

Even current attempts to forge political and cultural connections and alliances with members of other black communities both in Germany and abroad repeatedly falter on this issue, often coming into conflict at the moment when established histories of other black communities are imposed on Afro-Germans, who are assumed to identify with histories of struggle (most often those of Africans, Caribbeans, or African Americans) in which Afro-Germans are not seen as active participants. Their culturally specific struggles in the German context often go overlooked, along with the histories and existence of black Europeans altogether.

As a result, this essay is less about memory per se than about what happens in its absence. In other words, how does the discourse of diaspora play out in a black diasporic community where memory is quite palpably absent? What must be emphasized here is the extent to which memory plays a central role in constituting forms of diasporic identity and community. The direct and inherited memories of diaspora define and sustain a sense of relation among and between communities separated spatially in diaspora. As both remembrance and commemoration, this memory technology engages strategic forms of forgetting imposed institutionally from without as well as individually and collectively within specific communities. Memory provides the source of the defining tension of diaspora and diasporic identity: the dynamic play of originary and imaginary homes, and the complex networks of relation forged across national, spatial, and temporal boundaries.

In this way, Afro-Germans are positioned in a type of interstitial space—implicated and intertwined, though not fully encompassed by such a model of diaspora/diasporic relation. The waves of forced or collective migration that mark other black communities do not characterize the history of black Germans. And yet the individual journeys (voluntary except for the children of the postwar occupations and the scattered number of slaves brought by individuals to Germany) that led to the formation of this community might nevertheless be seen in relation to an alternative model of diaspora, albeit in a specifically German manifestation that has yet to find full articulation. The lack of recorded historical memories and the consequent difficulty of their public transmission and interpretation in turn further constrain the diasporic function of memory. Thus, the representation of Afro-Germans in larger historical narratives of nation, race, and place has only recently begun to occur, while this community's own work in establishing and claiming a "diasporic memory" still remains in its nascent stages.

"Spürst Du Denn, Dat Du Schwarz Bist?":
Feeling Black and the Difference It Might Make

My conversations with Fasia Jansen took place in Germany in 1992. At the time, I was a graduate student living in Berlin on a research fellowship that allowed me to work on my dissertation. It was the second of what would eventually be a six-year residence in Berlin, at a volatile time in the city's and country's more recent history. It was a crucial moment in postreunification Germany: between 1989 and 1992, Germany experienced a dramatic increase in racist and xenophobic violence. In April of 1991, a twenty-eight-year-old Mozambican man was killed by a group of neo-Nazi youth who pushed him in front of a moving tram in the East German city of Dresden. In September of the same year, right-wing youth firebombed a residence for asylum seekers and assaulted Vietnamese and Mozambican residents in Hoyerswerde. According to the Federal Office for the Protection of the Constitution (Bundesverfassungsschutz), 1992 marked the height of these violent attacks. In August of 1992 seven nights of violence occurred in the East German port city of Rostock, while in November of that year three Turks were killed in an arson attack in the small town of Moelln. In response, Germans staged a series of candlelight marches in Berlin, Munich, Hamburg, Bonn, and other cities, with more than three million people voicing protests against the violence. My interviews with Jansen occurred against this disturbing background of resurgent racist violence and resounding reminders of eras past.

As with all my informants, my initial contact with Jansen was facilitated informally, through a third party and mutual acquaintance. I received her name from a woman journalist whose documentaries on the history of blacks in Nazi Germany had been an important starting point for my research. My initial contact with Jansen followed what would probably be described as the most conventional rules of ethnographic or oral historical formality and etiquette—an initial contact letter followed by a phone call. I explained that I was interested in speaking to her as part of my dissertation research. Jansen was a well-known activist living in a small industrial town in the Ruhr Valley. Over the years, she had become a public figure of sorts and had developed a following among German trade unionists and in leftist, pacifist, and feminist circles, both within the region and in the Federal Republic more broadly, through her music and her dedicated work on these causes. Jansen agreed to speak to me after receiving my letter and on what I later learned was the enthusiastic recommendation of our mutual acquaintance. I conducted two interviews with Jansen over a two-day period; one of these was planned, while the other was a spontaneous follow-up interview that occurred a day later.

Our first interview took place in a political café near Jansen's home. The location was familiar to me not because I had ever visited it before but because I had been in countless cafés like it in other German cities. It was familiar as a result of my own political biography and activist work with feminist and antiracist groups in Berlin and in the cities to which my colleagues and I had traveled as part of this work. It was a place one could find in almost any German city. The café was part of a larger *Projekt,* one of the countless publicly funded local political projects that at the time were subsidized by agencies of the German federal, state, and local governments. The café was attached to a larger set of rooms used for meetings and other activities of the different political groups and alliances that worked out of the center. The café served as an informal *Treffpunkt* (meeting place) for activists and community members affiliated with or affected by the project's work. Unfortunately, Jansen and I never got around to discussing the specific nature of the work of this particular project—we were engrossed in her story from the moment I arrived.

Jansen had suggested that we meet at the end of her shift in the café and do the interview there. The café would be closed, and it was one of the few times she was available to speak to me. Jansen was a busy woman. She struck me as hectic on the phone, and I was intimidated by her assertiveness. I jumped at this small window of opportunity to speak with her and agreed to do the interview at the café, disregarding my own reservations about the potential noise and disruption of such a public place. As it turned out, the noise of café cleanup and the comings and goings of the project and café staffers were indeed quite distracting, but only to me—she was completely unfazed by it all. Until then, I had always conducted interviews in my informants' homes, a setting that I felt put them at ease and made them more comfortable speaking with a stranger. As I found out when I arrived at the café, location made no difference to Jansen, a gregarious, vivacious, witty, and outgoing woman who felt as much at home in the café as at her residence. It seemed somehow almost more appropriate to interview her there, since, as she later explained to me, she spent more time in such places and traveling between these and other sites of her activism than she did at home. In fact, in this semipublic place only I felt awkward—an out-of-place young American academic at a site of working-class struggle, asking this fascinating woman to reveal her innermost reflections on her complicated life.

But Jansen put me very much at ease. She had an easy way, and her charming manner allowed us to quickly establish a warm and open rapport. In fact, Jansen surprised me when, shortly after we met, she insisted that I address her with the informal *du*, rather than the formal *Sie*, traditionally used in German by a younger person to address an elder or a stranger. Yet it would be misleading to represent our exchange as a comfortable process of mutual and transparent comprehension, despite the warmth and honesty of our rapport. Indeed, in many ways, Jansen insisted quite strenuously on mutual respect as the basis of our dialogue, and in quite specific ways she defined the terms and delineated the boundaries of our relationship in the interview. For example, at the beginning of our second interview (which took place in her home), Jansen informed me that she preferred that we use the more formal *Sie*. I had never experienced such a reverse shift from the informal back to the formal, and I immediately thought I had done something to offend her. But Jansen explained that in her experience *Sie* conveyed a mutual respect that is quite often lost with the *du* form, even among good friends, and she recounted an instance with a close friend when such had been the case. In making this shift, Jansen established a particular form of formality between us. At the same time, it was also a gesture of control in that she effectively defined the terms of the level of intimacy and respect in our exchange.

Perhaps because of the fact that our rapport was so good, the seams and gaps in our communication became that much more visible, in ways that I found extremely revealing of the deeper texture of our dialogue. As we will see, this complex interaction can be read as a compelling commentary on the tensions within the relations of the African Diaspora in ways that urge us to consider the extent to which such relations are actively constituted at multiple levels in our crosscultural dialogues and thus can never be assumed as a simple fact of similarity, affinity, or commonality. Intercultural address is the one important site where both the texture of this complex ethnographic space and the dynamics of crosscultural diasporic relation were made manifest in provocative and compelling ways. In the following example of intercultural address, Jansen and I discuss our relationship to "Africa" as black women of different Western societies. We negotiate a popular construction of blackness that attributes to us a nonexistent relationship to Africa, a place that is foreign to both of us, whose social and cultural backgrounds lie outside the African continent.

> FJ: Later, [my sister] continued her studies in America. I don't know what happened then. We met again after the war.
>
> TC: Mmm, after the war.
>
> FJ: Yes—
>
> TC: Was that–
>
> FJ: I met all my brothers and my siblings then.
>
> TC: Here in Germany?
>
> FJ: In Germany.
>
> TC: How did that come about?
>
> FJ: One of them is director of geo-, geology—he does research on rocks and stuff like that and had some contacts in Hamburg. And then he heard that I was there and absolutely wanted to meet me. It was a terrible shock when a man came toward me who looked exactly like me. Exactly! It was my face. Yes. And it was so incredibly wonderful for me. He wanted to take me back to Africa. But I grew up here, and that's very, very hard. You see, I had no yearning for Africa.
>
> TC: Um-hmm. Um-hmm. And–
>
> FJ: I don't know how it is for you, if you have a yearning for Africa?
>
> TC: Not at all. [*Laughter*] I understand what you mean, because I'm American.
>
> FJ: Right.
>
> TC: That's it. Nothing else.
>
> FJ: That's it.[1]

In this passage, Jansen discusses one of her few encounters with her African siblings. In Jansen's comments "Africa" represents our common heritage as black women. However, in the German context in which we at the time both resided, "Africa" is constructed as implicitly opposed to Germanness and as the place where all blacks come from, belong, and/or should have some mythical longing to be. Both of us reject this construction of "Africa." But what constitutes the "yearning" or "longing" (*Sehnsucht*) to which Jansen refers? Jansen's comments put an interesting spin on the issues of relation and affiliation to Africa suggested by many scholars who emphasize the necessity for "diasporic Africans" such as Jansen to gain a greater appreciation of the significance of Africa and African culture in the development of their identities, communities, and social and political struggles. Her remarks highlight the tenuous nature of external attempts to define what this relationship should be, how it should look, and/or the terms on which it is or should be based.

The importance Jansen attributes to her contact with her African brother certainly affirms some sense of the significance attributed to contact with her African heritage. Yet Jansen's reaction to her brother's assumption that she would necessarily feel a natural connection to or affiliation with Africa seems equally worthy of comment. Jansen's brother's insistence that she return with him posits Africa as a lost homeland of sorts and intrinsically assumes either a return or, at the very least, identification and affiliation. Here, Africa is constituted as a mythic, transcendent signifier of diasporic relation, the site to and through which all routes lead as the link between black peoples. But in fact, it is less a site—that is a location—than a symbol that signifies connection in Jansen's case, anchoring a relation of kinship that begins with blood and for her brother ends with return. Yet for Jansen, like many Afro-German members of her generation, kinship with her African relations and culture is substantiated not by presence but by absence. For her, there were no shared memories or rituals of connections and few if any resources on which to draw in establishing any links of culture or heritage. Diaspora itself constructs such a relation, and Africa is its wholly symbolic vehicle. In her reaction to her brother's suggestion, Jansen asserts the limits of such a notion of diasporic relations. Her response engages Africa not as a symbol but as a peopled place of cultures and histories, a place to which, she emphasizes, she has no concrete relation: "But I grew up here, and that's very, very hard. You see, I had no yearning for Africa." Although links of kinship and heritage are important, Jansen underlines that hers are in Germany rather than in Africa.

At this point, Jansen's engagement of the limits of diasporic relation broadens when she transposes this thorny issue onto me by querying my understanding as an African American or my relationship to Africa. Her question, "I don't know how it is for you, if you have a yearning for Africa?" addresses me as a black woman who, like her, is also from a culture outside of Africa. Her query articulates a request for confirmation or rebuttal of her own sense of the limits of diasporic affinity and affiliation. Yet the effect of her question is to establish an ambivalent connection. By addressing me directly as a black woman and querying whether I have a relationship to Africa similar to that which she has just recounted in the story about her brother, Jansen initiates a process of interpellation that hails and thus produces me as a black woman, a hailing to which I respond with immediate affirmation. Not only do I feel recognized through her addressing me, but I also identify quite palpably with the awkwardness of the diasporic relation in which she is situated by her brother. Addressing her question to me effectively enables her to enact within the interview the same dynamic she has just described between herself and her brother. By asking me as another "sister" to position myself on the topic of my sense of my relationship to Africa—a place of tremendous symbolic significance in the discursive geography of the African Diaspora, yet a place to which I have no "real" substantive connection—her use of intercultural address puts me in the position of having to recognize the gap that exists between the two of us, a notion of diasporic relation that centers on Africa as a site of origin, and an assumed identity arising out of this site. In this process, her query effectively forces me to perform the same kind of positioning she did in relation to her brother, thereby beautifully making her point.

Intercultural address both points to the necessity of making this symbolic relation and concrete nonrelation explicit and makes clear the extent to which they remain present as assumed underlying relations in need of clarification. The fact that she asks me so pointedly where I "stand" in this relation strikingly attests to the truth of this paradox. In the end, we negotiate in this passage our relation to the diaspora, comparing our respective conceptions of what it means to be black and to not come from Africa—that is, to have a European or American socialization. In our exchange, the classic subject-object relation of interviewer-interviewee or speaker-listener dissolves almost completely in the context of our common rejection of a preexisting relation to Africa by virtue of race. In our discursive negotiation of the limits of diasporic relation, "Africa" at once signifies and facilitates the existence of our relationship to one another as black people and at the same time highlights the need to translate and specify such gaps in the diaspora rather than assume those relations, as well as their limits, on the basis of both commonality and, even more importantly, distinction.

The intercultural relations of diaspora are quite decidedly the ever present (sometimes explicit, at other times implicit) subtext of my interviews, both in the content of my questioning and woven through the fabric of our interpersonal interaction. Furthermore, intercultural address provides the vehicle through which this latent subtext repeatedly erupts into our interviews. The following exchange is a particularly evocative example.

TC: But what motivated you to do all this, all these political things and activities?

FJ: You shouldn't ask me about motivations and such things—you can't do that. It had to do with my being black.

TC: What exactly?

FJ: All the things that I experienced must never again [be allowed to] happen. I've seen too much misery, and [I] throw all the strength that I have into [political work]. But you mustn't think that I always—that I wanted to run around and play the heroine for justice. Instead it was always, always whatever was there—"Listen, you have to come," like that, right? Always pushing for something, [take for example] with the mills, get that through [. . .]. And then in the women's initiatives, the ones that fought for their husbands' jobs. They always came and got me.

TC: Came and got you?

FJ: And that's why—or went there—and that's why I didn't need a psychologist. I was able to get rid of all the anger that I stored up, you know, all of it.

TC: But what—

FJ: I've brought people to tears, but I've also made them laugh, and the reverse. And then, finally, I ended up in the women's movement. Good. Now you ask the questions.

TC: [Laughter] May I?

FJ: You have to now. It costs too much money in tapes.

TC: Yes. The question about being black. What exactly was it that, that connects your political work with your being black? How did you express it, or what did it give you?

FJ: You have to imagine, there was no black movement here. I was all alone with this, and I myself never felt that I'm black. The others have their problems [with it]. That was never my problem. [Laughter]

TC: Uh-huh. You never felt this yourself?

FJ: Do you feel that you're black?

TC: Yes!

FJ: How?

TC: Yes. Yes, I mean—

FJ: Yes, when you look at yourself.

TC: Well, you're right.

FJ: I said to the children, I say, "Imagine, I know that I don't have this racial problem with myself. If I have a problem with being black, then it's your problem, or your parents' problem."[2]

The sequence of intercultural address in this excerpt is embedded in our discussion of Jansen's political work. I begin by asking Jansen to describe her motivations for her activism. Her reply is unequivocal: it has to do with being black. She explains that her activism comes from a commitment never to allow what she experienced to happen again and that her political activism served as an outlet for her to work through many of her experiences. Later in the passage, I attempt to follow up on Jansen's original statement by asking for the exact nature of the connection between her blackness and her political activism. My intention was to obtain a more precise description of her personal understanding of this relationship. In response, Jansen initiates a subtle shift in our discussion, eliding the issue of blackness by referring to the absence of a black movement in Germany ("You have to imagine, there was no black movement here."). At first glance, Jansen's remarks seem almost to contradict her original statement that her political engagement was related to her being black. A superficial reading of this passage might lead one to interpret Jansen's reply as a misunderstanding, where Jansen mistakenly interprets my question to refer to her engagement in a black political movement. However, a closer reading of this passage offers a more plausible interpretation of her remarks.

Jansen emphasizes that she could not participate in a black movement because no such movement existed in Germany. As a consequence, she had no opportunity to work through her experiences as a black person in Germany with other blacks in Germany. Here her implicit reference seems to be the U.S. civil rights movement of the 1960s and 1970s. Jansen's emphasis on the absence of a black movement in Germany is a direct response to my question, despite the discursive shift with which she introduces the topic into our conversation. The lack of a black movement plays a primary role in explaining the necessity for Jansen's political engagement because the situation forced her to come to terms with her blackness alone ("I was all alone with this [*Ich was doch ganz alleine auf so was*]").

In many ways, Jansen's comments in this passage echo scholarly discussions of the diasporic resources and raw materials they describe as marshaled by black communities transnationally and used in strategic ways in the cultural, community, and identity formation of populations such as black Britons (J. Brown 1998; Gilroy 1987). Yet Jansen's comments also speak to her sense of the lack of availability of such resources to her in Germany at a key point in her life. Her awareness of and engagement with the struggles of blacks and women elsewhere, which she articulates throughout her narrative, makes clear that she did in fact draw inspiration from them. Still, Jansen seems to mourn the extent to which, regardless of their tremendous value to her, these struggles remain models and resources that are foreign and thus applicable only by extrapolation. Here again, the work diaspora seems to do is ambivalent, affirming the significance of access to transnational cultural and political models and resources while at the same time highlighting the extent to which they can always only be partial in their ability to satisfy the particular tasks, longings, and desires of specific communities in their equally specific cultural contexts. The kind of borrowing and adaptation so central to Gilroy's model of the syncretism of black expressive cultures is certainly important. Nevertheless, his model may not sufficiently account for the situations of populations like black Germans, whose very different historical trajectory and consequent marginality in the discourse of diaspora perhaps demand a different formulation.

Just after Jansen's reference to the absence of such resources for potential borrowing and adaptation, a more substantial shift occurs in our discussion via the phenomenon of intercultural address.

> FJ: I myself never felt that I'm black. The others have their problems [with it]. That was never my problem. [*Laughter*]
>
> TC: Uh-huh. You never felt this yourself?
>
> FJ: Do you feel that you're black?
>
> TC: Yes!
>
> FJ: How?
>
> TC: Yes. Yes, I mean—
>
> FJ: Yes, when you look at yourself.
>
> TC: Well, you're right.
>
> FJ: I said to the children, I say, "Imagine, I know that I don't have this racial problem with myself. If I have a problem with being black, then it's your problem, or your parents' problem."

In this sequence, our exchange moves away from the issue of the connection between Jansen's politics and her experience of blackness, beginning with her statement that she has never "felt" black. As an African American, I initially respond with skepticism to this remark. I am curious about why and how Jansen does not "feel" her blackness. Without reflecting on the implications of this statement, I implicitly attribute this phenomenon to Jansen's German cultural context. This assumption, along with my skepticism and curiosity, is expressed in my response to Jansen's statement, when I pose to her the question, "You never felt this yourself?" My question effectively sets up an implicit relation of difference between the two of us—a difference between two black women's understandings of the effects of blackness as more than "just" skin color. In response to this submerged level of my question, Jansen shifts the focus away from herself and directly addresses me, challenging me to reflect on the issue I have just directed at her. Jansen's counterquestion, "Do you feel that you're black?" rejects the assumptions of difference underlying my question, for Jansen directly takes issue with the subtext of my question: if I must ask why she does not feel her blackness, then by implication I (unlike her) must indeed be able to feel this aspect of myself. What follows is a fascinating exchange during which Jansen reverses the roles of the ethnographic encounter to query me on black identity and in the process foils my attempts to interpellate her as a black woman. Yet this role reversal also reveals an equally compelling process in which she comes to interpellate me on this same issue.

My comments to Jansen are made in response to her earlier statements that she grew up with little or no exposure to black people and that she lacked either a movement or a community of blacks with whom to identify. I assume, based on these remarks, that her comments are indicative of a lack of identification with blackness. I want to understand her comments in this way because, as an African American, I equate a lack of contact with blacks to a lack of identification with blackness. Indeed, as an African American, I have to acknowledge that my model of black identity fixes identity to a national community with whom one shares concrete ties of culture, history, and socialization. I also assume that the absence of these things as Jansen describes them in our interview would make such an identification improbable for Jansen, and I conclude all too quickly that her comments in this sequence are a direct reflection of that lack.

But Jansen's query as to my own sense of "feeling black" interpellates me to the extent that I feel called on to articulate this feeling as part of my identification as a black woman. From the moment Jansen begins to describe her experience of blackness in this sequence, I feel hailed to situate myself in relation to what I want to understand as our shared identity as black women. Unlike in the first example, though, this time it is a hailing to which I respond with suspicion, somewhat defensively. Although I feel directly addressed and recognized as a black woman by her comments, I am not quite comfortable with her particular citation (rendition) of the experience of blackness and black identity. When I attempt to relate Jansen's articulation of her understanding of what it means to be black to my understanding, this translation fails because I want to see her concept of blackness as identical to my own. I again confront an inevitable gap of translation—in this case, the gap between related notions of blackness and black identity that may share similarities but are far from identical.

But more important than the rapidity with which I jump to these conclusions are the assumptions that underlie them with regard to the relationship between my construction of blackness as an African American and Jansen's as an Afro-German. Equally significant is Jansen's response to my clumsy attempts to impose my own conception of blackness on her. The persistent skepticism I express, through my insistence on the fact that I, unlike her, can and do feel my blackness, functions as both an attempt to dispute the extent to which one can claim not to feel her race and an implicit attempt to impose an African American model of black identity on our exchange by contrasting my feeling with her lack. Indeed, by disputing her claim not to feel blackness, I seem intent on either exposing her denial or convincing her to acquiesce to the veracity of my position. Yet Jansen's response exposes my motives as well as the limitations of my narrow understanding of the dynamics of racial formation. Jansen articulates a complex sensitivity to processes of racial subject formation: she alludes to the fact that blackness has never been intrinsically problematic for her but rather has constituted a problem in what it is understood to mean by others and in how both we and others act on and thus produce it. Her counterquestions and challenges in this way school me, provoking me to recognize the ways in which I take for granted that blackness is a physical or material experience and one in which I act like I have cornered the market.

Jansen's questions forced me to understand the real message of her initial comments: that race and racial difference are the products of our social interaction and interpretation, and that those interactions occur not just in Germany between whites and blacks, and not only during the war, when race in Germany was an individual's defining feature. They also occur among blacks from different social and national contexts in our contemporary transnational encounters. In many ways, our exchange undeniably reproduces important tensions that might be seen as inherent to any cross-cultural dialogue between black people from different backgrounds. What is perhaps most instructive about our exchange is how the negotiation of our assumptions about our differences and similarities becomes manifest within the interview in ways that make them available to analysis and interpretation.

Such analysis nevertheless brings us back to the question of whether these negotiations can or should be seen as a reflection or expression of relationships that might be termed diasporic, and if so, in what ways and toward what ends. The question of what work is being done when such negotiations are conceived as diasporic forces us to consider the extent to which the type of queries and contestations that characterized my exchange with Jansen are both necessary for and inherent to the relations between members of different black communities and never in and of themselves either an explanation or an endpoint of such an analysis.

Diasporic Asymmetries

My interest in fleshing out the limits and tensions of diasporic relation arises out of my increasingly frequent confrontations with diaspora as *the* requisite approach or theoretical model through which one should (or perhaps must) understand all formations of black community, regardless of historical, geographical, or cultural context. In trying to understand the relationship of the history of black Germans to the histories of other black communities, it becomes increasingly apparent that diaspora does not constitute a historical given or universally applicable analytic model for explaining the cultural and historical trajectories of all black populations. Rather, we must engage this concept with an awareness and articulation of its limits in regard to those black communities whose histories and genealogies do not necessarily or comfortably conform to dominant models. Indeed, it is worthwhile to recall Gilroy's reminder that diaspora often serves to paper over difficult fissures and gaps within the affiliations constructed between black communities (1993). For a black community such as Afro-Germans, we must establish their specific relation to the concept of diaspora before assuming their inclusion within this model on an equal or universal status with other black communities.

In Jansen's narrative, intercultural address can be seen as a challenge that encourages us to reflect on the status of black America in relation to other black populations involved in the process of articulating their experiences and constructing alternative forms of black identity and community. Intercultural address asks us to take a closer look at the influence of representations of African American culture in these constructions. Each of these exchanges raises the question of whether these intercultural negotiations can or should be seen as a reflection or expression of relationships that might be termed diasporic, and if so, in what ways and toward what ends. And yet, although intercultural address presents itself as an obvious model for explaining the sense of relationship postulated through such crosscultural querying and citation, the question remains whether we can or should understand such citational imperatives as "diasporic" or as an expression or consequence of a "diasporic relation." Should the ways in which Afro-Germans draw on the African American context be seen as their use of some of the few diasporic resources available to them as black people lacking other indigenous narratives of belonging, community, and struggle—or, for that matter, access to the forms of collective or individual memory that sustain other black communities? In other words, can or should such references to black America be understood as necessary attempts to draw from elsewhere that which is lacking, though essential, to the constitution of very different notions of black identity and community at "home"? Or might such references also have everything to do with black America's emergent cultural capital, which increasingly allows it an almost endless capacity to proliferate and travel to many different global locations and thus become an available referent?

Although the concept of diaspora invites us to use it as an obvious model for explaining the sense of relationship postulated through such crosscultural querying, in some ways this invitation seems almost too seductive to be believed. One might ask whether part of the work diaspora does is to hold out a promise it cannot quite keep, the promise of transparent forms of relation and understanding based on links forged through shared histories of oppression and racialization. Indeed, the concept of the African Diaspora seems sometimes to invite us to forget the subtle forms of interpellation and incumbent gaps of translation that are a crucial part of all transnational dialogues. These gaps—inherent elements of all diasporic formations by virtue of the ever present diversity of black culture and community—cannot be negated, resolved, or erased. On the contrary, they are that which enables, rather than hinders both community and communication.

Each of the discrepant moments of diasporic invocation presented in this essay asks us to think about the stakes of diasporic relation and how those relations are structured as much through difference as through similarity and enunciated through complex modes of translation and interpellation that are anything but transparent. Engaging the tensions of diasporic relation as processes of translation and interpellation helps to explain how the diaspora and its diasporic links are produced both actively and strategically; how the discourse of diaspora circulates in uneven ways geographically, and within and between different communities; and how diaspora does indeed do interesting and important "epistemological work." The processes and practices of citation, translation, and interpellation that I have examined here are extremely illuminating and instructive when engaged with an eye toward understanding how they reveal the necessary if not crucial forms of distinction and commonality that characterize all transnational dialogues. But what is most essential to the future of African Diaspora studies is the project of making more explicit what exactly constitutes the links and relations between us and how they necessarily require translation (Brah 1996; J. Brown 1998; B. Edwards 2003; Gilroy 1987; Hesse 2000).

For those of us interested in reconstructing the histories out of which communities and identities emerge, the ways in which intercultural and transnational links, bonds, and affiliations between different communities are invoked and produced through nuanced articulations both by scholars and by individual members of these communities is a dimension of the study of the diaspora that should not be overlooked. Indeed, articulations like those explored here urge us to rethink the discourse of diaspora and the diasporic relations it references. We might more productively think of them as less a common trajectory of cultural formation or as a set of cultural and historical links that either precede or call into being particular community formations or identifications. Following Judith Butler, I would conceptualize the diaspora as space in which the relations, definitions, and identifications within and between communities come to materialize and to matter as "real" in ways that are strategically useful; these phenomena in turn "hail" and thus interpellate us in important political, symbolic, and often quite material forms (1993). Indeed, the links and relations of the diaspora are themselves enacted in and through such transnational exchanges in ways that are thoroughly strategic and deeply embedded in intricate social webs of power and hegemony. Hence, I propose that we think of the diaspora as less an answer or explanation than as itself a persistent question—in fact, the question posed at the beginning of this essay: What work does diaspora do?

My conversations with black Germans about their memories of their lives in the Third Reich forced me to contend with their often very different understandings of race and their status as raced social subjects, understandings that were not always compatible with my own. My status as an African American often became the site of challenge, as the ground on which complex contestations of difference and not simply similarity were waged. It is important to continually keep in mind that, like the category of race itself, our relation as black people to the diaspora is not something we all have or are born with. On the contrary, these relations are constructed through negotiations and contestations in specific ways that are not always or easily translated or translatable into our respective cultural contexts. Relations of diaspora forged on the basis of similar experiences of racialization are not transparent links between black people; rather, these relations are the products of highly constructed processes of cultural reading and interpretations that shape, define, and often constrain our ability to understand the differences between our histories and cultures. Although our experiences of living blackness may in some ways be similar, it is also necessary to consider the differences between our cultures and histories and to recognize how their specificities have come to bear on the ways in which the effects of race are lived and read.

Notes

1. Jansen interview, February 2, 1992.
2. Ibid.

"MAMA, I'M WALKING TO CANADA"

Black Geopolitics and Invisible Empires

NAOMI PABST

My title, as you may recognize, is a line from Alice Walker's canonical one-page vignette in which she defines "womanist." This of course comes out of her collection of essays *In Search of Our Mothers' Gardens* and is also anthologized in many women's studies and black studies compilations. In Walker's articulation of it, womanism is code for black feminism and as such encapsulates the basic tenets of a political and theoretical orientation that contends with race and gender simultaneously. More interesting for my purposes here, however, is that in this passage, one of Walker's metaphors for resistance, rebellion, and empowerment takes the form of an emboldened female declaring, "Mama, I'm walking to Canada and I'm taking you and a bunch of other slaves with me" (1983: xi). "Mama's" reply, "it wouldn't be the first time," denotes a long legacy of black American—female and male—freedom struggles, struggles against myriad forms of racial domination, the magnitude of which can hardly be overstated (xi). Walker's nod to Canada also suggests, rightly, that the U.S.'s neighbor to the north holds a special place within a genealogy of African American political projects and freedom struggles.

At the same time, in Walker's fleeting reference, Canada's significance is symbolic of freedom for African Americans. Canada as a symbol of liberation elides the fact of Canada as a geographical location, a place with a black population that is itself negotiating myriad forms of oppression that overlap with but do not replicate American ones. People have challenged Walker's "womanist" formulation, its side-stepping the "f" word (the "f" word being "feminism"), its spiritual undertones, its exceptionalist positing of black women. If it is becoming more prevalent in small academic circles to query, troping Stuart Hall, "what is this 'black,'" what is this oft-hailed signifier, it remains an inadequately explored trajectory (1993: 21). Even less developed, however, is the overlapping question of "*where* is this black," despite the growing popularity of academic constructions of "diaspora."

This essay foregrounds this question of "where"; it examines the relationship between black subjectivity and geopolitics as one transhistorical manifestation of globalization. As I use the term here, geopolitics is about the proverbial cultural studies homonym of "routes" and "roots." It is about identity in relation to "place," with place signifying dwelling and movement. It references where we're from, where we're at, where we've been, and where we're going, as individuals and as members of multiple categories of belonging. Geo*politics*, as the word implies, is also about politics, interactions of privilege and disadvantage, the intricate set of power relations embedded within the places, the ways, and the reasons we dwell and move, individually and collectively. Within this rubric of geopolitics, I will address the relevance of the Canadian scene to diasporic and American racial discourses. My essay is not *about* black Canada in a bounded sense. It is rather a scholarly meandering to and fro, in and out of Canada, a walk to Canada that attempts to realize the brash threats of Alice Walker's womanist persona.

The path to and in black Canada is well worn if unwieldy, and knowledge of it has been subjugated. This coterminous existence and erasure is replicated within two dominant conceptions about blackness in Canada, which would seem to contradict one another: One is that there are no black people there, and the other is that Canada was the terminus of the underground railroad. And it was the terminus only in a manner of speaking, as most escaped slaves remained in the United States, and for those who did opt for Canada the term "underground" was a misnomer in an abolitionist context in which escape routes were unhidden and public.

The history of offering asylum to American fugitive slaves is but one of Canada's many relevant appearances within even the most conservative African American studies canon. Canada was perceived by various African Americans as a prospective homeland. Mary Ann Shadd Cary and Martin

Delaney, for instance, advocated mass flight to Canada as the lesser of two evils for African Americans, yet they were nevertheless cognizant of the existence of racism in Canada, mindful of the fact that, in Delaney's words, "the Canadas are no place of safety for . . . colored people" (1968: 176). Mary Ann Shadd Cary, a charismatic nineteenth-century figure who has important implications for contemporary black feminism, spent fifteen years in Canada and took out Canadian citizenship before eventually returning to live in the United States. And her friend, Martin Delaney, made Chatham, Ontario, his home from 1856 through 1859. In fact, Delaney wrote his only novel, *Blake*, while involved in the bustling antislavery activity north of the forty-ninth parallel. Richard Wright spent a few months in Quebec, Jackie Robinson started his professional baseball career in Montreal, and the likes of A. Philip Randolph and Marcus Garvey advanced their political agendas in Canada.

The literal possibility of "walking to Canada"—which Josiah Henson and Harriet Tubman did repeatedly (both lived in Canada West, now Ontario)— underscores the presence and the proximity of the U.S.'s neighbor to the north. What also draws me to Canada, academically, is its status as an over-developed nation and its formal appellation, "cultural mosaic." Canada has officially institutionalized a policy of "multiculturalism," yet despite that, racism sets the terms of Canadian existence. The journalist Margaret Cannon has applied the term "invisible empire" to the vagaries of Canadian racism, hailing at once its strength and formidability but also its subtlety, its "invisi-bility" as it were. Racism in Canada is pervasive, empire-like in its reach and power yet prone to disavowal, and this "invisible empire" has, in the past and present, displaced, othered, and discriminated against black Canadians.

Contrary to Canada's national narrative and contrary to underground railroad mythology, there were two centuries of black slavery in Canada, if on a smaller scale and in a different form from that which emerged in the southern United States. Some scholars have noted that the existence of slav-ery in Canada is constantly being rediscovered, then reforgotten, forever resubsumed by the dominant narrative of Canada as a haven for fugitive slaves. Moreover, while Canada may have come to oppose slavery, it did not do so in an antiracist context. Escaped slaves were welcomed into Canada not just for benevolence's sake but as cheap labor. After slaves were emancipated in the United States, Canadians encouraged blacks to relocate there. And after emancipation many blacks voluntarily left Canada for the United States, not only to return to kin but also to flee Canadian racism. At the same time, African Americans continued to migrate to Canada to seek opportunities that were routinely denied to blacks in the United States. For black people, the border between the United States and Canada has been extremely porous.

If racism in Canada, historically and in the present, can be considered an "invisible empire," at once ignored and endowed, we could, at the same time, extend Margaret Cannon's metaphor to Canada itself. Canada, as a nation, can be considered something of an "invisible empire," as a huge geographical space. A nation with privilege, it is an uncentral yet certifiable member of the overdeveloped world. A case could also be made for the applicability of the term "invisible empire" to the erasure of Canada within discourses on blackness. Again, the terms "invisible" and "empire," taken together, eschew victimology, insist on simultaneous privilege and disadvantage, and observe patterns of exclusion and their consequences.

To exemplify this, I turn to another familiar instance of black border-crossing between the United States and Canada. The first meeting of W. E. B. Du Bois's Niagara Movement, which later became the NAACP, was held in Fort Erie, Ontario in 1905. The symbolic significance of the venue in light of Canada's role in African American history has been widely acknowledged. The meeting was, however, supposed to be held in Buffalo and was only relocated to Fort Erie as a result of exclusion from accommodations, a form of American racial discrimination that underscored the importance of developing this sort of civil rights organization. At the same time, as scholars such as Rinaldo Walcott and the late Robin Winks have pointed out, black Canadians were denied the opportunity to participate. As Walcott puts it: "The fact that many of the 'Canadian' blacks who would have gladly participated in the inaugural meeting were born in America, or were immediate descendants of African American slaves who had escaped to Canada, makes this exclusion interesting" (1997: 19). The exclusion *is* interesting, though Walcott does not mention how it corresponds with other omissions based on gender, class, and status. Gayatri Spivak's by now overinvoked but I think still useful term "strategic essentialism" hails the ultimate impossibility of *not* closing ranks, the impossibility of engaging in infinitely inclusive political struggles. She also deems this arbitrary, unavoidable closure a grave problem.

These overinvocations of Spivak's concept have most often been employed to justify rather than problematize exceptionalist claims. And indeed, as Spivak emphasizes, that does raise serious problems. For instance, because the participants in the Niagara Movement were fighting a closure of ranks by white Americans, one might expect their own political project to be more, rather than less, inclusive. And again, those black Canadians who were de-

nied the opportunity to join the Niagara Movement were connected to African America by way of geographical origins as well as cultural and political
affinities. That these Canadian blacks had direct ties to black America means
theirs was a transnational subjectivity, one with multiple reference points,
one that exceeded national borders. The disavowal of transnational overlap
implied by the moment of black Canadian exclusion from an African American political project, even as Canada was being touted as a symbolic site
of freedom for African Americans, is revealing. It points to the inadvertent ways that hierarchies and patterns of exclusion are reinscribed within
counterhegemonic projects, the ways that discourses and political agendas
sometimes unwittingly reify that which they oppose. This matters for contemporary black studies and for academic constructions of a black diaspora. If diaspora gestures to simultaneous difference and sameness among a
transnational circuitry of subjects partially descended from Africa, it is also
about geopolitical power differentials, erasures, and ongoing renderings of
invisibility.

The black or African diaspora is a contested category that has been defined in myriad ways, running the gamut from Afrocentric to pan-African to
postmodern in orientation. In none of these formulations is diaspora a
pretentious internationalism or an abstract "vision" as some have dismissed
it as being. It is rather a cartography that takes blackness to be a local and
global phenomenon, influenced, indeed constituted, by long-standing interactions of dwelling and movement. While the forms of and motivations for
black movement have been diverse, my walking metaphor underscores the
history of on-foot, overland, literally on the ground, back and forth human
traffic across the border between the United States and Canada—human
traffic whose affiliations, both real and imagined, included not only those
two but also other geographical sites. Transnational articulations of black
subjectivity also render nonsensical an invocation of an absolutist black experience, within a U.S. context and elsewhere. The more compelling diasporic castings of blackness are about neither nostalgia for lost origins nor
the claiming of an unruptured link to an invented homeland. Stuart Hall, for
instance, advocates rather for a sense of a dispersed, multiply situated subjectivity that claims that identity is not a matter of "essence or purity" and
recognizes "heterogeneity and diversity . . . transformation and difference"
(1994: 401–2). Such a contention with alterity is possible even while retaining
at the fore the serious political considerations and varying issues of domination that confront black people globally.

While blacks are dispersed transnationally, there is a certain centrality, as some scholars have observed, of African American sign production to global black standards. This is primarily a function of globalization and American imperialism, and in noting this global prominence, I mean not to apportion blame, guilt, or innocence, nor to oversimplify what are obviously complex matters. First of all, African American sign production is far from uniform. American definitions of blackness are, and have always been, disparate and debated. Not only is U.S. black subjectivity contested terrain, but it is differently rendered across space and time. Moreover, in arguing for combined local and global analyses of culture and power, Arjun Appadurai is persuasive in his oft-hailed reminder that an overemphasis on Americana as a circulating commodity can downplay the extent to which "the United States is no longer the puppeteer of a world system of images, but is only one node of a complex transnational construction of imaginary landscapes" (1994: 327). Here we should also note Appadurai's related caveat that when global subjects encounter Americana, whatever cultural forms are incorporated are also customized, adapted according to the specificities of their new location.

But the status of the United States as a dominant world power nevertheless renders it, in ways unrivaled and unreciprocal, a source of "global cultural production and circulation" (S. Hall 1993: 21). By extension, blacks outside the United States are often on some level in contention with black America, whether they wish it or not. As many have observed, black subjects globally are affected by African American political and civil rights struggles, as well as by other widely circulating African American discursive technologies and cultural forms, such as literature, scholarship, music, dance, fashion, and so on. This is especially the case in nearby Canada even though Canada is almost always overlooked within the writings that make this type of argument.

A number of popular sayings in Canada speak to the impact of the United States. One is "When the United States sneezes, Canada catches pneumonia." Another talks about what it is like to sleep next to an elephant. This suggests a significance of U.S. affairs to Canadians, a sense of contingency that is not mutual. Similarly, but also differently, black Canada is in contention with black America—in ways generally more apparent for those north of the border. The fact that these categories overlap as a result of proximity, porous borders, and historical ties is one reason. This observation is meant also as a qualification that my employment of terms such as "black Canada" and "black America" is strategic and mindful of hybridity, interstitiality, and overlap.

Aside from proximity and historical ties, Canada's institutionalized multiculturalism emphasizes national origin and heritage and encourages the celebration of cultural difference, at least in government-designated allowable manifestations. As Chris Mullard has put it in a widely cited quote, Canada's multiculturalism is basically about the three s's—"saris, samosas, and steel bands," and it is certainly not about the three r's—"resistance, rebellion, rejection" (quoted in Mackey 1999: 66). Canada's heritage project, its "multivulturalism," as it is sometimes called pejoratively, espouses color blindness and yet constitutes itself as the "great white north." What arises, then, is a brand of disavowed racism, in which black people are perceived as "cultural" rather than "racial" others. This then translates into blacks often being treated as literal foreigners, aliens within Canada's national boundaries. "Where are you *from* from?" or "What island are you from?" are questions often encountered by Canadian blacks, who may themselves make such inquiries of other blacks. It is significant that the majority of black Canadians claim as part of their legacy voluntary migration during the post–World War II era, but it is also the case that Canada traces its black presence to the early 1600s. Black people are not new to the Canadian scene, contrary to popular Canadian belief. A dub poem by Lillian Allen sums up one general motif well when the black Canadian persona is constantly greeted with the proclamation:

Oh beautiful tropical beach
With coconut tree and rum
Why did you leave there?
Why on earth did you come? (1986: 74)

The poem's persona is associated, synecdochically, with exotic landscapes, warm, tropical places quite the opposite of Canada's icy climes. This state of affairs reverses conditions in the United States wherein immigrant blackness is overshadowed by particular discourses and dominant narratives of African Americanness. For instance, the conditions for blackness in Canada would stand in contradistinction to, say, Mary Waters's (1999) assessment of U.S. immigrant identity being subsumed under race in her book *Black Identities*. What also arises in Canada is a notion of blackness as an American phenomenon. Blackness is seen as American, while Canada's foremost national bond, according to countless polls, is a collective sense of self as *un*-American. When the most notorious "invisible empire," the Ku Klux Klan, was established in Canada in the 1920s, anti-Americanness was part of its platform.

This would seem to underscore Appadurai's notion of the ways American imports are adapted in their new contexts. In fact, Canadian Klaverns emphasized that they had "no connection to the Klan in the United States . . . and no right to bear the blame for what the Klan in the United States might be doing" (Winks 1997: 323). Among Canadians with un-Klanlike sensibilities, Canada's much publicized and much celebrated history of offering asylum to escaped slaves lends itself to widespread Canadian self-perceptions as antiracist, especially relative to the overtly racist United States. And yet, the notion of blacks having asylum in Canada, being tolerated but not really belonging, endures.

Canada's institutionalized multiculturalism is deliberately designed as a would-be superior antidote to the American melting pot and its implications of a cultural homogeneity that is managed through forms of racial and cultural exclusion. And yet, this same multiculturalism fosters perceptions of blacks as having non-Canadian origins, a form of displacement, alienation, and expatriation (or repatriation) from the imagined community that is Canada. In the United States this type of association is uncommon for blacks and more common for, say, Asian Americans, who are often treated as recent immigrants, for instance, being complimented on their English, even if their Americanness extends back many generations.

If black Canadians are cast out of authentic Canadianness, they are similarly cast out of discourses of blackness. Walker's nod to Canada in her definition of womanism suggests its special place within a genealogy of African America, a special place which, like the Africa in Afrocentricity, is symbolic of freedom for African Americans. Womanism then, in Walker's definition, articulates a politics of race and gender that does not incorporate *geo*politics. Black American feminists have been exemplary at cultivating intersectional analyses of race, class, gender, and sexuality and my own scholarship—including this attempt to write geopolitics into that very equation—is indebted to some of those enunciations.

Valerie Smith writes astutely of the interaction and unfixity of race, class, gender, and sexuality in her book *Not Just Race, Not Just Gender: Black Feminist Readings*. Others, as diverse in orientation as the Cohambee River Collective, Patricia Hill Collins, Kimberlé Crenshaw, and bell hooks, have incorporated gender specificities into traditional masculinist constructions of black identity and black progress and have problematized the privileging of black male oppression as more grave and urgent than that affecting black females. Works by Barbara Smith, Audre Lorde, Essex Hemphill, Rhonda

Williams, and Marlon Riggs critique homophobia and heterosexist discrimination in generalized and racialized terms and also address the issue of being cast out of blackness from a narrow but widespread notion of blackness as rigidly coded "straight." Marlon Riggs's film *Black Is . . . Black Ain't* is a riveting exploration of the many ways in which black identity is regulated and policed *by* black people in detrimental ways. One of the film's most poignant moments comes when Riggs, a gay black man, queries, "When the people sang their freedom songs, do you think they also sang them for *you*?"

It is the same logic that has prompted some to note that blackness, unqualified, is often coded as American. The anthropologist Michel Rolph Trouillot, for instance, conjectures that "the U.S. monopoly on both blackness and racism [is] itself a racist plot" (1995: 71). The politics of place, the issue of geopolitics, is every bit as consequential an aspect of identity as race, class, gender, and sexuality. Here the title of Gloria Hull, Patricia Bell Scott, and Barbara Smith's ground-breaking anthology from the 1980s is suggestive: *All the Women Are White, All the Blacks Are Men, But Some of Us Are Brave* signifies that "blacks" unqualified tend to be men and "women" unqualified tend to be white. Other volumes that affirm this logic are *Black Feminist Thought* (Collins 1990), *Homegirls: A Black Feminist Anthology* (Smith 1983), and the early 1970s compilation *The Black Woman* (Rodgers-Rose 1980). Again, these are incisive texts, particularly within their respective historical contexts, whose titles usefully hail the interaction of race and gender. But even in light of the global circulation of these texts, the fact that "all the blacks are American" goes unqualified. Non-American black discursive interventions are far fewer and have titles like *Black **British** Feminism* (Mirza 1997), *Showing Our Colors: Afro-**German** Women Speak Out* (Oguntoye et al. 1991), *Black Like Who?: Writing Black **Canada*** (Walcott 1997), and *Cultures in Babylon: Black **Britain** and African America* (Carby 1999) (bold added). A recent anthology, *Black Feminist Cultural Criticism* commendably juxtaposes race and gender (Bobo 2001). But the text notes neither its situatedness within an American context, nor its especial relevance to that context, and it features only American contributors.

My point here is not merely about the politics of inclusion. Rinaldo Walcott says it well when he insists that it is enough that "black Canadas exist and will continue to do so" (1997: 17). But it is worth noting the consequential fallout for those transnational black subjects inside and outside the American context who become black "others," inauthentic and inappropriate blacks, in the wake of circulating ideologies of African Americanness that unintentionally set a standard for blackness locally and globally. Canadians, for example, read black American discourses to the same extent that Americans do, a result of American primacy in publishing and other mechanisms of knowledge dissemination. And in terms of black Canadian identity formation, African American discourses named simply as "black" assist in establishing tropes, themes, and models that elide the specificities of the Canadian context.

To further exemplify this situation, a number of black American feminists have problematized Gerda Lerner's status as a white scholar who is unduly, in their opinion, touted as a pioneer in black women's studies, a reputation that resulted from her book *Black Women in White America*. In "The Occult of the True Black Woman," for instance, Ann du Cille writes that despite prevailing misconceptions of Lerner as the "first" to compile "a book length study devoted to African American women," she was "by no means the first" (1996a: 89). She also critiques Lerner for having purported in that compilation to "let black women speak for themselves." While these are salient critical interventions, American black feminists have not tended to inquire into matters of which "black women" in which "white America." When I told a couple of Canadian friends about my research on black Canada they laughed as they recalled being assigned Lerner's *Black Women in White America* as university students in the 1980s. They were amused in hindsight at the extent to which the book obscured the specifics of their Canadian and black diasporic heritages, even though at the time they and their black peers relied heavily on the volume in their racial identity construction during their college years. This tale bespeaks a type of North American black heterogeneity that is not always portrayed within discourses of blackness and points also to a disavowal of the ways in which processes of racial formation, even if reflexively counterhegemonic, are in part extensions of nationhood.

George Elliot Clarke, a noted black Canadian writer, tropes Du Bois's famous representation of his induction into racial consciousness, the instance in the early pages of *The Souls of Black Folk* when his classmate refuses, out of hand, to exchange visiting cards with him. As a result, the young Du Bois first realizes he is different from his childhood peers. But George Elliot Clarke's initiation into a consciously black identity is doubly mediated when at age four in Nova Scotia he is met with racial epithets. In Clarke's early childhood consciousness of race he considers himself "African American," an identification that later in life transforms into a more reflexive African *Canadian* identity, a subjectivity that remains in dialogue with and informed by

African Americanness but that more accurately marks his geographical and ideological placement within Canada. In my illustration of this process of self-definition, George Elliot Clarke is not meant to stand in for black Canada as a whole. While his experience is not unique, it is also not necessarily the norm, as black Canadian social locations vary tremendously and there is no dominant narrative of blackness in Canada. Other black Nova Scotians of American descent would loudly reject a claiming of these origins. In joining the call for reparations, for instance, Halifax blacks, mostly of U.S. American descent, are seeking compensation from the Canadian, not the American government, on the grounds of Canada's disavowed history of slavery. What is revelatory about George Elliot Clarke's story is how in a predominantly white, racially integrated Canadian context, when a person inevitably bumps up against his or her racial *différance,* one readily available model of black identity is an explicitly American one, albeit rarely named as such.

The unwitting influence of African American sign production on perceptions of blackness outside of the United States combined with widespread Canadian ignorance about race played a central role in a custody case that was settled in the fall of 2001 by Canada's Supreme Court. For the two years until it was resolved, this widely covered media event functioned as a western Canadian equivalent to the Elián Gonzalez saga in the United States. The case was the topic of a conference at York University in Toronto, where academics from multiple disciplines debated issues of race, color, belonging, and the lawful kinship of a young boy, Elijah Edwards. Elijah, four years old at the time of the Supreme Court verdict, was born in Vancouver to a white Canadian mother and a black American father. The Supreme Court awarded custody to the mother, stating that in its decision, "race was not an important consideration." This ruling overturned an earlier one by British Columbia's lower court, which had granted sole custody to Elijah's father, Theodore "Blue" Edwards, a former professional basketball player for the NBA team the Vancouver Grizzlies.

While the case raised difficult dilemmas along inseparable lines of race, color, class, nation, gender, sexuality, and kinship, the lower court unanimously held that it had based its ruling on the importance of the child being raised in a black rather than a white context. Even more importantly for my purposes here, the court questioned whether Canada had a black community, per se, and suggested that as a member of an American family the child could access a more authentic black experience than he could in Canada. Technically, custody was awarded to "the black American community" more than to the child's father, who was established by that same court as a man with "character flaws," a man less committed to the son than the mother, and a man who had been on the road for the past nine years living "a glamorous life in which he frequently indulged in extramarital sex" (quoted in Wattie 2000: 1). The father was awarded custody because, as the court put it, "in a part of the world where the black population is proportionately greater than it is here . . . Elijah would in this event have a greater chance of achieving a sense of cultural belonging and identity" (2).

The main point I wish to make in sharing this story is that its outcome illuminates the troubling ways that issues of black authenticity play out in relation to interraciality, widespread Canadian ignorance about race, and African America's inadvertent international influence. The lower court's decision was on one level a deportation of a black subject to the United States, to a country seen by some within Canada as more natural and more suitable for blacks. This of course is reminiscent of the concerted efforts of the colonization movement in the 1800s, which attempted to relocate U.S. blacks to West Africa, which was seen as a more natural and suitable location for blacks than the New World. Without erasing the many nuances of the Elijah case, we can also observe how it reifies Canadian histories of racism that took the form of encouraging blacks to relocate to the United States after emancipation. It also recalls the barring, in the first half of the twentieth century, of black immigration into Canada on the grounds of a purported unsuitability for the Canadian climate.

The British Columbia court's interpretation of the ways that race, culture, and nation merge points to the urgency of a widespread recognition of the vicissitudes of blackness and whiteness in Canada, as they converge and diverge. These vicissitudes include an active repression of black cultural contributions to the Canadian social and discursive landscape and active antiblack discrimination, historically and in the present. American racial discourses often point to disproportionate black victimization along institutional lines, including lack of access to quality education, lack of adequate, affordable health care, and continuing de facto segregation. Canadians, in contrast, tend to boast (in many instances quite literally) that they have a more socialized political and economic system than that of the United States, with quality and equally funded public schools, affordable, universal health care, less disparate class divides, and virtually no segregated neighborhoods. None of this, however, translates into equal opportunity or an antiracist context for Canadian blacks. While Canada appears to be a context in which "the conditions for procuring 'freedom' [are] . . . evident" (Walcott 1997: 21), it is also a place where, to borrow Frantz Fanon's words, "an existential deviation" has been forced upon black people. According to Walcott, the "writer George Elliot Clarke describes contemporary Canadian racism as including: the shooting downs, in cold blood, of unarmed black men by white cops; the pitiless exploitations and denials of black women; the persistent erasure of our presence; the channeling of black youth into dead-end classes and brain-dead jobs; the soft-spoken white supremacist assumptions that result in our impoverishment, our invisibility, our suffering, our deaths" (xx).

This sort of maltreatment is similar to that which occurs in the United States, which underscores obvious national overlaps. But despite sharing certain manifestations of racial oppression, black Canada is not a replica of black America, nor does racism in Canada replicate that of the United States. For despite Canada's considerable history of antiblack racism, the black/white binary is not the primary racial formula in Canada, nor has antiblack racism been institutionalized in the way and to the extent that it has been in the United States. Canada, once again, is, by governmental design, multicultural, a mosaic of varying ethnic, cultural, regional, and linguistic constituencies, and its black collectivity fissures along similar lines, preempting the possibility of and in most cases the desire for racial solidarity, and preventing the emergence of a dominant narrative of Canadian blackness.

Scholarly examinations of blackness in transnational perspective, most notably within the British context, have fruitfully influenced conceptualizations of blackness inside and outside the American context. Stephen Small holds in tension simultaneous difference and sameness between the United States and Britain throughout his book, *Racialised Barriers: The Black Experience in the United States and England in the 1980s*. In that volume, he defends the utility of a comparative approach to black cultural contexts, as "many benefits would accrue to those involved in attempts to combat racialized inequality" (1994: 179). The feminist scholar Susan Friedman takes the argument in favor of transnational comparativism even further, noting how it enables "a kind of categorical 'travel' that denaturalizes 'home,' bringing to visibility many of the cultural constructions we take for granted as 'natural.' Sharp juxtapositions of different locations often produce startling illuminations, bringing into focus the significance of geopolitical mediations of other axes of difference. Comparativism and the 'glocalization' of a transnational methodology are not mutually exclusive. Indeed, these practices complement each other as constitutive parts of geopolitical thinking" (1999: 114).

Transnational comparisons, for instance juxtaposing Canada and the United States, and noting both differences and similarities can shed light on the nuances of black subjectivity in both places. Developing geopolitical thinking would also include studying localities other than our own and taking seriously external or outside opinions about our particular social and geographical locations (yes, often plural) while attempting to deconstruct binaries of "self" and "other" and avoiding locational parochialism (Friedman 1999: 130–31).

The stakes in negotiating the geopolitical axis of black subjectivity are apparent in the fiction and critical reception of the Haitian-Canadian writer Dany Laferrière. Laferrière, though scarcely heard of in the United States, is better known in Canada and is a household name in Francophone Canada and France. Because his writing addresses a number of the political and theoretical considerations that I have outlined throughout this essay, its short remainder will engage two of his fictional works and some critical responses to them. Each text features black displacement in the form of transnational border crossing, though one is set in Montreal, Quebec, and the other features a road trip throughout the United States undertaken by a black Haitian-Canadian protagonist. This latter book can be loosely classified as travel writing, though it defies categorization within a genre, just as its author, Laferrière, similarly defies absolute categorization of any kind. The text is, at once, a novel, a set of riffs, a series of loosely related vignettes, and a scathingly humorous and artfully offensive social commentary. The author believes in the power of a provocative title, though this book's title, *Why Must a Black Writer Write about Sex?* (1994), is quickly revealed as having slightly more to do with shock value than with the book's actual content. The book is above all a set of "field notes" taken throughout the road trip, a series of musings about race, class, gender, sex, and fame as they pertain to blackness in the United States.

Laferrière's protagonist is clearly an unveiled alter ego of Laferrière himself, though I will continue to refer to "the protagonist" as such, so as not to conflate the author and his fictionalized self-depiction. Throughout the narrative, the protagonist occupies the position of an "inappropriate" or "inappropriat*ed* other"—Trinh Minh-ha's term for the perennial "insider/outsider" or "other-within" social location (1990: 375). This is so in that Laferrière emphasizes the protagonist's simultaneous difference and sameness, his insider and outsider status in relation to American blackness and Americanness. The story begins with the protagonist being asked by an

American publishing interest to embark on a road trip throughout the United States and document his observations. In a spoof of America's wealth, the road trip is funded by "the Ford Foundation, and the Getty Foundation, the Mellon and the Morgan and the Rockefeller Foundations" (1994: 12). Before accepting the assignment, the protagonist asks, "Why don't they get a real American black?" (1994: 11), which from the outset raises the issues of racial authenticity and alterity.

Why Must a Black Writer Write about Sex? excavates ethnicity, transnationality, class, gender, and sexuality as they intersect with geopolitics. Moreover, Laferrière's reliance on such literary devices as humor, farce, irony, paradox, contradiction, satire, parody, and antagonism double as cultural polemics, or "freedom tropes." We can, and perhaps should, legitimately question at whose expense his scathing humor is employed. For instance, one of the reasons I gravitated toward critically engaging his work in the first place is that it begs for a feminist analysis of the ways he portrays white women and black women, when he portrays black women at all. And yet, his text is an assertion of freedom, a creative insubordination, that takes the form of impiety, a refusal to enact what some might consider to be categorical imperatives, a refusal to enact the role of an "appropriate black subject." Moreover, the humor suggests a pattern of laughing to keep from crying, as it were, for the perpetual laughter in the face of adversity does not entirely mask a weariness and despair. Laferrière's is an ambivalent, impious, yet politically charged representation of a Haitian-Canadian's misadventures in American and African American social contexts respectively.

During the road trip, the protagonist confronts select Americanisms. According to his observations, "America is an overfed infant. And Americans live as if no one else existed on the continent. On the planet . . . Each of their movements seems absolutely new, as if they weren't connected to the human chain. They are unique . . . the world is like a baby's rattle in their hands. They break it; they fix it . . . They are gods. And their blacks are demi-gods" (1994: 15). The protagonist also makes a series of assessments, some celebratory, even worshipful, some not, about a selection of specific African American "demi-gods," ranging from Spike Lee to Ice Cube, Miles Davis, Toni Morrison, James Baldwin, Jean-Michel Basquiat, and Billie Holiday.

The protagonist also attributes to the United States shocking class divides that are clearly racially marked. Yet he also perceives overly rigid black/white binaristic constructions of race and racism, perceptions of power as an issue of A-over-B, an obsession with "success" and the "American dream," as well as a rigid policing of black identity engaged in by some of the black people he meets. One of these self-appointed, black-identity policemen is a Nigerian immigrant cab driver, who himself fails to fit into his own rigorously defended, essentialist definition of blackness. By making and voicing such loaded observations as these throughout his road trip, Laferrière's protagonist is repeatedly greeted, within the United States, as a race traitor. The vehemence of this charge of "sell-out" is only magnified within the text when the protagonist is revealed as having authored the 1987 novel *How to Make Love to a Negro Without Getting Tired*. The protagonist learns that in the United States, more so than anywhere else, the text's very title is sufficiently off-putting to warrant constant charges of his being a race traitor. The Haitian-Canadian protagonist in turn questions whether one can sell out of blackness, or rather out of African Americanness as it were, if one never bought in, if one is, to begin with, in it but not of it. That is to say that even as the cultural signifiers and categorical imperatives associated with African Americanness are unfamiliar to the protagonist, he is expected to conform to them and deemed a sell-out when he does not.

Why Must a Black Writer Write about Sex, then, is a spin on the American national landscape in general, including antiblack oppression by whites, but more so the regulation of black identity by blacks. Alternatively, *How to Make Love to a Negro*, Laferrière's first novel, is about the constant indignities heaped upon a black Haitian-Canadian immigrant named "Man" and his Senegalese-Canadian roommate, "Bouba," in the predominantly white context of Montreal, Quebec. It eschews depictions of pure victims or oppressors, opting instead to represent more ambiguously and complicatedly the layerings of everyday life in Montreal during two summer months. Another central component of the plot is the writing of a novel within the novel, as Man, the protagonist, attempts to document his escapades in literary form.

The books *How to Make Love to a Negro* and *Why Must a Black Writer Write about Sex?* were published in English translation by Coach House Press, an Eastern Canadian publisher. Canadian reviewers, Francophone and Anglophone alike, evidence Margaret Cannon's notion of racism as an "invisible empire" within Canada and show a shallow understanding of the ways race and racism operate centrally within Laferrière's writings, emphasizing instead the humar and ribaldry of a seemingly unracialized sexual politics. Meanwhile, American critics are more savvy in emphasizing the obvious centrality of race within Laferrière's writing, but in assessing his works they tend to ignore the geopolitical axis, the Haitian-Canadianness, writ fluidly, of the books. Instead, American critics interpellate Laferrière into a recognizably American blackness. For example, a glowing *Village Voice* review describes *How to Make Love to a Negro* as "a fresh version of Zora Neale Hurston's delectable self-revelation ... a psychic tussle that resonates with the furious stuff in James Baldwin's essays, or Louis Armstrong's smiling trumpet, or Martin Luther King's oratory" (Wood 1989: 47). Here Laferrière is compared only to American blacks.

There are, of course, overlaps and parallels between black diasporic cultures, a sameness in difference, or as some have called it, a "changing same." But what we see here once again is that aforementioned slippage of "black" and "American" and a reduction of the politics of place to the level of irrelevance, in this case Laferrière's Haitian-Canadian background and the Québecois setting of *How to Make Love to a Negro*. The *Village Voice* reviewer continues by suggesting that Laferrière's writerly sentiments "are true-to-life, confused, *real American* thoughts" (Wood 1989: 47, italics added). Another scholar published an article in *Callaloo* that advocates for increased attention to Laferrière's works by American scholars, an admonition with which I would unhesitatingly ally myself. The essay, however, is entitled "Meet Dany Laferrière, American." The article does not clarify upon what grounds Laferrière is defined or redefined as an American. Perhaps it is Laferrière's Haitian background, as well as his links to the United States, and he does have tangible links to the United States. But the temptation to translate "American" here into its larger signifier of "New World," from its northernmost tip to its southernmost, creates a bit of a glitch, as it ignores the fact that those north of the forty-ninth parallel generally opt out of the contest for inclusion within the sign of Americanness. Yes, critiques abound in Canada about how problematic it is that residents of the United States have co-opted the term "American" for themselves, but statistically speaking most of the imagined community that is Canada imagines itself first and foremost as patently "un-American," black Canadians not exempted.

We might call this a "geopolitical illiteracy" that is evidenced in the *Village Voice* and *Callaloo* articles on Laferrière. And these are not isolated incidents. Rather, they are symptomatic of a pervasive treatment of U.S. black culture as a general index for blackness, of a not uncommon elision of blackness and African Americanness. Even given the increasing currency of black diaspora paradigms in U.S. intellectual circles, there remains a limited fluency in the transnational circuitry of blackness as a major operative force inside and outside a U.S. context. I have engaged in this provisional analysis of the black

Canadian scene as juxtaposed with select American and diasporic discourses of race and freedom not because I see this particular project as the ultimate black studies mandate or as African American studies' ultimate missing link. Nor is mine a call for increased virtuosity or expertise on specific sites of blackness scattered throughout the world, for never can we know enough even to pretend to understand them all. My concern is with the stakes in negotiating geopolitics in general, a call for increased reflexivity and awareness about the fields of power and patterns of exclusion that are embedded within the ways blackness is studied and represented.

My argument for the importance of geopolitics is very much about "the cultural politics of difference" in general, the ways in which, as Stuart Hall has put it, "questions of mobility and unity are now always questions of difference" (1987). If black subjectivity is mitigated by ethnicity, gender, class, and sexuality, it is also mitigated by geopolitics. Diversely motivated and varying forms of transnational border crossing shape the cultural, political, and ideological parameters of blackness. Just as the sign of blackness on a global scale is constituted by varying and overlapping national, ethnic, and cultural locations, blackness within U.S. borders is complex and differentiated. Contending comparatively with the local and the global then, taking seriously the geopolitical axis of subjectivity, can compel ever more discerning, efficacious articulations of blackness, wherever its location.

MAPPING TRANSNATIONALITY

Roots Tourism and the Institutionalization of Ethnic Heritage

KAMARI MAXINE CLARKE

One of the most important issues in the anthropology of Africa of the late twentieth century has been the "invention of Africa."[1] Valentin Mudimbe (1988) has demonstrated that, in addition to the existence of particular forms of native logics, colonial constructions of history, classifications of ethnicity, boundaries, and the imposition of European languages have informed the discourses through which Africans understand each other and themselves. This "invention" of Africanness has been revived by some black Americans in the United States, who, looking to Africa for ancestral roots, have reinvented themselves as both Africans (through descent) and U.S. Americans (through lived experience).

It should be no surprise, therefore, that two of the most powerful ideological narratives of U.S. black nationalist imaginaries that took shape in the mid-1960s and continue to circulate in the present are the "slavery narrative" and the "African nobility-redemption" narrative.[2] The slavery narrative (Martin Shaw and Clarke 1995) is based on notions of ancestral and therefore biological commonalities among black people. It narrates how Africans were torn from Africa, how they were enslaved because of racial oppression and brought to the New World. It also highlights how, despite the oppressive conditions under which they lived, enslaved Africans produced "diverse cultures" and maintained a fundamental connection to their African past. Through the symbolics of blood[3] and diasporic displacement and suffering, these narratives signify a connection to Africa that produces notions of ancestry as being constituted through and from one black ancestor to another. It describes black Americans as surviving incarnations of preslavery African societies, thereby enabling a self-identification of black Americans as not simply racialized but as fundamentally embedded in genealogies of heritage.

The African nobility narrative, on the other hand, legitimates the centrality of slavery as the basis for African American connections to Africa while also eliding it as secondary to the pride of black heritage. By highlighting the idea that African Americans are not merely victims of slavery but descendants of an African noble and religious elite who are, at the present time, culturally imprisoned in the racist United States, the African nobility narrative ambitiously links the noble African past with African American hopes for an institutionally empowered future. Because black Americans are seen as having "lost" their "traditions" and "culture" to white America, the nobility narrative offers them the promise of reclaiming their "true African selves" by embracing "African" traditions. This narrative incites black Americans to take control of their destiny by reclaiming their ancestral identities.

Since the late 1960s, these narratives have come to represent a popular common sense that links blackness to Africanness, thereby reinscribing the signs of slavery and nobility within transatlantic global circulations, past and present. Admittedly, ideological attempts to create linkages between the Americas and Africa long preceded late-twentieth-century shifts in global capitalism, since a cultural politics of black racial belonging to Africa was central to many late-nineteenth-century and early-twentieth-century black nationalist formations. However, as a result of both nationalist and transnational forms of agitation during the cold war, and with the post–World War II emphasis of the United States on democracy and economic integration, there was also an ideological shift within U.S. educational, governmental, and cultural domains that institutionalized the heritage model as the basis for contemporary identities.

In this essay, I argue that as a result of the globalization of cultural heritage opportunities, claims to African membership are becoming increasingly deterritorialized and far more negotiable and manipulatable today than ever before. Yet the development of diaspora studies in the United States has contributed to place-based conceptions of racialization and cultural formations. The very term "diaspora"—a Greek word whose roots, *dia* and *speirein*, mean "through" and to "scatter seeds" respectively—refers to the scattering of people's offspring. Thus, the term African Diaspora is often used to refer to the dispersal of black people from Africa to the Americas.[4] By the 1970s and 1980s, African Diaspora studies not only overdetermined the homogeneity of race and culture but also created an approach to diaspora that charted migration as a unipolar link from Africa to its *elsewheres*. By emphasizing Africa as the originary homeland of black people, the myriad circular influences between (and within) the Americas and Africa were ignored, and the institutionalization of African American studies in the United States presumed teleologies of ancestry that were unipolar and racially constituted. The problem with this approach to race and diaspora in contemporary studies is that it presumes the possibility of finding an "authentic" articulation of origins (which depends on Africanness as being produced in Africa alone) and maintains biology as the basis of this linkage.

Analyses of diasporic circulations should instead demonstrate how, through particular complex interactions between Africa and the United States, diasporic identities and consciousnesses are made, and therefore how narratives of descent are constructed in historically constituted ways. Approaches to diaspora should detail the ways that agents, institutions, state actors, and markets selectively set ideological roots where physical and material routes do not always exist (D. Scott 1991). In what follows, I examine how late-twentieth-century conceptions of racial belonging were embedded in a more aggressive form of capital institutionalism conducive to the marketing of black Americanness as a sign of African slavery and the glorification of a preslavery past. By focusing on what Ariana Hernandez-Reguant (1999) has referred to as the ethnicization of the African Diaspora, I explore new cartographies of blackness as they are taking shape in culturalist terms.

My points of departure for this exploration emerge from data collected in Ôyōtúnjí African Village in South Carolina and while traveling with them to Yorubaland in southwestern Nigeria (seen as their homeland). Named after the once powerful West African Ôyō Empire of the sixteenth to eighteenth centuries, Ôyōtúnjí African Village is a black nationalist community that was founded in 1970 by African American religious converts to Yorùbá practices who have reclaimed West Africa as their ancestral homeland. By the late 1970s, the village boasted a population of 191 residents.[5] For those living there, five thousand miles from the westernmost tip of West Africa, Ôyōtúnjí represents the home of black people in America whose ancestors were enslaved, sold to traders, and transported to the Americas as slaves. Because revivalists in

Ôyōtúnjí believe they have a right to control the African territory that was their homeland prior to European colonization, they claim diasporic connections to the ancestral history of the Great Ôyō Empire of the Yorùbá people and so have reclassified their community as an African kingdom outside of the territoriality of the Nigerian postcolonial state. The community's ultimate force, however, is in its national and international network of cultural, economic, and political linkages. As such, I begin with a description of our arrival in Lagos, Nigeria, in which Ôyōtúnjí African Americans and Africans are engaged in an airport encounter. I then proceed to examine the ways that various imaginaries about African heritage are shaped by particular changes in transnational axes of power. These revivalists' production of identity provides a springboard for a discussion of how new ideas about diasporic belonging are constituted by (and, to a degree, also constitute) changing political and market forces, forces that have also shaped the institutionalization of racial categories over time.

Roots Tourism and the Institutionalization of Race as Culture

"Welcome to Lagos, Nigeria," read the tattered white sign above the stairway encircling the airport. It was dark and windy by the time the plane landed on the Lagos runway and we disembarked. As the king of Ôyōtúnjí African Village and the six members of his entourage walked down the plane's steel staircase, he fell to the ground to kiss the cold white concrete. Some members of his entourage helped him to stand up as he embraced himself, raising his fists in the air to signal victory.

His facial expression changed from that of someone involved in sobering prayer to enthusiasm, as if to say, "The hardships are over. Africa, I'm home."

"I don't know, I think I'll wait for the broooown soil," muttered Adé Bíólú, one of the younger members of the contingent. "This concrete isn't the real Africa," he added.

For Adé Bíólú, as a first-time visitor to Nigeria, the airport runway's concrete was not satisfyingly symbolic of what constitutes appropriate "African" soil. For the king, in contrast, as he later stated, "the fact of arriving [in Nigeria] is the homecoming, not the way [that] it's been colonized."

As the six other members of the entourage walked to the terminal building with the other passengers who were on the plane, I noticed Adé Bíólú greeting many of the staring workers and observers. "Àlàáfíà" (Peace), he saluted them in Yorùbá, continuously initiating eye contact with the native onlookers. The interaction resembled the arrival of a delegate who had just descended from a private jet and was greeting his fans. However, most of the onlookers reacted nonverbally by nodding, smiling, or waving; others ridiculed him with nearby coworkers or companions. Most of the watchers refrained from responding in Yorùbá, perhaps because they assumed he would not understand their response or perhaps because they did not speak Yorùbá at all.

Adé Bíólú was the first from our group to approach the line for immigration clearance. The rest of us followed him, chatting quietly among ourselves and laughing at what we referred to privately as his bluff—the pretense of familiarity and assumption of acceptance. When it was our turn to proceed to the front of the line, Adé Bíólú greeted the officer by saying "Àlàáfíà," this time in a more serious tone.

"Good evening," replied the official in his crisply ironed police uniform and curved hat, as if to correct him. "You are visiting," he declared without asking. "What is your country of citizenship?" he demanded, staring at Adé Bíólú with an outstretched hand to signal for our passports.

"United States," the others replied in staggered order as Ade Bíólú turned to us to collect our passports.

"Canada," I chimed in.

The officer looked at them and then at me. We were dressed in "African clothes," with cowrie shell jewelry and common beads around our necks. A few seconds later the officer seemed to notice the *ilà* (tribal scarification designated to show tribal descent from Ôyō) on the faces of my companions. He stared at one of the darker-complexioned people in the group, whose ilà were prominently figured on his upper cheeks, and in a new turn of disbelief he asked, responding to our statement of origin, "All of you?"

I looked at everyone in our group. Half of us had dark brown complexions, the other half was lighter skinned. Together, we were distinctly different shades of brown. We wore the "traditional" "Nigerian" clothes that Ôyótúnjí residents are expected to wear—the women with elaborate head wraps and colorful garments, the men with their fílà (a Yorùbá traditional hat) and traditional cotton pant suits—known in Yorùbá as *aÿö òkè*. I looked to the back of the line and observed men, women, and a few children with faces darker than ours, who were wearing plainly colored Western clothes. We North Americans, it seemed to me, were the only people in this section of the airport who were wearing what was seen as "traditional" Nigerian clothing. Twenty men with brown, black, or beige jackets or shirts, carrying briefcases and multiple large bags, and women with varying hairstyles—chemically straightened hair, loosely curled, long, braided, and unbraided "weaves" — watched us with curiosity, amusement, and perhaps even disdain.

"Purpose of your visit?" continued the immigration officer as he looked at our passports, eventually raising his eyes to study us.

"Educational," responded Adé Bíólú, just as seriously.

"Vacation," someone else in the group said, immediately and loudly, as if to correct Adé Bíólú and hide the ritual initiation and learning goals that inspired their travel.

"What kind of education?" the officer asked as he looked toward those standing near Adé Bíólú.

"Traditional education," Adé Bíólú replied. "I was born in America, but Africa is my home. We have all come home," he added, moving his hands slowly as if to encircle all of us in his description of a homecoming—all of us, including the unimpressed officer. The officer's serious and unwavering frown turned into an unflattering smirk, perhaps a response of disbelief, nonacceptance, or offense at Adé Bíólú's attempt at so liberally remapping us as African citizens.

"What are those marks there?" continued the officer, cutting off Adé Bíólú's "homecoming" performance and instead pointing at the cuts on the upper cheeks of three of the lightest brown people in the entourage. As he looked at the last person's ilà, he exclaimed self-assuredly as he shook his head and smiled, "Why did you let them do that to you? These Nigerians will do anything for money."

"They're ilàs," Ìyá Sisilum responded boastingly. "And we did it. We do this in America too, you know, and . . ." she hesitated and speaking in Yorùbá this time, overemphasizing what should be tonal inflections with standard American English ones, "Àwa Â lö Abëòkúta and Ôyö" (We are now going to Abëòkúta and Ôyö).

"O kú isë! (Well done!) Obìnrin (lady), you speak Yorùbá!" responded the officer approvingly and with a smile. He looked over to one of his colleagues, who had already been listening to our interactions and looked amused. They both raised their eyebrows and the officer who had been questioning us said quickly and with a chuckle, "Òyìnbó ní they are African!" (White man say they are African!).

As both of them chuckled together, Ìyá Sisilum added charmingly, as if to indicate that she understood the paradoxical subtext, "Bëê ni, a wá kö èdè Yorùbá!" (Yes, and we are here to learn more Yorùbá).

Without an attempt to request a bribe for not harassing us, clearly tourists, the officer chuckled and, as he opened each passport, looked at the picture and matched it to the correct person, saying "O.k., a dúpë" (thank you) or "You can go now." Ìyá Sisilum's passport, though, he put aside.

After ushering all of the men through and then me, he handed Ìyá Sisilum her passport, and with a sly smile he said, "Olúwa yíó pànà mō (The Lord will keep you safe on the trip!), American Nigerian lady," and then he asked, in English, if she had anything for him.

"A dúpë púpô" (Thank you very much), she responded, flirting with a bashful smile, as if to misunderstand his question as a request for a bribe and not as a potential future meeting or date. As she walked away, both of the officers waved good-bye to all of us and chuckled, watching Ìyá Sisilum's buttocks as she walked toward the baggage and customs area.

Rethinking Race through Ancestral Heritage

The above vignette raises questions concerning whose "Africa" is "Africa"? Whose "Africa" is "African"? Which patterns of cultural production are "authentic"? And with what authority do diverse actors speak, judge, and shape the processes of cultural production and the diverse implications these processes have for claiming a "black," and African, and African American raced identity? Here, the encounter between African American heritage tourists and Nigerian governmental officials is part of a larger political economy in which Western tourists seek cultural heritage experiences from the non-West. Disjunctures in formulations of belonging, on both sides of the Atlantic, highlight the complex (and sometimes conflicting) basis upon which membership is forged and the institutional norms through which meanings are understood. For many Nigerians, for example, the terms of Yorùbá membership may be understood in relation to both norms of state citizenship and sociocultural laws of paternal descent (as the term òyìnbó suggests). For the Ôyōtúnjí revivalists, membership may involve racial ancestry as well as historical connections that predate the formation of the Nigerian colonial state. Ultimately, members of both groups seem to desire what the other group has and the existing features of desire and belonging continue to be deeply rooted in economic conditions of possibility and production. Nigerian Òrìsà practitioners, for example, tend to want access to the resources and connections of the West; Ôyōtúnjí revivalists, predominantly heritage travelers, want the knowledge of ritual through which to develop increasingly independent deterritorialized mechanisms for reclaiming and legitimizing their ancestral membership—what they see as their birthright (see also Ebron 2002). However, because these dialogues between black American heritage tourists and religious revivalists on one hand and African-born practitioners on the other are embedded within particular relations of power, the contours of their exchanges are unequal and asymmetrical. And despite the differing claims to membership, the criteria for legitimacy are still connected to particular institutional norms.

In understanding the development of roots tourism and the institutionalization of "Africa" as the homeland for black Americans, it is important to recognize that the publication of *Roots: Saga of an American Family* by Alex Haley and its subsequent broadcast as a television miniseries was critical to new imaginings of the African past.[6] As the third most watched program in the history of television—130 million people, representing a broad spectrum of viewers worldwide, were estimated to have seen it—*Roots* contributed to the production of collective memory of an already marginalized U.S. community. As time progressed, the nobility of the African past featured prominently in the development of cultural blackness as a heritage identity. Bringing to life narratives about the complexities of African American enslavement, loss, struggle, victory, and survival, the *Roots* story began with the birth in 1750 of the protagonist, Kunta Kinte, in a West African village in the Gambian River region. Detailing the trials and tribulations of seven generations of Kunta Kinte's descendants in the American South, *Roots* ends in Arkansas with the life of Alex Haley, who traces his family history back to its African origin. Declaring his ancestry as a narrative of African continuities and freedom, redemption and triumph, Haley follows the movement of Africans to slavery in the American South, to freedom, and, finally, to their empowerment in mainstream America. By creating a narrative by which the cultural politics of blackness merged with the ancestral history of slavery, *Roots* brought to life a history that was not part of the personal experience of African Americans but which became part of black popular social memory in the United States—a memory of the production of subservience, which had relevance in their personal lives.

Locating *Roots* as a key force in the shift in black American imaginings of their connection to the African heritage is critical for understanding the establishment of a new commonsense notion of racial categories in heritage terms. The early twentieth-century dominant textual narratives of slavery— that is, Africans being captured, enslaved, and sold to white traders, and suffering at the hands of white plantation owners—were reconfigured with what became a different public discourse about black American connections to African kingdoms. In the late twentieth century, these new constructions of the incorporation of the nobility of the ethnic past did more for the development of a widespread commonsense notion of the African roots of black American identities than any other back-to-Africa social movement in the United States. Ultimately, these nobility narratives contributed to the establishment of ideological terms for ongoing black American genealogical roots of African nobility.

In addition to foregrounding the centrality of slavery in transporting African captives from Africa to the Americas, *Roots* contributed to a narrative shift from what was popularly represented in schools as black Americans being victims of slavery who were saved by Abraham Lincoln to blacks as noble survivors and agents of their own freedom. Blackness became a popular signifier of cultural heritage and ethnicity emblematic of the multicultural principles of a post–Jim Crow, post–black power "American society," and it signaled a classificatory shift in categories of U.S. citizenship. For, unlike past pan-Africanist and black nationalist movements of earlier centuries, the mass circulation of *Roots* contributed to the widespread invention of an African ethnic identity constituted as a derivative of African Atlantic heritage. It followed a wave of wide-scale demands for American civil rights that reconceptualized black America's inclusion as one of a larger pantheon of American ethnic histories. After *Roots*, tracing genealogies of ancestry became a popular activity among Americans in general, and for African Americans in particular assertions of their African heritage began to overdetermine perceptions of racial belonging as cultural belonging. Given that black Americans could not draw on the experiential memory of transatlantic slavery, in the collective experience of a nation watching the story of slavery unfold, *Roots* brought to life the remaking of a collective memory of subordination that gained its experiential power through the power of association and rearticulation.

In 1999, some twenty-four years after *Roots* was published and televised, Henry Louis Gates produced *Wonders of the African World*. Though *Wonders* did not circulate as widely as *Roots*, this documentary also represents a significant moment in the history of black studies in the United States, having rattled the American academy by disrupting dominant institutional representations of slavery as a product of white Europeans and Americans exclusively. Unlike *Roots*, which reinforced a predominant narrative about European and Muslim participation in the transatlantic slave trade, *Wonders* invoked the grandeur of African civilizations by pointing to the complicity of Africans in contributing to the enslavement of Africans. *Wonders* had been preceded by another significant televisual moment—the airing, in the 1980s, of Ali Mazrui's *The Africans*, a PBS television series about colonial and contemporary African politics that also emphasized the cultural attainments of the precolonial African past. Following up on a theme set by its two most influential predecessors, *Wonders* highlighted a noble African past that had been rendered invisible in Eurocentric histories. Gates's retrieval of this precolonial past as a site for the acquisition of African American heritage established a new intellectual discourse about Africa's contribution to world "civilization."

Structured as Gates's pilgrimage back to the symbolic "homeland," the filmic text is organized as a travelogue, a personal voyage that was also a homecoming, in which Gates—a successful Harvard professor, family man, and tourist—returns as the distinguished son of the formerly enslaved who has embarked on a leisurely trek in search of Africa's wonders. Rather than focusing on an imaginary of shared roots, *Wonders* signaled the nobility of the African past as well as the complex relationships between Africans and African Americans. By highlighting the complicity of Africans in the enslavement of Africans, while at the same time unraveling the negative image of Africa as a dark and primitive continent that lacked "culture" and promoting an image of "Africa" as a place of great civilizations, *Wonders* foregrounded a dialectic of slavery and nobility. The documentary incited controversies within U.S.-based African and African American Studies programs that centered around three key problems. First, by limiting his focus to precolonial African civilizations, Gates was accused of decentering the importance of contemporary African concerns and sources of pride. Second, by highlighting African participation in slavery, he was accused of placing the minor role of Africans on par with that of the European machinery of the slave trade. And finally, by claiming to be the voice of Africa's prodigal son returned home with riches, Gates's success, on one hand, was a statement about middle-class black America's place in the new world order, and, on the other, raised issues regarding how (and by whom) African history should be represented for mainstream America. Despite the outrage, however, *Wonders*, like *Roots*, responded to an absence that addressed a social void, providing alternatives to imagining the African past.

The content of the representation in *Roots* and *Wonders* and the role of presenting alternatives to reconceiving the African diasporic past have contributed to new forms of black social memories. Yet, traditional debates in the anthropology of the African Diaspora have tended to address issues of cultural transmissions in relation to asymmetrical flows from homelands to places of migration—from Africa to the diaspora. Such approaches have established the presumption that the only practices that are authentic are those from so-called source counties and have neglected to recognize the ways that African peoples also incorporate and refashion Western practices as their own. As Eric Hobsbawm and Terrance Ranger (1983) have shown us, even the practices seen as the most "traditionalist" are often themselves equally dynamic and have changed over time and space.

Nevertheless, in highlighting the connections between Africans and African Americans as a result of slavery, these films not only began to highlight the complicity of African and European slavery, they also left an opening for rethinking African enslavement as an experience of a long and sophisticated African heritage of empires and rulers. And by providing knowledge about the "secrets of the African past," black public intellectuals contributed to the setting of new terms for the ways that commonsense notions about slavery and the African American past were to be understood. Moreover, because communities of black cultural nationalists became willing to claim a different narrative about Africa and slavery, new consumer demands for an African heritage industry took shape. The eventual proliferation of heritage literature, market products, heritage days, popular public artists and celebrities, and public intellectuals, such as Ali Mazrui and Henry Louis Gates, were possible as a result of the creation of a population willing to consume the productions of a growing heritage market. In order to understand what is new about contemporary U.S. workings of race and the invocations of diasporic connections to heritage, therefore, we must recognize the workings of transnational capital in the production of a new heritage consumer.

Capitalism, Mass Media, and Institutions of Belonging

The mercantile and transatlantic slave trade set in motion the ideological terrain for particular forms of racial mappings, and the eventual globalization of transnational capital has further reinforced preexisting norms by which notions of difference were demarcated, thereby setting the terms for territorialized black heritage claims to Africa. The spread of televised political forums, characteristic of the changing domain of the modes of communication, led to the development of an imaginary about shared black political struggles. Satellite television has thus played an important role in the late-twentieth-century development of pan-Africanisms and related forms of black nationalism.

Several scholars have examined the ways recent transformations of mass media have contributed to a shift in the centrality of information technologies in people's lives by examining the role of telemedia in shaping subjectivities (Abu-Lughod 1989, 1993, 2005; Appadurai 1996; Larkin 1997; Mankekar 1999). They have demonstrated that these technologies required the development of new daily practices and new ways of imagining social relations that, in turn, led to a distinctive reorganization of space and a shortening of temporal horizons—the time-space compression (Harvey 1989: 147). The burgeoning mass media also played an important role in publicizing black complaints about the institutionalized racism black Americans encountered on a daily basis (Van Deburg 1992). And though Martin Luther King's 1963 March on Washington was televised nationally and internationally and made U.S. racial inequalities public, the growing reach of the media, especially telemedia and radio, captured and sensationalized the rising tide of protest throughout the United States in the 1960s. Despite the political success of civil rights activism that ushered into law the Civil Rights Act of 1964 and the Voting Rights Act of 1965, U.S. social and political institutions were as politically regulated and racially divisive as ever before. As a result, many black activists were convinced that civil rights, as a means to an end, could not be the only goal of black self-empowerment in the United States.

By 1966, advocates for civil rights had developed a more radical social movement—one that advocated black power as the basis for racial equality. Black power ideologies extolling positive black self-esteem, social empowerment, and self-determination were incorporated into organizing strategies as an attempt to challenge racial hierarchies. Accompanying the development of black power identities was a shift from "being a Negro" to "becoming black," a shift that also signaled African pride as the term "Negro"—a term associated with slavery and the biological justification of racial segregation—was exchanged for the term "black." In this way, empowerment was connected to black (and eventually African) pride, and blackness became a form of "consciousness" that black Americans needed to undergo. The cultural politics of blackness, then, involved a multilayered and increasingly transnational ideological movement advocating a revolution through which black people attempted to transform the cultural tenets of European influences in their lives.[7] One of the famous slogans of black power, "Black is beautiful," was incorporated as a challenge to dominant signs of whiteness as superior and blackness as primitive. By expressing black aesthetic virtues and solidarity against white racism, members of the growing black power movement self-consciously recast the centrality of whiteness in their lives, rendering it marginal but curiously dialectical. By rejecting their given names as residual names from traditions of slavery and changing them to African names, and by using African-derived kinship terms such as "brother" and "sister" as new ways of communicating racial unity, black power adherents reeducated themselves about the existence of African civilizations, village life, and "traditionalist" lifestyles. And even though black power had the effect of acknowledging linkages in biologically racial terms, becoming black and conscious was a fundamentally cultural process.

By the early 1970s, black power sentiments became increasingly radicalized when Stokely Carmichael,[8] of the Student Nonviolent Coordinating Committee (SNCC), told reporters on the nightly news that "the greatest hypocrisy we have is the Statue of Liberty. We ought to break the young lady's legs and point her to Mississippi" (Carmichael, quoted in Karim 1971: 131–32). Carmichael was expressing the sentiment held by many black activists that the Statute of Liberty was a contradictory symbol of liberty, contradictory because though they were born in America they had not experienced the benefits of liberty and equal rights. By capitalizing on controversial statements like this one, media forums played a fundamental role in not only sensationalizing racial strife but also rendering trivial the grievances of black people in the United States. Black organizing was often labeled by the press as violent and radical, and black protests were often depicted as militant and therefore too radical for white America to take seriously.

Carmichael and many others began to develop larger cultural organizations in which they rejected the possibility of claiming rights to America, instead, in the most radical innovations, claiming transnational linkages to diasporic homelands outside the United States. In the case of the Black Panther Party, for example, which implemented revolutionary and community-based approaches to black Americans' social problems, these links were often forged ideologically through their sympathetic ties to communism. Despite this, their activism was decidedly grounded locally—they promoted black health and educational programs, the "Buy Black" protests, as well as the "Don't Buy Where You Can't Work" calls for economic solidarity, prison outreach and education programs, welfare counseling, security programs, and a voter registration drive as an attempt to put more black people on juries. Other organizations also proliferated during this period, including the Revolutionary Action Movement, the Black Liberation Front, and the Black Liberation Army. They followed the ideological principles of the BPP but adopted covert approaches to defending their communities against what was, at the time, a white backlash against the integration of predominantly white institutions.

Black nationalist Islamic movements also provided forums within which black people could claim self-determination based on shared racial oppression and religious convictions. The spiritual leader, Elijah Muhammad, became a prominent icon of political significance, especially in the urban U.S. North, and popularized the Nation of Islam as a political alternative to racial marginalization. The Nation of Islam extolled black personal empowerment as a tool for social change and insisted that participation in pilgrimages to either Mecca or the African continent and learning about the Koran should constitute critical components of self-teaching. The range of black Islamic movements that developed in the United States was, unlike that of the multiracial religious Islamic networks worldwide, often highly racialized (Turner 1969). Black Muslim political leaders such as Malcolm X, for example, also advocated black empowerment and racial justice, inspiring thousands of black Americans to convert to Islam. Blaming white racism and the political domination of black people as the basis for the growing poverty in inner cities, Malcolm X attracted hundreds of thousands of black Americans to follow his leadership.

Islam was one of many growing religious movements that provided an alternative to Judeo-Christianity. Other religious movements, for example, African-based religious practices, became popular in the black American search for non-European religions. It is here that the roots for new formations of back-to-Africa cultural movements took shape with the development of African-based religious diasporic movements such as Ashanti Ghanaian, Haitian Vodú, Brazilian Candomble, and Yorùbá Orisa revivalism, with the latter finding its most radical form in Ôyótúnjí African Village and other intentional religious communities in the rural American South. These religious awakenings not only became increasingly lucrative institutions from which to create a new market for narratives of slavery and nobility, but they also led to reconceptualizations of citizenship that extended beyond the nation-state. These reconceptualizations are of considerable significance for understanding the forces of power that shape who can access new forms of citizenship or who controls new maps of cultural belonging.

Toward Institutional Shifts in Belonging

By the 1980s there had been a more general shift in heritage consciousness, a shift that complemented new forms of post–cold war national consciousness. This shift was institutionalized within educational institutions as the idea of learning about one's heritage became framed as a right and was increasingly accepted over time. Students around the United States lobbied for the formation of black studies departments and demanded that university administrations provide African studies courses with tenure-track jobs for black faculty. They also agitated for the recruitment of black students and faculty into predominantly white universities. The eventual proliferation of African and African American studies in universities and community colleges throughout the United States overlapped with the curriculum of already established disciplines such as anthropology, sociology, and political science. In response, activists demanded separate programs to further promote racial and national origins, as well as gender studies, thereby leading to the establishment of Africana (African and African American) studies, as well as ethnic and women's studies programs on educational campuses. The institutionalization of these special programs marked the beginning of a significant shift in new approaches to origins and heritage as the basis for the widespread importance of "roots" as central to the learning and teaching about human civilizations.

The development of multiculturalism in U.S. colleges was accompanied by a critical legislative shift. In 1980, the U.S. census for the first time used ancestral heritage as the official unit of difference through which American differences were classified. Where once the U.S. census had organized identity according to racial groups—"Whites, Orientals, Negroes, Amerindians, and Non-Whites"—the census now shifted the terms of classification from race to ethnicity (Hernandez-Reguant 1999). Ancestry, such as country of parental birth, became the form of classification by which Americans were asked to identify themselves. This led to a shift from a bureaucratic politics of racial biology to an incorporation of new heritage standards by which U.S. belonging was framed through hyphenation. Similarly, the category of "African American" was used by the Reverend Jesse Jackson in his 1988 presidential campaign to recast the centrality of slavery in the lives of black people by laying claim to the noble African "origins" of black Americans. Jackson popularized "African American" as a middle-class household term that would fuse an idea of ethnic origins with U.S. citizenship. Further, his notion of the "rainbow coalition" linked African Americanness to other hyphenated identities that were simultaneously entering the American mainstream. These relations of belonging—though inscribed within modern notions of race, biology, descent, and nationhood—cultivated the virtues of ancestry that it valorized.

With the development of African American and ethnic studies programs in U.S. colleges and universities and the proliferation of a heritage agenda, a multicultural curriculum was integrated into schools around the country, and African American subjectivities as ethnically African took on a new meaning. Where race had been the basis for African and black American unity during earlier periods of social protest, blackness now came to stand for African heritage and, more importantly, for the right of black Americans to reclaim the heritage taken from them as a result of the history of transatlantic slavery. The educational system was not the only institution through which new variants of classifying difference were redefined along ethnic lines throughout the 1980s. The governmental institutions that regulated laws; the cultural and religious intermediaries that interpreted religious knowledge; the international organizations that convened conferences; the shopkeepers, traders, and manufacturers that sold ritual and cultural commodities; the corporations that looked for commodity possibilities; as well as academics and amateur historians, music companies, and jazz and rap artists all became conduits for a new (ethnic) expression of subjectivity. With the already developing global demands for these heritage artifacts, the commodification of African heritage gave rise to markets of transnational travelers.

To fill the demand for knowledge about the transatlantic slave trade and the precolonial African history that preceded it, black bookshops proliferated in U.S. cities. Not only were books about African history readily available for purchase outside African countries, but in the mid- to late 1980s, with increasing numbers of literate and educated populations[9] and a wider range of black university-trained graduates, a new middle-class black American consumer developed. Some public intellectuals, self-trained or recently trained in urban college programs, contributed to the development of new networks of African knowledge and of a black history industry.[10]

In satisfying the demands of this new market of heritage-conscious consumers, black-owned publishing houses used newly emerging computer technologies to either reinvigorate or create new African-centered black and

Third World publishing houses,[11] such as Africa World Press (AWP), Third World Press, and Black Classic Press.[12] While corporate mergers dominated the late 1980s and many small mainstream American publishing houses were subsumed by larger national and international corporations, in some cases publishing houses negotiated contracts with smaller presses to reprint key bestsellers. For example, Grove Press, through Vintage Co., sold the rights to publish *Malcolm X Speaks* (1965) to its new corporate parent, Grove Weidenfeld, then a subsidiary of the Getty Corporation, an oil conglomerate. The reissue of *The Black Jacobins* by C. L. R. James, first published in 1938 and reprinted in 1963, was another example of both changing public interests and business responses to new market demands.

The development of a black history industry also led to a new crest of black cultural nationalism, starting with the celebration of black American history. A special day in February, called Black Heritage Day, was set aside to commemorate black history. By the early 1980s, Black Heritage Day had been officially renamed Black Heritage Week, and eventually the week developed into a full-fledged monthly celebration supported by educational and governmental institutions. With February marked as the month for celebrating African culture and history, cultural nationalists began to participate in the celebration of black American and African history, arts, literature, and music. The concept of heritage months spread throughout U.S. social institutions in the 1980s, and African American history month was vertically incorporated into U.S. educational programming, again institutionalizing the shift from biological race to cultural race.

Throughout the 1990s, with the development of computer technology and the Internet, the transnational marketing of heritage products—music, art, books, rituals, and travel packages—increasingly occurred in cyberspace and through merging of the interests of African exporters and American importers and consumers. Corporations and small-business investors participated in the production of African linkages to American blackness by marketing the symbolic nobility of black history. African trading corporations worked with small and large U.S. corporations to export increasing numbers of African-related commodities. Some of these included kente cloth and prints,[13] as well as African jewelry, artifacts, food, and accessories. U.S. corporations such as McDonalds, K-Mart, JC Penney, and a range of other urban department store chains began to sell what many store managers referred to as an Africa-friendly image to mostly middle-class black Americans. Their consumers were black middle-class women and men who were interested in African-centered images, self-help books, fabrics, artifacts, and tourist packages and who were willing to wear African clothes and embrace African history.

Furthermore, with the increasing affordability of air travel in the 1980s, increasing numbers of corporations marketed heritage tourism to a range of regions. These included West and Central Africa in search of slave castles and heritage lessons; East and South Africa in search of game safaris, ancient ruins, and unspoiled wildlife; and North Africa, especially Egypt, in search of noble civilizations and the cradle of humanity. The expansion of heritage tourists and the development of commemorative events further propelled the institutionalization of African American heritage identities. Those who were able to afford travel to various African regions did so, and for many others the development of African rituals—such as manhood training programs and Kwanzaa[14]—further propelled the institutionalization of the narratives of African slavery and African nobility. Black cultural nationalism, then, was an extension of the rights revolution. It produced an African-heritage movement that, through the workings of market mechanisms, went from occupying a marginal place of radical black power to a multimillion dollar industry in mainstream America. While the middle-class appeal of the developing cultural nationalist movement broke down in the 1990s as some youth embraced a counterculture of African-invoked pride and American-based protest, the proliferation of films, events, music, consumer goods, and black academic production that emphasized an African heritage forced a fundamental rethinking and reworking of the racial imaginary at the end of the twentieth century that was unlike earlier forms of black nationalism.

Cultural Heritage, African Pride, and Global Capital

As I have shown in this essay, blackness in the United States was reconfigured institutionally through diasporic reformulations of roots, and racial categories were reconstituted through a quest for humanity. These shifts operated on a terrain of protest that also worked toward better working and social conditions, access to employment, gender egalitarianism, and overall equality for dispossessed people. New conceptions of race through the prism of rights and heritage have not supplanted biological conceptions, but the development of a post–cold war democratic politics of rights and shifts in market technologies worked alongside economic and political institutional transformation to produce new institutional mechanisms through which race could be classified in terms of culture. This shift from racial classifications that were regulated through governmental policies manifest in the body to the concepts of culture and ethnicity reflects how conceptualizations of race have been tied to developments in capitalism, new technologies, and the intensification of a maturing rights tradition which displaced histories of insubordination and struggle and recast them in noble terms.

The changes in classifications of black subjectivity within the context of a rights "culture" has implications for how we approach the category of "African Diaspora" in the twenty-first century. Because diasporic connections have been made and remade through time, scholars need to go beyond the mere charting of modern notions of territorial descent and instead demonstrate the ways race and diaspora are shown to be processes in the making rather than stable categories. We must strive to understand the selective processes through which diasporic formulations of blackness are shaped, and we must focus far less on prescribed attributes of race, religion, and presumptions of a unidirectional homeland. In doing so, we will need to be far more attuned to changes in relations of global power and how these changes are producing different lines of alliance and circulation. And we need to focus on the making and disjunctures of diasporic connections, and on the specific ways diasporic formations are embedded in hegemonic institutions of power, including its language of inclusion.

Notes

1. Special thanks to the following people for their feedback on earlier drafts of this piece: Mihri Inal, Jennifer Burrell, Randy Matory, Carolyn Martin Shaw, Laura Nader, Donald Moore, Brian Axel, William Safran, Naomi Pabst, Cori Hayden, Galen Joseph, Deborah Thomas, Charlie Piot, Lee Baker, Jacob Olupona, Kwame Z. Shabazz, Brackette F. Williams, Ariana Hernandez-Reguant, and Feyi Adunbi. I also thank the participants at the following places where this article was presented as a work in progress: University of California, Berkeley; Duke University's Department of Anthropology; and Harvard University's Center for International Studies.

2. By black nationalist and black cultural nationalism I refer to the loosely configured conceptualization of nationalism that transcends statehood and instead converges around racial biology or symbolics of ancestry.

3. By symbolics of blood I am referring to Michel Foucault's (1978) invocation of blood as biology, thus lineage.

4. It was not until after the 1965 International Congress of African Historians that the African Diaspora, as a subject of study, was introduced to the academy as an

intervention into the survivals discourse and as a popularized intellectual linkage between Africa and its history of African dispersal and exile.

5. Ôyōtúnjí is a small community built to accommodate up to twenty-five housing compounds with a potential capacity of over five hundred people. It is organized around three main sectors—religious ritual and organizations, political governance, and a small-scale market economy—through which practitioners enact a politics of redemption from slavery as a response to the hierarchies produced within U.S. society as a result of racism.

6. First published in condensed form by *Reader's Digest* in 1974, and then in its entirety by Dell in January of 1976, *Roots* was televised by ABC over an eight-night period in 1977.

7. The fundamental principles of becoming black included: (1) nurturing a positive self-image, (2) reaching a state of black self-actualization, (3) seizing the power to shape black images and creating new symbols of black lifestyles that would lead to the production of a new and unique form of African American culture, and (4) the reclamation of black manhood and family.

8. In 1978, Stokely Carmichael changed his name to Kwame Ture, an African name.

9. In 1980, 1,028,000 black Americans were enrolled in undergraduate study, up from the 950,000 black Americans enrolled in similar study in 1976. In comparison, 66,000 American blacks were enrolled in graduate study in 1980, down from the 72,000 enrolled in similar study in 1976. In the *Digest of Educational Statistics* (National Center for Education Statistics 1989), 194.

10. Some of these include Dr. Henry Clarke, Ivan Van Sertima, and Dr. Ben among hundreds of others.

11. The following is a list of African American publishing houses that spread throughout the 1970s to the present: Africa World Press and Red Sea Press; African American Images; Ananse Press; Basic Civitas Books; Beckham Publications Group, Inc.; Black Classic Press; Black Words, Inc.; Empak Publishing' FIRE!! Press; Fitzgerald Publishing Co., Inc.; Holloway House Books; IC Publications; MG-Publishing Company; Mind Productions, Inc.; Rapture Publishing; Sohaja Publishing Co.; Urban Research Press; and Waverly House Publishing.

12. Of the black-owned presses, some of their best sellers were: Wade W. Noble's *African Psychology: Toward Its Reclamation, Reascension and Revitalization* (A Black Family Institute Publication, 1986), Molefi Kete Asante's *Afrocentricity* (Africa World Press, 1988), Maulana Karenga and Jacob Carruthers's *Kemet and the African Worldview: Research, Rescue and Restoration* (1986), and Chancellor William's *The Destruction of Black Civilization: Great Issues of a Race from 4500 B.C. to 2000 A.D.* (Third World Press, 1987). In the 1990s, books such as Dr. Frances Cress Welsing's *The Isis Papers: The Keys to the Colors* (Third World Press, 1991), and Carter G. Woodson's *The Mis-Education of the Negro* (1933) predominated cultural nationalist circles.

13. Kente cloth is a Ghanaian fabric that became popular in North American cities with predominant black populations.

14. Kwanzaa was first celebrated in 1966 in Los Angeles at the height of the black power movement. Invented by Maulana Ron Karenga, a black nationalist who was interested in focusing on cultural nationalism instead of following a strictly Marxist ideological approach to black liberation. Kwanzaa is based on the celebration of seven principles—Unity, Self-determination, Collective World and Responsibility, Cooperative Economics, Purpose, Creativity, and Faith—that were seen as necessary to rebuild black families and redefine the nation.

EMIGRATION AND THE SPATIAL PRODUCTION

OF DIFFERENCE FROM CAPE VERDE

KESHA FIKES

This essay contributes to methods of analysis, like labor and psychology, which describe how race operates in practice. I focus on travel or spatial mobility as a medium that produces and recognizes 'difference' at state and popular levels. The migratory context in which Cape Verdean racial politics historically emerged provides a unique opportunity for observing how spatial movements create social meaning. Interestingly, this particular inquiry urges that the sending and the recipient contexts of migratory communities should not be assessed in isolation; in the case of Cape Verde, for instance, both spatial contexts mutually shaped a generalized perception of Cape Verdean racial identity under Portuguese colonialism. Subsequently, an understanding of Cape Verdean raciality, or the possibilities of raced identification within Cape Verdean communities, at least until independence in 1975, requires a dialogue on how the sending and the recipient contexts cumulatively produced a racially "flexible" Cape Verdean subject under colonialism. What follows is an overview of competing narratives of Cape Verdean history, with attention to the importance of the concept of indigeneity within it. Here, indigeneity is referenced as the sign for Africanity and/or "absolute" blackness. The concept is important because it was used to legally discern voluntary from forced labor status. As such, I try to show how local ideals of raced

difference were conceived through one's legal relationship to free or indentured travel. I discuss how Cape Verdeans' varied use of Portuguese nationality documentation (from the late nineteenth century through 1975)
became a means to entering voluntary and non-Portuguese regulated labor
activities.

Until independence the idea of the migrant Cape Verdean subject—whether
from Portuguese colonial ethnologies or popular racial discourses within and
beyond the Portuguese empire—is commonly problematized within discussions of racial ambiguity.[1] Portuguese colonial anti-miscegenation arguments on the unstable emotional and social destiny of the Cape Verdean
"mulatto" (especially in the 30s and 40s) (see Tamagnini 1934; Corrêa 1943;
Lessa and Ruffié 1960) and G. Freyre's suggestion that Cape Verde occupied
the infant stages of a miscegenation process like Brazil's (Lopes 1956),[2] have
contributed to scientific and popular statements that emphasize a racial
crisis. Such argumentation, cumulatively, positioned the Cape Verdean subject as disconnected from its political reality. But under what logics were
claims of racial ambiguity made intelligible? What aims were serviced by
politics that targeted racial practices deemed unstable? In short, at the same
time that this essay observes the mutual importance of sending and recipient
locations within the production and perception of Cape Verdean raciality,
from the abolition of slavery (1853–1878) to independence (1975), the essay
also questions the political productivity of ambiguity. Specifically, if states
(the Portuguese metropole and the countries that received Cape Verdeans)
created policies with effects that simultaneously managed perceptions of
Cape Verdean raciality, how can we rethink the circulatory value of narratives
of racial ambiguity? Or, how might attention to transnationally coordinated
emigrations recast narratives of ambiguity as institutional resources?

The Emigrant Logics of Cape Verdean Raciality

The Cape Verdean archipelago—annexed by the Portuguese in the late fifteenth century, and consisting of ten islands, nine inhabited—is located
within the Sahel wind belt. It has subsequently suffered from vicious drought
and periodic famine cycles that date from occupation through the mid twentieth century. This drastic ecological circumstance was such that most Cape
Verdeans had to emigrate to survive. Overtime, as described below, the blend-
ing of local practices of difference recognition and the development of state
managed emigration made travel a social and political tool. For instance,

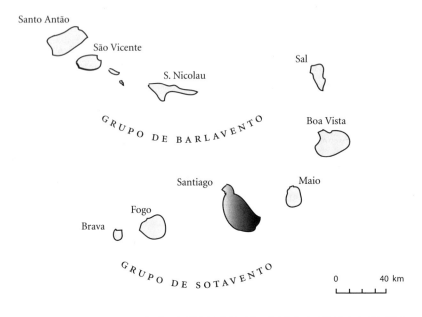

Santo Antão

São Vicente

S. Nicolau

Sal

GRUPO DE BARLAVENTO

Boa Vista

Santiago

Maio

Fogo

Brava

GRUPO DE SOTAVENTO

0   40 km

Cape Verdean Archipelago
(The archipelago is situated in the Atlantic, about 250 miles west of Dakar)

Portuguese subjects born in Cape Verde, and Cape Verdean non-slave communities (prior to emancipation), were able to travel under desirable conditions. In other Portuguese African locations (Angola, Mozambique, São Tomé e Príncipe, Guinea-Bissau) they worked as administrative officials. Beyond Portuguese space—in the Americas and in western Europe in particular—they led lives that evaded the confines of their colonial origins. Importantly, by contrast, enslaved populations were forced to emigrate; they were sent to plantations in Portuguese Africa where they labored under harsh conditions. In short, how, where and whether one moved made and unmade one's social essence; and one's essence—by the late sixteenth century—was interpretable through raced discourse. I argue that these forms of raced recognition were activated and materialized through travel.

Between 1861 and 1863 pre-abolition labor codes reinforced the link between migration and island geography. One's island affiliation within the archipelago was legally attached to one's migratory status as voluntary or indentured labor. For example, the first series of legislation on indentured emigrations named and targeted the island of Santiago (see Meintel 1984). And subsequent legislation in the early twentieth century protected targeted northern islands from participation in indentured work. Accordingly, for emigrants, one's racial location—as negro and indigenous-like, or mestiço or branco—was confirmed or transformed once one was distributed (forced or voluntarily) as unit of mobile labor. What's more, the Portuguese colonial administration partially sustained the Cape Verdean economy through forced and voluntary labor remittances. What mattered to the Portuguese state, thus, was the potential exchange value of Cape Verdean raciality within the recipient labor markets of Cape Verdean migrants; specifically, their recognition as racially viable migrants (particularly in the early-twentieth-century United States and in western Europe) affected Portuguese profits. Further, Azorean and continental Portuguese nationals carried the same nationality passports as Cape Verdeans; and visible "diversity" within a single national community meant that their identification as racially uncertain could facilitate their entry into places that racially profiled potential immigrants. Hence, at the same time that the metropole demanded financial returns from remittances, the Cape Verdean migrants' survival depended upon the ability to assume an identity that could safeguard one's entry and residency. In short, race was a political object that state and society acted upon for profit and survival, respectively.

Perhaps the vagueness surrounding the "racial character" of Cape Verdean communities begins with the popular narrative of Cape Verdean history, a product of colonial ethnology. The most widely known ethno-historical accounts suggest that the recognition of racial difference in Cape Verde is self-evident. Specifically, inter-racial unions across the archipelago, within the eighteenth and nineteenth centuries, are treated as naturally occurring, self-selective practices whose "frequencies" varied by island. These stories of degrees of miscegenation are then oddly mapped onto the notion that some islands were more civilized—as evidenced by the development of advanced school systems on select islands—while others remained more "African." These "self-evident" distinctions prompt one to question the aims of the standard historical narrative. I begin then by presenting the popular version; next I propose an alternate one.

Competing Racial Narratives

In the popular version the ten-island archipelago of Cape Verde, discovered uninhabited in 1460, is situated within the Sahel wind belt. Subsequently, it has suffered consecutive cycles of drought and famine. Portuguese colonial administrators and appointed Cape Verdean and Portuguese physical and social scientists produced volumes of ethnological texts that categorized and detailed difference by island, over time. (For colonial ethnologies see Pusich 1860–61; Barcellos 1899–1900, 1904; Lessa and Ruffié 1960; Mariano 1959.) To summarize these accounts, they describe the historic settlement processes from the early sixteenth to eighteenth centuries. Settlement experiences are organized into linear progressions, the point of origin being the colonization of the island of Santiago by crown-appointed Portuguese administrators and slaves from the Senegambia region. Next, subsequent colonizations of the islands of Fogo and Brava by Santiaguense slaves and European travelers and administrators suggest the ways that racially and culturally mixed descendants from these three southern islands (or the Sotovento group) slowly populated the remaining five islands (or the northern or Barlavento group). Over time the development of schools (especially a seminary school in São Nicolau) in the Barlavento group, in addition to lucrative port activities on the island of São Vicente, from the late eighteenth century through the early twentieth, allowed for creolized-mulatto communities to develop a self-reflexive sense of community in a nationlike sense that elite, early-twentieth-century Cape Verdean writers, the *Claristas,* defined as the essence of *creolidade* (creolization): it made them neither African nor European, but somewhere in-between. This experience was coupled with the defining sense of *saudade* (longing), which is treated as the emotional response to physical separation from those who emigrated or were left behind; this understanding is intertwined with the experience of creolidade for the important writers.[3] Celebratory representations of this hybridity—shifting vaguely between biology and culture[4]—were recognized in juxtaposition to failed attempts to promote civility on the island of Santiago. Santiago was the port of entry for new slaves from the continent and it was represented as a haven for "unruly" maroons and maroon-descended peoples.[5]

By contrast, an alternate version of this narrative begins with the same date, 1460. However, according to unedited accounts that António Carreira found, dated in the late eighteenth century, the island of Santiago was already inhabited by people from the Senegambia region (Carreira 1983: 281–320). Thus rather than focus on origins events (see D. Scott 1999) I emphasize how particular engagements with travel generated ways of understanding social difference across the archipelago and beyond. In particular, indentured and voluntary migrations—in response to the crisis of drought and famine—organized and deciphered the significance of social life in Cape Verde.

Since as early as the sixteenth century, if and where one moved became a racially inscribing practice. Those whose "origins" tied them to the Senegambia region tended to be divided into different classes of slaves. Literate and Christianized slaves were generally sent to Europe from Cape Verde, while "underskilled" slaves were divided into those who would be shipped to the Americas and those who would remain within the archipelago for experimental agrarian projects. Others were captured and then released to work as official bureaucrats or traders. Such individuals often had access to property and slaves, which would confuse the imaginaries of European maritime personnel and traders who stopped temporarily in the islands to refuel and/or to pick up slaves. By the mid- to late eighteenth century this economy had officially extended into voluntary and involuntary migrant markets (especially to the *cacau* plantations in São Tomé and Príncipe) in a process that coincided with Portugal's deteriorating imperial economy. Importantly, by the eighteenth and nineteenth centuries, one's potential for mobility—be it forced or voluntary, labor- or government-related, temporary or permanent, or within or beyond Portuguese colonial space—cumulatively organized a field of tangible power recognition. One's racial positionality would be conceived in connection to the spaces one had or could inhabit, via island and family origins and/or one's migrant labor status.

Thus, in contrast to the standard narrative which approaches migrant labor opportunities and racial positionality within an evolving island settlement schema, letters and records dating from the sixteenth through the nineteenth centuries indicate that Santiago always hosted a diverse community of free Africans, in addition to freed, self-liberated, and enslaved communities whose experiences with Portuguese planters and administrators were no less diverse—in a "contact" sense—than those on other islands. Repetitive famine crises, particularly since the metropole marginally protected planters and administrators, meant that drought cycles affecting the lives of slaves and planters alike disrupted the social order. From the eighteenth to the mid-twentieth centuries during famines, plantations were commonly lined with the carcasses of slaves, planters, and elites alike (Carreira 2000). What's more, each of the newly settled islands, which were represented as hosting creolized-mulatto populations, continued to absorb new slaves from the continent until the mid-nineteenth century. In fact, to conceal any "demographic" similarities between Santiago and the northern islands, Amaral (1964), drawing from Senna Barcellos's work (1899–90), suggests that one way of controlling the growing mulatto populations in Santiago was to send them to Brazil. Importantly, the objective here is not to represent these racial communities—African negros and creolized-mulattos—in fixed terms, nor to assume that negro meant slave or that mulatto signified freedom. Rather, I hope to point to ways that such representations signified categorical realities: race and the limits of freedom were made recognizable in relation to different practices of labor mobility, over time. These practices required the idea and presence of racial ambiguity for the purpose of being able to respond to the labor demands of different Portuguese African and non-Portuguese markets, especially in the early twentieth century. Thus skewed representations of geography (which mapped racial progress and degeneracy through island affiliations) are reflected in the uneven history of the making and dismantling of migrant labor practices; it would be the representation of African negros and creolized-mulattos as absolute categories that produced the facade of racial certainty. Subsequently, the idea of Cape Verdean racial ambiguity was produced when Cape Verdean workers changed markets and spaces (internally and externally). Arguably, it is for this very reason—the transit circumstances that yield recognition of racial ambiguity—that the interdependent political system of migration and labor requires close examination: race and island origins could mutually signify each other; they "blackened" or "hybridized" communities as necessary.

Racializing Island Origins

Colonial practices of "blackening" in Cape Verde were essential to the eighteenth century economic development of São Tomé and Príncipe, a set of cacau-producing islands whose export earnings and contracted labor profits (from non-Portuguese companies) would be used to support the metropole. The problem, however, was that by the late eighteenth century substantial numbers of men who were avoiding contracted labor began to participate in various undocumented maritime activities, namely the Atlantic whaling industry. Subsequently, dependable pools of labor dwindled. By the mid- to late nineteenth century, as the colonial administration contemplated the consequences of the abolition of slavery, it called for the greater management of the extraction of raw materials and plantation cultivation on the continent and especially within the islands of São Tomé and Príncipe. The implementation of policies of forced labor recruitment for disciplinary purposes camouflaged the continuation of slave labor. In reality, by the turn of the twentieth century, the new "freed" peasantries from *each* of the islands participated in the forced labor emigrations, particularly to the cacau plantations. Their numbers by island varied considerably, with the majority representing Santiago (Carreira 1977; Meintel 1984). But only one island was designated in the preabolition indentured labor laws that would protect cacau production;[6] that island was Santiago (Meintel 1984).

While in theory, as of 1910, Cape Verdeans were no longer Portuguese citizens (G. Fernandes 2002)—though travelers recognized by the Portuguese state continued to carry Portuguese nationality passports—they were neither indigenous subjects of the empire. Legally, they were provisional subjects of the Portuguese state. But the process of targeting Santiaguense workers into labor networks that legally named and targeted indigenous continental Africans (from Angola, Mozambique, and Guinea-Bissau) unofficially treated Santiaguense workers as indigenous subjects. Subsequently, the colonial administration related to them as *continental* Africans, or persons whose origins, by law, forced them to contract themselves to plantations to avoid criminal punishment. Santiaguense would be treated as indigenous workers until forced labor laws were abolished in 1959. In practice, curiously, other islanders from Santo Antão, Fogo, and Maio, who were likewise contracted to the same plantations, would also be treated as indigenous workers. This is evidenced by the language of their individual labor contracts, the outlined terms of their working conditions, and how they were identified within documented complaints by planters and administrative officials. But racialized narratives of their labor potential never matched those from Santiago.

Importantly, references to island origins should not be treated as real or absolute; Cape Verdeans migrated between the islands and hence always had family or social connections that linked communities across the archipelago. Hence, ideas about island space were produced through migrant labor practices that were intelligible through the fixating effects of race. In this sense, the argument is not simply that island origins determined spatial mobility; island particularity was likewise an ideological production that relied upon the certainties of racial *essence*.

Race and Indigeneity

The legal aims of the discourse of indigeneity, within the context of eighteenth- and nineteenth-century Cape Verde, focused on the benefits of turning "nonassimilable" *vadios*, or vagrants, throughout the archipelago into productive workers of the Portuguese Empire (see Moutinho 2000; Silva 1953; Pereira 1984). Importantly, the term vadio was used to describe any individual who appeared "idle" (see Pereira 1984). By the nineteenth century, as evidenced within the travelogue section of the Cape Verdean *Boletins*—weekly colonial administrative reviews—popular references to Santiaguense islanders emerged as interchangeable with a new category of identity—*Badiu*— derived from vadio.[7] It was used to identify local islanders who refused to participate in domestic and migratory slave labor. Within the historical literature on Santiago absentee landlord patterns on plantations are described as the underlying reason for Santiaguense "ruggedness." Likewise, the mountainous areas of Santiago, which often served as a refuge for runaway slaves, are used to substantiate this argument. Importantly, both Fogo and Santo Antão also had mountainous areas and absentee landlord practices. What's more, Santiaguense residing in the interior of the island never lived in isolation because the constant threat of famine meant that they were always connected to the urban center for food security purposes. Bravan and Barlavento island life, in contrast, are described as "close-contact" farming situations between slaves and colonial owners, which "naturally" provided the ideal environment for assimilation experiences to occur on their own over time. These juxtaposed narratives have lead many to argue or presume that Santiago remained the most racially and culturally "African" of all of the islands in the archipelago. While it is true that as a primary port of "African entry" Santiago experienced its own cultural particularity, future studies of Santiago will have to contend with the political implications of such representation, particularly since Santiaguense (though black-identified) do not necessarily articulate their daily Cape Verdean experience as African (though "black" and "African" can be treated as synonyms) and since the legacies of such representation are intimately tied to colonial economic interests. For example, the colonial bureaucrat and anthropologist Mendes Corrêa made the following remark (quoted in Andrade 1998: 31): "For them [referring to designated *mestiços*] manifestations of African origins did not survive and nor are they remembered, being that they [African manifestations] exist only (survived) in Santiago; on the other islands, what's been proven, in reality, was a simulation with a predominant Portuguese element."[8] Here, he contributes to a rationale linking indentured status to Santiaguense identity.

As representations of Santiaguense islanders fixated upon negro identity—while "other" islanders were understood to be creolized-mulattos—future studies will need to assess the discursive history of race distribution and categorization within the archipelago, from colonial settlement through independence in 1975. Notably, the works of Onesimo Silveira (1996), Daniel Pereira (1984), Gabriel Fernandes (2002), and José Carlos Gomes dos Anjos (2002), in particular, have already contributed considerably to this line of discussion. In that color is also a symbolic reference to power, a discursive legacy of colonial and plantation politics, it is also, as Frantz Fanon (1967) and Stuart Hall (1996) remind us, a sliding signifier whose meaning is politically situated. Given this sliding significance, phenotype—in terms of analysis—is marginally treated here; the categories "mulatto/a," "mestiço/a," and "negro/a" are not entertained as solid realities. As Santiago is centered within the history of Cape Verde, and its spatial signification is centered within labor migrations, Badiu identity (in relation to Santiago) is treated as a temporal and spatial signifier that was essential to supporting Portugal and its cacau industries after emancipation. Notably, the treatment of Santiaguense inhabitants as Badius not only guaranteed the availability of Santiaguense workers but likewise became an infinite solution to camouflaging or "blackening" the realities of contact in Santiago.

Labor Emigration to the Metropole, Portugal

The signifying capacity of Santiago, from the colonial administration's perspective, continued until approximately the mid-1960s, when Portugal began to reroute workers from each of the islands to Portugal. At this moment racialized worker distinctiveness was slowly removed from the language of labor policies on migration to Portugal. Cape Verdeans were recruited to replace male Portuguese workers who emigrated to the northern part of western Europe and/or to the Americas during the 1940s and 1950s, or who were either killed or injured in battle during the colonial wars on the continent between the late 1960s and the early 1970s. Cape Verdean men worked primarily in construction, mining, and carpentry. Simultaneously, Cape Verdean women from each of the islands and from different class locations also emigrated to Portugal. Some middle class women were employed as nurses, while working-poor women received family reunification visas to help "domesticate" their working male partners or family members (Fikes n.d.). Cape Verdean womens' migrations to Portugal were key to the transformation of the idea of indigeneity; as noted by Meintel (1984), Santiaguense women were represented as masculine and ferocious. In part, these discourses emerged in connection to their scrutinized participation in state-documented food revolts that date from the early nineteenth century through the mid-twentieth.[9] Subsequently, the relocation of Santiaguense women to the metropole would challenge how ideals of feminine respectability would likewise foreground the association of Santiaguense identity with indigeneity (Fikes n.d.). The discussion that follows attends to voluntary Santiaguense movements as a way of illuminating not only the operative qualities of Badiu identity but also the fragility and uncertainty of creole-mulatto status as evidenced by Portugal's changing relationship to Santiago. Importantly, the eventual change in Cape Verdeans' nationality status—because of the loss of Portuguese passport privileges at independence—likewise diminished the international exchange value once attributed to internally recognized racial heterogeneity. At independence, those who could not hold onto their passports legally became "sovereign" African nationals.

But in addition to Portugal's engagement in practices that would transform its labor relationship to the Cape Verdean archipelago, what else was serviced by recruitment to the metropole? From the Portuguese colonial administration's perspective, or so it seems, the objective was to disrupt the possibility of Cape Verdean anticolonial activity while filling construction, mining, and carpentry jobs that were vacated by Portuguese workers who went abroad. As fighting never occurred in Cape Verde but rather took place in Guinea-Bissau, Cape Verde's independence partner, one could argue that the colonial administration's attempts were somewhat successful. However, I would also consider the importance of the future consequences of the recruitment program. The recruitment program not only included a racially and sexually stigmatized island community within the archipelago—the Santiaguense, but it also simultaneously disrupted cultural practices of race recognition by 1) allowing Santiaguense to enter into a space (Portugal) that previously could only be occupied by Cape Verdean elites, clergy, and temporary maritime personnel, among the few, and 2) by enforcing labor practices that did not acknowledge (in policy or practice) differences between workers, regardless of island affiliations. In essence, the recruitment program to Portugal (among other transitional events) disrupted the ways that the capital potential of creole-mulatto particularity could "materialize" or be interpreted through transnational movements; creolized-mulatto particularity, from the position of Portugal, became blurred, or "black."

Immediately after Portugal's own revolution for democracy in 1974, which coincided with the independence movements in Portuguese Africa, the new democratic Portuguese government created its own constitution; the issue of overseas colonial citizenship was one of its key priorities (see Esteves 1991). The law that attended to overseas national status and citizenship—Decreto-Lei #308-A/75—stated that Portuguese citizenship could be maintained or acquired by those who were either born in Portugal or had at least one Portuguese parent who was born in Portugal. Importantly, Portuguese parents include contemporary Cape Verdean nationals who were legally recognized and documented as Portuguese citizens—and not simply Portuguese nationality passport holders—prior to Decreto-Lei #308. Otherwise, Portugal recognized them as sovereign Cape Verdean nationals who belonged to sub-Saharan Africa.

The loss of Portuguese nationality passport privileges meant that the terms for acquiring western visas changed, especially for new African national subjects. Subsequently, traveling Cape Verdeans who did not or could not hold onto their Portuguese status—regardless of their island origins—became African nationals overnight. The argument here is not to suggest that Cape Verdeans with opportunities to travel beyond the Portuguese Empire did not understand themselves as black and/or African when holding Portuguese documents. The point is that they lost the right of use of Portuguese nationality, which facilitated their entry requirement into select places and markets. This process, importantly, meant that Portugal also ceased recognition of differences in the cultural "potential" of Cape Verdeans, by island, in part because it had to dissolve any confusions (internationally) pertaining to similarities with Portuguese continentals and Azoreans. Subsequently, from the perspective of the international community, Cape Verde was now a sovereign African nation whose subjects—regardless of class or racial location—were one and the same. This instance raises important questions pertaining to sovereignty after independence. For the efforts of decolonization, in the end, were never simply about independence from Portugal. Arguably, the dissolution of the West's recognition of Cape Verdeans as Portuguese nationals is likewise reflective of new practices for deciphering race from nationality and/or citizenship globally. Today, with the exception of those migrants who were able to maintain or acquire Portuguese, American, or other Western citizenships, contemporary Cape Verdeans are not really moving in and out of different markets where race is managed differently. Instead, the politics of sovereignty are such that race—in light of increasingly centralized immigration technologies and the globally recognized citizen-status of the sub-Saharan African national—is increasingly operating, uniformly, across space. Digressing, one might even argue that the transnational networks that constitute this moment of globalization are merely about the spatial terrain upon which the management of social life and social difference has been expanded geographically.

Postcoloniality and Creolidade:
Reconfiguring the Signifying Potential of Labor Migrations

Since independence the relationship between racial positionality and island origins has shifted. In postcolonial Cape Verde the representation of cultural diversity and racial miscegenation is subsumed under a universalizing concept of creolidade. This contemporary concept differs from its colonial predecessor, however, as the term could previously operate as a synonym for *mestiçagem*, or miscegenation. Today it refers to pan-archipelago nation building and it is thought to be politically neutral; it is used to celebrate Cape Verde's unique form of Africanity in connection to its historic transatlantic experiences of contact and cultural hybridity. In theory, creolidade includes the Santiaguense. Likewise, the Santiaguense embrace this term as they situate their Cape Verdean identity both within and beyond the archipelago. But in practice something different seems to be happening and there is tremendous uncertainty around the representational role that Santiaguense identity may or may not be playing within the contemporary make-up of democratic cultural and political practices in Cape Verde (see Furtado 1993, 1997). This ambiguity, arguably, is grounded in migration-related demographic transformations in Santiago, where some 60 percent of the nation's inhabitants from across the archipelago reside. Santiago hosts the archipelago's capital city, Praia.

Today, creolidade, as a pan-archipelago experience, could be interpreted as trivializing the unequal historical circumstances that racially encoded voluntary and forced migrant labor practices. Not only is there little political space for debating island politics in conversation with race, but the state's agenda is so focused on the dilemmas of urban and rural poverty throughout the archipelago—as it should be—that poverty can only be criticized within a pan-archipelago context. In essence, after independence, class—which is treated as mutable and potentially controllable by the state and supporting donor agencies alike—is that which is recognized as being at stake; race is effectively blocked from debate. Hence, this pan-archipelago vision is not the only idea that is grounded in the transitioning status of the discourse of creolidade. In consideration of the very real poverty that affects Cape Verde, and the difficulties with access to water that continue to disrupt the possibilities for normalcy, it is important to acknowledge how the transimperial and transnational circumstances that once racially empowered creolidade through emigrant practices are increasingly dissolving, from the outside.

Conclusion

Understanding the legal capacity of race in transnational perspective is key to the study of transmigratory phenomena. Such perspective not only enables us to question the social logics of settlement in recipient settings, but it also enables us to assess how local imaginaries of social distance and proximity were institutionalized in tandem with those very settlement possibilities. The absence of this attention makes it difficult to historicize how politically diverse Cape Verdean communities were collapsed into a single nation according to the entry guidelines of Western receiving nations at Cape Verdean independence. For the process of recategorizing new Cape Verdean nationals

as sub-Saharan Africans versus Portuguese nationals is central to understanding how external legal frameworks are intimately and globally connected to Cape Verdean forms of social practice. Moreover, current local
struggles are about the assertion of control over one's relationship to the
possibilities of spatial movement, and hence one's livelihood, and the ways
that such control can mediate local experiences of national belonging in the
archipelago. In brief, subjects do not simply emerge in connection to the
spaces in which they "originate": the relational or dialectic quality of subjectivity is always constituted within the relationship that binds different
geopolitical locales.

These arguments should not be read as appeals to any form or practice of
raciality: this is not the point. Rather, this engagement is simply about questioning how the representational value of Cape Verdean raciality has serviced
diverse transnational interests: the mutual consequence, in the end, has been
the production of a dehistoricized or "questionable" racial subject. Plainly,
the production of the Cape Verdean subject as a unit of mobile Portuguese
labor is obscured at the same time that politicized ideals of racial consciousness are construed independent of the emigrant logics that texture(d) Cape
Verdean subjectivity. As a consequence, little room is left for considering how
whiteness—the effaced possibility through which difference and ambiguity
are made recognizable (Fanon 1967), and which renders the interpretation of
Cape Verdean raciality questionable in the first place—remains obfuscated in
the company of conversations that emphasize "passing." Significantly, degrees of difference can only be constituted or recognized in reference to
nonwhite racial subjects. How thus should we interpret the project that
requires or compels recognition of Cape Verdean raciality as ambiguous? In
what ways do discourses of racial appropriateness produce synchronized
forms of regulation that institutionally stabilize appearances of race and
racial order across space? Responses to these questions might best be framed
within what David Scott (1999) has referred to as the moral-political dimension of criticism, or the politics that ideologically shape how we interpret
events and practices. Narratives of colonial Cape Verdean politics and history
are accompanied, compulsively, by questions aimed at fixing who Cape Verdeans are racially; as such, one is not only required to confront the potential
effects that such narratives have on the representational status of Cape Verdean identity before independence, but also to consider how such circulating
discourses are in fact producing racially ambiguous Cape Verdeans in advance of the political histories that have positioned this community as such.

Notes

1. With the exception of a few texts (cf. Halter 1993; Meintel 1984) that attend to popular ideologies pertaining to Cape Verdean racial subjectivity in the United States, there is little textual "proof" that can speak to the prevalence of popular ideas regarding Cape Verdean raciality. What is significant, however, is the circulatory or oral nature of this information. When giving talks I am often asked "What they are?" or "What do they think they are?"

2. See Lopes (1956), a transcribed radio interview in Mindelo, São Vicente (Cape Verde). Here, Lopes, a Cape Verdean intellectual, criticizes Freyre's perception of Cape Verdean identity politics, arguing that Freyre could not conceive of the idea that Cape Verdeans were already culturally evolved and defined versus being in the early states of cultural or racial evolution.

3. Here it is essential to note that this colonial, prenationalist experience of "in-betweenness" was not conceived in terms of a logics of whitening or what it means to continue to evolve, "upward" or racially. Instead, as stressed by Baltasar Lopes, the founding intellectual of the Clarista movement, creolidade was understood to be a stable cultural experience that had *already* arrived or evolved. It was a cultural phenomenon in and of itself.

4. See Tamagnini 1934; Corrêa 1943; Lessa and Ruffié 1960. Notably, the Lessa and Ruffié reference is the collaborative product of Cape Verdean and European intellectuals and social scientists. The articles in this volume are driven by research questions that link biology, or rather blood studies, to ideas about culture.

5. See a critique of this idea in Pereira 1984.

6. See the proposed articles for legislation and letters to the governor of Cape Verde on the recruitment of Santiaguense workers, in the *Boletins Officiais do Governo Geral de Cabo-Verde,* 1862 through 1878.

7. This idea is also suggested in Pereira's work (1984) on Santiaguense identity politics in late-eighteenth-century Santiago. See also G. Fernandes 2002 and Gomes dos Anjos 2002.

8. Original Portuguese text: "Para eles, as manifestaçes de origem africana no passam de sobrevivencia ou de reminiscências, existentes sobretudo em Santiago; nas outras ilhas, o que verificou, na realidade, foi uma simbiose com predominância do elemento português."

9. Popular narratives of Badiu identity were intertwined with fantastic stories of resistance and vulgarity. While archives and letters documented the presence of slave uprisings on other islands (namely Fogo and Santo Antão), stories of trickery, aggression, and violence commonly characterized "Badiu" revolts. The reality is that Santiago was always the most densely populated island. During drought crises that led to famine, infamous Santiaguense revolts occurring in 1811, 1822, and 1835 (see Tomazinho 1996) coincided with periods of mass death. Moreover, the politicized participation and leadership of women in rebellions further served the purpose of

representing Santiaguense as savages, particularly at a time when "other" women began participation in migrations to the United States (see Halter 1993 on migration to the United States). Romanticized and antagonistic tales of self-liberated and fierce negro women with knives and machetes, coupled with the sudden deaths of food-hoarding landowners (see Meintel 1984) consummated the idea of Badiu identity. Gendered representations of Santiaguense identity as negro and aggressive were essential to discursively discerning mestiço from negro identity. And it was the racialization or rather "blackening" of Santiaguense identity that served the purpose of the illusion of Badius as masculine and vulgar, regardless of sex. Thus, as mestiço identity was imaginatively constitutive of ideas of mutability, Badiu identity controlled Santiago by "blackening" it. Further, as the fetishized synthesis of black and indigenous status, and mestiço and assimilated status were solidified, these discourses systematically racialized necessary pools of mobile labor, such that travel simultaneously situated one's racial and gender positionality within local politics.

FOLKLORIC "OTHERS"

Blanqueamiento *and the Celebration*

of Blackness as an Exception in Puerto Rico

ISAR P. GODREAU

In March of 1995, *The San Juan Star*, one of Puerto Rico's leading newspapers, announced that "Puerto Ricans will 'bleach away' many of the physical traces of its African past by the year 2200, with the other Spanish-speaking Caribbean following a few centuries later" (Bliss 1995: 30).[1] The article, which was written to commemorate the 122nd anniversary of the abolition of slavery in the island, also seemed to be commemorating the future "abolition" of blackness itself. "In two centuries," said the historian Luis Díaz Soler, one of the experts interviewed, "there will hardly be any blacks in Puerto Rico" (ibid.).

This racial forecast and concomitant claims to the gradual disappearance of black cultural manifestations reinforces ideologies of *blanqueamiento* well known and thoroughly documented in Latin America (Burdick 1992; de la Fuente 2001; Skidmore 1974; Stephan 1991; Wade 1997, among others). Scholars and activists have shown that such notions of whitening often go hand in hand with discourses of *mestizaje* (race mixture) that tend to exclude blacks, deny racism, and also delegitimize indigenous claims and demands (Hale 1999; Helg 1995; Whitten and Torres 1998). To challenge the silencing effects of such nationalist ideologies, Latin American activists have responded by developing important social and political movements that stand for black affirmation, the raising of black consciousness, and the nurturing of Afro-diasporic solidarities that extend beyond and complicate the regional boundaries of Latin America (Hanchard 1994; Gordon 1999; Wade 1997). These documented activities of affirmation and celebration mostly operate in contention with state agendas, national elites, or ideologies of mestizaje.

The purpose of this essay, however, is to examine what happens when celebratory renderings of blackness are appropriated by those who control the state apparatus. My goal here is to analyze some of the contested terrain in which blackness is accounted for, celebrated, and represented institutionally as part of the nation. As a case study, I will discuss a government-sponsored housing project developed to honor the community of San Antón in Ponce, Puerto Rico, as a site of black folklore. I argue that this inclusion and celebration of blackness is not distinct from but instead complements ideologies of blanqueamiento because it is rooted in some of the same ideological principles that distance blackness, geographically and temporally, from the imagined margins of the nation. This distancing has the effect of locating the phenotypic and cultural signs of blackness "somewhere else," and in premodern times of idealizing black people as happy and rhythmic tradition bearers who still inhabit supposedly homogeneous and harmonious communities.

Defined as the gradual "purging" of black features from the general population, blanqueamiento not only encourages but also enables dominant, romantic representations of black communities as remnants of a bygone era. Because discourses of whitening are also part and parcel of modernity and of the modern need to "rescue" national traditions in Latin America, I show how such dynamics of objectifying heritage through distance and nostalgia are particularly nourished in Puerto Rico by this "wishful thinking" over the supposedly vanishing qualities of blackness.

The critiques I outline here share commonalities with other globalizing and transnational dynamics discussed in this volume which address the commodification of blackness, the racialization of space, and the transnational referents and associations that nurture such racializing dynamics. In Puerto Rico, the key ideological points of reference in the construction of blackness and blanqueamiento extend well beyond the island boundaries as ideas about race and nation are inextricably tied to the island's colonial and transnational ties, first to Spain and after 1898 to the United States. Puerto Rico is not a sovereign nation but an unincorporated territory of the United States. Claims about who or what is a Puerto Rican and the arguments used to sustain such definitions thus have to be reconciled with the enduring effects of colonial discourses that associated Europe (Spain) and later the United States with ideas such as civilization, progress, and modernity. Because discourses of whitening are also part and parcel of modernity, claims about the gradual purging of black features or about the folkloric exceptionalism of blackness in Puerto Rico often make reference to the "civilizing" influence that Spain and/or the United States has had upon the island. Furthermore, the massive migration of Puerto Ricans to the United States over the past five decades coupled with the intense penetration of American capital, commodities, and media into the island make transnational referents such as the United States unavoidable in discussions about "the Puerto Rican nation" and the preservation of its cultural heritage. In fact, the United States often figures as a powerful counterpoint against which authentic Puerto Rican culture is defined (Dávila 1997; Duany 2000). In this context, deploying the ideology of racial mixture and democracy becomes instrumental because it serves to distinguish between a mixed and supposedly harmonious Puerto Rico and a deeply segregated U.S. "other."[2]

Constructing Distance and Nostalgia in San Antón

San Antón is a poor community currently consisting of approximately three hundred families. It was established during the 1800s by freed slaves (*libertos*) in the municipality of Ponce, an extremely important port during the heyday of sugar production in the island (Scarano 1992). Residents familiar with the barrio's history link its development to the sugar plantations that flourished nearby during the late nineteenth century. The community, however, is best known in Ponce and in Puerto Rico for its *bomba* and *plena*, which are two music genres that rely heavily on dance and the use of drums. These rhythms constitute the most explicit, celebrated link to the island's African presence (Blanco 1953; Barton 1995; and Banco Popular de Puerto Rico 2001).

Because of San Antón's reputation as the birthplace of plena, residents of Ponce and Puerto Rico consider the community a traditional site of black culture. This folkloric status is actively sustained and promoted by a select group of community members in coordination with different government agencies in charge of managing the city's historic and cultural development. The housing project I discuss as a case study in this essay was also developed in coordination with these agencies. The main goal of the project is to answer the needs of San Antón residents who for decades had endured decaying conditions by providing new and better quality housing facilities. The housing development, however, also intends to mark the community as a site of Afro–Puerto Rican traditions by preserving features that architects and city planners deemed to be typical of this community.

A number of forces backed this preservationist approach. Tourism was one incentive, but it was not the main target since San Antón falls outside the official boundaries of Ponce's historic tourist district and trolley routes have not been established yet to bring outsiders to the barrio.[3] A second, more powerful stimulus for the housing project came from Ponce's staff of architects and urban planners, a team of relatively progressive, young, well-educated, light-skinned professionals who felt committed to developing San Antón in a culturally sensitive way. Yet a third, more immediate motive for the construction of the first phase of the housing project was the 1996 general election campaign and its heated debates about the issue of national identity. In the context of heated disputes about Puerto Rico's political status vis–à-vis the United States, Ponce's mayor used the housing project as a political platform that would evidence his defense of Puerto Rican traditions and national pride.[4]

The Housing Project and the Re-creation of Family Patios

The construction of the first twenty-four houses in San Antón began in March of 1996. Before trucks began to pivot and load San Antón's fertile soil, Ponce's mayor Rafael Cordero visited the community to promote and justify the imminent intervention. In his speech, he declared: "In this soil where I am standing today, here the Africans contributed what they had to our race [*nuestra raza*]. And our race is nothing else than the mixture of the African, the Spaniard, and the Taíno Indian and from there comes the Puerto Rican race. . . ."

Residents were eager for the change. Community members had actively denounced San Antón's decaying housing conditions since the 1970s, but it wasn't until 1994, two years prior to elections, that the municipal government began to address the problem assertively. Mayor Cordero announced in the newspaper that: "The rehabilitation will respect the *patio*s [yards of various families] . . . as well as some trees where people used to gather and still gather to dance the bomba and plena" (Millán-Pabón 1995: 5).

The explicit attempt to "respect" San Antón's patios was articulated by architects and planners as one of the most innovative elements of this new development. A patio can be roughly defined as a small plot of land occupied by an extended family. Approximately 68 percent of all the families in San Antón were established in this arrangement before the housing project began (Urbain 1997). Patios vary in shape and composition. The smallest patio was made up of three persons, the biggest of approximately fifty-seven.

Patios in San Antón typify the settlement that took place in this region of Ponce among free blacks in the 1900s, a pattern documented in other parts of the Caribbean as family land (Besson 1984; Olwig 1998). Much has changed since the 1900s, however. In the past fifty years different housing and infrastructure development projects turned what used to be a vast sector into a much smaller and divided community. Nevertheless, patios are still an important reference point for community residents. They facilitate familial bonding, support, and socializing among family members and friends. Structurally, the patio adds an outdoor dimension to a home. Outdoor spaces located between houses are often swept, cleaned, and kept regularly just as if they were another living room. Although some patios are accessible to pedestrians, these spaces are considered private. An outsider is not supposed to just "walk right in." These spaces are also gendered, as it is often women who adorn and maintain them regularly.

The housing proposal for San Antón adopted the idea of the patio as an organizing principle for the spatial distribution of living units in the new development. Houses would have frontal access to the street and a back door facing a common green area in the center. This common area and the houses surrounding it in block formation were to be occupied by members of the same extended family. In fact, the architect provided a tentative assignment of blocks for each family in the proposal.

Houses built in the new development, however, were not to be raised over communally owned land. Instead units were parceled out into single plots to be owned individually by particular family members. In this way, the government replaced the principle of communal ownership with one of familial proximity. Yet, because the plan sought to reproduce, at least formally, the principle of connectivity and communal interaction, plots were not fenced. In fact, the project contemplated a series of semipublic corridors that would connect yards and street.

According to government officials, the reason for not simply restoring existing houses in order to maintain the original patio configurations was that original patios connote clustering (*hacinamiento*) according to urban policy regulations. Leaving these houses where they were would not have eliminated the overcrowding or the access problems for ambulances or fire trucks. Another reason preventing the restoration of existing structures was the fact that not all residents owned the land or the houses they occupied. This ownership factor prevented the government from making a permanent investment in certain housing units, since absentee landlords could ask residents to leave at any moment. To solve this uneven ownership situation, the government bought land in San Antón from residents and nonresidents, parceled it into individual plots, and then sold those plots to residents.[5]

The implementation of this complex transaction and development initiative required a tenacious approach on the part of architects, planners, and administrative officials. The staff also had to maneuver around various financial and political obstacles to get the project going. For example, funding sources targeted for historic sites were difficult to obtain because the barrio did not fall within the official zoning parameters of the historic district of Ponce. Thus, the team had to adopt creative funding strategies to research San Antón's patio configurations. Constructing wooden houses also required some extraordinary procedures because under federal regulations the standard material used for the construction of low-income housing in hurricane prone areas is cement, not wood. Still, the director of the Housing and Communal Development Office explained that "because of the barrio's typical nature, we succeeded in getting their approval for this project."

The perseverance and creative strategies adopted by these government officials are indicative of their understanding of San Antón as a deserving site of cultural recognition and of their interest in preserving what they perceived to be residents' communal practices. Yet residents received and interpreted these well-intentioned gestures somewhat differently.

Challenging Folkloric Housing

"All governments cheat the poor!" said Evelyn while I paid for a soda at her small store in San Antón. "I might be stupid, but everybody knows when they're being deceived." Construction of the housing project was already well underway. Besides criticizing the new houses for their small size, and for the proximity of the units, residents also criticized their high cost and the fact that they were made out of wood. Residents also complained about the uncertainty of not knowing what would happen to their property. Could they choose not to participate in the project? Would the government expropriate their land if they refuse to sell? If they moved, whom would they live next to? These questions remained unanswered. Other factors, such as the lack of parking space for a car or for cultivating plants also figured in the long list of complaints.

In the process of voicing those complaints, the heterogeneity of San Antón became evident as residents proposed different alternatives to their housing needs. Arcenia, for example, favored a linear setup similar to that of more "modern" urban neighborhoods. Armando, in contrast, thought that the best solution would be to give each household money so that families could fix their houses as they pleased. Guillo, the owner of the convenience store, thought the houses should be left as they were, but he suggested that the municipal government build new houses on an empty plot of land adjacent to his establishment. Another resident said the government should give money to people to move and buy houses elsewhere. In spite of differences in opinions, the general consensus among residents was that this was not the housing project they had hoped for. An old-timer baseball player, David, whom I had never heard complain, said, "Those houses are a scam!" And while he looked toward the construction site from his usual afternoon bench he added, "This is gonna' cause an uproar!" (¡Aquí se va a formar un revolú!).

The uproar took place. Within the next two weeks the community was meeting in front of television cameras and radio reporters to make their concerns about the housing project public. The president of the newly formed Committee in Defense of San Antón (Comité Pro Defensa de San Antón) explained their plea to one radio reporter in the following way: "We are owners of the land that we live on. They intend to expropriate the land and the homes, businesses won't work either, to then make us . . . because it's been done arbitrarily and unilaterally, to make us contract an unwanted debt. . . . What's happening here is that due to a lack of information, uncertainty reigns." As for the issue of historical preservation, the committee's vice president told the reporter: "This is simple, in other words, you can't move history from its place. History is where things take place. History is born, you can't take, for example, make one of the houses that are being built over there and give it to the Franceschi family and then bring the tourist and say 'This is where Juan Franceschi [the famous athlete] was born.' You can't move history from its place." After his intervention, the reporter asked about the communal design of the new patios. "But what patios?" said the vice president. "What patios? That's an Indian reservation. In other words, there is no patio, Penchi, there is no patio."

Invented Traditions

Scholars interested in the social construction of nations have argued that the collection and rescuing of traditions, whether real or invented, is a prevailing nation-building practice (Bendix 1997; Hobsbawm and Ranger 1983; Handler 1988). Virginia Domínguez has suggested that all traditions, and not just specific traditions, can be considered inventions motivated by the desire to find legitimacy through history (Domínguez 1986: 550). This is because history is often constructed as a narrative of truth (Price 1998; Trouillot 1995; Yelvington 2002). García Canclini has linked such validating processes to elite readings of folklore, arguing that part of the reason those in power show interest in the preservation of "popular traditions" is because it strengthens their legitimacy to rule (García Canclini 1989: 194).

In places like Puerto Rico, where national culture is often perceived to be threatened by U.S. influence over the island, the showcase of folklore as historical evidence can bestow political authority onto those who seek to administer the "colonial nation." In that sense, the new patios of San Antón tell us more about those who implemented them than about those who occupy them. They speak, for example, about how those in power attempted to gain support for the upcoming elections by presenting themselves as the true upholders of Puerto Rican culture.

The intent of salvaging the "traditions" of San Antón in the name of Puerto Rican culture also reproduces discourses of authenticity and romance found in other contexts, where the objectified properties of the nation appear to exist naturally and independently of the power relations that mold them and give them contemporary significance (Bendix 1997; Handler and Gable 1997, 1988). In Puerto Rico, bomba and plena are celebrated as one of those objectified traits of culture. However, state-sponsored performances of bomba and plena rarely make reference to how such creations were forged in the context of discriminatory practices that still persist. Thus, the positive value assigned by the government to these "black" working-class settlements might seem patriotic. Yet the controversy in San Antón evidenced the inadequacy of an approach that romanticized the patio without considering the social relationships of power that determined it, and—more importantly— without discussing its implementation with residents.

For the people of San Antón, it was not choice but rather need or lack of resources which determined most of what was considered typical housing in this community. Consequently, although patios and their wooden houses may seem quaint to the eyes of outsiders, they may or may not be valued as the most beautiful or the most desirable way to live by residents.

At the same time, those families who did wish to continue living in patios did not recognize the government's reinvention of this institution as their own. Some feared the new patios could be used by drug users or drug dealers. Others, like this young man and his female neighbor, thought these spaces would be used by tourists.

> YOUNG MAN: So that tourists can come in the trolley; they sit there and people dance bomba and plena for them . . . And I don't know what bomba and plena they're going to get . . . What they might get is shot!
> MARÍA: So a space that can be used for us is going to be given to them?
> YOUNG MAN: Imagine those gringos coming here to laugh at us. How ugly, what savages.

Keenly aware of the exotic gaze of others who associate blacks with ugliness and primitiveness, this young man's critique of the *patio-placitas* also speaks to the objectification of the community as a place of racial difference.

Blanqueamiento and the Spatial Distancing of Blackness

Scholars have underlined the importance of region and racial geographies for understanding how blackness is constructed in the Americas (Wade 1997; Whitten and Torres 1998), highlighting the singularity and social hierarchy of racialized regions. It is equally important, however, to underline the role of discursive distance in constructing blackness as a singularity, exception, or vestige of the nation. Such racial maps of distinctiveness become increasingly problematic in Cuba, Santo Domingo, Puerto Rico, and Brazil where one might not want to consider black people a minority. Certainly, the question of who is black and how one defines it is always a slippery one (Godreau 2000). However, there are important demographic factors tied to the historic development of the plantation economy and to patterns of Caribbean migration that distinguish the Hispanic Caribbean and Brazil from other countries in Latin America that were not so strongly influenced by transatlantic slavery.

Approaches to the issue of blackness in the Hispanic Caribbean and in Afro–Latin America, however, have tended to focus on communities that are deemed "different," given their predominance of black people, in order to document the prevalence of African cultural traits or survivals (Herskovits 1941). In spite of important contributions, theoretical conceptualizations of black identity in these studies are often construed as unambiguous, and blackness is often conceptualized as something that can only be found in a specific sector. Thus, while regions such as Bahia in Brazil and Oriente in Cuba are marked and celebrated for their "cultural distinctiveness," the nations to which they belong are overwhelmingly represented by light-skinned individuals in the media and in a wide range of nationalist events (beauty pageants, tourist campaigns, museum exhibits, and so forth).

In Puerto Rico, this maneuver of whitening appears in representations that locate blackness only in the northern coastal town of Loíza or in the bodies of immigrants from the Dominican Republic.[6] Such displacements of blackness also take place in Ponce, as people often refer to San Antón as "the place where black people live." This characterization indirectly constructs Ponce and Puerto Rico as not black. People in San Antón are thus celebrated as traditional but simultaneously excluded from the nation for not being mixed enough.

In displaying the "traditions" of San Antón, Ponce's municipal government also constructed the barrio as a site of "racial difference." The main designer of the project, a young, white, European man who lived in Puerto Rico, stated the following when I asked him about the criteria he used for the design: "I see it in terms of the barrio's urban organization: how the houses are organized, how the family has characteristics that are essentially more African than Latin [sic], apart from any influences that it has received from outside. . . . I see it as a foreigner, I guess. I came to this barrio about four years ago . . . and it seems to me like something totally distinct within Puerto Rico. . . ."

In another interview that took place after he read my dissertation (Godreau 1998), the architect clarified that he did not think San Antón's patios were of African origin. His perceptions, he said, had more to do with the community's family structure, particularly with the relationship between the patio and the extended family as a key aspect of San Antón's traditions. In this posterior interpretation, it was not Africa but the idea of extended kin networks that sustained his reading of San Antón's uniqueness.

A related interpretation, which was documented in a newspaper article, is that such kin networks were gendered since women, many of whom were prominent community leaders, often headed households. An individual interviewed for the article described San Antón as "a matriarchal community where women assume an active voice and where her figure plays a pivotal role in the struggles for a better future" (González 1995: 4). Immediately after the quote, the reporter linked such leadership to the bomba and plena traditions of San Antón, reinscribing once again the presence of racialized subjects in this particular place. Certainly, women in San Antón have played a key role in community struggles as well as in the everyday maintenance of networks and institutions such as the patio and exchanging goods, labor, and emotional support. Yet similar support networks of extended kin, often headed by women, can be found throughout Puerto Rico and the Caribbean.[7] However, the racialization of the community as different because of its blackness contributes to the casting of these and other gendered dynamics as "unique or exotic manifestations."

Ironically, residents rarely described their patios as "traditional" or "matriarchal," much less as African in our interviews. Patios were, in fact, rarely mentioned as something I as a researcher should see or take note of. Furthermore, very few of the residents I interviewed shared this notion of San Antón being different from the rest of Puerto Rico. Some even questioned the characterization of San Antón as a black community. For example, Libertad, a long-time resident, said:

> It may be true that we have a sad color [que somos tristes de color] but to say that we are a barrio of blacks . . . that word! They could say we are a barrio of people who are *trigueños* [wheat-colored[8]] but not to be so rude. We're mixed with African people, but that's going too far. Because there's racism in the U.S. and there's racism in Puerto Rico also. But the type of racism that's coming now is too much. It is true that we are black, it is true that we have a sad color, but you don't say that word like that . . . As a black woman I feel proud. Black people are a pride, but that does not mean that other people can behave with such despotism. We know what we are and that's enough.

As an outsider to the community, I also came across residents who expressed concern over the possible implications of being labeled black by me.[9] On one occasion, a female resident of San Antón told me, "Most people here in San Antón are not black, black. If you want to study black culture you should go to Loíza. People are *really* black over there [ahi sí que son bien negritos]." Her response also indicates that in Puerto Rico, even in San Antón, blackness is always located somewhere else.

This deployment of discursive distance also prevails in interpretations of the African influence in the Puerto Rican body. For example, kinesthetic, rhythmic, and sensual qualities associated with blackness are often described as remote or "hidden traces" that may surface at particular moments. Commonly voiced phrases, such as "Se le salió lo de negro" (the black came out of him), and words commonly used to talk about the African heritage, such as "roots," "veins," and "blood," show that this legacy's contribution is understood as residing in a distant place that lies deep within one's body.

The representation of blackness as a distant, different, and exotic element of Puerto Rican culture emerges out of dominant discourses that rendered Hispanic heritage as the essence of the nation. Deployed throughout Latin America during the late nineteenth century and the early twentieth, this notion became particularly popular in Puerto Rico among an elite group of educated men and public figures who sought to counter U.S. political hegemony over the island during the 1930s (Ferrao 1993). Nationalism was at that time linked to Europe and to the racial properties of whiteness. As a result, many Puerto Rican intellectuals upheld whiteness as a necessary component for self-government (Rodríguez-Vázquez 2004). Anchoring the origins of "the nation" in European heritage, the Catholic religion, and particularly the Spanish language also became an important strategic discourse to differentiate Puerto Rico from the United States and legitimize its potential as a nation. Africa, in contrast, was construed as a destabilizing disturbance, an element that had been culturally assimilated and should continue to be biologically subdued through gradual blanqueamiento.

Temporal Displacement, Race Mixture, and Modernity

The distancing of blackness in national discourses is not only manifested in spatial range or body depth but also operates in terms of time. In fact, the temporal distancing of blackness is one of the most constitutive elements of mestizaje and blanqueamiento in places like Puerto Rico, Cuba, the Dominican Republic, and Brazil, where Africa is recognized, albeit marginally, as part of the national heritage. In Puerto Rico, for example, state representations of the racial triad construct the Spaniard, the African, and the Taíno Indian as ancestral symbols that have left a cultural trace in all Puerto Ricans, regardless of their color. Racial purity is, in that sense, only recognized in the past, while mixture is understood as the mark of the present. Yet, while race is mixed and de-essentialized at this point, the cultural outcome of that hybridity is construed as a homogenous national product. As a result, when the phenotypic and cultural signs of blackness are celebrated in their own terms they are often rendered as remnants of a past era that has been replaced by a modern, mixed present.

In displaying the "traditions" of San Antón, Ponce's municipal government also constructed residents of this community as authentic trait bearers who could easily amuse others with the enchantments of their barrio. Ponce's mayor, for example, declared in the newspaper that the rehabilitation of San Antón would preserve the trees where "people used to gather, and still gather, to sing the bomba and the plena" (Millán-Pabón 1995: 5).

However, bomba and plena were rarely heard or danced in San Antón on a regular basis. Even community gatherings I attended, such as Christmas dinners or Mother's Day celebrations, did not display these folkloric rhythms. Rather, it was the rhythm of *salsa*, *merengue*, rap, and contemporary pop songs that were most popular, especially among the youth. Older folks also listened to *boleros* or *música de trio* (trío music). Bomba and plena, in contrast, were genres reserved for performances in which the "outside" community was the main audience.

As a discursive strategy, the temporal displacement of blackness is closely connected to state modernizing agendas, which were first carried out in Puerto Rico under the leadership of Luis Muñoz Marin during the 1940s and 1950s. Like other populist figures in Latin America, Muñoz sought to lead the country toward economic development while promoting the preservation of traditional practices and national values as necessary identity tools for withstanding the impact of modernity. This kind of romantic gaze, however, often inhibited the possibility of situating *lo popular* (the popular) in relation to structures of dominance (García Canclini 1989). In Caribbean nation-states where tourism is a key economic resource, the practice of constructing people as "traditionally picturesque" becomes increasingly important for attracting investors (Patullo 1996). Although tourism was not an immediate objective of San Antón's housing project, developments there were somewhat similar because the state also intervened to objectify the community and the patios in ways that obscured particular histories of oppression and social inequality. On one hand, officials constructed the common, everyday aspects of the patio as "black folklore." On the other, they operated as if the folklore of bomba and plena was part of the everyday lives of people in San Antón, continuous "traditions" that would justify their preservationist intervention. What we see then is a failure to recognize that residents of San Antón were also "modern," that some of them no longer wanted to live in patios or in wooden houses, and that certain cultural practices such as the bomba and plena had been replaced or combined with new ones such as rap, salsa, and merengue.

I have argued that this oversight is not only informed by modernizing state agendas but also operates in consonance with ideologies of blanqueamiento that represent blackness as a different and vanishing element of Puerto Rican culture. Behind such representations lies a longing to recover a black essence whose loss is only meaningful within the context of elite discourses that define the nation as not black. Thus, rather than being motivated by the fear of losing the black subject, state-sponsored constructions of blackness can best be understood as informed by an anxiety over its contemporary presence. At the same time, identifying only certain black expressions as authentic has the effect of constructing other more contemporary manifestations as illegitimate, impure, or Americanized. Hence, music genres commonly associated with blackness or Caribbeanness, such as salsa, merengue, rap, and reggae, or body styles popular among the youth, such as dreadlocks and corn-rows, are displaced from the boundaries of the nation as foreign or inauthentic, thereby reducing even further the repertoire of national signifiers that claim to be "black." This reduction operates alongside the whitening of other national symbols such as the *jíbaro*, documented in traditional Puerto Rican scholarship as a light-skinned peasant of Spanish heritage (Pedreira 1935, Alonso 1974 and Dávila 1997).

The craving for premodern, localized, and bygone black authentic expressions also informs the romantic construction of San Antón as a homogeneous and harmonious unit. The open spaces and yards, the semipublic corridors, presuppose agreeable and congruous relations between family members and among different family groups. Thus, while the government approached San Antón with temporal and spatial distance, they expected residents to live in seamless proximity. In this process, racism within and toward the community was construed as a nonissue while notions of "culture" and "African heritage" were deployed as heuristic devises that supposedly allowed "others" to understand black people and their "special" or, in this case, spatial needs.

The Aftermath: Modern Solutions to a Folklorizing State Approach

Despite criticisms, when one compares the approach of Ponce's municipal government in San Antón to previous development strategies of the 1950s and 1960s, which displaced entire communities to public housing projects (Duany 1997), this housing initiative represents a significant improvement.

One noteworthy aspect of the project was that it did not force residents to leave, neither during the renovations nor after their completion. This accomplishment results from previous struggles and public protests waged by residents who had been displaced during the 1960s and 1970s. Their trajectory of community activism coupled with the liberal outlook of the architects and planners in charge produced a relocation strategy that broke with traditional models of displacement. Finally, and most importantly, once residents mobilized in opposition to the project, government officials incorporated some of their demands into future plans for the community.

As a result, new houses were constructed in spaces that were originally intended for communal use, altering, in some cases, the family-block model. The Comité Pro Defensa de San Antón (Committee in Defense of San Antón) also managed to arrange a personal meeting with the mayor in which he reassured them that participation in the project was not mandatory and that no one would be obliged to sell his or her land.

On July 3, 1997, one year after the controversy, the first twenty-four houses of the housing project in San Antón were inaugurated. The day after, the people I talked to expressed satisfaction with their new homes. "Now people are going to live decently," said an older resident. There were residents who had refused to move to the new project, but those who did move seemed to be content. No one in the community, however, spoke of the new block arrangement as patios. In fact, living arrangements looked very different from the original projections of the master plan. Members of one family, for example, occupied houses on one block, but there were members of other families scattered within that same block. In addition, only three small communal areas remained, out of six that were originally envisioned. One of them currently remains empty. The other two have been cultivated, beautified, and claimed by residents as part of "their property." Residents also lobbied to get permission to fence their property, and some have separated their plots from neighbors and family members. Libertad's household, for instance, took advantage of fencing but also of the open-yard model. She integrated her plot with those of her sister and her niece by fencing the three properties off from those of other surrounding family members. In this way they created a communal space, shared by three households, and equipped with chairs, swings for grandchildren, plantain trees, and domestic animals.

In a survey I conducted in January of 2002 among residents of the housing project, 60 percent of those interviewed reported they were very satisfied with the project. Among the advantages listed were living more comfortably, better conditions in terms of housing and infrastructure, having family members nearby, and being property owners (45 percent of those who moved to the project were not landowners previously). Ironically, those aspects causing the most dissatisfaction among residents had to do with the reinvention of the patio structure and residences. For example, 73 percent of all residents interviewed said they disliked the fact that properties were unfenced; 65 percent said they disliked the fact that the houses were made of wood; and 80 percent expressed dissatisfaction with the corridors that connect streets and properties. The reasons were unwanted noise and disturbances, fear of drug trafficking, and the desire to protect their family members against police harassment.

These and other ongoing developments in the community reveal the desire of San Antón's residents for modernity as inscribed in the claim for privacy, comfort, security, and the clear demarcation of private property. Rather than endorse these desires uncritically, my goal has been to point out the limits of a folklorizing and patronizing approach that did not consider them initially. Future phases of the housing project contemplate building even more houses. These phases will probably beget new and different kinds of controversies. Whatever the outcome, these transformations must now take into account the militancy of San Antón's residents. That militancy forced the government to engage them in the development of San Antón's future, problematizing, in the process, folkloric discourses that render black people as distant and bounded tradition bearers. I take their commentary and practice as an important critique of how blackness is showcased by those who claim to have "better wisdom" and the power to implement their imaginations.

Notes

1. I am most indebted to the people of San Antón who have shared with me their time and their views throughout the process of research and writing. This article is dedicated to the memory of Doña Judith Cabrera and the example of her community activism. I am deeply grateful for the support of the Ford Foundation and the Wenner Gren Foundation, which funded research for and writing of this article. I would also like to thank the Department of Anthropology at the University of South Florida, and especially Kevin Yelvington, for supporting and facilitating my research endeavors as a postdoctoral fellow at the USF. All oversights are my own.

2. Similar dichotomies have been drawn to support nation-building projects in Latin America and the Caribbean. In fact, key ideologues of mestizaje such as Freyre in Brazil, Martí in Cuba, and Muñoz Marín in Puerto Rico construed their corre-

sponding versions of racial democracy in explicit comparison with the United States and in transnational dialogue with U.S. institutions and thinkers.

3. San Antón figures in government publications as a place of historic interest, but it is unclear whether the municipal government plans to bring tourists there in the future. Residents mentioned seeing the tourist-trolley drive by occasionally. However, according to the director of Ponce's Office of Tourism, the government has no immediate plans of incorporating San Antón into the city tour.

4. Ironically, this "patriotic move" in San Antón was funded, like other housing initiatives for low-income families in Puerto Rico, with U.S. government funds from HUD. Specifically, the project relied on grant money provided by HOME and section 108 of LGA (Loan Guarantee Assistance).

5. Those families who owned property in San Antón had to sell it to the government, divide the money among the rightful heirs, and use that amount to buy the new property. Because the project is heavily subsidized by federal funds, residents who did not own property are currently paying monthly mortgage payments that fluctuate between fifty-five and seventy-five dollars. Many of those who owned property (houses) were compensated by the government and have used part of that amount to pay the total cost of the new house. In a recent survey (2002) all of those making monthly payments said they considered the amount reasonable.

6. For an excellent analysis of how Loíza has been romanticized in Puerto Rican literature see Giusti Cordero 1996. For an assessment of the impact that Dominican migration to Puerto Rico has on discourses of national identity see Martínez-San Miguel 1998. For an assessment of the situation of Dominican migrants in the island see also Duany, Hernández Angueira, and Rey 1995.

7. Traditional anthropological literature treated such a family structure as a "different" if not deviant aspect of Caribbean social life by pointing to the absence of male heads of households. Other scholarship interpreted aspects of black family structure as African retentions (E. Clarke 1957; Herskovits 1947; R. T. Smith 1956). The question of how such gendered notions of the black family have affected the folklorization of blackness in San Antón merits further interpretation but is beyond the scope of this essay.

8. This is the literal translation. In everyday contexts, however, the term *trigueño* is used to name someone who is perceived as darker than white but lighter than black. The term is also used as a euphemism for "black" in those instances where people might consider that calling a person black is an insult (see Godreau 2000).

9. I am a light-skinned woman with features, such as very curly hair, that can be associated with blackness. Thus the way people identified me racially or identified themselves in relation to me varied. Most frequently, especially at the beginning of my fieldwork, San Antón residents identified me as "white." At other moments and for various reasons people identified me as *jabá*, a term used to name someone who is black but exhibits features such as light skin or green or blue eyes. This term would be the equivalent of "high-yellow" in the United States, although it does not always carry such pejorative connotations.

GENTRIFICATION, GLOBALIZATION, AND GEORACIALITY

JOHN L. JACKSON JR.

Peircian Harlems

There is a bookmark floating around Harlem, New York, that does a great job demonstrating the complicated mathematics of Manhattan. I first spotted it during the summer of 2003. Disseminated by a local real estate company, the bookmark serves as its calling card and is prominently displayed in the entranceway to its tiny, cluttered storefront office. It is an office space in one of those subsections of northern Manhattan that asserts its symbolic distance from the rest of Harlem with recourse to ever quainter, lofty, and deracialized place-names such as Morningside Heights, Hamilton Heights, SoHA, NoHA, SpaHA, and, in this particular instance, Manhattanville.[1]

The realtor's bookmark is simple and ingenious, really. On its front side, the company's name, phone number, and website frame a full-color repro-duction of Manhattan's portion of the New York City Transit Authority's iconic and ubiquitous subway map, with only a hint of the Bronx and a sliver of Queens peeking in from the corners. On its flipside, another listing of the company's URL crowns its "Arithmetic of the Avenues" chart, introduced as follows: "Here's a simple way to locate the cross street for an address on an avenue. Just take the number of the avenue building, cancel the last digit and add or subtract the number below. That's the nearest cross street." Under-neath those very instructions, 1444 Amsterdam Avenue, a Harlem address, is provided as illustration: one removes the final 4 from 1444 to get 144, divides 144 by 2 to get 72, and then adds 59 for a grand total of 131, which means that 1444 Amsterdam is closest to the intersection of Amsterdam and 131st street. Every single Manhattan avenue is then listed below, along with a truncated version of each avenue's respective equation: for Columbus and West End Avenues you add 60, not 59; for St. Nicholas and Lenox Avenues, you add 110; for Avenues A, B, C, and D you add only 3; for Riverside Drive you divide by 10 (instead of 2) and add 72 for your answer. Then there are avenues such as Fifth and Broadway that require a variety of additive amounts based on different groupings of street numbers, some even calling for subtraction instead of addition to determine final locations.

This is clearly a very useful device for many of the realtor's prospective homebuyers, especially outsiders who want to locate properties as efficiently as possible so that they can beat their competitors to the bargaining table. However, in all my previous years of researching and residing in Manhattan, I had never before taken note of such a master key to the city, despite the fact that several popular magazines and local phonebooks regularly publish the same wallet-sized "Street Finder" (minus the real estate company's contact information) for their own citywide readerships. As a minor consolation, I realize that I am not nearly alone in my imperceptiveness. This bookmark provides a distillation of Manhattan addresses that was unknown to almost all of the Harlem residents I ever asked about it. Of course, this hardly means that they are bumbling around the city missing appointments everyday because they cannot quickly figure cross streets; it does, however, highlight an otherwise commonsensical recognition that the lived experiencing of a neighborhood does not cultivate such strict mathematical formulas for rendering geographical certainty: Lexington Avenue, add 22; Madison Avenue, 27; Park Avenue, 35 (not to be confused with Park Avenue South, where you only need to add 8).

These different ways of parsing place resonate with what the French philosopher Henri Lefebvre famously described as the relationship between "quantified" and "qualified" spaces (Lefebvre 1991). For Lefebvre, these two spheres frame a related series of dialectical contradistinctions: abstract versus concrete space, public versus private space, productive versus unproductive space, and *capitalist utilizers* of space versus *community users* of it. He tries to provide a neo-Marxian argument that distinguishes quantified "spaces of consumption" from the more emancipatory and qualified "consumption of space." Quantified spaces are predicated on exploitative surplus values above and beyond already corrupted exchange values, a clear geographicalization of Marx. Qualified spaces bespeak the egalitarian impulses of an unapologetically nonproductive use-value that short-circuits and counters "bourgeoisified" utilizations of social space. Lefebvre tries to theorize along the fault lines of an ecological "class warfare" pitting "quantifiable, profitable, communicable and 'realistic'" considerations of space on the one hand against more subjective, proletarian, lived, imaginary, and ideal spaces on the other (362).

In this essay, I want to rewire Lefebvre's distinction between "real" and "ideal" spaces to a consideration of hot-button urban issues in contemporary black America—specifically, to the potential threat that gentrification poses for a place like Harlem, which is statistically portrayed as some five square miles and three hundred thousand residents, predominantly poor and working-class African Americans and Latinos.[2] Understanding some of the conceptual routes back and forth between the *real* and the *ideal* Harlems, real and ideal Harlemites, might be a useful way of comparing "a history of neighborhoods to a history of the techniques for the production of locality" in a self-consciously global twenty-first century (Appadurai 1996: 182). Moreover, since this essay examines the linkages between gentrification and race in America's urban core, it is also, quite clearly, a story about globalization— even though certain provincializing assumptions within American anthropology today (and within American ideologies more generally) might imagine globalism to be far better spied in other parts of the world, with the seemingly more exotic instantiations of racial difference found in places other than those conspicuous, local black ghettoes often abutting the very same academic campuses where scholarly research on globalization and race often gets conceptualized and debated. I am interested in the realisms and idealisms of everyday forms of African Americanness, everyday forms sometimes obscured from ethnographic view as a function of their taken-for-granted proximity and visibility.

There are many different ways of charting such pathways linking real spaces to ideal ones, connecting the seen to the unseen in contemporary black America, but they probably take an entirely different math from the variety offered up by that Harlem realtor's aforementioned bookmark. The bookmark's Manhattan-by-numbers recipe is reminiscent of a similar kind of globalization-by-numbers ethos that often entails little more than counting up the millions upon millions of bodies that cross different nation-state boundaries, imagining ourselves able to locate the specificity of globality in these traveling individual, political, and corporate entities. Instead, I am thinking here of a more mystical and slippery mathematics—a mathematics of illusion, allusion, ephemerality, and contingency, a burlesque mimicking of realness that might comprehend globalization more through sympathetic magic than improved empiricism.[3] One way to hint at such a seemingly oxymoronic notion (of supposedly mystical mathematics) is to invoke the late-nineteenth-century scholar Charles Sanders Peirce's mathematician father, Benjamin Peirce, who reveled in his intellectual incomprehensibility to such a degree that he proudly proclaimed that the anthropologist Louis Agassiz was the only person in all of Harvard University capable of consistently understanding him (Menand 2001).

Benjamin Peirce was clearly a well-respected mathematical mind of the mid-nineteenth century, but he was also notoriously impenetrable. And this was not so just because the concepts he talked about were difficult to understand. His math was also laced with just the kind of mysticism I am looking for. As an example of such myth-making mathematics, Charles W. Eliot, a former president of Harvard University, once told the story of "an intelligent Cambridge matron" who remembered one specifically cryptic line from a Peircean public lecture delivered in 1862, a line that has been offered up time and again as an example of Peirce's intellectual eccentricities: "Incline the mind to an angle of 45°," he is quoted to have said, "and periodicity becomes non-periodicity and the ideal becomes the real" (Eliot 1925: 3).

Here we have one mathematician's cryptic directive for travel between ideality and reality. There is a geometry at play here, but its lines reek of allegory. They stink with the stench of synecdoche. I want to invoke a similarly figurative and funky mathematics to talk about Harlem's ideal and real instantiations today—imagining Daddy Peirce standing on his soapbox at 125th Street, leaning against a lectern on the corner of Lenox Avenue, a bushy head cocked slightly to one side (at a 45° angle, no doubt), eyebrows scrunched, eyes squinting, in an attempt to see the everyday differently, to spot chaos where others would believe themselves to find clear and universal patterns, the sharply obvious contours of a matter-of-factly real world. But what happens when we look at the commonsensical, stereotypical, and over-studied Harlem with Peirce's canted and curious posture? What do we notice about the place that we have not quite seen before? Is there anything we recognize anew? And how can we even trust what we think we see? I want to look at how local Harlemites see Harlem and determine belonging in that upper Manhattan neighborhood, and I use Lefebvre and this notion of a metaphorical mathematics to frame and bookend my ethnographic examination of globality by way of its local instantiations.

To invoke a Harlem of the present is to talk, first and foremost, about pressing and controversial issues of gentrification—local, national, and international processes of urban change and conflict that have many suburbanites salivating, many grassroots activists agitating, and more than a few low-income tenants quaking in their boots. A discussion about gentrification also demands engagement with Harlem's storied history, along with the neighborhood's self-reflexive capacity to invoke that past as a way of vouchsafing particularly imagined futures. Founded in the seventeenth century as a rural outpost and built up in the late nineteenth century for a burgeoning, white middle class, Harlem is now globally recognized as the small-scale geographical quintessence of black racial difference. A racially segregated housing market combined with the great migration and white realtors' miscalculations to spawn an early-twentieth-century overcrowding of the community with black migrants from the southeastern United States, West African nation-states, and various islands in the Caribbean (Osofsky 1966; W. James 1998; Stoller 2002). However, that alone does not explain Harlem's international notoriety. The area is most famous today because of the cultural and literary "renaissance" it housed in the 1920s and 1930s, a time that grounds current neighborhood nostalgia about figures such as Langston Hughes, Rudolph Fisher, and Zora Neale Hurston—and how they once traversed this neighborly landscape. Here again, we find an analogy to Lefebvre's distinction between quantified and qualified assessments of place. There are more black residents in other American locales (such as Chicago and even the borough of Brooklyn right across the East River), but Harlem's symbolic purchase is imagined to outstrip strict demographic calculations—even as a certain understanding of racial demography is also considered the founding principle for its irreducible difference. There are black bodies in Harlem today, but that fact alone does not exhaust the explanations for Harlem's symbolic racial value. Numbers do and do not clarify what makes Harlem *Harlem*.

Varying assumptions of belonging in contemporary Harlem (assumptions translated through Lefebvre's quantified/qualified dialectic, assumptions that help explain Harlem's worldwide reputation) underpin fundamental disputes about class, race, and community in urban America. For example, one might say that there are two distinctly quantified notions of space (two mathematics of membership, if you will) at work in present-day discussions about gentrification in Harlem. One emphasizes the market as the final arbiter of residential validity, while the other highlights the purported dislocation of low-income residents as a deal-breaking by-product of renewed middle-class and corporate interest in once forgotten urban cores. The first claim is a mathematics of the marketplace (privileging housing prices and residential demand); the second, a mathematics of mobility (highlighting urban pioneers and concomitant displacement). The contrasts between these two interconnected claims help to disentangle two distinctive brands of privatization, one based on neoliberal assumptions about market-can-do-no-wrong social policy-making (a version of Lefebvrean quantification), the other an extension of more qualified space-making, what the theorist Pierre Mayol describes as the "insides" of local neighborhoods, those "third spaces" of playfully "poetic geographies" that create local intimacies within the most global of cities (de Certeau, Giard, and Mayol 1998: 11).

Lefebvre's critique of quantified social spaces privileges a class-based analysis that is more than operative in Harlem today, but I want to argue for an accompanying engagement with the quantified/qualified fault lines of *race*, an equally important analytical lens for spying space, place, struggle, and globalization. Some provincial assumptions about contemporary Afro-America notwithstanding, to theorize gentrification in Harlem is always already to theorize the global, a notion of local living that is inextricably linked to international tracks of racial mobility and processes of racial segregation. This is what I want to call a kind of *georaciality:* the transnational ebb and flow of people through local places that demand certain affective investments from them, including qualified and quantifiable racial frameworks for determining community and reckoning belonging. With America's current "war on terror" and its implications for theories of supposedly "new" and "multitudinal" imperialisms, it is important to remember that any articulation of empire's "changing sameness" must also help explain just what the global looks like in places like Harlem, New York (Hardt and Negri 2000; Gilroy 1991; Harvey 2003). Similarly, theories of globalizing "flows" and transnational "scapes" must account for the entrenched and institutionalized non-*flow*ingness and ine-*scap*ability of race in contemporary American society—and all around the world (Appadurai 1996; Jameson 1998). The culturally specific incarnations of racial reasoning found in different countries and continents belie an overly coherent organizing principle for planetary inequality mappable along a selfsame epidermal ladder from light to dark bodies. Today's Harlem, a gentrifying Harlem, is also shot through with such color-coded significances, a color-coding that tints the lenses local residents use to see international influences on their small upper Manhattan community.

Gentrification Studies

The study of gentrification has clearly become a veritable cottage industry within the social sciences.[4] Coined in 1960s England, the term is usually offered to mark middle-class reclamation of formerly forsaken urban regions (Glass 1964). In the United States, most renditions of gentrification start with a discussion of deindustrialization and suburbanization in the middle of the twentieth century (K. Jackson 1985; N. Smith 1996). Improvements in transportation technology, expansions in highway construction, and precipitous rises in service-sector employment helped to spawn a middle-class exodus from teeming urban centers (W. Wilson 1987). Corporate disinvestment accompanied this urban evacuation, as middle-class suburban families spent their disposable income at the cash registers of increasingly transnational big businesses, disposable incomes not believed to exist among the lower-class urbanites left behind, urbanites unable to afford the financial price tag of suburban relocation.

By the 1970s, as a function of this other "great migration," most academic and popular stories about urban Americana understood it as little more than a class-specific locus of poverty and deprivation (Gilder 1981). When that same discussion was linked to considerations of race and ethnicity, the out-migration of middle-class African Americans was utilized as a trump card for claims of urban cultural pathology and social marginalization (C. Murray 1984; Mead 1992). Once the black middle-class began following their white counterparts out of already racially segregated urban areas, the stage was set for arguments about the intergenerational transmission of familial dysfunction within poor black and Latino communities as a function of their social and cultural isolation. This social isolation was asked to explain perpetual black poverty from the political left and the political right (Reed 1999; W. Wilson 1978). Inner-city communities were conceded to the poor, while "equalizing institutions" like schools and other important governmental interventions were weakened by the disappearance of urban tax dollars (Murnane and Levy 1996).

In that context, cities were said to require more, not less, federal and corporate support, and intended improvements entailed cajoling corporate

America and middle-class families back into urban centers, a task that is slowly but surely being accomplished in places like Harlem. With renewed middle-class in-migration comes an increase in resources for local services, especially public schools, an attractive consumer base for corporate reinvestment, and what is imagined as a redevelopment circle that builds on itself to drastically enrich depressed urban locales. This notion of gentrification as urban salvation is, of course, only half the story. Many detractors (and in Harlem, they are organizing and mobilizing every day) argue that renewed middle-class interest in urban areas means low-income tenant dislocation and displacement. Apartments and houses that were once priced at below-market rates have risen to meet the market—and with this rise, poorer residents are said to be priced out of the homes and neighborhoods they once occupied.

Much of the literature on gentrification interrogates this dislocation hypothesis, often with differing definitions of displacement and less-than-perfect measures for comparing displacement rates in gentrifying and non-gentrifying neighborhoods.[5] Most recently, studies in Boston and New York City have argued that the assumed displacement believed to accompany gentrifying forces might be mitigated by the existence of already vacant apartment buildings—and by poor tenants' dogged determination to stay put and take advantage of their slowly improving local environs (Vigdor 2001; Freeman and Braconi 2002). These studies attempt to problematize simple arguments about gentrification as low-income dislocation and offer up a more complicated picture of gentrification's ills and gains. In Harlem, where residency has always historically included a certain embrace of racial community, these same debates about residential dislocation fuel cultural conflicts that power the engines for various kinds of racial politicking.

As late as the 1980s, Harlem was still considered somewhat gentrification-proof, specifically due to its symbolic connection to African Americans and its stereotypical media representation as violent and dangerous (Smith 1996). However, even before Harlem's congressman Charles Rangel helped to usher in a new era with the 1996 empowerment zone legislation, Harlem's outer edges, along stretches like 110th Street, touching the northern end of Olmstead's Central Park, were already sites of renewed middle-class residential interest and reoccupation. With the empowerment zone, hundreds of millions of dollars worth of government loans and subsidies have made it all the more enticing for stores such as Disney, Pathmark, Old Navy, and Starbucks, and enterprises such as the Magic Johnson Theaters to take a chance on the

Harlem consumer, and many residents welcome this renewal of retail variety. The argument that is offered up is simple: Harlem should have what any and every other community boasts (fancy cafés, convenient movie theaters, huge shopping centers), and corporate America should provide it. Anything short of that is deemed a slap in the face, a disrespectful dismissal of African Americans' identity and social value.

Housing Hoodoo

I am sitting in an eatery around the corner from that aforementioned bookmark-disseminating realty company, speaking with a competing realtor about the relatively new and much publicized interest in Harlem's high-end housing. She has been in the realty business for just a couple of years, but even in such a short time she has noticed substantial shifts in local demand and desire. She starts to tell me this story by summarizing a movie—or, at least, a movie pitch, one of her many screenplay ideas, this one based on the life of a fictitious Harlem realtor who gets killed by a crazed client obsessed with one specific nineteenth-century brownstone on one particularly quaint Harlem street. She is one of four realtors I will meet over a five-day period who are writing or selling original screenplays. The plot for this realtor's script pivots on a century-old curse that turns one Harlem house's Queen-Anne quaintness (its hand-crafted oriel windows and remote, recessed porches) into an intoxicatingly mind-altering and deadly preoccupation. The story's violence is not about gunplay; she makes that clear. ("We have too much shoot-em up already.") Instead, the film ends with the realtor, the story's main character, being slowly choked to death by an otherworldly (or othertimely) aberration in the house's small, overgrown yard. The realtor is left limp and breathless under a large, full moon. The ghost, a former resident of the house, possesses a local crack addict and forces the junkie to do the suffocating deed. The realtor-screenwriter is still working the kinks out of her script's third act, but she promises to send me a copy when the first draft is done. I tell her I cannot wait—and that I think it is just brilliant how she supernaturalizes history's constraints on Harlem's present. It came to her in a dream, she says, "clear as day" in her mind, but she wants to start typing it out with her Final Draft software before too long. "I'll email it to you when it's done," she says. "I promise."

This titleless horror story is not the only one that she is working on, either. There are several, at various stages of near completion. She thinks of herself as more of a frustrated writer and video director than a real estate agent. She lives in Riverdale and only sells real estate in Harlem for a couple of days out of the week. The rest of her time is spent doing unrelated office work in downtown Manhattan—that is, when she's not plugging away at her scripts and story ideas. Most of these stories, she assures me, have little to do with Harlem real estate, but she does see things that merit fictionalization each time she visits her work site in Upper Manhattan, with every single house showing or sale.

That very week, a different screenwriting real estate agent had witnessed an exchange that epitomized Harlem's fast-paced, gentrification-motored changes. She described a house off Mount Morris Park as completely gutted and sandwiched between two equally dilapidated row houses (one of them with a "deranged squatter" living inside). As if all of that were not enough, she said, the house also flaunts a caved-in roof that had somehow plunged all the way down to the ground floor. When you open the front door and walk inside you can look up and see the sky. A few years ago, even completely refurbished (and not yet replete with its windowless sunroof), the owners could hardly have gotten more than $100,000 for that house, the realtor guessed, and even that would have been wishful thinking. Now they are asking for $700,000. Not only that, they have already turned down a $675,000 offer. "The roof's in the basement," she reiterated. "Did I tell you that? I did say that, right? That's the kind of Harlem housing [market we have] right now. People are losing their minds. They see green, and they know it."

As I sit across from her in a Manhattanville eatery, I jot down the numbers feverishly, wanting to make sure that I get things exactly right: $675,000; $700,000. I have a cassette recorder in my bag, but she is leery about being taped, so I scribble sloppily instead. As I do, she reminds me that this very restaurant, the one I have taken her to for lunch this Saturday afternoon, is also a beneficiary of gentrification's changes, being the newest and most upscale business on a city block it shares with one Senegalese diner, several bodegas, and a Chinese take-out restaurant at the far northern corner. It is the latest addition to a bustling streetscape full of Latino toddlers and pre-teens on bicycles, African American seniors toting shopping carts from the catty-corner housing project, and white Columbia students softly disappearing into and out of their upstairs apartments.

The realtor emphasizes the fact that all the other patrons inside this restaurant are white, every last one, that is, except for the two of us. I assure her that I had already noticed and jotted that fact down: seventeen patrons, nineteen including us. She then launches into her theory of "the neighbor-hood squeeze," a version of social mobility in Harlem that is related (but not reducible) to gentrification. African Americans are in the middle of a double push, she says. Gentrification prices them out from the top; they cannot afford the rents for renovated apartments, she argues, which is why you have more and more Harlem restaurants patronized by more and more white customers. At the same time, "the rug is being pulled out from beneath them," as poorer Latinos and Africans, "people from overseas," are will-ing to pay more money for cheaper, unrenovated housing units. "They get squooshed in the middle," she offers, and they will eventually have to leave. "It's sad," she admits, "but I don't think it's anybody's fault. That's just how things go. You have to educate yourself if you want to stay here. They have to learn how to take advantage of the changes, if they can. If not, you won't be here for long."

Helping Homebuyers

I am using a Sony mini-DV camera to videotape the last-minute preparations for Harlem's Sixth Annual Community Homebuyers Fair. Everyone at the Greater Harlem Real Estate Board, a seventy-five-year-old nonprofit organi-zation, "the oldest African American housing trade association in the United States," is comparing notes for the next day's eight-hour event. They are expecting some fifteen thousand attendees, which would make it "the largest community-based Homebuyer's event in the nation."[6] With fiscal sponsor-ship from every major bank in New York City, the Homebuyer's Fair is billed as an opportunity to do exactly what the Harlem realtor-screenwriter advises: promote homeownership among poorer Harlem families. The fair does this by providing attendees with one-stop access to everything they might need for the process: "realtists, realtors, developers, building contractors, sup-pliers, mortgage lenders, financial planners, insurance specialists, architects, non-profit housing specialists, and government agents . . . free credit re-ports, pre-purchase affordability tests, as well as pre-qualifications and pre-approvals for mortgages," according to the *Harlem News*. There will be work-shops, seminars, and appearances by local and national celebrities—along with free Mister Softee ice cream for all those who arrive before supplies run out, not an unimportant perk on a hot July in the city.

Earlier that month, the head of Harlem's Real Estate Board took part in a Harlem Homeowner's event inside the Adam Clayton Powell State Office

Building, the very architectural backdrop for their Harlem Homebuyers Fair—and where I first met the aforementioned realtor and received my own "Arithmetic of the Avenues" bookmark. That same real estate company had sponsored a small gathering for current homeowners (the other side of that housing market transaction), giving them a sense of all the assistance potentially at their disposal whenever (and if ever) they decide to sell their Harlem properties. So you did not need to be actively selling anything to attend. Organizers just wanted homeowners to meet real estate agents who could answer any questions they might have about home-selling procedures. Again, I wielded my video camera, interviewing everyone I could find (estimators, lawyers, realtors, contractors—each with his or her own pamphlet-laden booth), asking them about what they stood to gain from such an event. Down to a person, they all toted basically the same party-line about making sure Harlem homeowners know they are around and available for consultation. The turnout was not as large as the real estate company had hoped, but it was still an upbeat afternoon, with attendees exchanging business cards and stories about their Harlem properties. "It is just about making contacts," one realtor offered, "a way to get your name out there and see where other people are at."

The executive director of the Harlem Real Estate Board was there to promote his upcoming Homebuyers Fair, along with a longer series of workshops throughout the year that were billed as "powerful, cost-effective homebuyer training services that inform, educate, empower, inspire, and motivate." They promised to "transform local residents into local Homeowners." He agreed to let us videotape their preparation for the Homebuyers Fair, which is why I had my camera in their faces as they went over last minute details before the big event. There were still portable toilets to pick up, workers to enlist, a few final hundred flyers to distribute, and a huge outdoor tent to construct. The main organizers (a group of some five part-time workers and a few more familial volunteers) mapped out their every step and stayed up all night to make sure that everything was taken care of. The next morning, on the day of the event, several thousand people (just about all of them black and/or Latino) snaked themselves around the block as they waited to register for admittance. Once they made it to the other side of the police barricades and into the tented affair, they found applications for unfinished townhouses and apartment buildings and over-sized blueprints and drawings, which were propped up securely on contiguous fold-out tables. They found booths full of legal aid attorneys and real estate developers. There were newly published homebuyer reference guides and table after table of soliciting realtors.

One of the first tables, closest to the entrance, included a pile of booklets on "Tenants' Rights," booklets produced by the state attorney general's office—the "tenant," of course, being the most explicitly invoked explanation for the homebuyer's fair in the first place. Turning renters into homeowners is the very raison d'être of the Harlem Real Estate Board, which has consulted with over 800 families and helped some 160 of them into their own new homes. After seven hours in the blazing sun, with Mr. Softee long gone, and even Congressman Rangel's rousing speech a distant memory, I see several journalists interviewing attendees about their assessments of the day's event. In a few days, local weeklies will officially proclaim the Real Estate Board's fair to be an unequivocal success, but for now the tents are not even down before organizers start thinking aloud about next year's exhibition. They might be able to get twenty thousand people out next summer.

Tenant Activists

There are clearly many more renting tenants than the Harlem Real Estate Board can ever fully house—and that lopsided fact is exactly what Netta Bradshaw, a local Harlem tenant activist, wants everyone to remember. She is part of a citywide network of urban activists from places such as Harlem, Chinatown, the Lower East Side, and Flatbush, Brooklyn, who are intent on keeping poorer tenants housed in their apartment buildings—even and especially in response to gentrification-specific pressures to oust them. Many of Bradshaw's clients could be found roaming around the tables at the Homebuyers Fair, trying to imagine a life without landlords and threats of eviction. In the name of these same tenants, activists like Bradshaw designate certain neighborhoods "Gentrification-free Zones," areas from within which they refuse to allow a single local tenant to be removed without public demonstrations and legal appeals.

"Everybody can't own a home in Harlem," Bradshaw says to me as we race through an obstacle course of people on Harlem's main thoroughfare. She is on her way to yet another meeting, already late and making it clear to me that my incessant questions will cause her to be even later. Still, she offers her take on things. It is important to debunk these myths from all comers, she says, to get the truth out there. "That's just unrealistic [thinking everyone can own a home]. We have to make sure that anyone can live with dignity and self-respect in this community. They don't deserve to be harassed by landlords or ignored by politicians because they don't have campaign contributions. That's what we're fighting against."

According to some activists, market-based incentives for removing tenants have seduced many an unscrupulous landlord into filing frivolous lawsuits in the hopes of ousting long-term tenants. And whom do they go after? Often, not so much African American residents as Panamanians, Dominicans, Haitians—and especially elderly female tenants for whom English is not their first language. This is one obvious inflection of gentrification's global relevance to local stories of residential displacement, an understanding of gentrification that spies a patterned manipulation of what might be called diasporic differences in the service of profiteering, with African Americans proportionally represented among the ranks of these overly litigious landlords. For Bradshaw, this is not just a race issue. It is also about class. "Owners and tenants have different incentives," she says. "And a lot of people will try to make money at the expense of other people if they have half the chance. And we don't want to give them that chance. Black, white, or whatever."

There are, according to Netta Bradshaw, at least two black middle classes in contemporary Harlem: the old guard that never left, and a newer group that has recently arrived. For many of the Harlem activists, these two black middle classes represent diametrically opposed interests—not least because the older guard views the younger set as a threat to their local authority. When newspapers and magazines represent the black powerbrokers of Harlem, they also use this dual model of older, liberal, civil rights patriarchs in one corner and newer, conservative, corporate-friendly upstarts in the other (Horowitz 1998). As overstated as the distinction might be, there are many ways in which activists like Bradshaw attempt to use such frameworks to re-educate tenants about class politics, complicating binary racial formulas for a schema that pits the older middle-class residents against newer ones, with poorer local tenants using that rift as a leverage-point for getting their demands heard and their needs addressed.

This discussion of the black middle class would also need to delineate another major fault line between and among Harlem's middle class members: (a) middle-class Harlemites who explain their relationship to the community in purely materialist, market-based claims, and (b) those who justify their presence as a function of race-based social community and commitment (M. Taylor 2002). For some, the aforementioned old-guard/new-guard divide graphs easily onto what I would call a market/membership distinction. For others, market and membership drives dissect old and new black middle classes alike. According to a long-time Harlem book vendor and resident, most of these newer middle-class arrivals are not even African American. "Just because somebody's got dark skin," he offers, smilingly, as Bradshaw and I stop to peruse the books displayed on his vending table, "that doesn't mean they deserve to be here. People fought for this community, and we got folks from all over the place coming in to capitalize on it, except for us, and not the *us* that just got off the boat from Africa or somewhere setting up a business to sell us nonsense. We gotta get rid of that foolishness. Black people gotta be smarter than that. These other people come here and buy cars and homes and live the lifestyle we say we want. They take our women, they take our money, and they take our destiny."

Veronica Boynton is head of a local homeowners association in Central Harlem. She arrived from Ohio over twenty years ago and was able to buy a brownstone in the community during Harlem's below-market, pregentrification days. She takes me on a tour of "the ruins," a local name for the string of nine infamous turn-of-the-century row houses that were seized by the government under eminent domain in the 1960s and slated for a drug rehabilitation center. Amid fierce resistance by nearby residents who were opposed to having such a center in their neighborhood, the plans were scrapped and the buildings left mostly in decay. Only the corner edifice was constantly used, most recently as a women's jail. The Community Preservation Corporation has finally turned the strip into a series of market-rate condominiums slated to sell for at least $225,000 each. To many tenant activists, this is just another example of "unbalanced" urban growth that privileges middle-class interests over the needs of poorer local Harlemites. For other residents, like Boynton, it is simply another feather in Harlem's cap—and a nice end to a long, embattled saga. Any other interpretation is just ridiculous.

"If you want to stay in Harlem," she says, "just pay your rent. That's it. Sure, we don't want landlords taking advantage of poor people, but we have courts to take care of that. It may not work perfectly, but it works. The only people not safe are those who don't want to pay their rent and need to be thrown out of here, and that's just a portion of the people who live here. Besides," she adds, "you look at some of these [tenant] activists; I never see black people in their offices. I used to work next to one, and I would watch the people who went in and out of there. They were all white people, so what kind of community are they talking about helping?"

Boynton and I are sitting at Settepani's, a two-year-old gourmet bakery on

Lenox Avenue, one of a cluster of smaller local businesses that are competing with corporate America for storefront space and empowerment zone money. My tape recorder rests on the table between us. I sip my iced tea and watch pedestrians traipsing past us on the sidewalk space out front. Settepani's is a trendy new business co-owned and run by an Ethiopian woman who greets me with a friendly smile of familiar recognition after only my second visit. Its well-prepared offerings are small and pricey; the menu is based on light tuna salads and an assortment of coffees; the staff is diasporic and multihued. It is the kind of establishment that members of both the new and old black middle classes look upon with pride. It is where Maya Angelou, a recent Harlem homeowner, takes many of her neighborhood meetings, where I once spotted Kareem Abdul-Jabar window-shopping outside, where residents convene midday for coffee and conversation. Well, maybe just certain residents.

Settepani's marks itself (and its surrounding sidewalk space) as a decidedly middle-class location. Across the street and within a stone's throw of Settepani's corner sign, abandoned buildings and un-air-conditioned chicken shacks serve as the stony backdrop in front of which local Harlemites chat and pass their time during the day, sitting atop milk cartons and fold-up chairs, sometimes playing dominoes, sometimes listening to music, sometimes just ogling passersby. Directly in front of Settepani's, however, the outdoor space is much more carefully configured. A row of too-small, lightweight dining tables and chairs align the storefront's exterior wall, chained and padlocked to one another and to the store's metallic storm gates. These outside seats and tables are as much about performances of middle classness as anything else. This is a rendition of public space with recognizably middle-class implications—and it signals, from afar, just who belongs and who does not. It is the counterpoint to the chicken shacks and graffiti-laden front stoops of establishments just across the street. It is a direct refusal of (and rejoinder to) these presentational alternatives. It is also what potentially flags the space as feminized and homosexual. One twenty-five-year-old Harlemite I know only ever describes the place as "faggoty." With clear implications for residential disqualification, this homophobic characterization is his most often-invoked reason for not wanting to eat there—an articulated connection between middle-class identity and sexual orientation that distinguishes their purported softness from more stereotypically hardened black masculinities.

These class-specific (and homosexualized) markings of space are some of the more obvious sites for social antagonisms and clear-cut displacements in a gentrifying Harlem. Whether or not poorer Harlemites are being displaced from their homes (with questions about just how quickly and substantially), there are very obvious examples of the ways in which middle-class usages of space (and a concomitant Disneyfication that evacuates all conspicuous class differences from the public sphere) evince a certain social displacement from public view, an obviously class-inflected loss of access to certain public locales (Zukin 1995). It is a displacement that, coupled with "quality of life" policing, fuels the fires of antagonism and rage along the cement sidewalk space of many urban cities.[7]

These kinds of class-related uses of sidewalk space are specifically important when we think about how public places gain personal, political, and private significances. Residents' paths to and from, say, laundromats and corner bodegas, Chinese or Senegalese restaurants, their children's public schools, and so on, become tiny patches of peripatetic privacy within an overdetermined landscape of market-based privatization. Pierre Mayol also calls these kinds of personal pathways forms of "privatization," a wonderful counterpoint to neoliberal notions of the private as ineluctably and exclusively linked to property ownership (de Certeau, Giard, and Mayol 1998). These intimate paths through public space are not equivalent to individual ownership in any simple sense. If anything, it is an ownership of space that money cannot actually buy.

Such a realization (that gentrification is as importantly about reprivatizing public spaces as it is about evicting building tenants) might mean imagining the activist and corporatist renditions of space (their mathematics of mobility and marketability, respectively) as two sides of the same quantificatory coin, analogous in many ways to the "Avenue of Arithmetic" equations that offer bird's eye and mathematized views of contemporary urban living. Instead, local actors can be seen vying for authority in a discussion about who is and is not a real Harlemite, about who does and does not truly belong, as a function of more than the fact that there are poorer residents who cannot afford six dollar salads at Settepani's. It is the same kind of distinction that frames conversations between (a) utilitarian neo-Harlemites who are unapologetically relocating for its cheaper rents and lower mortgage payments and (b) the counterclaims of racial communality that other middle-class blacks invoke to justify a belonging based on more than strict market privileges. This is just one of the fault lines along which a quantitative/qualitative divide organizes discussions about belonging—and about how a look at the remainders (what's left out of popular mathematics of Manhattan) might also allow us to spy other forms of urbanity in contemporary black America.

Notes

1. The acronyms refer to South (of) Harlem, North (of) Harlem, and Spanish Harlem. These names operate as euphemisms for the designation Harlem, which connotes a world of African American residential difference and danger.

2. For other recent ethnographic engagements with contemporary Harlem as a demographic site, see J. Jackson 2001, Stoller 2002, and M. Taylor 2002.

3. For a critique of statistical mobilizations of race, see Zuberi 2001. For a discussion of anthropological roots in realism, see Elliott 2002. For an argument about what a different kind of visualization might add to multivariate statisticalization, see Krempel and Plumper 2003. For an overview of "rule bound systems" analysis as a mechanism for using math to test certain cultural characteristics and trait frequencies among social groups, see Ballonoff 1976.

4. Grier and Grier (1980) provide an early operationalization of dislocation; Lee and Hodge (1984) exempt occurrences like natural disasters and come up with a national rate of 3 percent. Ley (1993) compares six Canadian cities in the 1980s. Schill and Nathan (1983) focus exclusively on rates of dislocation in gentrifying neighborhoods, while Atkinson (2000) compares gentrifying neighborhoods with nongentrifying ones.

5. Working with Boston data from the late 1980s, Vigdor (2001) finds that "low-status families" in gentrifying neighborhoods have lower rates of displacement than do other families in the same gentrifying circumstances. Freeman and Braconi (2002) make a similar argument based on New York City data from the 1990s.

6. These quotes are all from the organization's in-house pamphlets, posters, and other literature—as well as an article about the fair in a free local weekly, *Harlem News*, July 21, 2003: 9.

7. For a discussion of "quality of life" policing, see Wilson and Kelling (1982).

RECASTING "BLACK VENUS" IN THE "NEW" AFRICAN DIASPORA

JAYNE O. IFEKWUNIGWE

There are a number of ideas that attempt to draw together new African diasporas by looking backwards to an ideal African homeland and to sets of Afro-centric values that stream from this common origin. Beneath the pan-African imagined global networks, however, run fluid discursive structures that blur conventional and taken-for-granted classificatory practices with emergent nodes of cultural identity that we have yet to imagine.... There is no trans-historical box large enough to contain such disparate and heterogeneous processes, rather linkages must be accounted for with greater care and specificity.

—Donald Carter, Preface to *New African Diasporas*

Much theorizing on and periodizing of the African Diaspora[1] either privileges the narrative of transatlantic slavery or addresses the social and historical processes of imperialism and (post)colonialism (Koser 2003).[2] These earlier circuits of trade, processes of settlement, and political economic regimes created similar and different points of reference for African diasporic constituents, be they in the Americas, the Caribbean, or Europe. However, in the twenty-first century, there are new epistemologies of the African Diaspora, which are not predicated on current problematic distinctions between "authentic" diasporas of transatlantic slavery and to a certain extent (post)colonialisms and *faux* diasporas ("economic" migrations) (Butler 2001). In particular, I am referring to clandestine movements "by any means necessary" of the unwanted and the impoverished from structurally (mal)adjusted West African urban centers to economically and demographically restructured western and southern European metropoles (Harding 2000). What motivates West African migrants is the promise of European Union (EU) wages "10–15 times higher than in Africa . . . [given] the [GDP] gap between the EU and the less-developed non-EU Mediterranean [and sub-Saharan African] countries" (Gold 2000: 133). At every stage of the migration process, strategies are highly gendered (Morris 2002). That is, West African clandestine migrant women and men may share a similar destination, but by virtue of their "glocalized" (Robertson 1995) structural positions, their destinies will be very different: "If one asks a recently arrived migrant woman today where the opportunities for work lie in Europe, she will tell you that apart from sex work or domestic work, the avenues for employment are closed to her" (Westwood and Phizacklea 2000: 131). Conventionally, these contemporary continental African dispersals have been analyzed either utilizing traditional tropes of "push/pull" migration or place them within the broader contexts of European asylum and immigration discourses. I argue for the reassessment of recent clandestine West African migrations as culturally specific, differentially gendered, and similarly racialized new African Diasporas, which are situated inside, and not outside, the latest political economic circuits of global capitalism (Akyeampong 2003; International Organization for Migration 1996). By placing trafficked Nigerian migrant women sex workers in Italy at the center of my analysis, I intend to provoke a rethinking of what constitutes volition, agency, and victimhood in theorizing about the politics of race in the African Diaspora in particular and diasporas in general (Braziel and Mannur 2003; Anthias 1998).

This essay represents one facet of a broader ongoing theoretical project, which, using the transnational circulation of people as a paradigm, rethinks the gendered relationship between continental Africa and the African Diaspora. Rather than treating contemporary processes of continental African migration as separate entities outside the diaspora paradigm, I outline a theoretical formulation that assumes their interconnectedness and demonstrates their dynamism. To test this reformulation in current everyday lived contexts, I address the newest layer of African Diasporas, which have resulted from recent continental African dispersals to Europe. These transnational migratory processes include the smuggling of West African (and North African) women and men via Morocco to southern Spain—the gateway to Fortress Europe (Harding 2000); the trafficking in West African (in particular

Nigerian) women to Italy as part of the global sex trade (Aghatise 2002); and the strategic and "voluntary" migrations of West Africans (once again mostly Nigerian) to the Republic of Ireland (E. J. White 2002). In the cases of both Spain and Ireland, the arrival of pregnant West African migrant women, who subsequently give birth on Spanish and Irish soil, has generated significant religious and political debates about the limits of citizenship and contingent definitions of family (Lentin 2003).

In the following discussion, I will highlight two of the theoretical strands that comprise my current thinking on complex, compound, and new African diasporic formations (Koser 2003; Stoller 2002). First, I position contemporary documentary film representations of trafficked Nigerian sex workers in Italy in dialogical relation to nineteenth-century discourses of black sexuality—in particular, Sharpley-Whiting's reinscribed "Black Venus master narrative"—and assess historical and geographical (dis)continuities in their modes of signification. Second, by linking endemic factors feeding the supply of Nigerian women for the purposes of (in)voluntary participation in the Italian sex industry, such as the localized feminization of poverty and regionally specific perceptions of sex work as a temporary economic strategy, I address the extent to which women can both be victims and exercise agency. Their victimization stems from their plight as unemployed or unskilled young women with a limited range of available options "back home." Even if agency is partial, delayed, or never achieved, for conscripts and their extended families back in Nigeria, (in)voluntary conscription for participation in the migrant sex worker industry in Italy holds "the promise" of economic empowerment. The emergent and existing literature on trafficked Nigerian sex workers in Italy does not explore the full extent of this individual and familial strategizing. In this new trade encounter, the ways in which old racialized stereotypes about black female sexuality are trafficked and commodified have also not been scrutinized in relation to the changing relevance of race and blackness in particular. This essay outlines a dialectics of structure and agency (Alexander and Mohanty 1997) as well as the feminized interface between processes of racialized embodiment and sexualized commodification (Collins 2004).

In the next section, I critique a 2002 Channel Four British television documentary on the politics of illegal immigration in Italy that highlighted the status of two groups of undocumented youth who are both workers in the informal economy: trafficked Nigerian sex workers and smuggled Albanian migrant men. This critical reading, which specifically addresses filmic repre-

sentations of only the first group of "subjects," is the starting point for a
" 'deterritorialized' practice that deals with inequities not only in that 'other
[Nigerian] place,' but also in one's 'own' [European] community" (Behar
1995: 22). My deployment of documentary film, which relies on "evidence" to
verify its authenticity and reliability, is not accidental (Trinh 1991). In this
genre, the subject, in this instance black female undocumented migrant sex
workers, must submit to the higher power of the filmmakers and their audience (Trinh 1989).

(Mis)Representing "Foreign Bodies" in the Italian-
African Diaspora

I also hope to avoid the rather wooden presentation of notions of "Otherness," so common in
work on representations of the socially oppressed, whether women, black people or working-
class people. This ends up by placing the oppressed as objects within a previously concep-
tualised framework that denies them any conscious potential to refuse their place within this
framework or to challenge it. We can certainly try to deconstruct images to attempt to
understand their meanings in terms of ideology and how that ideology is visualised, however,
every deconstruction is also an act of construction.
—Gen Doy, "More than Meets the Eye"

In an unspoken negotiation, creators and spectators retrieve mythologized
images of both the hypersexual black female and the clandestine migrant sex
worker as polluted interlopers, which provide missing symbolic links between
what exists on the moving frame and "realities" before and beyond: "The new
sociohistorical text thus rules despotically as another master [mistress]-
centered text, since it unwillingly helps to perpetuate the Master's [Mistress's]
ideological stance (Trinh 1991: 42). In my reframing, I inscribe both a "black
female gaze" (Roach and Felix 1989) and a critical black anthropological
perspective that problematize the ways in which dominant Eurocentric and
essentialist ideologies of Africa and the African Diaspora are reproduced
(Ginsburg 2002; Harrison 1991). By an oppositional black feminist gaze, I
mean an engaged and enraged standpoint that is situated in alternative and
empowering frameworks (hooks 1992; (charles) 1997; Abraham 2002).

I am mindful of the possibility that in the process of constructing counterhegemonic discourses (Harrison 1995) I am indeed reproducing the precise iconography I am attempting to critique: "the insistence of the image and
its signification, in this case the sexualised, colonised female African body,

can simply collapse into restatement" (Edwards 2001: 196). I may also be accused of reinstating a First World feminist hegemony (Ong 1995; Spivak 1988). Oyewumi's astute terms for this imposed recapitulation are the "bio-logic of the sisterarchy" (1997: 11). Neither is my intention. Instead, the plight of debt-bonded Nigerian sex workers in Europe functions as a symbolic lens through which to critically view the "changing same" economic, social, and political positions of multiplex black women in the African Diasporas (Gilliam 2001; Terborg-Penn and Benton Rushing 1996).

On January 13, 2002, here in the United Kingdom, as part of a Channel Four series on contemporary Tuscany, a program aired which dramatically destabilized notions of social progress in media portrayals of contemporary, gendered, African diasporic processes. The piece, entitled "Foreign Bodies," addressed the plight of young Nigerian women who had been trafficked for the purposes of participation in the lucrative global sex trade. What was most troubling was the sensationalized and overtly sexist and racist angle chosen by the filmmakers. The English producer of the series, Catherine Bailey, and the Italian director of "Foreign Bodies," Enrica Colusso, are both white. Their intentions may have been honorable—they did highlight forms of victimiza-tion and agency—and their primary motivation may have been to expose these young women's desperate situation. Overall, though, their particular portrayals of black women reproduced negative representations (hooks 1991) and thus indicated the extent to which, in the words of the late great Audre Lorde: "the work [and experiences] of women of Color is [still] being ghet-toized by a white [wo]man dealing only out of a patriarchal western euro-pean [sic] frame of reference" (1984: 68).

The opening description by the documentary's male narrator falls into the problematic trap of describing black women as part of the naturalistic sur-roundings: "an extraordinary spectacle" dotting the Italian landscape. The objectifying description of the behavior of the arrested Nigerian prostitutes as animalistic and "primitive"—"biting . . . smearing police with menstrual blood . . . raining voodoo curses" (Channel Four, 2002)—is consistent with nineteenth-century 'race' science fictional representations of black and Afri-can people as socially and morally degenerate (Abraham 2002; Collins 1990; Walker 1971). A white male journalist, who reviewed "Foreign Bodies" for the New Statesman, also fails to contexualize, humanize, or address the political and economic complexities of this "phenomenon" and instead asserts his male privilege as the spectator not the spectacle: "I once nearly crashed a hired car on the road from Siena to Florence. I would have plead temporary insanity, caused by the sudden appearances around the corner of a flock of beautiful black African women dressed in bras and hot pants—a vision I would have dismissed as a trick of a diseased mind, had the scene not been repeated shortly afterwards, thigh for thigh, in Bernardo Bertolucci's film 'Stealing Beauty' " (Billen 2002).

There are disturbing parallels between the early-nineteenth-century objectification and exploitation of Khoikhoi Saartjie Baartman, also known as the Hottentot Venus, who due to the size of her protruding buttocks was exhibited in London and Paris as a representation of deviant sexuality, and this film's lingering shots of Nigerian sex workers' backsides (E. F. White 2001; Hammonds 1997). In her insightful and provocative book, *Black Venus: Sexualized Savages, Primal Fears and Primitive Narratives in French,* Sharpley-Whiting (1999) refers to this as an invocation of the "Black Venus master narrative." Though primarily engaging with nineteenth- and twentieth-century French representations of black women from the Hottentot Venus to Josephine Baker, throughout the text and explicitly in the epilogue, Sharpley-Whiting argues that the Black Venus master narrative is reasserted in other European/colonial milieux and in contemporary historical moments: "Black women, embodying the dynamics of racial/sexual alterity, historically invoking *primal fears* and desire in European (French) men, represent ultimate difference (the *sexualized savage*) and inspire repulsion, attraction, and anxiety, which gave rise to the collective French male imaginations of Black Venus (*primitive narratives*)" (1999: 6, emphases in original text).

Sharpley-Whiting's study is also a critique of the influential work of Sander Gilman (1985a and b), in particular *Difference and Pathology*, wherein he argues that the black female body was the lens through which forms of deviant white female sexuality were viewed. Gilman's metaphorical white-centered stance provides the reader with very little information about Baartman[3] herself, rendering her at once highly visible but yet textually silent. In "Foreign Bodies," the "subaltern does speak" (Spivak 1988), but her words are drowned out by the deafening voices of patriarchy, scientific racism, and neocolonialism (Hammonds 1997).

The film highlights the fact that the Catholic Church is one of the main Italian institutions campaigning for the emancipation of Nigerian prostitutes and administering aid. The rehabilitation strategies of church-based "protection" programs encourage victims to atone for their transgressions by denouncing their traffickers and/or madams. In return, they are offered "salvation" in the form of accommodation, employment, residency permits, or repatriation and family reunification (Crane 2001). This paternalistic intervention is a thriving relic of the civilizing missions of the past wherein religion was part and parcel of imperial conquest (Oyewumi 1997; C. Hall 2002).[4] What this documentary does reveal in a lucid fashion are the gendered and racialized hierarchies within global sex work, which force feminist debates beyond issues of morality, prevention, and protection.

By reinscribing "Black Venus," I am not simply suggesting that Khoikhoi Saartjie Baartman from the Cape Colony, South Africa, displayed in nineteenth-century Paris and London, and Bini women from Edo State, Nigeria, working in the sex trade in twenty-first century Florence, are the sum total of their inscribed black bodies (Marshall 1996). Such an oversimplification feeds into the false European "brain"/African "body" dichotomy (Bordo 1993; Butchart 1998; Davis 1997), perpetuates the Africa as monolith figuration (Appiah 1992; Mudimbe 1994) still prevalent in media imaginings of this vast and heterogeneous continent,[5] and ignores the ways in which conceptions of black female sexuality shift across time and space (Gilliam 2001; Shaw 2001). Rather, as Magubane argues in her brilliant critique of the "theoretical fetishization of Hottentot Venus":

> Baartman represented far more in the European imagination than a collection of body parts. Indeed, closer examination of the furor that ensued in the wake of her exhibition demonstrates that what she represented varied (as ideologies are wont to do) according to the social and political commitments of the interested social actors. Baartman's exhibition provoked varying and contradictory responses. These responses are better understood if they are analyzed as part and parcel of larger debates about liberty, property, and economic relations, rather than seeing them as simple manifestations of the universal human fascination with embodied difference. (2001: 827)

When recasting "Black Venus" in the contemporary transnational sites of Italy and Nigeria, Magubane's conceptual frame facilitates a deeper understanding of complicated and triangulated dynamics involving various "social actors" with differential access to liberty, property, and economic resources. Severe poverty "back home" rather than the marketability of black female sexuality "abroad" is the main catalyst for the migration of young female labor (Ume-Ezeoke 2003; Okojie et al. 2003). This "skin trade" conscription process involves multiple actors and agents, including entire families, who may be partially motivated by the prospect of status enhancement:

Our study has confirmed the hypothesis that sending female children abroad has, in most cases, become a sort of status symbol for families. This is as a result of the breakdown of social and cultural values, the disintegration of traditional family structures, and the lack of valid, efficient social reference models in substitution. Most families interviewed tacitly accepted the idea of prostitution as a solution where extreme poverty has made life difficult. They were, however, less ready to accept this when the violence and humiliation involved in it was made clear to them. Thus feminisation of poverty comes to have the greatest expression in the sale of female children into trafficking for prostitution. (Aghatise 2002: 7)

Once trafficked to Italy, in presentations of self and the provision of sexual services, "*Italos* in the skin trade"—the Nigerian term used to describe the workers and their work—actively deploy prevailing universalized stereotypes of deviant black female sexuality as "marketing strategies" (Spanger 2002). Writing about the ways in which the sexual iconography of the Hottentot Venus in particular and black women in general represented unbridled sexuality, Gilman suggests that "the primitive is the black, and the qualities of blackness, or at least of the black female, are those of the prostitute" (1985b: 99). These Italos are themselves controlled by madams,[6] who dictate the stringent terms and conditions of their employment. Both madams and Italos are economically dependent on the demands of their indigenous Italian male clients for Nigerian female sex workers: "how the body is marked is integral to the commodity exchanged" (Sanchez Taylor 2000: 50). What I am arguing is that although nineteenth-century colonial stereotypes of the Third World woman of color as exotic and sexually uninhibited are recycled in the twenty-first century global sex trade (Kempadoo 1998, Sanchez Taylor 2000), the gendered, racialized, and economic relations of power deeply embedded in all of these encounters and negotiations must be interpreted inside not outside the feminized circuits of global capitalism and underdevelopment (di Cortemiglia 2003; Prina 2003).

The Cultural Politics of Transnational Sex Work and the Traffic in Nigerian Women

Trafficking in women is an international problem often involving complex transnational and criminal elements. It is also, however, simultaneously an immigration issue, a labor issue, and a gender issue, requiring a frame that encompasses analyses of immigration, labor, race, and gender (Berman 2003: 39). In this section, in an attempt to rethink the changing face of race in the globalizing context, I will address endemic factors feeding the supply of women for the purposes of sexual exploitation, such as the localized feminization of poverty as well as the ways in which the social functions of sex work intersect with other Nigerian social relations. Under capitalism, sex work becomes wage labor and thus is susceptible to exploitation (Weitzer 2000; Hennessy 2000).

Although transnational sex work is not a new practice, as capitalism has globalized in search of cheap labor so has the sex industry (Ryan and Hall 2001; Kempadoo 1999). In other words, the ideology of cheap sex is synonymous with the ideology of cheap goods and cheap labor (Clift and Carter 2000). It is "exotic" migrant women from eastern Europe, Asia, Africa, and Latin America who satisfy this First World consumer demand for inexpensive and "unique" sexual services: "Prostitution across borders has increased in the last twenty to thirty years . . . the number of women who migrate to richer countries from poorer and work in prostitution has also grown. The differences in circumstances of migrant prostitutes are vast. Some may have been cheated or forced into the trade; others have chosen it voluntarily, knowing what the work entails, and some have had experience of prostitution both at home and abroad before travelling" (Thorbek 2002: 1).

Of the myriad routes into transnational migrant sex work, the most disempowering and exploitative is via trafficking, wherein the inflated and exorbitant debt for services rendered by traffickers and their associates (provision of false documentation, arranging travel, securing accommodation and employment in destination countries) is recovered from the young woman or child's limited future earnings (E. Taylor 2002). In the case of trafficked Nigerian migrant sex workers in Italy, the imposed and enforced debts range from "sixty million Italian Liras (ITL) (about USD $30,000 by current exchange rates) to a hundred and twenty million ITL (about USD $60,000) . . . the girls charge an average of twenty thousand ITL (USD $10/15) per client and at times, as little as ten thousand ITL (USD $5)" (Aghatise 2002: 5). While the existence of this new form of sexualized globalization is rarely disputed, due to its clandestine and illegal nature there are significant discrepancies in "official" statistical accounts of its extent (Thorbek 2002). In an important analysis of European sex-trafficking discourses, Berman observes:

The International Organization for Migration's (IOM) estimate of 500,000 women annually trafficked into Western Europe redundantly appears in media and official documents, adding social scientific authenticity to the claim that this is an immense problem. Figures range from "175,000 women and girls . . . taken into the EU illegally every year" to "epidemic proportions" of "700,000 to 1 million women and children sold into modern day slavery. . . ." The United Nations estimates the worldwide profit to be "$7 billion a year" while others claim that "mobsters on every continent . . . pocket an estimated 12 billion each year from the sex trade." (2003: 65)

In contrast, there is consensus regarding the ways in which the increased presence of Third World trafficked women in First World sex industries further complicates debates on the empowerment and/or victimization of "working women" (Andrijasevic 2003; Pattanaik 2002).

In the global sex work literature, the term "sex worker" is advocated in order to distinguish the pathological social characterization "whore" from the form of income-generating labor performed by women (and men) (Doezema 1998). If prostitution is seen as work, then the rights of those exploited can be protected. Current debates center on the extent to which sex workers can both be victims and exercise agency (Chapkis 2000). In addition, distinctions are made between voluntary ("guilty") and forced ("innocent") prostitution, that is, women who have been trafficked and are thus in debt bondage—a form of slavery (A. Murray 1998). As Bindman suggests: "in the case of the sex industry, the ending of slavery-like practices is held back by the distinction between sex workers or prostitutes and other workers" (1998: 66). Global sex work activists argue that a strictly abolitionist agenda deprives sex workers who have not been trafficked of their human rights as laborers: "We in the human rights field must work alongside efforts towards economic justice, towards viable economic alternatives for everyone, ending vulnerability to slavery-like practices. . . . Let us fight laws which exclude women in the sex industry from society and which deprive them of the rights that everyone else enjoys, at least on paper. Let us fight exploitation in every form" (Bindman 1998: 68). As such, sex trafficking is at once a development, a feminist, and a political economic problematic.

It is worth noting that just as not all sex workers are trafficked nor is all trafficking in women confined to sex work, "'traffic in women' is a broad category covering various forms of exploitation and violence within a range of informal labor sectors that migrant women work, including prostitution, entertainment industries and domestic work" (Wijers 1998: 70). Trafficked women in general are extremely vulnerable and are frequently at the mercy of violent criminal networks (Bales 2000). What is particular about trafficked sex workers is their double stigmatization: first as illegal migrants and second as prostitutes (Lederer 2001). The Italian findings of a recent multisited (Nigeria and Italy) collaborative social science research project on trafficking from Nigeria into Italy, which was commissioned by the United Nations Interregional Crime and Justice Research Institute (UNICJRI) as part of the Programme of Action against Trafficking in Minors and Young Women from Nigeria into Italy for the Purpose of Sexual Exploitation, support the notion that trafficked sex work is a double bind:

> Even for those who choose to come to Italy knowing that they are coming to prostitute themselves, the discovery of the way of work, the entity of the debt that must be repaid and the conditions of life and work ahead of them produces discouragement and rethinking. What prevails at this point is a sense of impotence and isolation. The girls find themselves in a foreign country, without family support and without any possibility of contact [sic] friends and parents possibly present in Italy or Europe. . . . Without documents, taken away or immediately destroyed, without the minimum idea of how to escape their destiny, frightened by the threats of action against the family and with the fear of the negative influences of wodo,[7] sometimes subjected to physical violence, they wind up doing the will of their "owners"[:] starting the activity of a prostitute. (Prina 2003: 47)

These unnamed migrant sex workers comprise an ever expanding army of Nigerian surplus labor: "None of these girls or women would be in the streets of Europe and the other parts of the world selling their bodies had IBB [Ibrahim Badamosi Babangida] and Abacha not handicapped Nigeria and bequeathed economic hardship upon us. It is true that prostitution is a problem, but we need to put the blames [sic] where they belong" (Evbayiro 2000).

Their passages from Nigeria and processes of settlement in Italy are frequently orchestrated and facilitated by crime syndicates, which, capitalizing on desperation and misery, run a lucrative trade in female cargo. These carriers are part of but not necessarily connected to a global, highly organized, and sophisticated communication system for the transportation of undocumented sex workers: "We are talking about a country [Nigeria] that is increasingly claiming the premier position in the exportation of prostitutes to Europe. . . . Our exports in this regard are equaling our oil exports to the western world" (David-West 2002).

The Nigerian research team's extensive report, which was produced for the aforementioned collaborative UNICJRI social science research project on trafficking from Nigeria into Italy, supports David-West's claim:

> The scanty data available suggest that trafficking in women and minors to Italy has been increasing over time, from when the flow started in the late 1980s. . . . Most of the women trafficked out of Nigeria for prostitution are from Edo State. Some of these victims are minors, that is, they are below age 18 years. . . . Reasons why Edo women are involved in trafficking include: the low valuation of women reflected in limited access to education, employment and income earning opportunities. Other reasons are poverty, greed, peer group influence . . . ignorance of the types and conditions of work in Italy. A few success stories, usually of victims who have become madams, have proved sufficient to lure young girls and their relations (parents, brothers, sisters, and even husbands) to be involved in trafficking. The devaluation of the Naira whereby a few units of foreign currency convert into thousands of Naira also encourages the youth to desire to leave the country to do any type of job. (Okojie et al. 2003: 127)

The most intriguing finding of Okojie et al.'s (2003) study, which has also been reported elsewhere (Ume-Ezeoke 2003; Prina 2003; di Cortemiglia 2003), has to do with the overrepresentation of women from one particular region in southern Nigeria. That is, it is estimated that up to 80 percent of girls and women trafficked to Italy from Nigeria for sex work come from Edo State in general, Benin City in particular (Aghatise 2002). There are two explanations for this trend. The first, a multifaceted structural and political analysis, has already been provided by Okojie et al. (2003). The second is that since the late 1980s as a direct result of the failed structural adjustment regime implemented by the IMF/World Bank, Nigerian women and men have been smuggled or trafficked into Europe, where they have contributed to informal economies, such as itinerant tomato picking in the Italian agricultural industry (Ume-Ezeoke 2003). Over time, laborers drifted into cities, and the women discovered another market within which to sell their labor, so much so that turf wars ensued between Nigerian and Italian sex workers. Benin City gained a national reputation as the headquarters for illegal immigration fixers (Advocacy Project 2003).

Therefore, some migrant sex workers may not "originate" from Edo State, but that is where their hopeful journeys begin. In this twenty-first century skin trade, though the modes of transport and the destinations have changed, Benin's former prominence as one of West Africa's slave trading centers has been restored.

There are other complex reasons for this booming export business, which have less to do with the victimization of vulnerable young women and more to do with the problematics of cultural translation and (re)territorialization (Inda and Rosaldo 2002). In their trail-blazing work, Nigerian scholars Amadiume (1987) and Oyewumi (1997) compare the more egalitarian gender systems which existed in pre-colonial Igbo and Yoruba societies to the Western binary sex/gender system predicated on the devaluation of women (Goddard 2000), which was inherited by Nigeria as part of the British colonial project. They also demonstrate the deleterious impact on local "traditions" of these racist and patriarchal institutions, which were maintained in the (post)colonial milieu (Amadiume 1987; Oyewumi 1997). As such, in form and function, localized and indigenous Nigerian conceptions of sex work both differ from and mirror their Western counterparts. More specifically, sex work did exist in precolonial Nigeria, was reinvented as part of the colonial encounter, and has been transformed in (post)colonial Nigeria (Little 1973; Mama 1997).

In his survey entitled *Prostitution and Society: Primitive, Classical and Oriental*, Henriques (1962) identified three types of African sex work, which included precolonial forms institutionalized by both the Nupe and Hausa of Nigeria in order to circumvent strict traditional codes of sexual morality. In (post)colonial Nigeria, the dividing line between social relations and sexual services is not clearly demarcated:

"So common has prostitution become, and so widespread, that some are unable to see a distinction between prostitutes and those who are not. In Akure, the capital of the cocoa producing Ondo State, residential prostitutes are scarcely to be found. Yet girls, especially students of secondary schools, colleges of education, as well as workers, can be seen laundering their boredom at drinking and eating places, waiting for customers" (*African Guardian* 1987 cited in Amadiume 2000: 139).

What these fuzzy social borders illustrate is how in a context wherein

40 percent of the "developing world" lives in cities, "structurally adjusted urbanism" becomes a way of life (Centner 2002). That is, global economic policies do have an impact on local urban social practices (Ogden 1996). Nigeria is the most densely populated country on the continent and one of the wealthiest, yet nowhere are the failures of structural adjustment and fiscal mismanagement more apparent than in Nigeria (Maier 2000). An attorney and a former senior investigator for the U.S. Senate, Jack Blum (2002) estimates that since colonial independence from Britain in 1960, at least $120 billion has been stolen from the government's coffers by corrupt politicians and military dictators such as Babangida and Abacha.

The on-the-ground ramifications of such poor governance have a human cost and more specifically a female face. That is, on the African continent in general and Nigeria in particular, women from particular regions (i.e., Edo and Delta States) and specific sectors of society (young, poor, relatively uneducated) are increasingly embracing sex work as an economic survival strategy, what Iliffe describes as "subsistence prostitution" (cited in Farmer et al. 1996a: 159). Ifi Amadiume (2000) attributes its feminized persistence and its growth to the unhealthy state of the Nigerian economy as well as to the failure of the aforementioned externally imposed but locally implemented structural adjustment programs:

> Because of the direct economic relationship between women and prostitution, we find that prostitutes are mostly mothers—widows, divorcees and unemployed teenagers. Most Nigerian female prostitutes go into the business to raise the capital to begin a trade or to educate their children. Many "retire" after they have achieved their goals, and many become "somebody." The post-colonial culture in Nigeria is such that "money talks"—i.e. wealth is respected, regardless of the means by which it is acquired. (Amadiume 2000: 138)

A study of sex workers in Nigeria, cited in John Anarfi's chapter on Ghanaian sex workers in Cote d'Ivoire in *Global Sex Workers*, also highlights the perceived "use value" of sexual labor in the present as a means of securing economic stability in the future: "A recent study of prostitutes in Nigeria (Orubuloye et al. 1994) asserts that the women who engage in prostitution regard it as a transient phase in their lives. The study notes that in order to ensure a later life of marriage, business ownership and respectability in one's area of origin, it is necessary that the transient period as a prostitute be spent far away" (1998: 112).

Niger-Thomas's research among women smugglers who operate between Cameroon and Nigeria illustrates a direct link between sex work and other income generating activities: "There is indeed an historical connection between prostitution and trade: an occupational shift from prostitution to entrepreneurship. Some of the women smugglers were former prostitutes who were used to money, nice clothes, good food and drink, and other forms of luxury and saw smuggling as an easy way to earn more money" (2001: 63).

To summarize, after first situating this case study within the broader contexts of the global sex work and migration literatures and their concomitant feminist debates, I have then highlighted the different "glocalized" ways in which sex work is deployed by young Nigerian women as a mode of either survival or economic enhancement.[8]

Conclusion

With the strategies and struggles of trafficked Nigerian sex workers as my object of analysis, I have illustrated the complexity of gendered life ways in the age of globalization and transnationalism, wherein universalist conceptions of sex work as merely the exchange of sex for money are entirely too simplistic (Tandia 1998). I have demonstrated that sociopolitical constructions of "Nigerian women" can no longer be exclusively confined to national boundaries or specific localities (Mustapha 1985) or simple conceptions of race or citizenship. Trafficked Nigerian sex workers exemplify the intersectionality of continental African and "new" Italian-African diasporic subjectivities (Greenleaves 2000). There is a lived tension between the migrants' desire for eventual repatriation back to Nigeria (with elevated status and a bulging bank balance) and the harsh social realities for undocumented trafficked migrant workers owing huge debts to their sponsors. This dialectic is emblematic of the Nigerian-diasporic nexus (Marble 1996). Young women's initial and strategic embrace of sex work in Italy as a temporary economic strategy is motivated by a genuine wish to provide for themselves and their extended families "back home" (Sassen 1999). Once settled in Italy, their vulnerable status as illegal immigrants deprives them of the rights and entitlements afforded citizens and designated refugees (Daniel 2002). This marginalization is compounded by everyday racism and threats of violence (Prina 2003). Daily survival dictates that young women create support systems, pool resources (i.e., share housing and information), maintain transnational links (i.e., send remittances and correspondence to family in Nigeria), and re-negotiate meanings of community and belonging:

> The cosmopolitanism of migrants has entailed the proliferation of illegal or clandestine spaces. This can be seen in the existence of genuine un-official towns constituted by so-called illegal immigrants. It can also be seen in the flexible practices adopted by illegal immigrants in the country of reception, and in the xenophobia which contributes to confining them to legal obscurity. In these spheres of illegality, marginality might favor the reconstruction of complex forms of community life. (Mbembe 2001b: 11)

Regarding this transnational circuit between Nigeria and Italy and the domestic deficits in knowledge and opportunity that perpetuate the cycle, developmental, discursive interventions tend to emphasize the victimized status of women at the expense of their current agency and future empower-ment (Mama 1997). Amartya Sen's insistence that the ultimate goal of de-velopment is freedom strikes a more appropriate balance: "The extensive reach of women's agency is one of the more neglected areas of development studies, and most urgently in need of correction. Nothing, arguably, is as important today in the political economy of development as an adequate recognition of political, economic and social participation and leadership of women" (1999: 203).

In the long and the short term, ameliorating poverty and gender inequali-ties must be at the top of any development agenda and is an important route toward the sustained empowerment of African girls and women in all their diversity (Moser 1993; Kolawole 1997). There have been successful initia-tives, which simultaneously address processes of underdevelopment, gen-der inequities, and human rights (Brussa 1998; "Ending the Global Sex Trade" 2000). These more multipronged interventions do acknowledge the voluntary/involuntary sex worker distinction but the intervening emphasis is on female educational empowerment and poverty reduction in "sending" countries and immigration policy reform and the decriminalization of un-documented migrant sex work in "receiving" countries (D'Cunha 2002; Giammarinaro 2002).[9]

The trafficking in Nigerian women for the purposes of (in)voluntary participation in the Italian sex industry is but one example of the gendered dynamics of clandestine global migration processes:

The growth of a global economy has brought with it an institutional framework that facilitates cross-border flows and represents, in that regard, an enabling environment for these alternative circuits. It is increasingly on the backs of women that these forms of survival, profit making and government revenue enhancement operate. . . . Linking these counter-geographies to programs and conditions at the heart of the global economy also helps us to understand how issues of gender enter into their formation and viability. (Sassenb 2000: 512–13)

The case study of Nigeria shows us that the human face of global migration is increasingly young, female, black, and African (Joyce 1999; Kofman et al. 2000). These new nomadic communities are part of the latest global forced migration system, which in turn grew out of the earlier globalizing phases of transatlantic slavery and empire (Narayan 1997). They represent what Catherine Hall (2004) describes as a "reconfiguration of colonial relations," wherein the North and South are still connected by the sinews of inequality and subordination (Hardt and Negri 2000). In light of these (re)territorializing processes of migration, which transport workers from African to European metropoles, new gendered African diasporic differences must be situated in appropriate historical, social, cultural, and geopolitical contexts, which we must now refashion as merely "one node in a [post]national network of diasporas" (Appadurai 1996: 171). Rethinking African Diasporas necessitates the simultaneous pivoting of the conceptual axes of time, space, and shifting condition (Gilroy 1993; Schipper 1999). Rather than mapping specific diasporic communities on to particular (post)colonial landscapes, the analytic framework within which we must build new theories is one based on the simultaneity of transnational existences and of (post)national life-worlds and material-worlds rooted in multiple fusions and confusions (Busia 2000; Westwood and Phizacklea 2000; Sassen 2000a and 2000b).[10] More recent migrants and refugees from continental Africa have different shared narratives of home, community, longing, and belonging than their predecessors (Chabal 1996; Drachler 1975; Drake 1987, 1990).

Notes

1. Borrowing from the seminal essay "Unfinished Migrations: Reflections on the African Diaspora and the Making of the Modern World," co-authored by historians Patterson and Kelley (2000), I refer to African Diasporas not simply as political *spaces*

but also as *processes* and *conditions*. That is, first, contemporary African diasporic processes extend the links of the migration chains, which originated in the historical moments of the transatlantic slave trade and the rise of European empires (Ford 1999). As a result, two adages pervade the collective consciousness of the older African Diasporas of transatlantic slavery and (post)colonialism respectively: "We are here because you brought us here" or "We are here because you were there." Second, contemporary African Diasporas are spatially constituted wherever African (post)colonial and transnational constituents find themselves, be that conventionally in the Caribbean, North and Latin Americas, or Europe (Torres and Whitten 1998; Green 1997; Modood and Werbner 1997). Their spatial and "racial" locations as both gendered African diasporic agents and former black colonial, tribal, and island subjects inscribe sameness as they mobilize and politicize (Adi 2000; Gilroy 2000; Obichere 1975; Bousquet and Douglas 1991). Finally, African diasporic conditions persist and are transformed by the interface of transnational African diasporic traditions of resistance, protest, and cultural innovation with global economic, political gendered, and racialized hierarchical structures which exclude as they appropriate and commodify (Rose 1994; Chuck D 1997; H. Campbell 1985). In other words, local and dynamic diasporic spaces, processes, and conditions intersect with and in fact are produced by transnational identities, translated cultural commodities, and global political strategies (Browning 1998; Lipsitz 1994).

2. This chapter has been enhanced by many stimulating exchanges with colleagues at countless invited seminars, symposia, and conferences both in Europe and the United States. I am thankful to all who have provided such constructive feedback and engaged so enthusiastically with my work. Special thanks to Kamari Clarke and Deborah Thomas for shrewd editorial assistance and collegiality as well as for inviting me to contribute to what is destined to be a groundbreaking anthology.

This work in progress is a think piece, which means my analyses are not based on ethnographic field work—the tool kit of my anthropological discipline. Instead, I have drawn from a limited but rapidly expanding pool of available sources, including four quite comprehensive and collaborative social science reports commissioned by the United Nations Interregional Crime and Justice Research Institute. In the future and as part of a larger enterprise on the transnational circulation of people and goods, I hope to make my own empirical contribution to this emergent and compelling problematic.

3. As a poignant postscript, on April 29, 2002, (post)apartheid South Africans won their long battle with the French government for the repatriation of Saartjie Baartman's remains. In a ceremony of "reconciliation" involving French and South African delegates, two crates containing a plaster cast of her body, her skeleton, and her preserved brain and genitalia were handed back to the South African government: "Finally, dignity was restored to a women [*sic*] who has become a symbol of the damaging effects of colonialism, sexism and racism. . . . In her address, Skweyiya [the South African ambassador] said this final journey of Baartman's symbolised freedom for African women. 'South African women fought a hard battle for equality and

justice. We join hands with all peace-loving people in the world to sustain the fight for women's human rights' " (*South African Times,* May 1, 2002).

4. In Nigeria, it is the Catholic nuns who are working with both repatriated trafficked young women as well as those who are perceived to be at risk of being lured into the trade. Though the humanitarian efforts of these nuns and priests are tainted by religious zeal, they and other nongovernmental organizations are not only genuinely assisting those who are already in "bondage," they are also trying to stem the tide.

5. I spent Christmas 2003 in Los Angeles, California. One of the evenings, I was captivated by a special programme entitled "Oprah in Africa," which was broadcast on national television. Oprah Winfrey was in conversation with the highly esteemed news broadcaster and journalist Diane Sawyer. Their exchange was interspersed with film clips from Oprah's recent visit to Southern Africa in general and South Africa in particular, where she performed astounding acts of philanthropy in an attempt to ease the material circumstances of young children and youth, many of whom had been orphaned by the HIV/AIDS pandemic. Though at times both moved and inspired, I became increasingly annoyed at the frequency with which both the interviewer and the interviewee referred to "Africa" rather than naming the historically, politically, socially and culturally complex and specific country in question—"South Africa."

6. Unlike other prostitution rings in Italy, such as eastern European one wherein those in control are pimps (Andrijasevic 2003), the Nigerian women are controlled by women in the form of ex–sex workers turned madams: "Once they are able to make it to Italy, they are distributed to areas where their services are in demand. Before distribution, the Madame of the apartments where they are accommodated set the condition for engagement and remittance of proceeds from the trafficked woman's new trade of prostitution" (Ume-Ezeoke 2003: 17).

7. In order to avoid reproducing some of the ethnocentric and racist stereotypes I have already critiqued, the prominent role of "voodoo" in the recruitment, coercion, and exploitation of trafficked Nigerian sex workers is one that must be analyzed with care and sensitivity. Such a detailed analysis is beyond the scope of this particular essay. However, given its significance, Aghatise's discussion of its potent function is worth citing:

> Another cultural aspect of the trafficking in Nigerian girls for prostitution is the fact of their being made to undergo black magic "juju" rites to ensure their payment of the debt imposed on them. This is perhaps the most relevant aspect because of the subsequent effect. . . . The strong belief which they have in these rites coupled with an exaggerated sense of duty owed to their "benefactors" later develop into strong fear. This fear is up to the extent that even when they do succeed in paying all the "debt" to their exploiters, they still continue to live in the fear of some unmentionable misfortune happening to them or members of their family. Each and every misfortune they may suffer is attributed to the rite they were made to undergo. (2002: 7–8)

8. It would be naive and irresponsible to focus entirely on agency without also addressing the link between African sex worker status and susceptibility to HIV/AIDS (Farmer et al. 1996). Unfortunately, within the confines of this argument, there is not ample textual space for me to address such a critical issue. Nevertheless, without falling in to the pathologizing trap which presumes that sex workers are the primary vectors for HIV, there are significant implications for its transnational transmission in light of both the trafficking in women from West Africa to other parts of the continent and to Europe as well as their potential repatriation via escape or deportation:

> The policy of deportation. . . . adds to the stress of the women (many of whom are infected with the HIV-AIDS virus) and makes their reintegration in Nigeria much harder. . . . According to one prominent advocate in Benin City, the girls are medically screened in Lagos, whether they like it or not—and the results are then sent back to Edo State. . . . The results are supposed to be confidential, but the statistics are available. We were told that the rate of HIV infection among the returning girls is in excess of 50%. (Advocacy Project 2003)

If accurate, such statistics are indeed alarming and are in accordance with disproportionate and mounting HIV infection rates for sub-Saharan Africans as a whole and young African women in particular (Gysels et al. 2002). However, just as the microstructural reasons why (young) women become involved in sex work and/or are susceptible to HIV/AIDS are many, varied, and complex so must be the macrostructural antidotes and analyses (Simmons et al. 1996).

9. For examples, in Nigeria: Women's Consortium of Nigeria; Idia Renaissance; Sisters of Sacred Heart, Benin City; National Council for Women Society; International Association of Criminal Justice Lawyers; Movement Against Trafficking in Persons; and Girls Power Initiative; in Italy: TAMPEP; New Wings; and Caritas; and in the United States: the Advocacy Project and the Protection Project.

10. Whither the nation-state? This complex and highly contentious debate is one that I do not have time to address adequately. However, what I have tried to illustrate is the extent to which the nation-state is both extraneous to transnational identities formation and integral to the everyday policing, surveillance, management, and containment of gendered and racialized diasporic bodies.

"SHOOTING THE WHITE GIRL FIRST"

Race in Post-apartheid South Africa

GRANT FARRED

They shoot the white girl first. With the rest they can take their time.
—Toni Morrison, *Paradise*

In Paul Gilroy's provocatively entitled work, *Against Race* (2000), the opening chapter is both an acknowledgment of the efficacy of raced struggle and a caution against its uncritical future usage. "The currency of 'race' has," Gilroy argues, "involved elaborate, improvised constructions that have the primary function of absorbing and deflecting abuse. But they have gone far beyond merely affording protection and reversed the polarities of insult, brutality, and contempt, which are unexpectedly turned into important sources of solidarity, joy, and collective strength" (Gilroy 2000: 12). It is in the description of exceeding easy conceptualizations of race, in "going far beyond" easy binaries, that the sharp edge of Gilroy's critique can be located. In the attempt to transcend polemicized thinking, *Against Race* (or *Between Camps*, as the book was titled in Britain) refuses to reduce race to the physiognomic. *Against Race* will not accede to a "raciology" of the body, to the overdetermined enunciations "blackness" or "whiteness." Gilroy is equally wary of locating race in culture, the sociopolitical practice that is too often rendered as the racialized metonymic, that expansive cluster of signs that compose and substitute as the discourse of racial difference.

It is precisely because Gilroy goes beyond racial conflict (or, more importantly, race as the telos of conflict), beyond the "polarities of insult, brutality, and contempt," that *Against Race* compels a different engagement with race. In unmooring race from the body, from culture, and, even, from its colloquial and "commonsense" history, a new set of interrogations becomes imperative: What has race become? How does it function? What has the struggle for racial equality become, into what kind of political tool has it been transformed? Cynically phrased, does the "race card" have any contemporary veracity or efficacy? Has the privileging of race, the calling attention to itself as an experience (of racialized subjugation, degradation, or grounds for exclusion), become merely a political expediency?

Refusing the location of a racialized identity in the physiognomic, Gilroy designates the body as considerably more than an unreliable marker of racial knowledge: it is also the site of ontological anxiety because it provokes a questioning of the "essentialized" self. *Against Race*'s determination to resituate blackness emerges not so much "externally"—a narrow conceiving of racial antagonism; or, blackness under threat from the usual protagonist, "whiteness," or, more crudely conceived, "whites"—as from within the discursive changes wrought by the conditions of a "post"-bioculturalism. The "crisis of raciology" is located firmly within the (black) body, a process that destabilizes race as a secure and reliable political category. If race can no longer be considered equivalent to "culture," if the (racially) agnostic "black" body can not rely simply upon that hard-won right (secured through the critique of liberalism[1]), the speaking of racialized self to assert its social identity, then the Foucauldian "bio-political" sphere has to be reexamined.

The nonracialized or antiracialized identity can only be thought beyond the somatic markers. The "appearance," in Gilroy's allusive terms, "of a rich visual culture that allows blackness to be beautiful also feeds a fundamental lack of confidence in the power of the body to hold the boundaries of racial difference in place" (Gilroy 2000: 22). The racialized body is not a sociopolitical entity convinced of either its sustainability or its ability to "hold the boundaries of racial difference in place." This ontological uncertainty injects a precariousness into racial discourse: if "difference" cannot be maintained, what will become of racial identity and the racialized politics founded upon it, in different forms, for centuries?

Both the literal and the fictional black body, as twentieth-century authors from James Weldon Johnson (*Autobiography of an Ex-Coloured Man*) and Nella Larsen (the novellas *Quicksand* and *Passing*) to Toni Morrison (*Paradise*) and Philip Roth (*The Human Stain*) make clear, should not be easily trusted. The body can lie: the (black) physical, as in Johnson's (early-twentieth-century) and Roth's (fin-de-siècle) stoic male protagonists, Larsen's tragic mulattas (Harlem Renaissance), and Morrison's (late- twentieth-century) racially "indistinct" convent women, is not the site of the ontologically "confident" but the embodiment of "raciological"—Gilroy's term—uncertainty. The (black) body is often something—or someone—other than what it is racially deemed to be. The "black" body is frequently revealed, in fiction and in the "scientific" moments in *Against Race*, to be hybrid, if not putatively "white."

The impulse to think beyond race, to produce a paradigm that enables an alternate, transformative view of social arrangements is an old but by no means unimportant project. With its deep philosophical roots in the ostensibly egalitarian paradigm of Enlightenment subjectivity, the desire for a structure of sociopolitical sameness has animated and sustained antiracial struggles from slave rebellions in the antebellum U.S. South to Toussaint's campaign for Haitian sovereignty, from the mid-century anticolonial movements in the Asian subcontinent to fin-de-siècle Chiapas (which stands as its own kind of "autonomista" battle against imperialism, racial discrimination, and global capitalism). The struggle against racial(-ized) naming (so constitutive of Ralph Ellison's *Invisible Man*, whose many-faced protagonist is always slipping the yoke of naming) is, much like *Against Race*, about imagining a world in which the racialized body—the historically denigrated black body—is not always read a priori, and interminably, as a deficit; witness the "spook" of Ellison's novel, who understands that his lack, his invisibility is not "exactly a matter of bio-chemical accident to my epidermis" (Ellison 1987: 7). In resisting racism, the black body wages an epistemological campaign to refute its deficient representation, its enunciation as a lack, an absence, the Other, or an interrupted or suspended humanity.

The desire to think beyond race is, however, a double-edged sword. It marks the ambivalent process of mobilizing against racism and yet working within—and against—established racial categories. Race and racism are, for this very reason, not only dialectical but epistemologically foundational. It constitutes the very architecture within which the debate about race takes place: race cannot be transcended. It is impossible to be "against race" without, as it were, "doing" race—as a theory of politics or as a way of accounting for its deleterious ontological effects. It is for this reason that Gilroy, despite being "against race," acknowledges how ambivalent, contradictory, and potentially destructive (to historical subalterns) such an imagining might be: "the dramatic gestures involved in turning against racial observance can be accomplished without violating the precious forms of solidarity and community that have been created by their protracted subordination along racial lines" (Gilroy 2000: 13). Race constitutes a critical community; or, because of race and racism, sustainable communities of subjugated peoples are racialized into being; political identities emerge out of the historical process of racialization; constituencies, be they located in the diaspora or the periphery, are philosophically inconceivable without the experience of race and racism.

"Post"-racialism, however contentious such a condition might be, constitutes the dialogic project of recognizing race as the primary discourse to be at once engaged and disarticulated; postracialism cannot be achieved "without violating the precious forms of solidarity and community"—practices essential to sustaining a black biopolitics in moments of degradation, disenfranchisement, or repression. Within the discursive project of transcending racial affect and effect, race is centered even in the attempt to oppose it. Hence the paradox: race is constitutive and yet it can only be epistemologically liquidated—which is to say, worked through and beyond as a philosophical terrain—upon the terms of its historically racist making. Race is a politics that in-forms and de-forms, even in the efforts to disarticulate it, to take it apart, and render it sociopolitically null and void.

It is for this reason that the campaign against race is of especial significance in those societies where racial categorization has significant purchase, where race is at the root of societal conflict, where the very history of the locale is (over)determined by race. This essay explores the construction of an antiracist yet racialized politics in a society, South Africa, structured by specific, historicized racial hierarchies. It examines the entanglements of race as it obtains on the terrain of the nation's "politics," conceived here in both its electoral (post-apartheid) constitutional formation and in its "extraparliamentary," anti-apartheid articulation. The struggle against apartheid is located here in the "long" (specifically African) anticolonial decade, that protracted moment from the mid-1950s (when Ghana gained independence in 1958) to the late 1980s (when Zimbabwe in 1980 and Namibia in 1990 became sovereign) when the "political" consisted of predominantly "black"[2] opposition through nonelectoral strategies, some of them more violent than others.

South African politics in the "long decade" is not generated by historic turmoil, which we would expect to be most conducive to political change, but by a very different modality, that moment Fredric Jameson names the "suspension of the political" (Jameson 2003). In Jameson's conception (which is inflected with Carl Schmitt's notion of the political),[3] politics emerges out of precisely those moments when change, through either constitutional or revolutionary means, appears impossible: when the (apartheid) state, having secured to itself all the legitimacy it requires to exercise power, has worked diligently to block any efforts to effect social transformation. Historic turmoil, Jameson might argue, is produced precisely out of the subjugated's response to the suspension of the political. The political stasis, the enforcement of a Schmittian "order," sought by the state is, instead of quiescence, met with intense opposition. The modality of "suspension" constitutes that moment when any notion of democracy, which is founded upon the right to political disagreement, even disaggregation, is suspended. "Suspension" is how the political, instantiated as the sovereign white state, was lived in antiapartheid South Africa by the disenfranchised: the condition of racialized inequity. In South Africa, the moment of "suspension" proved decidedly generative in that it motivated black youth (in particular) to attack the state. It was during the long moment of "suspension" of normative, democratic politics, the apartheid era that lasted from 1948 to 1990, that unarmed or stone-throwing or Molotov-cocktail tossing black subjects took up the struggle against the might of apartheid machinery most committedly. The "suspension of the political" produces a series of protests against disenfranchisement—and its many manifestations—which result, "impossibly," in a democratic post-apartheid society. (The South African experience of the "long decade" finds its contemporary corollary in the Palestinian scenario—a politics crafted out of historic inequity in response to the seemingly unending "suspension" of the political.) In South Africa, racism formed the very basis for the "suspension of the political" which, impossibly, produced a (constitutionally) nonracial democracy.

In reading two speeches by post-apartheid South Africa's first two black presidents, the iconic Nelson Mandela and his successor Thabo Mbeki, this essay demonstrates how fundamental race is to political thinking in this newly democratic nation. The ways in which race and racism function discursively for both of these figures is instructive because of how they position themselves in relation to South Africa's apartheid past and because of how race is and will be instrumentalized in the post-apartheid present and future:

How, to reframe the issue, is race understood and spoken in that moment in which democracy has been achieved? What is the role of race in a nonracial democracy? Can there be a nonracial democracy? How do we think politically about race in a society where race thinking is implicitly verboten?

Mandela and Mbeki, in their different ways, confront the political task of addressing race at a conjuncture where race is the (over)determining and most visceral factor in South African life. This moment consists of a two-phase paradox: transforming the foundational element of the society, race and racism, from the defining trauma (apartheid) into a public speakability (this was the task of the Truth and Reconciliation Commission), and then into a (post-apartheid) discourse outmoded by the transcendent, incorporative commonality of national identity—the nonracially imagined community. Envisaged as the culmination of the post-apartheid project is, conceptually phrased, the replacement of race with racelessness. More specifically, race as the primary signifier of identity is liquidated by its modernist equivalent, the geopolitics of spatiality; racial affinity, imposed or otherwise, is superceded by national identity. The aporetic moment in this project of constructing a postracial/racist national identity, in the sense that the aporia indicates not simply a gap but a bridging, might be Archbishop Desmond Tutu's poetic vision: South Africans as the "Rainbow Children of God."

In the first instance, the "rainbow" symbolizes the disjoining of the "old" South Africa from the new; the rainbow of the present represents a "racially" complementary harmony as opposed to the apartheid past where the disunion of the various peoples was the predominant racist logic. In the second, it makes a metaphor of the splendid, "colorful" conjoining of all South Africa's racially distinct peoples. In the African National Congress's (ANC) vision of the post-apartheid future, the rainbow functions only as a temporary (national) emblem en route, ideologically, to nonracial South African sameness. The rainbow has to be superceded by that modality in which race has no purchase and the different colors of the (racial) spectrum have merged, through concerted political education, into a "colorless" singularity.

A Nobel Peace Prize laureate (like his countrymen Tutu and F. W. de Klerk, the last white president and the National Party figure instrumental in undoing apartheid), Mandela positioned himself as the Gandhi-like liberator of the black South African masses and the Toussaintian figurehead, the black leader who would protect white life and property under the terms of the Enlightenment constitution and who was committed to a harmonious, racially heterogeneous present (im)perfect. Racial reconciliation was always a project for Mandela, but he traded heavily on his own symbolism—the ex-guerilla, ex–political prisoner reincarnated as the post-apartheid "man of peace"—to advocate the possibility of overcoming historic racial enmity. For this complex of reasons, Mandela's presidency was symbolically critical: he the first black leader of a democratic South Africa, who offered, in a single rhetorical gesture, a racially loaded and racially transcendent vision of post-apartheid society.

It is in Mbeki's presidency, however, an infinitely less charismatic tenure (where the racial cleavages cannot be so easily disguised or "canonized" away by presidential aura), that the workings of race become more obvious, and more obviously discursively demanding. A dour figure possessed of no Mandela-like resonance with the South African populace, except the business community, Mbeki has used his notion of an "African Renaissance" (Farred 2003) to lay claim to "continental" leadership, both within Africa and as a representative to global capital and its major institutions, the World Bank and the International Monetary Fund. However, what is evident in the tenure of both of the nations' first democratic black presidents is that their rhetoric reveals how they are capable of thinking racially, of mobilizing racial identi-ties, even as they disavow race as a strategy for achieving electoral gains. Mandela and Mbeki demonstrate how race, when it is either affirmed or transcended, is always available as a first or last recourse in the post-apartheid democracy. Race is always, politically and philosophically speaking, in play in South Africa. In South Africa, to think politically is to think racially and, possibly, "racistly" (to coin an awkward term), so precarious is the epistemo-logical slippage between the two concepts.

Beware of Shooting the White Girl

The novel *Paradise* constitutes Toni Morrison's most ambitious engagement with the dialogic of race in America. Morrison's work is more often preoc-cupied with, in significant measure, the internality of black life in America, even though she is always aware of the white presence at its fringes that can impinge at any time—as is so patently obvious in *Beloved* (as Sethe flees from Southern slavery) and, as a haunting pathology (the desire for a white physi-ognomy), in the *Bluest Eye*. Whereas race is undoubtedly the dominant trope of the Nobel laureate's oeuvre—novels such as *Beloved, Song of Solomon,* and *The Bluest Eye* make this patently clear—it is in the dystopia named *Paradise* that racial identities are most concertedly unsettled. In *Paradise* Morrison crafts a narrative—which turns on the difficult, erotically entangled but un-speakable relations between the (re)constituted black town and the racially mixed, even indistinct, socioeconomic space that is the convent—where black and white is harder to pin down, sometimes even to name. Who, after all, is the "white" girl? Can we ever really be sure, given the complications of Morrison's postmodern tableau that is built around an oven that has to be disassembled, moved from the town of Ruby to the town of Paradise, and then reconstructed with every deracination?

Both the implicit invocation of "paradise" and its more racially resis-tant articulation, *Paradise,* resonate with the South African condition. In its "peaceful" transition from white minority rule to post-apartheid democracy, South Africa was heralded as a (putatively) postcolonial "miracle": the Afri-can state that achieved black majority rule with a "minimum" of violence. South Africa became, in and through this enunciation, an African "paradise," an ideologically and economically idyllic space because of its ability to ac-commodate all of its citizens in the postlapsarian colonial moment—the beacon of Third World hope after the postcolonial world's ignominious fall into corruption, disease, famine, war, and civil strife. In South Africa, unlike in Uganda and Kenya in the 1970s, the racially enfranchised and the histori-cally disenfranchised can coexist within the borders of the new postcolonial state. South Africa represents the exceptional African state, in the benign, American ("new Eden") sense, not in Agamben's more violently traumatic sense (where the state of exception produces the notorious "camp"). Post-apartheid South Africa is configured as the postcolonial democracy sans specters of fleeing white or Asian settlers (their capital in tow, their businesses abandoned). However, South Africa is also the incarnation of *Paradise* in that its new leaders, the various constituencies, its old but newly articulated mem-ories, and its new technologies of governance have to grapple with the project of assembling the "oven" of post-apartheid democracy—how will it work? How do its constituent parts fit together? Can the old and new modalities of race and ideology and different generations collaborate successfully in this venture to produce a new fractured and fissured yet functioning national identity? Can white and black citizens, for so long balkanized into their own separate and racially distinct mechanisms of social operation, work together on the new national undertaking? Can a usable sameness be fashioned out of historic difference, out of a rainbow of colorful component parts?

These are the metaphoric challenges that Morrison's work poses for the post-apartheid dispensation. It compels a thinking of race through the treacherous network of black and white epistemologies, self-conceptions, and pasts; it demands a racialized dialogic where the space between the fictional towns of Ruby and Paradise, the post-apartheid "paradise," and the border locale that is the convent, the apartheid past that lies at the forefront of the new nation's consciousness, has to be traversed from a racially dangerous terrain. The conceptual framework offered by *Paradise*, its complex figuring of the "raciological," anticipates and gives literary animation to the theoretical girding of Gilroy's *Against Race* in that both authors resist an easy recourse to uncomplicated racial binaries. "Race" has to be produced, or not, out of the text; it is not a concept, or an experience, or even an epistemology that can be imposed upon a historical (or fictional) moment. The politics of race can only be discerned by reading the fragments or corpuses of racial texts that constitute "paradise" or dystopia, or the dystopic elements integral to, and indeed constitutive of, the "paradaisical" construct, be that Ruby or post-apartheid South Africa.

Cast in the terms of *Paradise*, the state (or the party) is always willing to metaphorically "shoot the white girl first" if it believes that the "black girl" (the "ideally" constructed political subject, the metonymic subject being hailed through the white girl's abjection) understands herself to be (affirmatively) addressed through this act of semiotic violence. There can, as in *Paradise*'s convent, be no "white girl" to "shoot" if there is no racialized alterity: the black girl who is not yet shot. The "black girl" is saved, or her fate is suspended, precisely because the critical event of the "white girl" is framed as constitutive of the misogynistic social violence; the violence is also exemplary (in the Foucauldian sense) in that it prefigures what will happen to the "black girl." However, what the metonymic "black girl" has to grasp is that the symbolic death of her (white) sister who is also her enemy, since the two positionalities lie so close to each other within the logic of the older black men from the town of Ruby, has little to do with her own repositioning, reinscription, or advance. She is not able, literally, to move to another place that is not the circumscribed space that is the convent or house of domestic violence; she cannot relocate herself on the political landscape; she is unable to reconfigure a different, non-, or antiracial or antiracialized identity. On the contrary, who and what the black girl is has everything to do with the consequences that obtain from the white girl's figurative death.

The dead, reviled, racialized subject, the figuratively white body of *Paradise*, represents the (un)conscious force of race as a disciplinary mechanism. Similarly, the white apartheid past functions as an ideological tool with which to police the post-apartheid nation's political thinking. Violence demonstrates how race can be expropriated from the implicitly referenced black body, the black woman who is "hailed" without "language" through the death of her white contemporary in the convent, summoned unceremoniously into the service of racialized hegemony. Race is the discourse deployed only when the political shock of its violence can be heard, and, not simply heard but acknowledged as an incendiary speaking to whiteness. Whiteness is addressed only in the form of the threat: when its vulnerability is made public, when the apartheid past can be used to regulate the post-apartheid present.

Girding the political struggle against apartheid by organizations such as the ANC and the Non-European Unity Movement (NEUM), as it was then known,[4] was the vision of a nonracial society. A concept first coined and most carefully theorized by NEUM intellectuals, nonracialism proposed a social arrangement in which race was not (supposed to be) constitutive of citizenship or the determinant of human worth. First articulated in the 1940s, the principle of nonracialism was founded upon the Enlightenment epistemology that race was an "unscientific" discourse; NEUM's concept of nonracialism can be understood as a precursor to Gilroy's notion of "against race." Nonracialism was, and continues to be, in some quarters, a means of arguing against race in order to refute the apartheid categories of statutory racial difference—strictly hierarchized, from the white minority at the apex to the black majority at the base of the racial pyramid. Based upon a profoundly modernist European principle, nonracialism was an ideologically strategic means of agitating for legal equality for all South Africans.

Because the logic of nonracialism refused the philosophical grounds of racial difference, it revealed the fundamental flaw at the core of apartheid reason. The apartheid ideology of the ruling Afrikaner National Party (NP) premised itself upon the "Europeanness" of white South Africans; they were the bearers of white, Western modernity with the Calvinist mission of civilizing the "natives" but never recognizing their equality. The NEUM's nonracialism revealed how incommensurate NP logic was with the terms of progressive European modernity. Within a nonracial society, race could not be the very telos that decided whether or not people should be enfranchised, where they should live, work, attend school, whom they could marry. While the ANC was never as sophisticated in its thinking about race as the NEUM—it adhered to a concept of "nations" (each of the four apartheid communities, white, black, "coloured," and "Indian," were represented at the historic Congress of the

People in 1955)—the principle of nonracialism gradually emerged as the guiding principle in the anti-apartheid struggle (Lodge 1983). The boycotts, strikes, "rolling mass actions," innumerable protests, and the high-intensity "civil war" of the 1980s were motivated and sustained by an opposition to racial categorization. Nonracialism envisioned a nation in which race would be negated, where it would have no role or value. It was this guiding principle that the world celebrated in both 1990 and 1994: the first moment marked the unbanning of the black liberation movement and the release of political prisoners, the second marked the historic, inaugural, democratic elections.

Residual Race and Racism? Mandela and the New Racial Logic

It is against the backdrop of these two historic events that the last full-length ideological statement by then-president Nelson Mandela achieves such salience. Speaking to the ANC national convention in his final major address as party leader in December of 1997 (some sixteen months before the second democratic elections), Mandela focused his political sights on a single constituency: white South Africa. And he did so in a historically overdetermined guise. He addressed whites not as post-apartheid, rainbow-nation fellow-citizens but as a residual constituency: as inveterately, ahistorically apartheid subjects, those who represented nothing so much as an ideological time-lag (people who clung desperately, defiantly, to an earlier mode of being, which we might understand as racism), whites as reluctant citizens, as political recidivists, guilty of nothing so much as the crime of historic privilege—of implicitly remembering (and thereby tacitly regretting) the loss of inequity, of hierarchy. Speaking at one moment during his speech in defense of affirmative action, Mandela warned his colleagues: "even a cursory study of the positions adopted by the mainly white parties in the national legislature during the last three years . . . will show that they, and the media which represents the same social base, have been most vigorous in their opposition, whenever legislative and executive measures have been introduced, seeking the end of racial disparities which continue to characterize our society" (Mandela 1997: 3).

In the ANC's terms, South Africa was democratic but not yet egalitarian. According to Mandela, post-apartheid society remained steeped in racial inequity, an imbalance that the historically enfranchised were eager to maintain: "Thus, whenever we have sought real progress through affirmative action, the spokesperson[s] of the advantaged have not hesitated to cry foul, citing all manner of evil—such as racism, violation of the constitution, nepotism, dictatorship, inducing a brain drain and frightening the foreign investor" (Mandela 1997: 5). Departing from the same philosophical standpoint of being opposed to race, Mandela's pronouncements seem to throw Gilroy's project into sharp relief: even in a post-apartheid society committed to a nonracial future, every rhetorical attempt to transcend race confronts—either as an imagined, expedient opposition or a substantive socioeconomic force—itself, most frequently, as racism. This suggests that the ideology of *Against Race* is at once a complicated amalgam of the ideal, the politically naive, and the structurally impossible. Even those opposed to race as a mode of social arrangement and thinking find themselves mired its in several, all too manifest physiognomic and cultural-political realities. Being against race does not necessarily mean that it is possible to refuse its ontological purchase. Mandela's speech demonstrates how it is impossible to argue, in a putatively nonracial society, against race without being ensnared, subverted, and even possibly undone by it.

The process of transformation, the president held, "had not yet tested the strength of the counter-offensive which would seek to maintain the privileges of the white minority" (Mandela 1997: 1). Mandela's sudden (re)turn to a Marxist discourse is salient because it makes a sudden reappearance on the most public of party platforms—the annual, in this case fiftieth, party conference in 1997. It is possible to argue here that Mandela, as a socialist fellow traveler, was simply remembering the Trotskyist dictum that the revolution is never quite so vulnerable as in that period immediately following its completion. Beware the counterrevolutionaries, fear the white Russians, as Trotsky warned, was the message that came echoing fraudulently across the Russian steppes to the South African hinterland town of Mafikeng, which hosted the ANC conference. The racial commensurability between the white Russians and the white South Africans was convenient and especially apt for Mandela's purposes. But why, against the backdrop of a superficial Marxism, invoke the specter of race, the history of racism, when the political threat does not exist? Why recall a "politics of suspension" when a political democracy obtains? Why the temporal anachronism, the recalling of apartheid's racial logic, the strategic political disjuncture? What is Mandela's but an ideologically hollow call to "shoot the white girl first?" All of these questions provoke the more insidious inquiry, premised upon the "exceptional" Agambenian trajectory from the exception to the "camp": Who is next in line after the "white girl" has been dispatched?

First in line, clearly, is the "media," an institution of civil society that "represents the same social base" and is overly identified with white South Africans. But what other constituencies were also being indicted? Is there in Mandela's address, more ominously, a warning to black opposition? To black journalists who do not agree with the ANC's policies? Does it also contain a caution against any recalcitrance by the trade unions? Are all "counter-offensives" equally intolerable to the ANC government? These constituencies and institutions of liberal civil society, whatever critiques one may offer of that political construct, represent the real opposition, those forces who have been most willing to express their dissatisfaction with the new regime, who have been prepared to articulate the shortcomings of the post-apartheid society and to aim their critiques at the governments of first Mandela and then Mbeki as well as at the apartheid past.

Race and Capital: Critiquing Mbeki

The press, the trade unions, and the new black lumpen proletariat have, since Mbeki came to power, established themselves most vocally as the anti-Mbeki constituency. The political constituencies are all, in their own particular ways, suspicious of the new president, his relationship to capital, and his economic agenda involving big business, global capital, the World Bank, and the International Monetary Fund. Unlike Morrison's vengeful black men in *Paradise*, who can "take their time" because the convent where they will kill the "white girl" and all the racially "indistinct" girls is isolated and vulnerable to no one so much as the men of the all-black town of Ruby, there is not quite the same temporal luxury for the ANC's leadership. The ANC may have the "time" to expediently invoke race because there is no viable opposition to the government. But there are other factors mitigating against Mbeki. As an American journalist reported from Soweto in 2002: "Disappointment is clearly surging among the poor, the working class and the undereducated. Western officials have praised the black government for its conservative fiscal policies, but the nation has lost thousands of jobs in recent years as the previously sheltered economy has been liberalized" (Swarns 2002: 4). With the worsening economic conditions, the fissures within the black community have become more publicly obvious since Mbeki's ascent to power: " 'Things were better before,' said Kala Kgamedi, 33, who lost his job as a salesman two years ago. 'In the years of apartheid, things were running smoothly,' said Mr. Kgamedi" (ibid.).

In this instance, those against, critical of, or unsure about the post-apartheid dispensation demonstrate how the contestation is not reductively about race but, more complexly, about class, ideological differences within the black community, even a wistful remembering of the efficiencies of the apartheid dispensation, all of which produce a compacted political discontent. Under- and unemployed and leftist blacks alike are opposed to a black president who does not represent their interests, a president whose rhetoric on race is discredited by his alliance with global capital (which is identified as institutionally and figuratively white). Economic restructuring, approved of by "Western officials," has produced such dissatisfaction within the black ranks that the unthinkable, nostalgia for apartheid, is now a resonant trope in the black political imaginary: " 'We wanted to contribute to our country,' said Mr. Sibanda. . . . 'We fought so long for equal rights, to be respected, to be treated as people. I wonder now, the struggle, was it worth it? Here I am, young and qualified, and I cannot get a job. Why should I vote when I don't benefit from this government? They say they're trying to alleviate poverty, but I don't see it' " (Swarns 2002: 4).

While Mbeki may not agree entirely with his critic from the streets of Soweto, even as the most ardent proponent of attracting international capital for investment, the president recognizes how post-apartheid society has created new intraracial divisions. According to Mbeki, "The disparity in wealth and income between the black rich and the black poor has, in fact, become the distinguishing feature of the new South Africa" (Mbeki 2000: 4). It is not, however, a situation that Mbeki is considering rethinking. The impact of globalization and Mbeki's close relationship with the World Bank and the International Monetary Fund has produced a post-apartheid category of impoverished blacks dubbed, by one critic, the "poors." Entering the global economy as a democratic society has, for the historically disenfranchised, meant the destruction of the racially stratified apartheid welfare state and the loss of its not inconsiderable benefits. Apartheid provided decent health care, minimal housing, basic education, and, most crucially, a safer society than its successor. The "poors" (Desai 2003) are produced out of that unexpected conjuncture between globalization and post-apartheid democracy, between the failures of anti-apartheid and post-apartheid race politics, and between race politics and international capital.

The South African situation represents a complex intertwining of historical racism, the desired (but perpetually deferred, elusive) nonracial future, intrablack ideological disagreement, and a looming class conflict (uneven and varied as it is), all of which are eminently capable of working in multiple alliances with and against each other. In South Africa, for this reason, race can only—in its Gilroyian instantiation—be effectively contested by operating within a raced paradigm that is always alert to the functioning of global capital. In order to oppose the "shooting" of the symbolic white girl, to oppose and counteract an uncritical race politics, it is necessary to understand that while being cognizant of how economic inequity and exploitation can be subverted by recourse to racialized logic. It is imperative to recognize the expedience of the racialized logic of the post-apartheid black government: "If you are a black South African, you are most likely to have welcomed the end of apartheid in our country in 1994 with great enthusiasm. You would have seen this as an historic fact of liberation, indeed opening up the prospect of a better life. If you are a white South African, you are most likely to have welcomed this change with a certain degree of unease. Some would have wondered whether they, their families and properties were safe from black hordes that might go on the rampage" (Mbeki 2000: 2).

Black unemployment, poverty, and structural lack can always be explained (rationalized away) by the authority of presidential, racially inflected dictate. Mbeki's discourse is premised upon the political fallacy, what he projects as the new "racial common sense," that to speak of the racialized past is to implicitly invalidate other critical discourses. When Mbeki invokes racial difference and transubstantiates it into a historical absolute, his intention is to deploy race as a blunt but affectively potent ideological tool. Race is transformed by the black president into the political weapon of elite black censorship: to recall the apartheid past is to immunize, by affective contrast, the black ANC government from opposition by either other blacks or whites. Paradoxically, and insidiously, through Mbeki's representation of it race once again becomes an oppressive discourse for black South Africans. The black "poors" are punished, not once but twice, first by the white apartheid regime and then by the black post-apartheid government, in both cases because they represent a sociopolitical constituency opposed to the (white and black) ruling blocs. The memory of black orchestrated liberation is used against the possibility of other, future, race-based struggles that are equally rooted in and routed through class politics. The discourse of race, both Mandela's and Mbeki's speeches make clear, is always in the service of power.

Ironically, in post-apartheid South Africa, much as during the apartheid era, racial identities have hardened discursively. Post-apartheid racial identities function as signs of an unchanging same, concretized into articulations that permit only temporal—the apartheid era as opposed to post-apartheid era—but never conceptual notions of difference—ideological disparities are not permitted. South African identity, the intensely racialized self of the past and the present has, as in Gilroy's terms, "degenerated readily into emblems of supposedly essential or immutable difference" (Gilroy 2000: 101).

Essentialism inscribes within itself a history of a specific and crucial aspect: the lack or circumscription of agency. Essentialism is often not so much a strategic ideological choice as the only possible response to a variety of repressions, violence, and disenfranchisements. It is about the absence of real political alternative. Essentialism enunciates, in instances such as South African apartheid, a politics of depravation because it precludes, because of the conditions of racialized struggle, the material and psychic possibility of a different, more politically efficacious response. Essentialism is not always about the insistent, unreflexive, and intransigent maintenance of identity or ideological position. It is frequently, as is the case in South Africa, about race—about the denigrated historicity of the black body—as the final resort: as a genealogical marker of community, an immutability out of which an enforced solidarity—a sameness of the body that translates and widens into the sameness of lived experience—binds disenfranchised constituencies together. It is, not to put too fine a point on it, essential that these communities cohere in the face of hegemony—or, worse, state-sponsored repression. If they do not practice political essentialism, they render themselves even more politically, psychically, and physically vulnerable.

While Mandela and Mbeki may, with their different nuances and emphases, insist that in South Africa race is not the terrain of contestation, the transmutation of race into ideology—for a second time—signals a crucial postlapsarian conjuncture. Too soon after the fall of institutionalized racism, for the historically disenfranchised, race has all too evidently become the modus operandi of post-apartheid politics. A critical race politics has to be conceived of as an ideology that recognizes how various constituencies, black and otherwise, align themselves in relation to the functioning of global capital and its workings in postindustrial South Africa. At the level of the "second" struggle, that of the black "poors" against the black ANC government, the political project is to unyoke the uncritical ANC discourse that implicitly and cynically links post-apartheid race to the legacy of post-apartheid capital. This strategy amounts to little more than explaining continuing black poverty through the lens of historic white privilege in an era when the black elite has, courtesy of the ANC, "embourgeoisified" itself beyond the recognition of both the "poors" and the new elite's more modest apartheid status. The ANC has failed the black "poors" as much as it has advantaged the new black elite. In the "second" black struggle, apartheid's racial categories are fundamental but contextually and textually inadequate. The apartheid categories cannot simply be transposed into the post-apartheid context; race has to be contextualized into contemporaneity, it has to be made into a political text incorporative of the conjunctures of the new, conceptually unprecedented moment in South African history. The critique of post-apartheid economics has to be redefined on the occasion of South Africa's entrée into global capital as much as race has to be reanimated and retooled as a political discourse.

In South Africa race and class have historically been mutually constitutive. Thinking them discretely has never really been a viable political option except for the interregnum that was 1990 to 1994. Mbeki returned to this theme a couple of times in his short speech at the Youth Conference on Nation Building in 2000": "The racism . . . defined black people as sub-human, barbaric, incapable of sharing the same moral norms as the white minority, incapable of being civilized—and therefore menacing, requiring to be watched, contained and tamed at all costs" (Mbeki 2000: 2). At the very moment of nonracial inauguration, the new nation reveals itself to be racially discontinuous; the racial cleavages, "civilized" whites and their Conradian black counterparts who are too "savage" to be trusted to their own political devices, not only survive the end of apartheid but emerge at the beginning of the new century in sharper ideological outline. Post-apartheid society in 1994, where black "enthusiasm" contrasts sharply with a "certain degree" of white "unease," announces the revitalization of racialized discourse, affect, and identity. Race lives even as it is being constitutionally buried. In South Africa, race and racism constitute an (im)permanent conundrum, a conceptual incorrigibility in and for a society trying to imagine itself as nonracial.

Race and Nation

It is not surprising that race should emerge so regularly in the South African national discourse, or in the discourse of the insufficiently tentative project, or too balkanized girding, of nation building. As Mbeki phrased it in his address, "in our social psychology, our instincts and our perception of ourselves, we see ourselves as distinct elements of an agglomeration of different racial and ethnic groups whose interests we believe might very well be mutually exclusive" (Mbeki 2000: 2). What is significant, however, is the return to race in what should be the apogeic moment of nonracial triumph. Instead of celebration there is, when the government is confronted with the nation disarticulated by race, public admonishment of those who wish to "maintain racial disparities" by the iconic Mandela, the post-apartheid statesman. Instead, Mandela offers a relenting of, not a giving up on, the raced morality of the apartheid past. It is in this moment of racialized indefatigability, that moment when race and racism reveals its public sustainability, that the nation reveals itself to be in racial disarray. It is on these occasions that race and racism demonstrate how the post-apartheid nation is lived as a disjunctive if not yet dystopic construct. How is race reconstructed as an oppositional politics at a juncture when the establishment of the post-apartheid state publicly embodies its death? Is race and racism the perpetual South African political unconscious? Is race the historical condition, the historic experience, that is always invocable, inexorably subject to recall at strategic moments?

Problematic as Mandela's and Mbeki's expedient deployment of race is, it would seem that in South Africa—for now and the foreseeable future—the only way to think a nonracial society, if not a postracial future, is to engage the social construct through race bifurcatedly: through the dual and occasionally split lens of anti- and post-apartheid history. Such a modality requires an acute awareness and grasp of strategic moment, a critical consciousness about how and why race is invoked, the understanding and acknowledgment of Gilroy's critique; and yet such an approach is also predicated upon knowing that the project of nonracialism is premised upon thorny, uneven, entangled engagements with the history and consequences of race and racism. The black South African body, in other words, continues to possess both an ideological presence and an ontological saliency, a racialized memory, an apartheid sense of itself that makes it simultaneously wary of antiwhite rhetoric and strangely susceptible to that discourse—an ideological proclivity that Mbeki was clearly trying to invoke, if not explicitly exploit, in his "Youth Day" speech. This ontologized racial memory retains, furthermore, an ideological purchase precisely because of the conditions under which the newly enfranchised black citizenry labor: they are the "poors," still the economic subalterns, they have greater numbers of the unemployed in their ranks, they and their children are less well educated. In post-apartheid society, guaranteed equality by the constitution, they still live the socioeconomic experience of the black subject under apartheid. Their past is only constitutionally distinguishable from their future.

Black subjectivity remains anteriorized: located in and enfranchised by post-apartheid South African society, ideologically it is an anachronistic socioeconomic experience. Blacks continue to live, materially, in the time before—in the conditions of the original struggle except that the state is now governed by "their" representatives, speaking physiognomically. For the expanding class of black subalterns, race is not only the dominant language of their social existence, it is the lingua franca of their lives: they are nonracial citizens in a world still stratified by the inequities of the racist past, philosophically nonracial, economically racialized, negotiating not so much between the present and the past as between the past and its double-edged, shadowy, as yet unformed future.

Nonracialism is always lived imaginatively, at a historical distance, removed from and unavailable to the conditions of the present even while epistemologically girding—ideologically holding up—the present. In this scenario, nonracialism assumes a conceptual urgency and again offers itself as a struggle—as the condition to be achieved, again. Nonracialism cannot, because of the establishment of the post-apartheid state, be rhetorically postponed into the future: it has to have an envisioning in the present. Unlike the Morrisonian "white girl," nonracialism cannot be summarily "killed"; unlike the "rest" of *Paradise*'s convent women, its fulfillment cannot be postponed indefinitely. It has to have a presence, however ghostly, unhomed, or unachievable, in a society in which race functions as the founding myth. Even as the "white girl" is held metonymically accountable for the delayed nonracial condition, so the body of the historically privileged victim draws attention to its subreptitious absence. Subreption not only conceals strategic information, its speaking—the indictment of white South Africans—enunciates its foundational lacks: apportioning blame to whites as an explication for nonracialism inadvertently articulates the nonfulfillment of the historical pact.

As Mbeki, without any sense of historical irony, or, worse, historical foreboding, himself acknowledges: "If we do not address these disparities, which, like the land question in Zimbabwe, were central to the struggle for liberation in this country, at some point in the future we will experience an enormous and angry explosion by those [who] remain disadvantaged" (Mbeki 2000: 5). Invoking the specter of Robert Mugabe's expedient and economically devastating deployment of race politics in Zimbabwe (where five thousand white farmers have had land expropriated almost two decades after independence when ZANU PF was, not coincidentally, in electoral trouble), Mbeki uses the crisis in Zimbabwe to warn against race-based economic exploitation without any awareness of ANC accountability. Again, the specter of black violence of the anticolonial variety is used not to achieve equality but to hint at the potential fate of the "white girl." Zimbabwe allows for the metaphorical treatment of semiotic violence: it recodes the threat of violence for South Africa by geographical displacement. The "dispossessed" Zimbabwean peasants stand in for, and momentarily as, post-apartheid South Africa's historically disenfranchised underclass. Displacing accountability, playing the race card, in this case doubles back upon its speaker: despite the efforts to deflect it, nonracialism's nonexistence becomes—perhaps even demands—its own interrogation. If the language of race is always historically racialized, overburdened by inequity and injustice, then the discourse of nonracialism is similarly, constitutively, overwritten by race.

It is, as Gilroy suggests, an injunction to take seriously the "idea" that a "fundamentally shared identity becomes a platform for the reverie and of absolute and eternal division" (2000: 101). Within the South African context, the memory of race and racism has a powerful retention. It remains deeply present within the collective and "divided" consciousness of the new nation. Race is unarguably resilient in its capacity to shape thinking about the past, the current conjuncture, and the future, and it has obtained a haunting poignancy: that set of recollections of what the society once was, that memory of how the nation was once "absolutely" separate, divided into distinguishable entities. The apartheid past is, paradoxically, a source of ideological poignancy because the lines of division were not only sharper but more unambiguously etched.

In the apartheid past South African identities were experienced differently because they were firmly racialized—the "fundamental divisions" were different, ensuring that the new process of constructing a post-apartheid shared identity will be equally arduous, working against and along racial fault lines that the new nation is only beginning to map. It requires a process of suturing which it is finding incredibly difficult to do—necessarily so, one might add. It is in this way that arguing against race, working for its institutional death, means nothing so much as hand-to-hand combat with the workings, language, and consequences of race—of what it did, of how it imprinted a society, of how it coded civic functionings. It is about arguing not simply against race, but against the powerful authority of racialized "reverie"—of how things used to be, of how much that affects how the new nation no longer wants and does not want those codes—that fragmented conception of race—to work. It is about recognizing that nonracialism is not a "paradise," that it is in the convent that most instructive lessons about racialized identity are located, and that semiotic (or physical) violence against the white girl, shot first or last, is always only a political ruse. If the white girl's story is silenced through rhetorical death, then oppositional narrative of the black "poors" will surely follow. Under no circumstances must the white girl, or the black girls, be shot.

Notes

1. In the foreword to Carl Schmitt's *The Concept of the Political*, Tracy B. Strong critiques liberalism as that series of social processes that "wishes to substitute procedure for struggle" (Strong 1996: xv).

2. The term "black" is used in this essay in its incorporative anti-apartheid instantiation: it includes the three historically disenfranchised groups, "blacks," "coloureds," and "Indians"—those of south Asian descent.

3. According to Schmitt, the political is constituted out of sovereignty, the state as the "sole subject of politics," and the distinction between friend and enemy. See Schmitt (1996, 1985) for a fuller discussion of the political.

4. It was reconstituted in the mid-1980s as the New Unity Movement.

PART III

POPULAR BLACKNESSES,

"AUTHENTICITY," AND

NEW MEASURES OF LEGITIMACY

HAVANA'S *TIMBA*

A Macho Sound for Black Sex

ARIANA HERNANDEZ-REGUANT

Dicen que yo soy un niche
Mira: yo soy un niche educado
Cuando camino te digo
Que La Banda ha leido y estudiado.[1]
—NG La Banda

In mid-1990s Havana *timba* music saturated the air.[2] It was the worst economic crisis in memory, yet the blasting beat was everywhere, playing on the
radio along with new commercial advertisements and also live at nightclubs
and soirées throughout town. Despite shortages of food and utilities and the
merciless summer heat, people did not stop dancing, and the lusciousness of
timba's body shakes mesmerized the tourists who, for the first time in decades, roamed through the city. However, timba was no ordinary dance
music. Played mostly by Afro-Cuban conservatory graduates, timba was a
contemporary sound of racial pride that challenged official discourses which
did not assign salience to race as a marker of hierarchy and inequality. It was
only at this point in time—when the Cuban infrastructure of cultural production engaged in commerce with foreign parties, and when the tourist

industry brought large numbers of Europeans and Canadians to the island in search of sun, romance, and socialist exotica—that the cry of "I am black and I am proud" became louder than ever before, immediately rallying a mass public among Afro-Cuban youth.[3] No doubt the project of the undifferentiated revolutionary masses was in crisis, as was the link forged by the government between national identity and revolutionary allegiance. New and old identifications emerged, and more saliently perhaps, race reappeared as both a line of social segmentation and a powerful idiom of positive difference. Nevertheless, why only when life horizons seemed to expand to the whole of the capitalist world did blackness break free from silence and prejudice to become a positive signifier of difference?

This essay argues that in a new situation characterized by an opening of the economy to capitalist markets, and of society to a massive influx of foreign visitors, new opportunities arose for disenfranchised segments in Cuban society, specifically Afro-Cubans, to voice a positive discourse of identity and difference, thereby claiming a presence and visibility. Indeed, in the Special Period—the period following the loss of Soviet support—the crippling of the welfare state affected most negatively those without access to key employment sectors or to hard currency from, for instance, family remittances. The resulting social stratification strikingly followed a color continuum, with darker-skinned Cubans massively placed at the bottom. As if that were not enough, after decades of silence on the issue of racial inequality, prejudice was back with a vengeance, and that extended beyond speech to police harassment and employment discrimination, most notably in the tourist sector. At the same time, the ubiquity of interracial romances involving foreigners and Afro-Cubans became the talk of the town, the subject of scorn in jokes, plays, and novels, which revealed, above all, a status quo of segregated intimacy.[4] Afro-Cubans finally talked back. Even though they remained, by and large, peripheral to emerging financial networks, they had benefited from the social policies of the Revolution and had the educational capital to do so. Discourses of black pride found their way into popular music and identity narratives among Afro-Cuban youth. An embryonic rap movement was in the works in marginal urban neighborhoods, but it was timba, the most popular dance music of the period, which loudly put forth a counternarrative of race that disputed both the myth of the *mestizo* nation and the ideology of the color-blind New Man.

Timba's cultural nationalism did not look at a preslavery past nor was it a reaction to a very recent history of racial violence, as in the United States.[5]

Timba emphasized Afro-Cuban heritage as central to national culture. But there was more. Timba located the contemporary—more so than the past—black experience at the heart of what it meant to be Cuban in a post-Soviet era caught between the imperatives of socialist morality and market expansion. And by extension, it explored what it meant to be black in the new transnational predicament, where race was by no means superseded. Timba did not substitute race with ethnicity, nor did it propose a multicultural model of coexistence, much less a separate-but-equal scenario. Much to the contrary; it naturalized blackness, and along with it difference and inequality, but not exactly as it had so far played out in Cuban society. This time, a correlation between nature and culture situated the black male on top—male hypersexuality being a marker of superiority. The challenge, then, was to extend black male superiority—his power invested by sexuality—to the social domain, and now the opening of new affective horizons afforded such opportunity. That is, Timba fixed blackness as a naturalized category and assigned it value as a form of social capital vis-à-vis a global society—with the twist that this global society was perceived to be free from the historical prejudices of the postcolony. The new theater of operations offered the possibility of a clean slate. Black disenfranchisement thus appeared as contingent and historically specific, and therefore localized. Consequently, the expansion of the social world beyond the rigid boundaries of Cuban revolutionary society offered the possibility to turn blackness from a hindrance into an asset—a redefinition of identity in strategic terms in order to cope with new transnational scenarios is not unique to Cuba, existing as it does in other late socialist contexts such as China (Rofel 1999b). That is not to say that timba music became a global genre. It did not. Nonetheless, it connected with its public by assuming an imaginary framework in which capitalist globalization was not the apocalypses that the revolutionary government presented. Rather, it offered the possibility of liberation through a redrawing of hierarchies of power and wealth. Within this framework, a racialization of self was not necessarily a mark of internalized subjugation but an affirmation of positive diversity as well as a strategy for social mobility.

This essay further maintains that, in a context in which forthright dissent was not viable, public disidentification with the racial status quo contained a deeper social critique. The reformulation of race, gender, sexuality, and nation implicit in timba not only spoke of a new global imaginary in which new cartographies of power and experience disrupted relations of scale, and very particularly, those of intimacy and sexuality (Povinelli and Chauncey 1999; Rofel

1999b). It also spoke to its primary and historical referent: the racial prejudices in Cuban society inherited from the colony, which the Cuban Revolution only managed to hush up. Timba revisited the link between blackness and illicit sexuality dating back to colonial times, when colonial elites and metropolitan intellectuals imputed both a dubious morality and an unrestrained sexuality to colonized subjects in order to justify their domination (Fanon 1967; Helg 1995; McClintock 1995; Stoler 1995). In so doing, timba redefined the triangulation between blackness, sexuality, and the white gaze, problematizing them all. For instance, it sustained the myth of the luscious and exotic other, but with the transgressive particularity that the black other was now the black self, and that the white gaze was not authorial but spectatorial. By turning negative racial and sexual stereotypes of the black man into positive attributes in a new context requiring new strategies of sociability, timba's "booty call"— to borrow from Gilroy (2000)—sought the empowerment of the black man vis-à-vis both white men and black women. This was no simple reversal of categories but a type of discourse which José Esteban Muñoz (1999: 3) has labeled as "disidentificatory"—one that foregrounds, rather than silences, the object of disidentification "using the majoritarian culture as raw material to make a new world . . . by recycling and rethinking encoded meaning." At a more textual level, this is what Alan West-Duran (2004), building on Henry Louis Gates and in reference to later Cuban rap, has called, "signifying in overdrive"—a discursive strategy in which the parodic repetition of canonic works is used to debunk prevailing notions of race, authority, and power. These types of discourses, present in timba, establish new possibilities by echoing the old in ways that expose the rhetoric of state power.

Timba, nonetheless, spoke the language of the street, often making up expressions which immediately became part of youth's slang. In addition, in the absence of any reporting of urban everyday life in the controlled Cuban press, timba operated as a "social chronicle."[6] For the first time in the revolutionary period, a public discourse told it "like it is," openly and without metaphor, detailing the hardships and hassles of Afro-Cubans in Havana's mean streets during the Special Period. In addition, through intertextuality and even direct interpellation, timba musicians addressed each other in public, referring to their mutual whereabouts and lifestyles. As if that did not cause enough scandal, timba's sexualized performances and graphic lyrics relentlessly pushed the limits of expression and moral decor of late revolutionary Cuba. Rather than openly confronting revolutionary governance, timba's disidentificatory discourse of a sexualized blackness exposed the underlying structures of hierarchy and power—of race, gender, and sexuality—that sustained the socialist regime, pointing at their continuity since colonial times. Still, even as nonopen confrontation, timba shook the establishment with its dialectical stance (at once of embrace and rejection) toward the commodification of sex, pleasure, and sociability that resulted from the crisis of socialism.[7]

In this process, timba attracted a massive following, constituting a sort of "competing counterpublic" (Fraser 1992) that was not fully independent from either the state or market forces but, rather, encroached on both of them. Indeed, the socialist state's participation in capitalist markets, particularly in the field of cultural production, introduced the imperative to balance profit and ideology, allowing for new spaces for art, performance, and leisure which, in some cases, were able to project themselves beyond national boundaries. Timba, specifically, soon transcended its base of Afro-Cuban youth to form a transnational "interpretive community" of performers, audiences, media producers, and commercial stakeholders around a discourse of racial and sexual citizenship. But it was its spectacular popularity within Cuba itself which brought to the fore the embroidering of bureaucracies and markets, profit and ideology, the national masses and segmented publics. Thus, contrary to what social scientists might have expected on the basis of the late Soviet experience, economic reforms did not lead to the waning of the state's ideological control but rather to a negotiation between profit and critique, and between art and ideology. Thus spheres of critique were facilitated, to some extent and temporarily, by the state itself—by liberal sectors within the cultural bureaucracy—and were justified as both revenue generating and controlled outlets for leisurely discontent. Why and how one such arena emerged and persisted with a positive discourse of blackness is the subject of this essay.

The Holy Word of Timba

Esa música que heredamos
hijos y nietos de los africanos,
la que mezclamos con la española,
con la francesa y la portuguesa,
la que fundimos bien con la inglesa . . .
—Los Van Van, "Somos cubanos"[8]

No escondas los collares ni los santos
Por temor al que dirán
Porque los santos lo malo te quitan
Y muchas cosas buenas que te dan.
—NG La Banda, "Santa Palabra"[9]

In musical terms, timba is a hard-edged form of *salsa,* but unlike New York-style salsa, it is based as much on *son* as it is on *rumba, batá,* and other traditional Afro-Cuban rhythms. It features complex polyrhythmic arrangements, an aggressive brass sound, synthesizers, a standard non-Latin drum set in addition to a Latin percussion section and several lead vocalists. While its music, choreographies, and aesthetics incorporate elements of hip-hop, reggae, rock, and even flamenco, its lyrics mostly deal with the everyday urban experiences of black Cubans in the context of the economic crisis, often using a humorous language filled with neologisms and double-meanings. Catchy chorus lines lend themselves to a play of call-and-response between singers and audience—much in a form reminiscent of some African American churches—and sudden rhythmic breaks encourage dancers to improvise and engage in *el tembleque* (the tremor). In this dance, the woman performs a body shake based on a relentless circular rotation of the pelvis with arms thrown up, chest shaking, and head moving sideways. Standing close to her, either in front or behind, the man, with his legs apart, knees slightly bent, extends his arms outward, as if surrounding her space with his four limbs without actually touching her, while he rhythmically and frenetically shakes his crotch, mimicking the frenzy of sexual climax. In Cuban musicological discourse—lyrics aside—timba was considered the most highly developed manifestation of a musical type that began with Cuban rural *son* early in the twentieth century and that incorporated influences from jazz and various Caribbean dance styles, taking Cuban popular music to unprecedented levels of complexity.[10]

As the story goes, timba developed in the early 1990s, when classically trained Afro-Cuban musicians turned to popular music in reaction to a rigid education that emphasized traditions associated with European "high culture."[11] With a contagious dance beat, timba—pioneered by NG La Banda,[12] catered to inner-city youth, chronicling life in the Afro-Cuban barrios with unprecedented candor. The goal of these bands was—quoting NG La Banda leader Jose Luis Cortés—"to tune in with the language and experience of the inner city."[13] They exposed the contradictions of these difficult years through a self-consciously racialized lens, breaking one of the greatest taboos in contemporary Cuban society: racial prejudice.[14] NG La Banda, along with most timba bands, zeroed in on the dynamics of the alleged "racial democracy" with neorealist wit.[15] NG had made a name for itself by playing in inner-city neighborhoods and downtrodden slums around Havana, becoming a favorite of working-class black youth—those derogatorily called *reparteros* (from the "hoods") and *ropas nacionales* (domestic clothing, as opposed to imported)—picking up their slang and incorporating their world view into the lyrics.[16] Its 1993 dance number in defense of an interracial union was probably a first in revolutionary Cuba and revealed the difficulties encountered by such couples:

Por qué tu finges? Se te nota
Que no puedes soportar que sea mía
Me saludas esquivando la mirada
Y dejando entrever la hipocresía
Ella es blanca, yo soy negro
Los tabús del racismo ya pasaron
Los valores que profeso
Conquistaron sus caricias y sus besos
No te apures compañero . . .[17]

NG was a black band with a consciousness-shaping mission, and knew well that racism was not a thing of the past. A century after the legalization of interracial marriages in the late nineteenth century, these unions were still few and short-lived due to social pressure, and, according to polls, over two-thirds of the white urban population opposed them altogether (Fernandez 1996; de la Fuente 2001). Yet, challenges to the official denial of race divisions were typically met with the Cuban proverb, "Quien no tiene de Congo tiene de Carabalí" (Who has not of Congo has of Carabalí), meaning that everyone has a drop of African blood and that precludes racism. But by locating the alleged drop in a distant past (when African ethnic groups such as Congo and Carabalí were identifiable), whites exonerated themselves from further mixing. The mestizo nation was a myth of racial origin that continued to be invoked, as in the nineteenth century, to deny racial prejudice (Kutzinski 1993). At the same time, its cultural counterpart, the *ajiaco* or melting pot of cultural synthesis, continued to sustain the ideology of racial democracy. But both discourses were in crisis. Two out of three of the characters representing the Cuban population in prerevolutionary popular culture were bailing out: the mulatta—the embodiment of *mestizaje*—and the *negrito*—the embodiment of Afro-Cuban heritage, now refashioned as a *niche*—were ready to leave the *gallego*—the creole descendant of Spaniards—on his own.[18]

Ironically, the arrival in mass of white tourists to Havana and their immediate friendship with Afro-Cubans exposed this public secret, provoking an upsurge of expressions of prejudice on the part of the white Cuban middle class, which considered such alliances to be a form of social descending. However, the presence of these newcomers, in addition to boosting the state-run tourist industry, offered hope and opportunity to those who crowded the touristy old city, who were mostly Afro-Cuban and marginal to the new networks of wealth. An informal economy quickly developed to cater to tourists' curiosity about life under socialism, and in turn, Afro-Cubans acquired international visibility as integral to the tourist landscape. An aesthetic of socialist poverty gained currency in world markets—*Buena Vista Social Club* being just the tip of the iceberg—and the dilapidated downtown and its black dwellers were beautified in coffee table books, television documentaries, and travelogues all over the globe.[19]

In the meantime, a timid debate on race relations ensued at the instigation of Afro-Cuban intellectuals, although it mostly stayed behind the institutional walls that hosted it. Nevertheless, academic research on Afro-Cuban folklore received a boost, and a number of documentary films, art projects, plays, and publications resurrected the old *Afrocubanista* project while addressing the problem of "el negro en la cultura cubana" (the role of the black man in Cuban culture).[20] The state's concomitant promotion of Afro-Cuban folklore and religion in the tourist sector resulted in the higher visibility and acceptance by wider sectors of the population (see Hagedorn 2001). Ironically, the timba bands proliferating at the time stood in contrast to these various Afrocubanista projects, claiming the same landscapes but in all their sordidness—not in their glory of yesteryear but as live and integral to a present consciousness of race linked to an imagined capitalist globalization.

That was the case with the Afro-Cuban religion, Santeria, which is something that timba does not joke about—musicians wear the religion on their sleeves. In timba, ritual drums like batá are routinely included in the bands, and their associated rhythmic patterns are incorporated into many compositions. More explicitly, musicians loudly proclaim their faith and visibly display ritual protective beads (*collares*), which, for decades and due to the hostile religious environment, used to be worn inconspicuously under clothing. For religion was not something the Revolution had endorsed. Atheism was intrinsic to governmental doctrine and religious manifestations were repressed for decades. Religious allegiance was often kept private for fear of negative repercussions, particularly in the case of Communist Party members. Although popular dance music (*son* and *salsa*)—in addition to specifically religious music—never eliminated references to Santeria, it was only in the 1990s that an official relaxation toward public religious expressions fueled timba's vocal defense. Furthermore, timba was not "traditional" music, and its religious discourse had a new language, for instance, referring to religious saints in colloquial terms,[21] claiming the relevance of Afro-Cuban religion to the present woes and tribulations endured by the people of Afro-Cuban descent, and criticizing those who hypocritically worship in private but shun religion in public for fear of what people may say.[22]

Los Van Van—Cuba's most famous dance band since its inception in 1970, and one that has been integral to the timba movement of the 1990s—has pioneered what might be called a "charismatic" kind of timba. The band typically starts its performances with a musical intro which includes remarks on the religious initiation of particular band members, pointing out those who are full-fledged *babalawos* (the Santeria equivalent of a priest).[23] The band's 1995 album *Ay Dios Ampárame* (God protect me) pays explicit homage to the Afro-Cuban religion. Its cover features the green and yellow beads that symbolize the protection of Orula, the deity of divination and wisdom. The album includes "Soy todo" (I am all), which is one of the band's highlights during live performances and is a religious performance in itself. Beginning with a poem by the Afro-Cuban poet Eloy Machado, aka El Ambia, which defines man as a repository of the ancestors' wisdom, the singer launches into a long charismatic sermon in both Yoruba and Spanish, asking the Lord to protect the Cuban people and especially "the people of this color: the niche, the brown, who have arisen from the bottom struggling against so much hardship."[24] As the extemporaneous deliverance escalates in intensity and fervor, the public—possibly tens of thousands of people—extend their arms upwards and respond, echoing the chorus line: "Ay Dios ampárame." The emotional performance deeply involves musicians and audiences in a religious community that was presented as integral to national solidarity—a message that timba bands continue to bring to their international performances. In these contexts they stress the unity of all Cubans—not only in Cuba but also dispersed throughout the world.

Thus, timba performance connects with the public emotionally in ways hardly seen in Cuban dance music. Part of the reason why is that it points at the humble working masses as the repository of Cuban popular culture and therefore of Cuban identity at large. Take "Crónica social," a song that was censored and never recorded but part of NG La Banda's performance repertoire. In an angry and defiant tone, NG La Banda denounces the social distance between state officials and the people and recriminates an unnamed interlocutor, presumably a high government official who has scorned their music, for never having set foot in a *solar* (a crowded inner-city tenement typically inhabited by Afro-Cubans), and for being out of touch with the humble and hard-working people for whom popular music provide meaning:

Por eso que te digo
que no critiques mas
la música popular de estos tiempos.
Que son exactos,
Chabacanos?
Quien te dijo?Has ido tu a los solares de Cuba? . . .
Has visto a la gente que se levanta a las cinco de la mañunga,
a cogerla?
que son los que ponen la música popular . . .[25]

In a similar tone, Los Van Van, in "La bomba soy yo," accuse a *pancho* (a know-it-all)—typically a white man—of not being a good Cuban "because in music you have no rhythm, and in sports you don't excel, because you don't know anything about baseball, and you've never been in a *bembé,* and you don't know who Manuel Mendive is, so what can you offer?" And while not all Afro-Cubans may have rhythm, be good in sports, or know the work of the Africanist painter Manuel Mendive, most of them have at one point participated in a *bembé*—a spontaneous rumba performance occurring at informal gatherings. The point, however, is clearly one of exclusion. Whites cannot claim to be rightfully Cuban while they ignore the experiences and endurance of their black and mulatto counterparts.

In relation to this, timba identifies the *solar* as equally central to the Afro-Cuban experience. The *solar* was as much a product of socialist housing policies as of endemic racial inequality. Walter Benjamin (1978: 108–9), in his 1927 chronicle of Moscow's life under the Bolsheviks, observed a residential setting that could easily apply to certain buildings in Havana: "Apartments that earlier accommodated single families . . . now often lodge eight. Through the hall door one steps into a little town. More often still, an army camp. Even in the lobby one can encounter beds. . . . Curtains and partitions, often only half of the height of walls, have had to multiply the number of rooms. . . ." In Havana, early efforts at residential integration resulted in the introduction of *solares* in white neighborhoods, and the further marginalization of their Afro-Cuban dwellers. In public discourse, the *solar* became antithetical to socialist order: an infamous setting where crime, immorality, and subversion thrived; a sort of residential lumpen land for squatters and black marketers. Alternatively, literary and artistic representations of the *solar* depicted it as a stage for Afro-Cuban folkloric spectacles.[26] But in timba, the *solar* was the school of life where Afro-Cubans learned the values of solidarity and community.

An early CD cover by NG La Banda (*En la calle*) was one of the first to show a solar, even though it was still as a performance space—perhaps because foreigners were the main buyers of CDs at the time.[27] Thereon timba narratives focused, rather, on the *solar*'s everyday dynamics, which included music and performance, but also manicuring and hair dressing, hanging out, gossiping, making love, watching soap operas, and even hiding from the police. According to Issac Delgado's hit "El Solar de la California" (a timba version of "Hotel California"), the *solar* is not only a center for black culture but for the black market: where "love is made in colors" and "where the dollar value goes up and down." The solar, in sum, is seen as "the true Havana."[28]

By the end of the 1990s and following the migration of a new generation of Cubans to Europe and North America during the period, the *solar* also became a transnational site of Cubanness. In Los Van Van's first and controversial appearance in Miami in 1999, for example, the band called for unity and community between the Cubans "of here and there," adding positive commentary on the *solares* of Hialeah (a working-class Cuban community in Dade County) as emblematic of an extraterritorial Cuban national identity. Back in Havana, some time later, before thousands at the Malecón, Los Van Van's singer asked those living in a *solar* to raise their hand and say it out loud, adding that he himself lived in a *solar*, along with black people all over, from Hialeah to the Bronx. It was this fact which gave him and would give them the strength to carry the message of black pride all over the world.

Timba, in sum, proposed a brand of cultural nationalism that situated the racial experience—the lived experience—at the center of nationality. But this voice only reached the public thanks to the opening of discursive spheres following the state's concessions to market interests. Up until then, the Revolution sought to render the meaning of race irrelevant, promoting a political type of nationalism that built on citizenship, participation, and the moral idea of the New Man (Hernandez-Reguant 2002). Public debate on race relations was suppressed. Nevertheless, racial prejudice as well as racial identifications and their related social networks remained in place. As was the case with the resurgence of ethnicity in Eastern Europe after 1989, the state's silencing of these types of identities did not amount to their disappearance. To the contrary, socialist policies, along with a permanent economy of shortage, actually maintained networks based on ethnic allegiances through which necessary resources circulated (Verdery 1996). In Cuba, these networks were often based on the neighborhood. And since many neighborhoods remained, to a great extent, racially segregated, these ties still followed race and class lines. Thus timba's emphasis on blackness as a locus of identity in the 1990s cannot be attributed merely to its insertion in Black Atlantic circuits emerging from the underground thanks to capitalist globalization, as has been argued in relation to the later popularity of Cuban rap in certain neighborhoods of the capital city (Fernandes 2003; Pacini Hernandez and Garafolo 1999/2000; West-Duran 2004).[29] Rather, timba's spectacular growth paralleled the commercialization of cultural production by state institutions.

"From Cuba and for the World": The Emergence of a Timba Public

De Cuba y Para el Mundo
Llegó lo que tu esperabas
Lo que te gusta, lo que te encanta
Lo que revuelve La Habana . . .
—La Charanga Habanera[30]

Si vas a La Tropical
Si vas al Palacio de la Salsa . . .
Ni lo pienses, mi hermana
La música de hoy
Es la música cubana.
—Manolito y su Trabuco[31]

Timba became known, simply, as "the Cuban music" at a moment in which the definition of national identity was more uncertain than ever. During the Special Period and as the state's ideological hegemony was breaking down, timba acquired both media exposure and institutional support. In seeking innovative ways to keep afloat while confronting a postsocialist world market, the socialist government boosted the tourist industry and infused its cultural infrastructure with foreign capital. Dance bands playing the contemporary form of *son* that was known as timba proliferated along with the newly revamped hard-currency clubs, finding instant promotion on new radio and television shows, and signing record deals with foreign labels. Media exposure contributed to the celebrity status of musicians and their entourages of agents and managers. Furthermore, the introduction of commercial advertisements contributed to the association of these Afro-Cuban musicians with new capitalist opportunities as they often appeared in campaigns for consumer products like beer, rum, and tobacco. Their meteoric careers, along with their flashy looks and conspicuous spending, turned them into popular symbols of upward mobility and capitalist plenty. Although viewed with apprehension by state officials, they became heroes to their inner-city audience, to whom they remained loyal, playing for free in their neighborhoods and defending Afro-Cuban culture and lifestyles as key to both national belonging and transnational opportunity.

In the midst of water shortages, electricity blackouts, and scarcity of food and basic consumer items, and as popular discontent mounted throughout Havana, timba connected with the experiences of the Afro-Cuban working classes, inciting them to dance and making them laugh with stories of urban picaresque. In effect, the world created by timba through live performance and broadcasts was central to an alternative public sphere in which notions of race, sexuality, nation, and morality were increasingly at odds with revolutionary ideology. Timba offered a space and a language of critique that was permitted as long as it was confined to a nonpolitical arena. Most importantly, timba did not become the national music only because of a general trend to reclaim blackness within the Cuban melting pot. Rather, as the market became another element in revolutionary governance and society, financial considerations weighted heavily on its proliferation.

In such a context, the emergence of this arena of leisure and entertainment showed that alternative public spheres could be more flexible than those described by Habermas and his critics. Such spheres could coexist— with limitations—with a socialist regime, at the interstices of state and market. They did not have to be fully independent from the state nor speak in overt political terms in order to offer an alternative discourse. For as long as such discourses were formulated in nonoppositional terms and coded with a seemingly nonpolitical language they were able to pass the filters of censorship. Hence, semi-alternative public arenas emerged out of the precarious equilibrium—a dialectic—between a socialist administration and capitalist economic policies, an equilibrium that in the late Soviet experience did not last long. In the former Soviet bloc, economic reforms led to the formation of interest groups and ultimately to a civil society, which produced capitalist versions of democracy. In Cuba, however, this process was aborted and the socialist government remained in place. However, liberal sectors within the cultural bureaucracy were aware of the need to provide outlets to the most disenfranchised sectors of society in order to channel increasing discontent and ultimately safeguard revolutionary hegemony. Thus, it was in the realms of leisure and entertainment, of art and performance—realms of nonpolitics —that disidentifications with the socialist project found a sort of safe haven, at least temporarily. This was no civil society as is often understood. These arenas of contestation were encroached on both by the state and the market— they were alternative but not independent.

In the case at hand, timba thrived thanks to institutional support, which included the state and Communist Party—radio and television channels, recording studios, record labels, management agencies, neighborhood cultural centers, rehearsing spaces, music schools, nightclubs and dance halls; and, in sum, the entire state cultural infrastructure. In late socialism, the state, the market, and society were not neatly separated entities. It was in the process through which the revolutionary government sought to balance profit and ideology that new spaces of critique—"soft" critique—emerged. From the government's standpoint, timba's discourse of race, nation, community, and cosmopolitanism seemed a lesser evil, and, most pragmatically, it was one that generated foreign currency for the starved state coffers.

Timba was what García Canclini (1999) has termed "an interpretive community," an unstable and contingent public, gathered in informal participation in events, social networks, aesthetics, and modes of speech, and around the identification—and disidentification, to borrow from José Esteban Muñoz (1999)—with dominant ideologies of race and power. Neither were these "counterpublics" in the sense of organized arenas of "resistance" against a hegemonic power structure (Fraser 1993; Warner 2002).[32] Rather there existed a multiplicity of overlapping publics that were too loose and unstable to conform to the hegemony/resistance model implicit in the notion of counterpublic, and which, in this case, came together, first and foremost, in live performance. For instance, a notion of community was conveyed through a heavy intertextuality, that is, through the bands' use of musical and lyrical references and interpellations to each other as well as through media outlets which provided gossip commentary and delimited the in-crowd from those out of the loop.[33]

Timba's new ways to think and speak about self and other, nationality and community—in addition to its association with the new tourist clubs, which provided regular employment to the new bands, its commercialization by foreign record labels, and the touring of bands through Europe and North America—reflected an expansion of life horizons beyond the island nation. It was not capricious that timba's foremost radio show, *From Five to Seven*, started its daily broadcasts by greeting in both English and Spanish an audience that, according to the show's announcement, was located all over Latin America and the Caribbean. With a loud and dynamic pace, and a formula of music, commercials, entertainment news, and informal talk, the program achieved top audience ratings in Cuba's urban centers and blasted daily in homes, cabs, and cafeterias, becoming the country's main source of advertising revenue during its six-year run. Programming of the latest foreign salsa and *merengue* hits alongside information on the bands' international tours and promotion of foreign consumer products presented a seductive image of the capitalist revelry soon to come. The show made the bleakness of the Special Period go away in favor of a hip and cosmopolitan Havana that was home to a *farandula* (showbiz elite) of Cuban and foreign jet-setters—including the show's own producers. For the time being, being in *From Five to Seven* was prized, and priced, and ultimately accusations of payola brought the show down and off the air. But during its six-year run (1994–99), *From Five to Seven* constructed an alternative universe of celebrity culture, one that was, by and large, Afro-Cuban[34] and, in contrast to earlier elites, not impenetrable but, ironically, more democratic, as it could be accessed thanks to capitalist opportunity (Hernandez-Reguant 2002).[35]

From Five to Seven was no privately run show but a major program at a national radio station, Radio Taíno, overseen by the Communist Party. The Institute of Radio and Television converted Radio Taíno into a commercial-like station in order to obtain advertising revenue and finance its entire radio network. Timba was instrumental in attracting foreign advertisers, even though these were premises that sent chills to top Communist officials, who worried about the music's symbolic power in support of lifestyles contrary to socialist morality. The more liberal Cuban cultural bureaucracy, however, jumped on the timba bandwagon and generally adapted to the new business environment by introducing flexibility and autonomy in its dependent enterprises. The Cuban Music Institute—a division within the Ministry of Culture—dedicated the 1997 CubaDisco music expo to the genre in the hopes of turning it into a cultural export, and it also mediated the interest of foreign labels and sponsored an international tour of an All Stars timba band.[36] In exchange for their privileged lifestyle, bands often endorsed government campaigns of various kinds by participating in Communist-sponsored events.[37]

Timba bands, nonetheless, maintained their connection with those whom they viewed as their natural public, Afro-Cuban youth, and nothing evidenced their connection more than the weekly concerts at La Tropical. La Tropical was timba's undisputed cathedral. Initially a beer garden, it was an open-air dance hall located in a populous Afro-Cuban neighborhood. It was there where bands tested new tunes and dancers rehearsed new steps. La Tropical was the only timba club accessible with Cuban pesos; its cover charge was only costly enough to make the occasion special for its mostly Afro-Cuban patrons—for La Tropical was a marked space in terms of both race and class. As David Turnley's 2001 documentary film *La Tropical* poignantly showed, white Cubans would not mingle in the *ambientes* (circles) frequented by the *guaperia* (knife-carrying black youth). White Cubans tended to stay away, especially on timba nights, when brawls were said to erupt just as easily as cheap rum circulated throughout the dance floor. "That is not a place where decent people go," they would say. Indeed, the so-called "Cuban music" was considered to be the music of the most marginal and antisocial elements associated with the black market and the criminal underworlds, and therefore attracting violence, alcohol, and drugs. To validate these fears, La Tropical's gate was permanently flanked by police vans, are officers routinely frisked customers and infiltrated the crowds to look out for fights and drugs.[38] Prime bands like Los Van Van, La Charanga Habanera, NG La Banda, Klimax, Manolín, Bamboleo, Bakuleyé, Tamayito, and Paulito FG were often on the bill, and the regulars knew every one of their songs even before they were formally released. Spontaneous exchanges between performers and audience culminated in the blurring of the two, with singers eventually descending to the dance floor and people climbing up on stage—something not that unusual in Cuba, where even in large concerts the crowds were not physically separated from the stage, and where on more than one occasion the audience's actual invasion of the stage paralyzed the concert itself.[39] While at La Tropical things were usually more civil, the few foreigners attending would typically stay in the VIP section, safely watching the floor below from the balcony.

Whether alone or with a Cuban date, most tourists would rather go to El Palacio de la Salsa, El Café Cantante, or any other of the hard-currency clubs where the steep cover charge—fifteen to twenty dollars—was unaffordable to most Cubans, and where they would enjoy ample dance room, clean bathrooms, and designer drinks. At these, the scene was rather different. Under dim lights, small tables surrounded a clearly marked dance floor next to the stage. Patrons from Europe, Canada, and Latin America were usually accompanied by black Cuban dates. On weekends, young black men and women crowded the doors in the hopes of finding a foreigner willing to pay their cover charge.[40] Inside, single Afro-Cuban women in skimpy clothing pursued the mostly middle-aged European and Canadian men. On stage, the bands would use phrases in English and Italian and would call for the countries represented in the audience: Italy, Spain, the United States, Mexico, Brazil . . . One of timba's foremost bands, Klimax, would typically start its concerts that way, then, referring to the Cuban women on the floor, praise the virtues of the Cuban mulatta, and urge the foreigners present to repeat the chorus line, "Mulatta, take me home with you." Then, again addressing the Cubans in the house, the singer would empathize with their hardships: "Those here who want health and money, raise your hands!" "And those who want health, money, and a trip abroad? Raise your hands!" "Ah, everyone likes that!" The whole orchestra would then kick in as the audience seconded the chorus: "Yo lo que quiero es salud, dinero, y un viaje pa'l extranjero" (What I want is health, money, and a trip abroad).[41] Love was conspicuously absent from this wish list, perhaps because, in timba, more often than not, love is an obstacle, holding people back (home) rather than propelling them forward (abroad).

At this time, the associations between white foreigners and Afro-Cubans were highly debated moral issues. Many of these relationships were deemed, without further investigation, as based on interest and identified with *jineterismo*—the exchange of company and favors for favors rather than for a monetary fee as in standard prostitution. The phenomenon captured widespread attention in Cuba and abroad as the shameful side of capitalism for some—or of socialism for others. The fact that many of these relationships ended in marriage seemed irrelevant to their detractors. Severe travel restrictions imposed by the socialist administration on the population meant that marriage was—as it had been in the former Soviet bloc—a common strategy for legal emigration. Therefore marriage, in some cases in lieu of payment for services, was viewed as the price and prize of such associations. According to a report by Mauricio Vicent (2001), the Cuba correspondent for the Spanish daily *El País*, only 15 Spanish-Cuban marriages were registered at the Spanish consulate in 1990, but 670 were registered in 1993, 1,190 in 1996, and 4,169 in 2000. Vicent cited consular officials who stated that in 80 percent of these cases, Spanish men, usually middle-aged, wedded much younger women, "beautiful and mulatta," often with "a technical or university degree." Middle-class prejudice, weighing heavily in these types of characterizations, often portrayed the Afro-Cuban party as a hustler, the white foreigner as either a dupe or a pervert, and the entire interracial relation as invariably linked to self-interest and illicit profit.[42]

In contrast, timba songs defended such transatlantic love affairs, particularly when the Cuban party was male, and in so doing, they also sustained the myth of the luscious exotic other. The particularity was that now the "other" was the self, and that now the goal was not subjugation but the selective empowerment of black men vis-à-vis not only white men but also women—white, mulatto, and black. Timba stressed the link between blackness and sexuality but in a positive way and within a context larger than the colony. Timba contested not only the status quo in regard to interracial and heterosexual relations but also the hierarchy that placed white men on top by identifying sexual prowess as a key for upward mobility in a new transnational terrain. Timba's disidentifications, in sum, threw into question the very pillars of the status quo, exposing the reified hierarchies of race and sexuality which structured postcolonial society to the present day.

The Niches and Their Booty Call

Dicen que se comenta por toda La Habana,
Que estos niches están acabando
con todas las mujeres de La Habana
toditas las mujeres
Y no pasa nada . . .
—La Charanga Habanera, "Lo siento por ti"[43]

Pa que tengas lo que tenias que tener
Un papirriki con wanikiki.
—La Charanga Habanera, "El temba."[44]

In the new economy of affect manhood was sublimated first and foremost in the game of heterosexual seduction, which, in timba, was symbolically simulated in the *tembleque* along with a wealth of dance moves focusing on the sexual attributes of both men and women. These types of performances, not unusual in the African Diaspora, have been referred to by Paul Gilroy (2000: 266) as a "booty call"—defined as the "androcentric and phallocentric presentation and representation of heterosexual coupling." Gilroy situates these types of performances in contexts in which open political rebellion is not viable and interprets them as forms of biopolitical resistance. That is, where open attack on the body politic is not feasible, critical discourse may focus instead on the individual. In this case, as in other authoritarian contexts in times of political crisis, public eroticism and pornography became a language of resistance, a challenge to public morality as a form of expressing dissatisfaction with a political regime that is also a moral system. In Cuba, the provocative showcase of black sexual power in the mainstream worked to subvert the moral imaginary sustaining revolutionary governance.

Those involved in the performance and popularization of timba crafted an ethos of black machismo and a narrative of male hypersexuality to accompany timba's so-called macho sound.[45] Timba lyrics and extemporaneous talk at live performances often referred to black men's conquests, including boastful proclamations such as "They say that we niches are finishing up / with all the women in Havana / absolutely all the women / And nothing happens!"[46] It also included references to male sexual attributes, like "this little thing I have that gets up and not down," and to sexual exchanges, like "open your mouth baby . . . and suck my lollipop," "I give it to you in your size," "don't touch it so hard / be careful with my instrument," or "going down on you, no way."[47] Such statements caused the rage of orthodox sectors of the government, like the Federation of Cuban Women, headed by Fidel Castro's sister-in-law, which lobbied for and eventually succeeded at banning certain songs from public broadcasting.[48] Timba's spectacle of black sexuality was considered an attack on social decency and was labeled as *chabacana*, in bad taste—a charge contested in numerous songs.[49] These accusations revealed a subtle racism, and they were invariably put forth by whites in reference to the Afro-Cuban working class. Timba bands sided with NG La Banda's angry response in the aforementioned "Crónica social": "Yo no soy chabacano, lo que soy es tremendo cubano" (I am not vulgar, I am just a true Cuban). The point was that in a socialist society, in which value and identity hinged on labor and political citizenship, black males were representing themselves not only as forces of production but also of pleasure, and such a controversial stance—they insisted—was not any less Cuban. This was by no means a form of colonialist nostalgia, when the triangulation between blackness, sexuality, and the white gaze yielded such representations. Timba's public endorsing of past racist depictions amounted to an exposé of the public, yet shameful, secret. What timba put forth, therefore, was a discourse of power which sought to reorganize race relations, and there could be such reorganization because the composition and boundaries of society were in flux.

In the most graphic way, a 1997 album cover by La Charanga Habanera sexualized the black male body—from head to fingers—in clear "disidentification" with prevailing ideologies of race and gender inherited from colonial times.[50] In reference to a song promoting condom use—commissioned for an AIDS prevention campaign and a concession to government pressure— the front cover shows a cheerful black man carrying flowers in his hand and an oversized condom on his head. The graphic can be interpreted as forging a link between affection, symbolized by the bouquet, and recreational sex. Or perhaps the image implies that the main sexual organ is housed in the head. The back cover, in turn, depicts an older and dark-skinned band member dressed as a *negro calesero* (a colonial carriage driver), smiling and waving his left hand. Highlighted in red, his fingers are shaped like erect male organs, thus giving his salutation an obvious motive. The negro calesero was a frequent character in the early twentieth-century burlesque theater of white authors. Typically a slave, he was a shoddy yet harmless character who would make advances toward light-skinned ladies traveling in his vehicle (Moore 1997). Barely a hundred years after the abolition of slavery and national independence, La Charanga Habanera mocked this well-known guise—itself a mockery—by explicitly and proudly emphasizing the black man's sexuality, undomesticated by the servant's uniform. But the disidentification with the stereotype does not reside in its endorsement, nor in its rejection, but in its full disclosure. In this period of increasing globalization, black men rewrote the script and the negro calesero was no loser. As his placement on the back cover suggests, he was the last to laugh.

At the end of the twentieth century, the subservient negrito represented himself as a successful and proud niche, and in the process he refashioned the national triad in his favor, broadcasting his "booty call" to the entire country and beyond. His phallocentrism was a statement of superiority vis-à-vis not only white men, but also black women, whose independent strategies of survival he belligerently rejected. Indeed, timba's disidentificational stance is heavily male-centered. When it comes to the Afro-Cuban woman, timba offers no salvation. When the triangulation previously mentioned had at its apex the white gaze, the black body often was either explicitly male or female, depending on the gendering of the white onlooker, but not both, and the relation between the black man and the black woman tended to be overlooked. In timba, black men break this silence but not to seek justice for the black woman. As Brackette Williams (1996) has explained, competing nationalist discourses also establish a competition between racialized forms of masculinity, and by extension, domination. The Afro-Cuban man was male before Cuban, leaving the Afro-Cuban woman as a double other.

In timba, like in Cuban colonial and postcolonial literature, the mulatta— confident in her youth and beauty—is a conniving character with a deviant sensuality, one that "melts ice" but lacks a heart.[51] She is materialistic and unscrupulous to the point of bringing her man to bankruptcy, indigence, and even death. In song after song she is a "shopping maniac": a compulsive consumer of foods and goods;[52] a "super touristy" who will only go to the most expensive clubs and ride in hard-currency taxis; "a witch without feelings" quick to exchange a man's love for cheap thrills;[53] one who will allow a black man to shower her with love and affection only to extend a bill for services rendered, payable by "check, credit card, or cash."[54] As represented in La Charanga Habanera's comic strips included in their CD *Pa Que Se Entere La Habana*, women are insatiable. The beautiful "Super Turistica," for instance, is too expensive for the average Afro-Cuban man, even though they might have grown up in the same neighborhood. The tourist-loving mulatta prefers to work the streets and ride in cars with foreign strangers rather than being with a good-hearted but penniless black man.[55] According to this and numerous lyrics, the mulatta's love is up for auction,[56] and in the end, she commits the worse affront: she leaves the black man, not for a white Cuban, but for a foreigner, a *temba* (an older man), a *papirriki con wanikiki* (a sugar daddy with dough)[57] who can fulfill her frivolous needs and perhaps take her with him to his country. In so doing, she also abandons the project of the mestizo nation—however futile that project might have been anyway—and therefore her betrayal is not only to the black man but to the entire nation. For, in timba, it is the black man, and not the mulatto woman—nor the white revolutionary—who stands as symbol of a Cuban nation, now open to the world.

This collective trauma was evident at a mass concert in Havana's Malecón, when Los Van Van's singer asked the tens of thousands in the public to raise their hands if a mulatta ever left them for a foreigner, only to obtain a loud ovation in response.[58] After sharing that his mulatta, a beautiful woman of "hazel eyes, black hair and a mouth like a ripe mango," left him for an Italian, he warns that mulattas are two-faced and therefore not to be trusted. Should they want to come back, seeking the unparalleled sexual abilities of the black man, they are not to be given another chance. After all, mulattas are expendable—he continued—as Cuba produces them at a dime a dozen. Furthermore, unlike in previous historical periods, when immigrants to the island were mostly men, now foreign women provide additional options. Assuredly, black men's conquests—their "finishing up with all the women in Havana"— particularly those white and foreign, boosted their egos, and in broadcasting these relationships, timba musicians sent shockwaves through Cuban society, ending the societal silence on race and in the process challenging revolutionary discourses on nation and social equality.

Conclusion

By the end of the 1990s, the timba world was ridden with scandal. Its main radio show, *From Five to Seven*, went off the air following payola accusations; the Spanish labels that initially signed the bands went bankrupt and left Cuba; some of the nightclubs were closed down for alleged involvement in the sex and drug trade; and many musicians defected while on tour in Europe and North America. One thing remained strong, and that was the tembleque, and not just because Afro-Cuban youth adapted it to the beat of the new reggeaton craze. The tembleque officially engrossed national patrimony, and so by 1999 it was incorporated into the repertoire of the National Folkloric Ensemble; the sexy booty shake invariably causing respectable theater audiences to break into laughter. Likewise, the paradigmatic Solar de la California that inspired Issac Delgado was turned into an Afro-Cuban cultural center. The tremor of timba was now carefully choreographed by a professional troupe, and the social history of Afro-Cuban performance repeated itself in this trajectory from marginal *chabacanería* to folkloric spectacle. Once again, the state containment of Afro-Cuban performance intended to diffuse its subversive power, repositioning such cultural manifestations in delimited zones of social action. By this time too, economic reforms were stalled or reversed, and the government ostensibly returned to ideological orthodoxy, strengthening its repressive apparatus to exert control over discourse and practices.

From the onset, timba was controversial. In contradiction to a socialist doctrine which negated the existence of, or the place for, racially based identity, timba championed a discursive arena in which racial thinking was central. Moreover, its message did not stay underground. The contagious dance music grew alongside Cuba's opening to global networks of exchange, travel, and entertainment, benefiting from the spaces of expression facilitated by the incoming capitalism. In the Cuba of the Special Period, survival literally depended on the ability to skillfully navigate between the capitalist practices of incoming stakeholders and the socialist bureaucracy and its public morality. At the interstices of this encounter between socialism and capitalism—in the compromise between socialist ideology and market imperatives—was some wiggle room. Timba seized that space, and, at a time in which the imperatives of profit were hard to ignore, its immediate popularity gained it both a stage and media exposure. And as the state struggled to provide for people's material needs, race held a key to mobility for those who had nothing else. Timba musicians were living proof, for it was not only their musical abilities but their skills to market themselves for new audiences that launched them to fame and wealth. For their Afro-Cuban followers, they became symbols of an incoming capitalism, which, unlike the socialist revolution, did not purport to be race blind, but in which what kind of difference would translate into hierarchy was up for grabs.

Timba, at the forefront of this new racial consciousness, critiqued the model of racial democracy and normative sexuality promulgated by the revolution, implicitly exposing the social hierarchies upon which both the postcolonial nation and the socialist state were predicated. But timba's discourse of race and sex was not only in dialogue—and disidentification—with revolutionary ideologies of race, sex, and nation; it was also in dialogue with an "interpretive community" that extended to the transnational music industry as well as to a growing foreign presence in search of business opportunities, socialist exotica, and Caribbean romance. In this context, timba crafted an ethos of blackness linked to machismo and a flamboyant sexuality as a strategy of mobility for its primary public of disenfranchised Afro-Cuban youth. More precisely, as a new transnational economy of commerce and affect flourished, a kind of blackness identified with both masculinity and sexuality was relocated at the heart of what it meant to be Cuban.

It would be an exaggeration to say that timba ever became a global genre, or that it fostered transnational identities, like so many other Black Atlantic cultural manifestations. The music was rooted in Afro-Cuban rhythms, and its audiences for the most part were located in Cuba. However, timba's explosive popularity in Cuba during the 1990s was only made possible, precisely, by Cuba's emergent imagining of the global, by the newly acquired expectations, on the part of previously disenfranchised groups, of life beyond the horizons of revolutionary socialism. Timba echoed a new imagined landscape in which self and other were no longer placed, primarily, within the framework of the island nation (revolutionary or otherwise), or even within that of a greater *Cubanidad* encompassing the exile community, but within an envisioned framework of unbound transnational circuits. Nonetheless, timba remained quintessentially Cuban. And being Cuban during the Special Period meant pointing to, and planning for, new possibilities for life elsewhere.

The dialectics of power and intimacy expressed in timba showed that racial and gender hierarchies are always intertwined, and when they are linked to a nationalist discourse, they structure both class privileges and state authority. Timba proposed an alternative that took into account the reconfiguration of life horizons for inner-city Afro-Cuban youth—albeit not necessarily one leading to social justice. Timba was no mindless booty call or a remnant of earlier political rebellions—a free ass is not a step toward a free mind. Nonetheless, in the authoritarian context of late socialism, the booty and the brain, sexuality and ideology, race and power, were inseparable, and a booty shake shook, perhaps for more than a moment, the body social. Hence, the condom on the head.

Notes

1. "They say I am a nigger / Look, I am an educated niggah / My walk tells you that / in this band we are well read" (NG La Banda, "Los sitios entero," *En la calle*, Qbadisc 1992). The Spanish "niche" can be translated as the English "niggah" or "nigger." Although in some areas of the Spanish-speaking world the terms are equivalent, in Cuba *niche* lacks the U.S. connotations of racial violence and its consideration as a pejorative term depends on the context. Generally, niche describes a dark-skinned black male. In a friendly environment, its use is considered acceptable by blacks, even if used by whites. However, most whites consulted confirmed that their use of the term as an appellative would be "inappropriate" for them. The term, however, acquired a connotation of pride only when timba musicians began to use it. Only in recent times and in certain circles (such as among rappers), are some people becoming aware of the phonetic similarity between nigger and niche and investing in

niche the contextual North American meanings of nigger (see, for instance, Pacini Hernandez and Garofalo 1999/2000). Hence, some young Cubans consulted believed niche is a derivative of nigger.

2. In addition to all the people in Havana who, at one time or another during my several years there, shared my passion for timba, I wish to extend special thanks to my colleague and friend Paul Ryer, for agreeing to be my date on that fateful first visit to La Tropical in 1996. Many thanks too to Marcial Godoy, Dana Holland, and Kevin Moore for their commentary of earlier drafts of this work, and to Hourik Goulabi for the editing. In addition, I want to mention the *charangueros* who, during the long process of writing this paper, generously provided me with relevant materials, comments, and/or inspiring conversation: Ale Aragón, David Cantrell, Kamari Clarke, Darsi Fernandez, el Dongo, Ariana Hall, Jesús Jambrina, Bobby Jiménez, Humberto Manduley, Ivor Miller, Giraldo Piloto Jr., William Sauvorin, Monika Smith, and Ignacio Vera.

3. Although people in Cuba recognize a broad spectrum of shades in the white-black color continuum, the categories more widely used are those of white, black and mulatto. In timba, the term "mulatto" is hardly used in its masculine form. Rather, it refers almost exclusively to women, whereas "black" (*negro*) is most often used to refer to men. Broadly speaking, even a dark-skinned woman might be referred to as mulatta, whereas mulatto men might be included in the broader reference of black. In this essay, I use Afro-Cuban to mean phenotypically nonwhite and of visible African descent, and socially identified as either black or mulatto.

4. The revolutionary government had purported to end racial inequality when coming into power in 1959, but it did not push the issue in order not to antagonize the white middle class. Later the issue was swept under the rug following the idea that redistribution policies aimed at ending income differentials would take care of race and other inequalities. For an extensive account, see de la Fuente 2001 and H. Adams 2004.

5. Cuba did not undergo a history of rigidly enforced segregation and racial violence as did the United States, nor did Cuba have a civil rights movement. Racial discrimination and inequality were pervasive in Cuba, but were covered up by a collective censorship (as Sheriff 2000 has described for Brazil) and the belief that time and revolutionary policies of social equality would cure them. But the Special Period came and stratification hit Afro-Cubans hardest.

6. "Social Chronicle," or "Crónica Social" is the title of a song by Jose Luis Cortés, which was censored and never even copyrighted, much less recorded in a studio.

7. The stance was echoed by some of the so-called literature of the Special Period, exemplified by Pedro Juan Gutiérrez 1998. See also Whitfield 2002.

8. "The music we inherited / Africans' children and grandchildren / which we mixed with the Spanish / the French and the Portuguese / which we fused well with the British . . ." (Los Van Van, "Somos cubanos," from the CD *Llegó Van Van*, Habana Caliente 1999).

9. "Don't hide the beads, nor the saints / for fear of people's scorn / because the saints save you from the bad / and give you many good things" (NG La Banda, "Santa Palabra," from the CD *Échale Limón*, Artex 1992).

10. This was the thesis maintained by the documentary *Yo Soy Del Son a la Salsa*, and by musicologists such as Helio Orovio (1999).

11. Personal communications with Radamés Giró (2002), Juan Manuel and Jacqueline Castellanos (2003) on the history of Opus 13, a band that began at the Escuela Nacional de Arte.

12. NG stands for "Nueva Generacion" (New Generation). The band was the brainchild of the classically trained flutist Jose Luis Cortés.

13. Interview with Jose Luis Cortés in Aaron Vega's documentary, *NG Pa Rato* (1997).

14. A social silence on racial inequalities among both whites and blacks is not unique to Cuba. See Sheriff (2000) for Brazil.

15. An earlier NG La Banda song had provocatively included an exchange between a *negrón* and a blond "of the color of the sun but who likes black coral," but the flirtation was without consequence ("Te Confunde" [1990]; included in the CD *Best of NG*, Milan Music 1997).

16. Those were initially at odds with the *moñeros*—middle-class college-bound black youth who listened to U.S. FM stations and frequented clubs where they played R&B and North American music. As the 1990s progressed and racial inequality overrode class differences, timba brought the two groups together.

17. "Why do you pretend otherwise? It is obvious / that you cannot stand that she is mine / You greet me without looking me in the eye / and showing your hypocrisy / She is white, I am black / the taboos of racism are a thing of the past / the values I sponsor / conquered her caresses and her kisses / Chill out compañero . . ." (NG La Banda, "Búscate un congelador, camará," from the CD *La que manda*, Caribe Productions 1994).

18. For more on these characters of popular and comic theater, see Moore 1997 and Frederik 2001.

19. For an article on Havana, see Dopico 2002.

20. New research centers opened with that goal, and the Academy of Sciences led a multiyear research project on race and race relations (Fernandez 2001). For the first time since the 1940s, Fernando Ortiz's anthropological works were reprinted by a state press. For instance, Tomás Fernandez Robaina, at the National Library, published his influential book *The Negro in Cuba, 1902–1958* (1990), inaugurating a string of publications on the topic. Subsequently, influential publications such as *Gaceta de Cuba* and *Temas* devoted space to the issue. The films of Gloria Rolando are an example of this tendency.

21. For instance, in "Papá Changó," Changó is referred to as "the most super-stereophonic saint of the Yoruba religion" (NG La Banda, "Papa Changó," from the CD

En directo desde el patio de mi casa, Caribe Productions 1995). See also La Charanga Habanera, "Extraños Ateos" (from the CD *Me Sube La Fiebre*, EGREM 1993).

22. This is also the subject of the first-fledged timba track, NG La Banda's "Santa Palabra" (from the live CD *The Best of NG*, Milan Latino 1997), as well as of La Charanga Habanera's "Extraños Ateos" (from the CD *Me Sube La Fiebre*, EGREM 1993). Countless other songs take on religious themes and include references to them.

23. "Permiso que Llego Van Van," from the CD *Llego Van Van*, Habana Caliente 2000.

24. Los Van Van, "Soy todo," from the CD *Ay Dios Ampárame*, Caribe Productions 1995. A live version can be viewed on DVD: *Los Van Van, Live at Miami Arena*, Habana Caliente 2003. Also available is a live (pirated) recording of their concert in Havana's Malecón on August 26, 2001.

25. "This is why I tell you / to stop criticizing / the popular music of these times, / which are just fine. / Vulgar? / Who told you? / Have you ever been in the solares of Cuba? . . . / Have you seen the people who get up / at five in the morning / to struggle? / They are the ones who like popular music."

26. See, for example, *La Ultima Rumba de Papá Montero*, directed by Octavio Cortázar in 1991.

27. NG La Banda, *En la calle* Qbadisc 1992. The LP version, sold in Cuba in local currency, was different.

28. Issac Delgado, "El Solar de la California," from the CD *La Formula*, 2000, Ahi Namá Records.

29. In the early 1990s, popular dance music (salsa and timba) debunked *moña* (rap, R&B, Motown, and other North American genres followed on Miami radio) among Afro-Cuban youth. Until then audiences diverged in terms of class and educational level, with the better educated preferring moña. Later in the decade rap gained currency mostly in marginal neighborhoods, and its wide appeal was largely made in the United States. Rap had little media exposure and did not have a wide social following. In time, rap became considered a form of spoken word, not a commercial music that could be danced to or nonchalantly listened to. Its annual festival, which took place in a poorly connected area in East Havana, was seldom attended by people from other parts of the city. The Paris-based group Orishas, which received wide media attention after it recorded with the transnational recording label EMI, proved to be the exception to rap's lack of popularity. The opposition between timba and moña remained, mostly on the moña side, with songs referring to the violence present in timba performance and its apparent lack of social consciousness. By the turn of the millennium, some rappers had achieved a professional status through institutional affiliation, while timba was in steep decline in favor of the now ubiquitous reggaeton.

30. "From Cuba and for the world / what you were waiting for just arrived / what you like, what you love / what turns Havana upside down" (La Charanga Habanera, from the CD *El charanguero mayor*, JMI Music 2000).

31. "If you go to La Tropical / if you go to the Palacio de la Salsa . . . / Don't even think about it sister / Today's music / is Cuban music" (Manolito y su Trabuco).

32. At the turn of the millennium, underground dissident networks barely emerged as they were dismantled.

33. NG La Banda's song "Crónica Social" included a mockery of gossip columns by detailing the most inconsequential news about each and every one of the musicians in the main timba bands, as well as crimes and newsworthy occurrences taking place around Havana.

34. The show's director was one of the very few black program directors in a radio and television system known to exclude blacks.

35. *From Five to Seven* was not the only media outlet for timba music, but it was the most popular. Other radio shows at other stations programmed timba as well but could hardly compete with the resources of their competitor, Radio Taino, resources brought partly by advertising revenue, nor with the personal ties between *From Five to Seven*'s producer and timba's most famous musicians. In addition, there were two glossy magazines dedicated mostly, but not exclusively, to timba: *Salsa Cubana* and *Tropicana Internacional*.

36. The first CubaDisco focused on timba, featuring, among other events, the longest *son* in the world, which set a world record when timba and salsa musicians took turns jamming continuously for five days.

37. They also permitted state agencies to use their compositions in propaganda and even advertising campaigns without compensation. Manolin El Medico de la Salsa's hit "Somos lo Máximo" is one example. It was used in an anti-U.S. campaign sponsored by the Union of Communist Youth, much to Manolin's dismay, who, at that time, conceded the song in order to maintain his privileges.

38. Although in the 1990s La Tropical acquired a reputation for being a black club, that was a recent development. Since its inception it had been a beer garden frequented by patrons of all colors (Orellana 2003); during the revolution it became a place where workers would organize parties and where there were occasional concerts. It was in the late 1980s when dance bands started to attract all-black crowds. In the early 1990s, with the economic crisis, it was closed down for several years, and when it reopened it was the only dance hall in Havana that charged in pesos and was therefore affordable to poor people. At that point, it replaced Tropicana's Salon Mambí (now charging in dollars) as the prime dance hall for Havana's black population.

39. At an open-air concert by La Charanga Habanera during CubaDisco 2002, hundreds of people invaded the stage to the point that it almost collapsed and several people were wounded.

40. Cuban women were not allowed inside without a foreign escort.

41. The song has not been included in any of the band's recordings. According to band leader Giraldo Piloto that is the case "because it is just a live intro." He sent me an mp3 of it that was recorded live at Casa de la Musica some time in 2002.

42. The stories and novels of Pedro Juan Gutiérrez are paradigmatic in this sense.

43. "Everyone in Havana is talking / They say that these niches are finishing up / with all the women in Havana / absolutely all the women / And nothing happens!" (La Charanga Habanera, Ricky Rikon, *El charanguero mayor*, Karlyor 2000).

44. "So that you have what you deserve, a sugar daddy with dough." These lyrics are a spoof on a famous verse. La Charanga Habanera, "El temba," from the CD *Pa que S'Entere La Habana*, Magic Music 1997.

45. Cuban musicians often refer to timba's macho sound due to both the inclusion of a "macho" drum used in Santería performance and their bands' aggressive brass sound, which they contrast to the "hembra" (feminine) sound of North American and Puerto Rican salsa.

46. David Calzado, La Charanga Habanera, from the CD *El charanguero mayor*, Karlyor 2000.

47. The quotations are from five songs, all by La Charanga Habanera, respectively: "Sube y Baja" (from the CD *El charanguero Mayor*, Karlyor 2000); "Cristobalina" (from the CD *El charanguero Mayor,* SML 2000); "Cavillero Soy" (from the CD *Pa Que Entere La Habana,* Magic 1997); "Hay que Tocármela" (from a pirated recording from a 1998 Youth Festival concert in Havana's Malecón); and "Que tu Quieres de Mi" (from the CD *Tremendo Delirio*, Magic Music 1997).

48. La Charanga Habanera was banned from broadcasting in 1997 for six months precisely because of its provocative dancing and sexual references at a mass rally for international Communist youth.

49. For example, NG La Banda's "Crónica Social" and Manolito y Su Trabuco's "Llegó la música cubana."

50. The designs were made by the Spanish record label that released the CDs for sale in hard currency both in Cuba and Spain. Unlike most of the songs, which were broadcast and performed first and foremost within Cuba, the CD covers may not be seen by Cubans, who are unlikely to spend one month's salary on a CD.

51. NG La Banda, "La Película del Sábado, Camará," from the CD *La Bruja*, Caribe 1994.

52. Los Van Van, "La Shopping maniaca," from the CD *Te Pone La Cabeza Mala*, Caribe Productions 1997.

53. NG La Banda, "La bruja," from the CD *La Bruja*, Caribe Productions 1994.

54. La Charanga Habanera, "Hagamos un Chen," from the CD *Tremendo Delirio*, Magic Music 1997.

55. "Super Turistic" is included in the CD *Pa Que Se Entere La Habana* (Magic Music 1996).

56. Respectively, La Charanga Habanera, "Hagamos un Chen," from the CD *Tremendo Delirio,* Magic Music 1997; La Charanga Habanera, "Amor de Subasta," from the CD *Pa Que Se Entere La Habana*, Magic Music 1995.

57. The lyrics are a spoof on a poem by the revered Afrocubanista poet Nicolás Guillen. While in the original poem "Tengo lo que tenia que tener" (I have what I should) is intended as an endorsement on social justice over material things, in the

Charanga Habanera version, what should be had is a sugar daddy with dough. The poem was later "sampled" with yet a new meaning by a rap band, as documented by West-Duran (2004).

58. Los Van Van, from a pirated recording of their concert at Havana's Malecón on August 26, 2001.

READING *BUFFY* AND "LOOKING PROPER"

Race, Gender, and Consumption among West Indian Girls in Brooklyn

ONEKA LABENNETT

Brooklyn's first- and second-generation black immigrants from the English-speaking Caribbean negotiate between West Indian and American definitions of race, ethnicity, and gender.[1] This essay explores how West Indian adolescent girls in particular use cultural products such as music, fashion, and television in forming their gender and ethnic identities. Tenuously positioned between the stages of childhood and adulthood, and between West Indian and American ideologies of identity, my informants also negotiated between competing and, at times, contradictory definitions of race and gender. While several scholars have argued that West Indian immigrants create transnational identities by maintaining political and social ties in their home and host countries (e.g., Basch 2001; Foner 2001), my own research has revealed that West Indian adolescents employ different ways of forming transnational identities. Unlike their mothers, who formed transnational identities by literally crossing national boundaries on a frequent basis, by taking part in the politics of their home and host countries, and by sending home remittances, my young informants formed transnational identities by consuming music, fashion, and food from their home and host countries. Moreover, they did so as a way to act within and beyond American racial constructions.

Whether they claimed an affinity for Caribbean musical artists who were less well known in the United States (such as Spragga Benz) or mainstream American hip-hop artists (such as Sean "P. Diddy" Combs) was often times symbolic of whether my informants, in any given situation, were asserting American or West Indian identities. These identity claims and consumption choices revolved around race, ethnicity, and gender, and were negotiated in complex ways depending on many factors, including the girls' social settings. As such, the West Indian American adolescent girls among whom I conducted research consistently reinvented and reinterpreted the images and meanings of mass-mediated products to suit their particular realities (Miller 1994, 2001). Thus, in this essay I draw from theoretical literature on race, globalization, mass media, and consumption to analyze the meanings attached to first- and second-generation West Indian girls' consumption of cultural products such as television programs, hip-hop music, and fashion. In particular, I will explore the meanings surrounding my informants' consumption of the television program *Buffy the Vampire Slayer* (*Buffy*), along with the evaluations they made of particular female hip-hop artists and the styles of dress associated with hip-hop music as either "positive" or "negative," as windows into the processes by which they construct racial, ethnic, and gender identities for themselves.

The Field Site, Informants, and Methodology

The ethnographic data I am drawing from is based on twenty months of fieldwork in the Flatbush and Crown Heights sections of Brooklyn, New York—the neighborhoods that house the largest population of West Indian immigrants in the United States (U.S. Census 2000).[2] These neighborhoods have been characterized as ghettoes both by the largely minority communities that now live there and by the white ethnic groups whose exodus from the neighborhoods coincided with the influx of black immigrants from the Caribbean. My informants alluded to factors such as the presence of black poor and working-class families, what they saw as frequent police brutality against black men, and the absence of movie theaters and Starbucks stores as evidence of the neighborhoods' ghetto status.

Caribbean products and services also serve to characterize the neighborhoods of Flatbush and Crown Heights (Kasinitz 1992; Foner 2001). While conducting my fieldwork I observed and heard accounts of a steady transportation of cultural products such as music, food, clothing, and audio/video equipment between the Caribbean and Flatbush and Crown Heights. Flatbush Avenue is a major shopping thoroughfare that represents the main artery of the neighborhood that bears its name, and the multitudinous stores along Flatbush Avenue are indicators of the neighborhood's class and ethnic composition. These stores include Caribbean and Korean grocery stores, Caribbean and Caribbean/American take-out eateries, ninety-nine-cent shops, Caribbean record stores, Chinese restaurants, and Latino-owned bodegas. A walking tour of Flatbush Avenue would also give one a sense of the institutions used by the neighborhood's immigrant communities. Such institutions include numerous churches of various denominations and languages (English, Haitian French Creole, and Spanish being the most present), ROTC recruitment sites, and community gathering places such as the YMCA where I conducted most of my research. While Flatbush and Crown Heights are clearly multiethnic neighborhoods, my own focus was on West Indian immigrants from the English-speaking Caribbean. Yet, I include in this work the responses and experiences of peers who were Latina and African American in order to contextualize and problematize the notion of ethnic identity categories as static. As I hope to illustrate when I introduce a Latina named Veronica, the Caribbeanization of Flatbush has resulted in a selective appropriation of West Indianness by individuals who may or may not be West Indian.

As my focus is on consumption, I approached my informants in institutions of leisure rather than at work or at school. I conducted repeated interviews with girls ranging in age from twelve to seventeen who frequented two establishments: The Flatbush YMCA and the Brooklyn Children's Museum (BCM), which is located in Crown Heights. At the YMCA, I conducted interviews and participant observation with a group of thirty cheerleaders who practiced at the YMCA and cheered for its basketball team. Of these thirty girls, twenty-five were of West Indian descent. Of the remaining five girls, three were African American and two were Latina. At BCM, I conducted the same types of interviews with the adolescent girls who frequented the museum's after-school program. This program incorporated about thirty-five children aged seven to eighteen. The younger children received help with their homework from BCM's staff and from their older peers, and the older children (ages fifteen and older) worked as guides in the museum. At BCM, I interviewed eighteen girls, all of West Indian descent.

The girls' class backgrounds ranged from poor to lower middle class, with most of them coming from working-class homes. When I began my fieldwork I found it difficult to identify my informants' class backgrounds. Their class status here in the United States seemed obvious at first glance: The girls' mothers often worked in service industry jobs—such as cashiers, house-keepers, or hairdressers—and more often than not these women headed their households with little or no assistance from men. The girls' homes were cramped apartments in which they often shared bedrooms with numerous other siblings. And they attended public, predominantly minority schools that often had overcrowded classrooms, outdated textbooks, and many children who took advantage of the free lunch and breakfast programs. All of these factors might seem to place them in the working-class or poor segment of the U.S. population and it was factors such as these that my informants relied on in characterizing their neighborhoods as ghettoes. However, since I was working with an immigrant group, I also tried to take my informants' class status "back home" into consideration, as well as the changing circumstances occasioned by their aspirations to social and economic mobility.

Mass-Mediated Culture: *Buffy*

I was drawn to *Buffy* because, while it consistently renders blacks as nonexistent or peripheral, *Buffy* was immensely popular with the black West Indian youth I studied in Brooklyn. I therefore became interested in the ways American constructions of race had come to influence how my informants viewed themselves in relation to the television programs they watched. I understand this as a dynamic process, and for this reason I present my informants as active, discriminating consumers who think critically about the products they consume rather than as passive victims of the culture industries.[3] As such, this essay is an intervention designed to problematize both popular and academic discourses that present adolescents in general as devoid of agency, and black female adolescents in particular as invisible. With the complex and more often than not derogatory representations of African Americans in mass culture in mind, I wondered what it meant for black adolescent female West Indians to identify with a predominantly white television program like *Buffy*. Did it mean that my informants who identified with Buffy Summers (*Buffy*'s white protagonist) were distancing themselves from African Americans?[4] Were they denying their blackness? Were they obsessed with whiteness?

That black youth should prefer to consume images and products which reflect "positive" representations of African Americans is a view held by the youth I studied as well as by their parents. Academics such as bell hooks and

Michele Wallace have echoed this assertion, the latter referring to a now-famous study done in the 1950s by the psychologists Kenneth and Mamie Clark, which argued that because black children preferred to play with white dolls, and preferred to color pictures meant to represent themselves with white crayons, black children suffered from damaged self-esteem at the hands of racism (hooks 1992; Wallace 1990b). Other scholars have taken steps toward problematizing the notions that buying products such as black Barbie dolls necessarily represents more "positive" consumption and that youth are incapable of questioning "negative" products (duCille 1996b; Chin 2001). Throughout their history in this country, and perhaps most visibly in the 1960s and 1970s with the civil rights movement, African Americans have consumed certain products and boycotted others in acts of pride, resistance, and protest. African American youth, in particular, have been instrumental in developing what I call an African American culture of consumption. They positioned themselves in relation to the consumption of cultural products, and at lunch counter sit-ins, public performances, and bus station rest areas they demanded to have the same access to consumption that was enjoyed by their white peers. In doing so, these youth helped set the stage for current notions of identity politics—the notion that how one constructs one's identity vis-à-vis consumption has political significance. Yet, because the politics of consumption are contingent, what I hope to contribute to an understanding of the formation of contemporary West Indian racial identities in the United States is a sense of how race is socially constructed in relation to specific popular cultural products, products that have social lives and should be studied within their particular social and historical contexts (Appadurai 1986, 1996).

Late-twentieth-century Brooklyn boasted a pervasive mass-mediated culture in which consumption was reflected in " 'emancipated signs' . . . which no longer have any fixed referent" (Baudrillard, quoted in C. Campbell 1995: 99). Television programs such as *Buffy* exemplify this phenomenon. Sarah Michelle Geller is not only the protagonist on *Buffy*; she also stars in blockbuster teen-oriented films (*I Know What You Did Last Summer*, *Scream 2*, *Cruel Intentions*, and *Scooby Doo*), and is a television and magazine spokesmodel for Maybelline cosmetics. *Buffy* itself was one of its network's highest-rated programs, garnering both critical adulation and a cult following; although the program recently ceased production after seven seasons on the air, it continues to be broadcast in syndication. *Buffy* has also spawned an extensive popular cultural market with more than 320 unofficial websites devoted to the program, an Internet fan club, and merchandise lines including a comic book series, licensed novels, and other teen-oriented products such as student planners, video games, and calendars. Additionally, in 1999, The WB network introduced a *Buffy* spin-off series, *Angel*, which remains on the air and which chronicles the adventures of Buffy's ex-boyfriend, a vampire with a human soul. In its final seasons of production the program moved to the UPN network and had a production budget of $2.3 million per episode ("Slay Anything," May 21, 2001). While I was conducting research, therefore, teen consumers were confronted by images of Sarah Michelle Geller at almost every turn, and almost every one of the girls I interviewed at the YMCA and BCM said they watched and enjoyed the show.

Buffy the Vampire Slayer

When the program debuted in March of 1997, Buffy was a high-school freshman moving with her divorced mother to Sunnydale—a fictional California suburb plagued by demonic forces because it exists on an ancient portal to Hell, a "Hellmouth"—to start a new life (she had burned down the gym in pursuit of vampires at her old school). While Buffy may have appeared to be a "normal" teenage girl, she was actually one of a few "chosen ones" or "slayers," female teenagers with the ability to fight and slay vampires and other demons.

Each episode of the program showcases Buffy's physical strength, combat technique, and expertise with ancient weaponry such as stakes and crossbows. The general format of the program involves Buffy and her friends, including her "watcher" (a father figure and trainer in the form of a British librarian), discovering evil or supernatural wrongdoing perpetrated by vampires or demons. As each episode unfolds, Buffy and her cohort must defeat the vampires and other evildoers and restore some semblance of peace to Sunnydale. Buffy's special talents and duties as a slayer often made fitting in difficult for her in high school and continued to complicate her life in college. On numerous occasions she was called upon not only to save the unwitting residents of Sunnydale but also to save the *entire world* from demonic forces.

Buffy frequently had to lie to her mother who, until the third season, did not know Buffy was a vampire slayer. To complicate matters, Buffy fell in love with Angel, a vampire with a soul. Week after week, teenagers (along with preteens and adults watched as Buffy went through "normal" rites of passage with a twist. For example, she lost her virginity to a vampire with a soul, who, upon experiencing the perfect happiness of their union, triggered the reversal of a Gypsy curse—magically and heartbreakingly transforming the vampire back into a remorseless beast. It is this aspect of irony and masked social commentary (here, girls learn that teen sex can ruin a relationship) that I think makes the series popular with the adolescents with whom I worked. I would hasten to add that what also makes *Buffy* appealing to teenage girls and adult academics alike is the program's practice of flipping gender roles; the female heroine holds greater physical power and responsibility than any of the program's other characters, including her male adult mentor. Additionally, the program introduced a lesbian relationship into its subplot, when Buffy's best friend, Willow, began experimenting with witchcraft and sexuality during her sophomore year in college. Elements such as this same-sex relationship reveal the program's dialectical nature—it is both liberal and stereotypical in its characterization of the lesbian characters.

Representations of Blackness

While most of my informants were of African descent, the protagonist and all of *Buffy*'s regular cast members are white.[5] There have been instances when black characters have appeared on the program (I counted five black guest-starring actors in the first four seasons). These characters have often been represented as exotic others (examples include Kendra, a black slayer with a pseudo-Caribbean accent, Mr. Trick, a black vampire who worked for the evil mayor and was killed by another slayer named Faith, and "the spirit of the first slayer," the prehistoric, primitive creation myth to whom Buffy traces her identity). True to Hollywood form (especially the horror genre), these few black characters have all been either quickly killed off or otherwise written out of the regular story line.

Although the program frequently makes clever allusions to popular culture, *Buffy* almost never makes reference to rap, hip-hop, or African American popular culture. While the rest of American youth culture seems to be obsessed with consuming black cultural products—70 percent of all hip-hop albums are purchased by white youth (Kleinfield 2000)—it is startling that *Buffy* renders black youth culture almost completely invisible. The program has, however, periodically mined the culture and rituals of Africa for quasi-representations which support its science-fiction story lines (examples include an episode in which Buffy's classmates become possessed by Masai warriors' practices and hyenas' instincts, a plot in which Buffy's mother falls prey to the evil forces attached to an African mask, and two seminal episodes in which Buffy confronts the Neanderthal-like spirit of the first slayer who is the source of Buffy's power and is played by a black actress). When I asked my informants what they made of some of these episodes, instead of focusing on the derogatory images of blacks on the show, they engaged in conversations about issues such as Buffy's fighting techniques and her ability to overcome hardships. Yet, *Buffy* did not exist in a televisual vacuum and thus formed one part of a broader fictional universe through which West Indian youth negotiated their own identities.

When I asked Rebbie, whose mother and father are black Jamaicans, to list her favorite television shows she said, "Soaps, videos, *Fresh Prince, Martin, Seinfeld*—sometimes. *Moesha,* you know, ghetto shows. And *Buffy.*" In Rebbie's list, *The Fresh Prince, Martin,* and *Moesha* were described as "ghetto shows" not because they took place in ghettoes (in fact, *The Fresh Prince* portrays an upper-class black family in Bel Air and *Moesha* depicts a middle-class black family), but rather because they portrayed African Americans and were perceived as being appreciated by African Americans. To varying degrees these programs, regardless of their settings and the socioeconomic backgrounds of their characters, also reproduced television's conventional tropes of African Americans. Although these programs portray contradictory rather than completely stereotypical images of black Americans, few black sitcoms have been able to escape racial conventions that equate African Americanness with being poor or working class and with stereotypical markers of race. Rebbie's invocation of "ghetto" sheds light on how constructions of race in America have come to shape how my informants saw themselves and the programs they watched. The programs she described as "ghetto shows" were also seen as such by other viewers and by industry insiders because they have been "ghettoized" on lesser networks. Predominantly black programs such as *Moesha, Martin,* and more recently *The Bernie Mac Show, Eve,* and *Girlfriends* air on the UPN, Fox, and WB networks while the majority of predominantly white programs such as *Seinfeld, Friends, Frasier,* and *Home Improvement* originally aired on the primary networks, ABC, NBC, and CBS.[6]

It is therefore significant that Rebbie chose to qualify and separate the two predominantly white programs she watched. For Rebbie it was important to say that she only watched *Seinfeld* "sometimes." *Buffy* was added at the end, separately, but certainly not as an afterthought. Rebbie was not my only informant to make a distinction between black and white sitcoms. Keisha, a fifteen-year-old who emigrated from Trinidad when she was eight years old, listed *Party of Five* (which portrays a white family) as one of her favorite shows when I interviewed her alone. Yet, when I interviewed her again in the company of an African American friend, Keisha's friend gasped when Keisha mentioned *Party of Five*. Keisha quickly lessened her appreciation saying, "Yeah, I watch [*Party*] sometimes."

Keisha's behavior evidenced a tension between race and ethnicity that was rooted in the particular positionality of my young West Indian informants. Keisha's qualification of her tastes in the presence of her African American friend signaled a reluctance to admit a preference for a product ostensibly geared toward whites. As several scholars have pointed out, tensions between African Americans and black West Indians have often led to mutual negative stereotyping and tenuous alliances between the two groups (Kasinitz 1992; M. C. Waters 1996a; Rogers 2001). One outcome of this stereotyping has been that West Indian youth who do not adopt African American slang, who think of school success as a gateway to social mobility, and who do not actively stress their alliance with African Americans through the products they consume, are sometimes disparaged for "acting white." For the teenagers I studied, a primary method of either distancing themselves from, or allying themselves with African Americans was through selective consumption of products coded as white, African American, West Indian, or West Indian *and* African American. I was therefore interested in the role of a predominantly white program like *Buffy* within my informants' consumption preferences and categories. Additionally, I pondered why my informants were not troubled by the negative images of blacks on *Buffy*. Why didn't they see watching *Buffy* as a betrayal of racial and ethnic pride?

One of my informants, a thirteen-year-old of Afro-Cuban and Puerto Rican descent named Veronica, found moments of pleasure and identification in programs such as *Buffy* and *Charmed* (another predominantly white program on the same network as *Buffy* about three sisters who are witches). Veronica was one of a few girls of Latina rather than English-speaking Caribbean descent who frequented the YMCA. I found that her experiences shed light on the strong Anglophone Caribbean presence at the YMCA, and in Flatbush in general, because Veronica positioned her own ethnic identity within the context of Flatbush's Anglophone Caribbean community. Throughout our interview Veronica was very animated and spoke quickly and enthusiastically. She peppered her comments with slang terms and responded with good-natured sarcasm when I asked "dumb" questions. I asked her why she liked *Buffy* and *Charmed*:

> VERONICA: Oh, 'cause I like witches. I like witchcraft and stuff. I really believe in that stuff. I even thought I was a witch one time.
>
> OL: Really?
>
> VERONICA: Yeah. With some girls at my school. Because we all had the same mark on our arm. And we used to have these weird dreams. Yeah! We thought we were witches.

In the same interview, I asked Veronica about her favorite actresses:

> OL: Do you have any favorite actresses?
>
> VERONICA: I liked Queen Latifah in *Set It Off*. And I liked the girls in *Soul Food*. I can't remember their names right now. One is Vanessa Williams. And all the other ones. I can't remember their names though.
>
> OL: I think Nia Long was in it.
>
> VERONICA: Oh yeah, her and the other sister. I just can't remember their names.

Veronica's preference for *Buffy* and *Charmed* had to do with her specific interest in witchcraft and her identification not only with the witches on these programs but with her friends at school as well. But Veronica was also well aware of the importance of identifying with black characters and black celebrities. She named a host of celebrities whose images adorned the walls of her bedroom—all of whom were black. Veronica spoke of these celebrities on a first name basis as if they were fictitious kin—a family of blacks who had "made it." She evoked the language of kinship again when speaking about the actresses in the predominantly black film, *Soul Food*, calling them "sisters." Queen Latifah's character in *Set It Off*, one of Veronica's favorites, was a black lesbian bank robber. Though Veronica's identity politics were in part rooted in consuming images of empowered, unconventional, black "sisters," she also preferred white programs such as *Buffy* and *Charmed*, suggesting that her preferences, like her ethnic identity, were multilayered and resisted categorization.

When I asked other girls why they enjoyed watching *Buffy* I found that like Rebbie and Veronica, they saw *Buffy* in a different light from other predominantly white programs. Shauna, a twelve-year-old from Jamaica whom I interviewed at BCM said she "like(s) it when Buffy kills vampires but she goes through her own problems too." Another informant, Andrea, said she liked *Buffy* "mostly because it's different." For Shauna, like most of the girls I met, Buffy was a superhuman character (she had supernatural strength and is adept in martial arts and combat fighting) with whom they could identify because she had many of the same problems of regular teenagers (Buffy got poor grades, had trouble meeting boys, and worried about fitting in). I would posit, however, that a central reason my young informants so keenly identified with Buffy was because she, like them, was *not* a "regular" teenager. She, like the girls I interviewed, negotiated between two very different worlds. Similarly, Buffy's day job—being an adolescent student—was complicated by the fact that she moonlighted as a slayer. Buffy did not choose her special calling; her dual identity was one she reluctantly negotiated. In fact, a central theme on the program is Buffy's constant longing to live the life of a "normal" teenager.

The girls I interviewed also straddled class, gender, and ethnic identities that were complex to say the least. Their worlds at home, with either one or two parents from the Caribbean, were in many ways very different from their realities in the world beyond their homes. Michelle, a thirteen-year-old whose mother was from Harlem and whose father was from St. Kitts, remarked, "I'm both [West Indian and American]. I can't consider myself all American." As they negotiated these ethnic identifications, they also maneuvered between West Indian and American definitions of femininity. Girls like Rebbie felt it was unfair that they were expected to perform household labor, especially when their brothers were not required to do so. However, Rebbie rationalized that she "had to cook because in Jamaica the women stay home and cook." Implicit in Rebbie's statement was the notion that in America women were not expected to "stay home and cook." Also implicit was the understanding that the ethnic identity to which Rebbie must conform at home was different from the identity she could assert outside of her home. Mary Waters has noted that West Indian adolescent girls living in Brooklyn also have less freedom to travel beyond their homes than their male siblings (1994a, 1996b), and indeed, my informants contended that West Indian parents were stricter in regard to how their daughters spent their time inside and outside the home when they compared themselves with their African American peers. The girls complained that their time at home was often spent doing homework and household chores such as washing clothes, cleaning, and babysitting, and that unlike the mothers of their American peers their mothers felt they were too young to date. At the same time, my West Indian informants also learned the workings of an African American culture of consumption from their peers and from the popular media. They saw that they could assert and circumvent both West Indian identities and white Americanness by valuing particular African American cultural products. Considering their efforts to be both West Indian and American (and, especially, African American), it was not surprising that these girls appreciated Buffy's special circumstances. However, television shows are not the only arena through which West Indian adolescent girls in Brooklyn negotiated ideas about gender, race, and ethnicity. Shows like *Buffy* existed within a broader popular cultural sphere that included music as a dominant and dynamic referent for identity formation. Hip-hop, especially, came to index struggles over what it meant to be an American, an African American, a West Indian immigrant, and a young woman.

Hip-hop, Positivity, and "Looking Proper"

The cheerleaders I met at the Flatbush YMCA were not the "typical" American cheerleaders we see in films and on television. Their cheers asserted that they were neither blond nor obsessed with being thin but instead that they were tough girls from Flatbush. Nevertheless, three or four of my informants' mothers came to watch every cheerleading practice.[7] I learned from the mothers that they came because they were ambivalent about allowing their daughters to participate in cheerleading since they felt there was not enough adult supervision at the YMCA, that their daughters were in too close proximity with the predominantly male basketball team (for whom they cheered), and that the hip-hop music the cheerleaders danced to was "a bad influence." I also learned that the mothers felt that their primary duties as moms were to police their young daughters' access to sex and sexually explicit material. The mothers' main concern was shielding their daughters from teenage pregnancy and from sexually transmitted diseases. With their sexually explicit lyrical content, the hip-hop songs to which the girls practiced were viewed as just as potentially dangerous as the boys who vied for the girls' attention.

My informants' mothers' views of hip-hop suggest that cultural products understood as African American in origin were granted lower status than cultural products thought of as West Indian. Moreover, where hip-hop lyrics were seen as inappropriate, the equally explicit lyrics of West Indian dancehall artists like Lady Saw escaped criticism from the mothers who frequented the YMCA. The mothers' hesitancy to allow their daughters to practice cheerleading to hip-hop and their desire to shield their daughters from the op-posite sex were both informed by American popular constructions of race and gender which equate consuming hip-hop music and being sexually ac-tive as an adolescent with "ghetto-ness" and "blackness." Therefore racial and gender meanings attached to my informants' acts of leisure and consumption were negotiated with trepidation both on the part of my informants and their mothers.

When I asked one mother, who gave birth to her daughter when she was still a teenager, if her daughter listened to sexually explicit music at home, she told me the following:

> She listens to this song by Jay-Z [and when I heard] the uncut version of the song. I was like, "we're going to have to discuss this song." Because I want to know, does she really know what the words to the song are? Listen, I know when I got out the house I was listening to whatever I could listen to. I'm funny about what she listens to . . . The stuff is sexual . . . some people may think I'm obsessed with it but I'm really scared about it because . . . When I got pregnant with her, that was like the worse thing that could have happened—is me becoming pregnant. Now, the worse thing is you can get AIDS . . . So it's no joke. I watch my daughter.

This mother's fears echo the very real dangers faced by girls coming of age today. Significantly, this mother perceived a connection between the problem of adolescent pregnancy and two other social problems, AIDS and sexually explicit rap lyrics. The connection she made between adolescent pregnancy and explicit musical lyrics is a connection that has also been made by moral guardians (such as Tipper and Al Gore) and academics (such as Mary Pipher) and is one that positions girls' consumption of popular culture as a corrupting influence. Not surprisingly, the girls tended to view things a little differently.

While both the youth and the adults at the YMCA utilized a "positive" versus "negative" framework for interpreting consumption and leisure, the girls and adults implemented the model in different ways. For the girls, there was an acknowledgment that certain female hip-hop performers were "nega-tive" because they promoted female promiscuity and that others were "posi-tive" because they either connoted respectable femininity or female indepen-dence from males. Leisure activities were placed on a value scale in which "positive" was code for Caribbean, black (when opposed to white), respectable, and, I would argue, middle class. On this same scale, acts of leisure and consumption that were described as "negative" were more often traceable to African American origins, were indicative of female promiscuity or male violence, and were ascribed to poor or working-class values. In this framework hip-hop artists like Lil' Kim and Foxy Brown were "negative" role models because they were seen to promote wanton sexuality, conspicuous consumption, and "ghetto fabulous" styles. For example, when I asked Chandra her opinion of Lil' Kim and Foxy Brown, she curtly responded, "They're hookers." I hasten to add that the girls were also aware that musical artists promote images that are designed to sell records. The following quote from Foxy Brown is a self-characterization in relation to some of the girls' other favorites and illustrates that Brown herself adopts a framework similar to that of the girls: "Everybody has their gimmick. Lauryn (Hill) is very positive. Missy (Elliot) and Da Brat are sorta' fun and hardcore. Then you have Foxy, who is like, sex. I don't think my shit is a gimmick—I think it's real. It's what I am. Every woman has a Foxy Brown in her, meaning just that bad bitch who ain't takin no shit. But if someone thinks it's a gimmick, you know what my motto is? 'Just gimme my check.' " [Laughs] (Toure 1998).

Hip-hop artists such as Lauryn Hill and Missy Elliot were seen by the girls as "positive" due to Hill's middle-class respectability and her successful appropriation of West Indianness and to Elliot's androgyny and independence. Veronica, for example, had this to say about Missy Elliot: "She can sing and she can rap and she has nice lyrics. In one of her songs she says she don't make no boy walk all over her—if you want her, you gotta' look for her. She don't look for no boy."

However, while the girls argued that Lil' Kim and Foxy Brown were "bad role models," they surreptitiously derived pleasure from these artists and only selectively distanced themselves from these performers. For example, when I asked two of the YMCA cheerleaders, Andrea and Cheryl (best friends whom I interviewed together), if they liked the way Lil' Kim and Foxy Brown dress they said the following:

CHERYL: I like the way they dress—but I wouldn't dress in it.
ANDREA: Yeah, that ain't my style of clothes.

While in this instance Cheryl and Andrea shunned the notion of wearing sexually provocative clothing, I found that for them and the other girls, styles of dress had much to do with the absence or presence of adult supervision. On a number of occasions I discovered that girls had left their homes in conservative or "respectable" clothes only to change into far more racy out-fits after they arrived at the YMCA. In their valuations of rappers like Lil' Kim and Foxy Brown the girls oscillated between "looking proper" and finding pleasure in sexualized styles. Thus, the girls used performers like Lil' Kim, Foxy Brown, Missy Elliot, and Lauryn Hill as gauges to negotiate "respect-able," "positive," and racier roles for themselves, a process that invoked be-havioral expectations that were gendered, ethnicized, and classed.

This dynamic self-fashioning was exemplified one night when I observed a Youth Leaders Club meeting at the Flatbush YMCA. Ten boys and eight girls from eleven and seventeen attended the meeting that evening. While one of the youngsters in attendance was African American, the rest were either first- or second-generation West Indians or Caribbean immigrants from Barba-dos, Trinidad, St. Lucia, Guyana, and Haiti. The adolescents in attendance that night were dressed very much like all of the youth who frequented the YMCA. The boys wore baggy jeans, Tommy Hilfiger T-shirts, and basketball tank tops. While the Leaders Club president wore a conservative white shirt and black pants, the other girls wore jeans and "baby T-shirts" with single words such as "Angel," "Hottie," and the brand name "Baby Phat" (a label designed by the wife of the hip-hop mogul Russell Simmons) written in rhinestones across the chest.

The president of the club, a sixteen-year-old Trinidadian girl named Astride ran the meeting with order and precision. One of the issues discussed was a YMCA fundraising mission in which the Leaders Club participated. The members planned to visit the businesses along Flatbush Avenue, a busy shopping thoroughfare, to solicit donations. Astride instructed the members on how to dress while fundraising: "Look proper when fundraising. Guys, no pants with the butts hanging out. No mini-skirts and halter tops for the girls. Look proper! People put up a face in Leaders Club—I don't know how you dress when you're not here."

What was most significant about Astride's instructions is that she main-tained that it was important for *both* males and females to refrain from revealing attire. Here, she seemed to be contesting the sexual double stan-dard. Yet the dress she condemned as inappropriate (baggy jeans with one's behind exposed for boys and halter tops and mini-skirts for girls) were the styles most popular with Flatbush's African American, working-class, and poor youth.

The low-hanging, baggy jeans Astride described have come to symbol-ize "inner-city," black, hip-hop fans. A popular urban legend is that low-hanging, baggy jeans originated on New York's Rikers Island, North America's largest penal colony. The legend goes that the predominantly African American and Latino inmates at Rikers Island, prohibited from owning belts, wore their prison uniform trousers low, with their behinds partially exposed in acts of resistance against prison dress codes. Whether this legend is true or is an urban myth is less important than the common understanding that baggy, low-hanging jeans are indicative of a particular racial and class status—black and poor, working class, or criminal. Baggy, low-hanging jeans are also now markers of the distinctive material style of hip-hop consumers and performers. Astride was therefore not only influenced by Caribbean values of respectability, she was also cajoling the Leaders Club members to distance themselves from their African American poor and working-class peers. Gender and ethnicity were therefore identities that were constructed in relation to popular cultural products coded as African American, as Caribbean, and as American.

Conclusion: Theorizing "Positive/Negative" Consumption

For the youth who frequented the Flatbush YMCA and the Brooklyn Children's Museum, West Indian and African American identities could be asserted and circumvented through the appropriation of hip-hop and dancehall music. Moreover, girls of Caribbean descent used cultural products to negotiate between West Indian and American gender expectations. The lines between West Indian, American, and African American identities, however, are sometimes blurred and at other times made prominent, and the coexistence and intermingling of West Indian and African American cultural products such as food, music, and fashion in Flatbush contributes to this ambiguity. By watching *Buffy*, my informants found moments of pleasure, even empowerment. They also came to understand that being black in the United States often means that one is, at best, rendered invisible. And while they grappled with the "negative" images presented by African American artists such as Foxy Brown and Lil' Kim, neither my adolescent informants nor their mothers saw the consumption of a similar genre of West Indian musical products as "negative." Rather, they saw consuming West Indian products as "positive" because such consumption asserted their West Indian identities.

These paradoxes in my informants' processes of meaning-making speak to the contradictions inherent in notions of "positive" versus "negative" consumption, notions that beg deconstruction. In "Negative/Positive Images," Michelle Wallace's introduction to *Invisibility Blues*, she discusses this framework as it relates to the controversy surrounding black feminist writers' "negative" portrayals of black men. "Significantly," Wallace writes, "I have become convinced that the binary opposition of 'negative' versus 'positive' images often sets the limits of Afro-American cultural criticism" (Wallace 1990a: 1). Wallace goes on to argue:

> The negative/positive schema discourages us from looking at Afro-American mass popular culture from the crucial perspectives of production and audience reception. Who produces Afro-American mass culture, how and for what audience? Can this information be used to distinguish Afro-American popular culture from mass culture? Is the distinction viable? Moreover, how does black audience reception affect the production of mass culture. . . . What relationship do questions of consumption and commodification have to the viability of an Afro-American oppositional avantgarde or the potential for continuing or amplifying Afro-American practices of cultural resistance? (Wallace 1990a: 3–4)

While Wallace asks these questions in the context of African American cultural production and consumption, her queries also relate to West Indian American consumption. Considered from the crucial perspective of my informants, notions of "positive/negative" consumption are destabilized and problematized. Recall that while many of my informants characterized artists such as Foxy Brown and Lil' Kim as "negative," they still listened to these same artists and appropriated their styles of dress to varying degrees. Moreover, their identification with performers such as Missy Elliot and Lauryn Hill as well as with characters such as Buffy Summers and the lesbian bank robber Queen Latifah portrayed in the film *Set It Off* demonstrates that girls interpreted certain unconventional images of femininity as "positive"—physically and emotionally strong women who were independent of men and who exemplified talent and creativity.

Wallace's questions can also be extended to consider how black audiences interpret products that are not produced by blacks. My informants' consumption of *Buffy* exposes the contradictory and complex nature of "positive" consumption because they made distinctions between predominantly black programs (which they usually read as "positive") and predominantly white programs (usually read as "negative"). Still, the vast majority of them received pleasure from viewing *Buffy*—a predominantly white show—precisely because, like them, it was "different." Regardless of the races of its cast members, *Buffy* held a nebulous role between "positive" and "negative" and perhaps even between "black show" and "white show." As Wallace suggests, binary conceptions of "positive" versus "negative" consumption can serve to essentialize black consumers' identity politics by taking only one aspect of consumption into account while ignoring the complex nature of identity formation. Indeed, the girls among whom I conducted research revealed not only that consumers make real use of mass-mediated images but also that those meanings meet and interact with each other in an interdiscursive space between what Angela McRobbie calls different, youthful, subjectivities (McRobbie 1994).

Unpacking notions of "positive" versus "negative" consumption and exploring young peoples' efforts to consume "positively" emphasizes consumer agency. Seeing youth consumption, in particular, as a complex act of meaning making demonstrates that viewers are able to create their own, unexpected, alternative meanings that can counter hegemonic ideologies (Fiske 1987; S. Hall 1997). Whatever their preference, whether it was for West Indian dance-hall musicians such as Lady Saw, "good girl" personae such as Lauryn Hill, "ghetto fabulous" rappers such as Foxy Brown, or white supernatural characters such as Buffy, my informants demonstrated that they thought about the products and images they consumed. The cheerleaders at the Flatbush YMCA and the girls who frequented the Brooklyn Children's Museum positioned their favorite songs, styles, and television programs within larger discourses of race, ethnicity, and gender. Clearly, we must complicate our notions of consuming "positively" and problematize our interpretations of what it means to be black in the United States.

Paul Gilroy has argued that media such as television, music, sports, and fashion share common origins that feed the same uncertainties about race (Gilroy 2000: 23).

> Bodies may still be the most significant determinants in fixing the social optics of "race," but black bodies are now being seen—figured and imaged—differently. Thanks to Adobe Photoshop and similar image-processing technologies, skin tones can be more readily manipulated than the indelibly marked musculatures that sell the sweated and branded products of Tommy Hilfiger, Calvin Klein, Timberland, and Guess in the glossy pages of publications like *Vibe* and *The Source* that trade widely in aspects of

black culture but are not primarily addressed to any particular black reading public. This crisis has ensured that racialized bodies represented as objects—objects among other objects—are never going to be enough to guarantee that racial differences remain what they were when everyone on both sides of the line between white and colored knew what *"race" was supposed to be*. (Gilroy 2000: 23, emphasis mine)

For the young first- and second-generation West Indian girls with whom I worked, *Buffy* and other popular cultural products helped to depict not only what race was supposed to be but also what *they* were supposed to be. By identifying as both West Indian and American, my informants performed complex maneuvers that could not be reduced to whether they consumed black, white, West Indian, or African American products. Rather, they extracted what they could utilize positively and questioned those products they saw as undermining their identities.

Notes

1. My thanks to Kamari Clarke and Deborah Thomas for bringing the contributors of this volume together, with special thanks to Deborah Thomas for her editorial work on my essay. For comments and helpful suggestions on earlier versions of this essay, I thank an anonymous reader, Mary Steedly, Mary Waters, James L. Watson, J. Lorand Matory, Ann duCille, and Elizabeth Traube.

2. It is difficult to say precisely how many West Indians reside in Brooklyn due to the limited documentation on illegal immigrants. However, the 2000 Current Population Survey indicates that there are over seven hundred thousand persons of Caribbean origin living in New York City.

3. The notion that youth are thoughtful consumers rather than cultural dopes is one that has been contentiously debated within media scholarship (Pipher 1994; McRobbie 1994, 1999; Best 2000; Chin 2001).

4. New York's West Indian immigrants have had a history of both forming alliances with and distancing themselves from African Americans in relation to political activism (Watkins-Owens 1996, 2001; Rogers 2001) and in school and work settings (M. C. Waters 1994a, 1994b, 1999).

5. There is one black cast member on *Angel*, the *Buffy* spin-off series that debuted after my fieldwork was completed. Additionally, in a peripheral but recurring role, a black actor played the principal of Sunnydale High School in the sixth season of *Buffy*, which also aired after my fieldwork was completed.

6. This is both a racial and an age-based ghettoization of programs; the WB, UPN, and Fox networks are also the carriers for most of the youth-oriented programming,

including *Buffy*, *Felicity*, *Dawson's Creek*, *Party of Five*, and more recently *Gilmore Girls*, *Smallville*, and *The OC*.

7. Unlike the cheerleaders' mothers, the parents of the girls who frequented the museum's after-school program did not find it necessary to watch over their daughters during time spent at the museum. The museum's more intellectual and, one could argue, middle-class image (although frequented by working-class youth) was not questioned by parents.

THE HOMEGROWN

Rap, Race, and Class in London

RAYMOND CODRINGTON

It's down to an identity crisis. It's not to compare the U.K. to the U.S. because the U.S. are deep within their infrastructure. I mean six, seven hundred years. At the most blacks have been here (Britain) for one hundred years, and as a black force. In a way as [for] being a force to reckon with in British society it's only been for one hundred years and getting certain opportunities. As far as identity goes, we haven't actually established this proper black British culture. Even though we have a British hip-hop sound, people are not embracing it enough. That's the problem. That's the identity thing. You are not proud of it enough.

—Tony, a British rapper

Tony's comments encapsulate an aspect of the discourse around race among British blacks that relates to the impact of African American culture on black British young people.[1] While Tony recognizes and acknowledges that blacks in both the United Kingdom and the United States have lived in their respective countries for different periods of time, he nonetheless chooses to contextualize his discussion of race and cultural identity by using black Americanness as an established identity from which to gauge the validity of black British identity. Indeed, Tony's style of rapping has been developed through contact with his relatives in New York and Virginia, whom he would visit, returning to London with American phrasing and vocabulary. Yet, the accent that he raps in is reflective of his Jamaican and Nigerian parents and his upbringing in London. In this way, Tony, like other blacks, negotiates several sources of diasporic culture—the United Kingdom, the Caribbean, Africa, and the United States—forming them into what has come to be known as black British culture. These cultural influences are increasingly disseminated through forms of popular culture such as rap music and the wider hip-hop culture. This essay discusses the deterritorialization of racial and class identities that are facilitated by the globalization of popular culture (M. Waters 1995; S. Hall 1997), with a particular focus on how the globalization of rap music and hip-hop culture affect the definition of racial and class identity for black youth in the United Kingdom.[2]

Historical Context of the Black Presence

After World War II, there was a massive influx of black immigrants to the United Kingdom from the Caribbean, with the largest group coming from Jamaica.[3] They came in search of employment, called by the "mother country" to rebuild those areas of England that had been damaged by the war. Most often, Caribbean immigrants were steered into low-paying jobs in sectors with poor working conditions, such as transportation (London Transport) and the National Health Service (NHS), and were typically denied access to better paying jobs or job training programs regardless of their previous educational or employment qualifications (Harris 1993). In large part, this was the result of racial ideologies that relegated black workers to manual labor. This kind of racism often came as a surprise to West Indians who had been socialized in the Caribbean to feel that Britain was the "mother country." As one youth whose mother immigrated to London during this time remarked, "My mother felt the Queen was next to God." The discrimination directed toward blacks in the employment market extended to their access to housing and education. Essentially a color bar was erected between blacks and the rest of society that limited blacks' mobility.

In turn, West Indian immigrants in Britain became racialized in a particular way that conflated race with cultural and economic inferiority.[4] Consequently, the construction of race was not merely social but profoundly political in the sense that the state generated and authorized inferior racial and cultural identities as devices for the allocation and distribution of social and material resources (Carter et al. 1996: 153). Moreover, the debate around immigration control has been an area where the British state has played an active role in creating a particular image of black people not only to control the influx of (particular) immigrants into the country but also to legitimize racism directed against blacks in the country.[5] As part of anti-immigrant discourse, the concept of cultural difference between blacks and whites became a primary way to draw distinctions between those populations who were seen as either upholding or threatening the "English way of life."[6]

In the 1970s, notions of aliens overpopulating Great Britain gave way to more subtle forms of antiblack discourse. Although this new era's rhetoric of exclusion produced the same racist sentiment, the way in which antiblack sentiment was phrased relied less on stopping immigration into the United Kingdom. Instead, attention turned to the immigrants and their progeny residing in the United Kingdom, especially in the inner cities of the United Kingdom's major urban centers. Here, the British government and press constructed a dichotomy between foreigners and those who "really belonged" in a way that conflated race, nation, and culture in what came to be known as "commonsense racism." According to one commentator discussing the period, "Blacks are pathologized once via their association with the 'cultures of deprivation' of the decaying inner cities and again as the bearers of specifically black cultures" (Lawrence 1982: 56). In this setting, the discourse of racial difference was both biologized and socialized. Subsequently, racist policies directed at blacks became viewed as acceptable because these groups were *by nature* unlike the British. In this instance culture became an area where these differences were rationalized. These rationalizations generated a broad ideological assault by the media and politicians that established young blacks as a criminal element in British society (S. Hall 1978).

Racial conflict in areas such as Handsworth in Birmingham and Brixton in London not only revealed the increased animosity black immigrants faced but also invigorated the stereotypical public representations of black youth that were circulating. In 1981, youth in Brixton revolted against the increased police presence and unfair treatment resulting from "saturation policing," a strategy that had caused already strained relations between police and black communities to deteriorate even further. The rebellious actions by blacks in Brixton alarmed much of mainstream Britain as images of insurrection made blacks appear lawless and consequently further outside of the national identity.

During this time, artists began to form organizations—such as the Black Audio Film Collective and Sankofa—to address these concerns. As an outgrowth or stop-gap measure, black arts projects received funding while at the same time a burgeoning race relations industry began to attempt to address the tenuous racial climate of the period (Bianchini 1997). Underrepresented groups such as people of color as well as gays and lesbians began to receive funds for art-based projects in order to directly address the paucity of alternative representations of working-class histories. In this way, public representations became the key spaces in which racial and sexual identities were being produced and where the shifting realities associated with blackness were being debated and documented. As one official in the GLC's Arts and Recreation Committee stated, "Representation is not just a matter of parliamentary democracy, it is one of the principal means through which the cultural and political configurations of a social formation are historically produced" (109).

During the 1980s, Margaret Thatcher's neoliberal administration pushed to privatize the gas, steel, and telecommunications industries, resulting in a spiraling unemployment rate and cuts in funding for the arts, recreation, and youth centers. These are the conditions that spawned the emergence of rap in the United Kingdom, conditions that are similar to those that were occurring in the United States during the same period (DeMott 1988; Chambers 1988; Jones 1988).

While the early 1990s ushered in a new Labour government that under Tony Blair promoted a "Third Way," this period was still characterized by the privatization of industry, a moral and ideological backlash directed at the welfare state, and continuing high rates of unemployment. What was different from previous periods, however, was the emergence of a new cultural openness and the development of the ideology of "Cool Britannia." This term referred to London's cultural vitality, especially in the arts, design, and popular culture. Simultaneously, there was a marked increase in the use of the term "hybrid" in discourse related to the production of culture, especially the types of music produced during this period; in many cases the term was used to suggest the erosion of racial and class boundaries in major urban centers. During this time, the United Kingdom witnessed the cross-fertilizations of various indigenous urban music such as jungle, drum and bass, and two step, all of which fused forms of rapping and up tempo staggered beats with the production techniques found in hip-hop music—mainly sampling, looping, and the use of break beats combined with variants of dance music.[7] American hip-hop, then, became part of the British popular cultural scene, as second-generation West Indian youth began to look to hip-hop culture as an alternative cultural frame. In doing so, they forged a new identity—one that relied on the aural and oral imagery of expressive cultures from black America through the medium of hip-hop culture, adding a new dimension to what it meant to be young and black.

The Birth of U.K. Rap

The vocal styles that have emerged in U.K. rap use a Jamaican reggae-influenced pattern and delivery that bears similarities to the chatting and toasting of previous reggae sound system artists, alongside additional rap styles that use a traditional London accent. These styles reflected the varied cultural and racial backgrounds of the artists who comprise the rap community and called into question the boundaries of what is traditionally considered rap music. By writing and performing rhymes, young blacks in Britain disseminated ideas that reflect the diasporic nature of the music's elements and history while simultaneously representing the particularities of racial and class formation in multicultural London. At the same time, a generational shift was occurring among young working-class blacks and other disenfranchised racial groups, who increasingly turned their attention to the popular cultural forms developing in the United States. Mastermind Roadshow, a sound system that played rap and electro music, came into prominence during this time. Mastermind's members were well known for their sessions at clubs and especially at the Notting Hill Carnival.[8] Herbie, the founder of the Mastermind Crew, became interested in playing rap music after hearing the American hip-hop DJ technique of using two turntables to play records and manipulate breaks, creating extended mixes of songs.[9] Mastermind began to incorporate the two-turntable style, departing from playing primarily reggae, then a one-turntable technique.

This kind of transformation was seen as liberating by many young people. As one young man remembered, "When hip-hop came it gave man [people] an alternative. Hip-hop took people away from the reggae scene. You had the writers, the *Wild Style* movie.[10] My cousins who came from Canada showed me poppin' moves[11] when I saw them in Bermuda on vacation." For many of these youth, black America came to represent the racial and cultural vanguard because of its ability to create a globally accessible cultural idiom such as hip-hop. In addition, they used hip-hop to forge a new sense of racial community, one that was diasporic and multigenerational:

Even though we saw Puerto Ricans in the video, it [hip-hop] was expressed as an ethnic thing; it was something that minorities who had been undermined could [use to] express how they felt. How they were trapped in ghettoes, pushed to the bottom [of] certain things. It was an opportunity to tell people about how they lived. Whites had pop music and other mediums to express how they felt. We [blacks] didn't have anything. We had soul, but even within our soul and jazz music we couldn't get out to wider masses and some of this wasn't reaching the young kids. But hip-hop, it was something that no matter how old or young you were you could get involved.

Cassette tapes of New York hip-hop radio shows were traded in school yards, documentaries about U.K. and U.S. hip-hop were featured on television and in movies that passed through cultural channels between the United States, the United Kingdom, and the Caribbean. In this way, hip-hop became enmeshed in London's cultural fabric (Codrington 2001).

In his documentary *The Darker Side of Black*, the black British film director Isaac Julien explored the influence of rap and reggae on black identity in the United Kingdom: "Rap music has not the same importance in Britain as it has in America, except for the black diasporan communities in Britain and the Caribbean, where it has great influence especially in younger audiences. With regard to representations of black identities the homeboy image plays a transnational role to mythic dimensions in black youth culture" (Julien 1995: 2). Here, Julien is arguing that while young blacks in London were well versed in the intricacies of several different racialized music styles, a dominant style has tended to define individual allegiances to a particular musical genre at specific moments. The production and consumption of particular forms of popular culture, therefore, "express, construct and mediate a sense of internal collective equivalence and external difference" (Briggs and Cobley 1999: 342), a sense that is historically, politically, and economically contingent. This has also been the point of several scholars who have evaluated the more general experiences of people of African descent in the United Kingdom and who have understood identity formation as a process that is forged through the manipulation of diasporic practices within particular relations of power (J. Brown 1998; Fryer 1988; Gilroy 1987; Walvin 2000; Shyllon 1982; James and Harris 1993).

The fluid nature with which black British culture is created is evidenced by the production of music by the black youth among whom I conducted ethnographic research in the 1990s.[12] Through the consumption and production of these forms of music, black Londoners identified themselves in relation to each other and to other blacks in the diaspora, as well as to the rest of London more generally. While many Londoners were more knowledgeable about rap music being produced in the United States than they were about rap music being produced in their own city, this was changing owing to the increasing number of radio shows and television outlets that specialized in U.K. rap and the higher national profile of British artists who were beginning to gain exposure and sales.

During the early years no one commercial impetus dominated the production of rap music in London. As a result, artists tended to focus on a set of unique themes specific to working-class youth, with lyrics addressing conditions in London's inner-city areas. Topics such as lack of financial resources, the selling and use of drugs, lack of employment, and the dearth of political options were common, as were recreation and lyrical skill. A relatively relaxed commercial atmosphere around rap also provided a degree of self-reflexivity that communicated a less fantastic representation of reality in comparison to some subsets of commercial rap in the United States. In London rap, class was often stressed as a lived practice that was symbolically and materially grounded in daily activities. This was also reflected in the ways the music was produced. While rap was increasingly available in major retail outlets such as Tower Records, Virgin Records, and HMV, it was not uncommon for rappers to produce albums in homes or in the community studios located in low-income neighborhoods that offered working-class youth inexpensive access to recording and production equipment. Rappers also sold their music in these areas and in smaller specialty stores.

Nevertheless, the primary way in which rap records have gained public exposure has been through radio, particularly on the nationally broadcast Radio 1 Rap Show that was aired Friday and Saturday nights on the BBC (British Broadcasting Corporation). At the time of my research, one of the main local London rap shows was CHOICE FM's "Friday Night Flavors." CHOICE FM was considered to be a "community" station, which meant that it was aimed primarily at black audiences and that it had a weaker broadcasting signal than larger radio stations. Outlets of Sky TV, the satellite cable network owned by Rupert Murdoch, also played a number of rap and urban music videos. And BBC 1 showcased U.K. rappers on its urban music radio show called "Extra," which was available on-line and through digital television cable that featured U.K. rap shows. Finally, indigenous rap music was featured on pirate radio stations, illegal stations that tapped into available radio frequencies. Because the signal of pirate stations is regionally limited, artists whose music was played on these stations tended to develop followings in particular neighborhoods in particular parts of the city, further localizing their popularity.[13]

Black Hegemonies

A distinctive feature of the new Black British identity is the extent to which it has been Americanized. Its ideal images, its stylistic references are very powerfully Black American. Even though the style may be indigenized, given a British home grown stamp, all leads come from Afro-America. The lines of Black transatlantic communication grow ever more complex and intense. And that too has consequences for the relation to Blackness.

—Stuart Hall, "Frontlines and Backyards: The Terms of Change"

Stuart Hall's argument here positions black American popular culture in an always dominant position vis-à-vis black British identity. He sees blackness as a notion that is produced transnationally (and diasporically), but as one whose innovations are always generated by African Americans. Yet, in a study of the influences of African American rap on hip-hop in south London, the sociologist Les Back has emphasized the ways black Londoners recognized similarities between themselves and black Americans based on the conditions of economic disenfranchisement and racial marginalization; they did not just adopt African American rap wholesale. Back argues instead that rap in London "looks out and plots cultural connections with African Americans, while at the same time looking in and reconstituting the local aesthetics of South London. The language and style of South London are thus laced with symbols and cultural fragments from urban America and the Caribbean that are rearranged in a unique way" (Back 1996: 209).

Popular cultural appropriation is, in this view, a differentiated process, and it thus becomes important to situate what is being appropriated and why, and how this appropriation influences the formation of racial and cultural identities in black Britain at particular moments. In what remains of this essay, I will discuss three modes of appropriation that are apparent in London among the populations that collectively comprise the rap community.

A group that I refer to as mainstreamers comprises a visible component of the hip-hop community in London. This group follows the commercial rap music played on DJ Tim Westwood's Radio 1 Rap Show. Although ranging in class position, most mainstreamers that I knew were black working-class youth who consumed the commercial U.S. rap music whose images have come to be associated with a hip-hop lifestyle. In this instance, hip-hop culture was presented in a particular way through print media, music videos, and music. For example, this group dressed in current styles of hip-hop-related clothing that are made by particular manufacturers or labels such as Mecca, FUBU, and Avirex. They also read a number of mainstream publications, such as the British rap journal *Hip Hop Connection* and the American rap magazines *XXL* and *The Source*, and they watched American films such as *8 Mile*, *Belly*, and *Honey* in which rap artists played major roles. They tended to emulate popular modes of blackness that were generated by commercial rap in the United States, such as the gangsta (outlaw), the pimp (womanizer), the baller (wealthy/successful male), and the hoochie (female sex object). These kinds of characterizations—characterizations that were popularized by U.S. rappers such as Jay Z, 50 Cent, and Lil' Kim—were also echoed in this group's speech, for example in the use of the term "nigga" by young blacks in reference to each other.

These performative aspects of hip-hop identities were also associated with actual instances of violence and subsequent ideological developments that linked hip-hop to violence. For example, the month before I left London (July 1999), DJ Tim Westwood was involved in an altercation in which he was shot after a hip-hop event in South London. The press and others in the rap community suggested that he brought this type of violent incident on himself by playing "aggressive" rap music. Here, the link between the content of the music, the audience, and violent behavior was made clear. In addition, elements within both rap and garage music and club communities publicized their various tensions, or "beefs" as they are known in the United States. Members of this group of rap aficionados have also appropriated the tendency to foreground particular narratives about artists' backgrounds as drug dealers, playas, or serious gangstas in order to sell records. In London, this has taken on an almost surreal tone because the closely associated forms of material consumption and presentation of real and scripted violence found in rap music in the United States are rarely seen in the United Kingdom. These adoptions of U.S. style have contributed to an emergent moral panic regarding black popular culture and violence that has also been expressed by sectors of white and black communities in the United States and that has become part of Britain's public discussions about youth. These discussions portray rap as primarily a black art form that had somehow "infiltrated" sections of the white community. "Make no mistake," one writer from the conservative *Daily Mail* newspaper wrote, "this is not just a problem with inner city black youth; you can hear aggressive rap in pubs, shops and clubs across Britain" (Mooney 1999).

These kinds of violent incidents separate this community of rap enthusiasts from black Britishers who are interested in promoting different aspects of hip-hop culture. A young man in his mid-twenties explained the influence of U.S. commercial rap music on black youth in terms of generational differences between himself and this group, differences that are reflected in the kinds of images that are now circulating transnationally as the result of recent technological developments often associated with contemporary processes of globalization:

> They [black teenagers] are not into the U.K. stuff and they are not as proud of their music and know what kind of influence that they could get from their music. Instead they are building on Queensbridge [a part of Queens, New York that has birthed several well known current rappers]. These kids are influenced by trends. They are cable babies. We had that foundation of actually going to the jams at the Brixton Academy seven–eight years ago. We had the opportunity to see the tours. Biz, Shante [famous U.S. rappers]. We went to the Fridge [a London hip-hop club in the 1980s]. We had local gigs all around the area. Tabernacle, the Albany. Now the only concerts these youths go to are Mase and Puff, Wu Tang [U.S. rappers]. A lot of their success is based on image. Wu Wear [clothing line brought out by this group] is almost more important than Wu Tang. That's the foundation that these kids have.

What this speaker is arguing is that a previous generation of hip-hop aficionados experienced the musical culture "live and direct," while today's youth are left only to consume it, via U.S. media.

In essence, young people in the United Kingdom have been subjected to the hegemonic forms of blackness that are seen and heard in the United States, and they have emulated these images in similar ways as have American youth. However, the fact that this emulation occurs in a social and political context that is markedly different from that of the United States is masked because the images and lyrics associated with U.S. hip-hop are decontextualized through the marketing campaigns of transnational recording companies.[14] This has resulted in a predominance of images and themes that are presumed to resonate with urban working-class youth across the globe (realness, living on the streets, etc.) and at the same time the presentation of a very mainstream narrative around upward mobility. It is not uncommon, for example, for U.S. rappers to discuss their rise from poverty to recording popularity and to show the spoils that come with such success through their own consumption and by owning their own record labels. In U.K. rap videos, racial and class-based parallels with African Americans are being directly posited, both visually and lyrically. In this sense, the blackness that is viewed and emulated in the United Kingdom is that which is without local context and which therefore blurs the specificity of racial formation over time in both countries. Nonetheless, this commercial rap music from the United States has informed the ways in which some blacks in the United Kingdom have represented themselves and articulated critiques of British race relations. In London's increasingly violent areas, messages related to sensationalized depictions of this life in the United States are popular among youth who listen to U.S. hip-hop music, generating public discussions of race and class marginalization that have traditionally been side-stepped within the ideological context of multiculturalism.[15]

While I have discussed rap music and hip-hop culture as a hegemonic form of music that conflates particular instantiations of race, class, and culture, it is also being used to squarely reflect the experience of blacks in the United Kingdom in a clearly identifiable black British voice. One artist who embodies this Afro-British rap style is Roots Manuva. He incorporates West Indian and London-based language into his raps as a way of keeping his music, themes, and approach to rap locally grounded. He also uses both patois and London accents to reduce the degree of American influence on his music's vocabulary. Roots Manuva's style is also, in part, rooted in the mix between reggae and rap style that was popularized by ragga hip-hop groups that fused these types of music during the mid-1980s.[16]

This kind of Afro-British rap uses a traditional approach to rhyming with some added reggae influences in the vocabulary and delivery. It reflects the Caribbean heritage that influences many members of this group, yet this heritage is moderated by the black British space in which the rappers exist. Roots Manuva's style has a unique focus that uses a South London drawl with a delivery that maintains an off-and-on relationship with the beat. Rather than maintaining the same rhythm throughout the rap, he raps on and sometimes around the beat in a delivery that is calculated to exist in a rhythmic relation to the beat. Definitely experimental in nature, his flow is a good example of what London rap can sound like when it maintains a degree of West Indian influence, especially in the use of accent, beats, and rhythms. On his albums *Brand New Second Hand*, *Run Come Save*, and *Dub Come Save Me*, Roots offers examples of the full range of black British music, from hip-hop to ragga to drum and bass beats. The way that Roots raps—word choice, flow/cadence, and themes—are British. He remains within the genre of rap but with a voice and a style that are influenced by reggae, which provide some indication of the ways in which the boundaries of rap in the United Kingdom are stretched.

Another uniquely British voice in rap music is that of one of London's most popular rap artists, Dizzie Rascal. Dizzie is a British rapper of Nigerian descent in his late teens. His music melds elements of U.S. rap, garage, and rock through low-tech production techniques, which gives his music a stripped down, unencumbered feel. This musical fusion is characteristic of the new breed of rappers that are becoming popular. While Dizzie is heavily influenced by U.S. hip-hop imagery, style, and vocabulary, his thick East London accent, in conjunction with his raps that focus on life in London from the perspective of a young black male, make his music resonate with youth throughout the city. For example, his video for *Jus' A Rascal* features Dizzie rapping atop the deck of a barge floating down the Thames River while a large group of black youth dance and rap on the floor below. As the video progresses, major London landmarks such as Tower Bridge and the Millennium Wheel are used as backdrops, thus making the link between rap music and local institutions as spaces that can be inhabited by young blacks.

With Roots Manuva and Dizzie Rascal, hip-hop is used to challenge particular hegemonic forms of blackness within the United Kingdom. For example, Tim, a Nigerian youth, explained his reaction to hip-hop:

> TIM: A lot of people in this country grow up and attempt to be West Indian. Hip-hop gave me something else.
>
> RC: Your background is not ragga [reggae orientated] but you can appreciate it?
>
> TIM: Yeah, but I don't have to act it out and it's not the end all be all. I don't take it on and try to act like it. I don't forget where I come from. Hip-hop gives me an opportunity to act independently, ragga wouldn't give me that opportunity to chat lyrics. Ragga wasn't for me, so I turned to hip-hop.

Another youth of Nigerian descent suggested that in the past, Africans like himself disassociated themselves from African accents and music to take up the Jamaican influence so that they would not stand out in relation to other blacks. Yet now they have been able to negotiate their difference (from other blacks in London) through hip-hop, thereby displacing the local hegemony of Jamaican popular cultural forms. And a journalist related the following interaction with Dizzie himself: "He says he's often mistaken for a Jamaican or a Ghanaian, and because he prides himself on being hard to figure out, he can be playfully evasive on the question of ethnicity. 'I'm Cockney,' he said, half-smiling. 'That's about as white as you can get, innit (isn't it)' " (Sennah 2003).

Here, it is interesting that Dizzie downplays his Nigerian heritage and foregrounds instead his English background as his primary mode of identification. Such a strategy seems to be more commonplace in the United Kingdom now, a trend that leads us to question the place of diasporic roots in the formulation of identity. Yet Dizzie's problematizing of blackness here also questions the category of whiteness (here conflated as Cockney). This does not mean that blacks do not acknowledge the presence of West Africa or the Caribbean in their backgrounds, but it does mean that an attempt is being made to aggressively redefine what it means to be black and British through new sources of rap music and hip-hop culture that were previously either unavailable or unnecessary. Hip-hop, therefore, has created a space where dominant ideas about race are suspended and racism can be challenged.

Conclusion

I have been grappling in this essay with the extent to which British rap has created counterhegemonic possibilities for the expression and creation of identities and with the suggestion that popular culture provides a lingua franca for working-class youth of various racial backgrounds in multicultural environments (Back 1996). While I agree that hip-hop has brought groups together in certain ways, the terms under which these groups have contact, as well as the contexts within which these interactions occur, invite a different perspective on multiculturalism. Given the significant number of Africans and Asians living in London, discussions relating to the consumption and production of culture must increasingly address the presence of these groups. The question remains, however, as to how these groups will be included in wider discussions around blackness. In certain cases, individuals within these communities choose to identify with a larger black urban community, and rap and hip-hop culture becomes a way to define both individuals and solidarity within this community. At the same time, contextual changes transform the extent to which rappers identify themselves as either African, Asian, or British hip-hoppers. In spaces that bring together blacks of various backgrounds, hip-hop music and culture have become a bridge that has allowed young people to navigate complex understandings of blackness that are not dealt with in other segments of English society.

Taking cues from West Africa, the Caribbean, and the United States, blackness in Britain has been forged through public acts of consumption, production, and representation of cultural identity. The imagery used in the music and music videos by those rappers who are interested in creating counterhegemonic forms of blackness has focused on the mundane aspects of life in London, such as street scenes and shots of housing projects. Such an approach to visual representation is a function of low budgets for urban music videos but is also an attempt to link a particular urban aesthetic with a particular place. The use of housing estates, street scenes, and landmarks in videos stresses the importance of place and neighborhood to the particular artists and to rap more generally; these sites are marked with class indicators and imagery that address the range of everyday experiences of life in London (Foreman 2002). This mundane urban scape speaks to how global movements of images are used to actively create forms of blackness. The use of inner-city imagery draws parallels between various marginal urban locales and conditions taken from experiences related to similar processes of racialization and class marginalization occurring in different areas across the globe. As a result, the movement of rap music and hip-hop culture has facilitated the creation of divergent forms of black British identity by helping blacks redefine and recontextualize their local surroundings.

In all, hip-hop has become a way to level out some of the differences that obtain among blacks in Britain. For people of African and Caribbean descent, hip-hop appears to be a neutral space in which both can participate in creating and recreating a type of black urban identity that creates a shield of sorts in relation to both racial and class-based discrimination. This process has been influenced both by U.S. definitions and expressions of blackness, and by African American responses to racism, yet it is still particular to black Britishers' own understandings of and responses to state-based racism. In a diasporic context the production and distribution of forms of popular culture de-emphasizes the distance between populations and instead stresses the movements that facilitate new forms of identity creation among groups that are geographically dispersed. Through the manipulation of images and styles the globalization of hip-hop has allowed both for the reproduction of hegemonic notions of blackness and for the development of counterhegemonic racial expressions.

Notes

1. I would like to thank the members of the London hip-hop community who offered their time, patience, and stories, especially ACyde and Task Force. I would also like to thank the staff at the Center for Cultural Understanding and Change (CCUC) at the Field Museum for providing me with the time and resources as the Sandy Boyd Postdoctoral Fellow to write much of this essay.

2. Definitions of blackness are complicated by the political context of the term black, which in the 1970s included people of Caribbean, African, and South Asian descent. The scholar-activist A. Sivanandan (1981) viewed the position of South Asians, African, and Caribbean blacks as marginal. Hence they represent a stance from which to create an effective political movement and identity. Through their common exclusions, a political struggle could be forged. In contrast, Modood (1994) emphasizes the complexity in using the term black to refer to people of African, West Indian, and Asian descent. He suggests that the term in Britain is not inclusive enough to identify and mobilize different groups that have been categorized. In his opinion, black cannot be a viable political category, as this category does not address the historical, cultural, and political differences between people of African, West Indian, and Asian descent. I will limit the discussion to blackness as it relates to people of African descent.

3. While the post–World War II period does not mark the initial entry of blacks into the United Kingdom (see J. Brown 1998), it does signal a significant shift in the history of blacks in Britain.

4. For further discussions of the process of racialization see Omi and Winant 1986; Solomos 1989; and Gilroy 1987.

5. When concerns of being overwhelmed by immigrants were articulated they tended to reflect racist sentiments rather than concerns about actual overpopulation. While approximately 36,000 black immigrants entered Great Britain between 1950 and 1955, the 250,000 Southern Irish and other European immigrants who also entered during the same period were not subject to the same political rhetoric (Carter, Harris, and Joshi 1993).

6. The concern around immigration to the United Kingdom culminated in the infamous river of blood speech in 1968 by Enoch Powell, a Conservative member of Parliament. This speech deemed immigration a problem that threatened the English way of life and Powell suggested that immigrants and their progeny re-emigrate. For Powell, the presence of black immigrants in Britain would increase tensions between immigrant and native populations, with the potential effect of causing a similar racial rift as obtained, in his view, in the United States.

7. For discussions of British urban music genres, see Sharma, Hutnyk, and Sharma 1996; Eshun 1999; Briggs and Cobley 1999; Osgerby 1998; Hesmondhalgh and Melville 2001; and Oliver 1990.

8. Carnival is Europe's largest street festival and attracts more than a million people over several days. It is a celebration of soca music and is widely seen as a "black" event, although others participate.

9. Breaks are sections of songs that feature musical interludes such as drum or bass solos and are sometimes referred to as the most "musical" parts of hip-hop.

10. The movie *Wild Style* introduced much of mainstream America to hip-hop culture, and it is considered one of the most enduring hip-hop movies ever made. It is also a term used to describe a particular style of graffiti.

11. Poppin' is an early hip-hop dance technique.

12. I conducted ethnographic research among working-class young people in North London for fifteen months. The broader study of which the analysis here is a part examined the creation and practice of rap music by people of Caribbean, European, and West African descent. I evaluated different facets involved in the creation and practice of rap music and the wider hip-hop culture to which it belongs by including time spent with my informants in their homes and neighborhoods. In addition, I integrated myself into the rap community by attending U.K. and U.S. hip-hop performances, hip-hop recreational events (jams), in-home and studio recording sessions, and video-taping events, by listening to weekly hip-hop radio shows, by interviewing U.S. and U.K. artists, and by writing for U.S. and U.K. hip-hop publications. The recreational events were particularly revealing because they allowed me to gain a wider ethnographic perspective in relation to the racial and class demographics of the rap community. In other words, it was difficult and somewhat rare to find autonomous spaces where only blacks were present. This absence reflects the demographic marginality of the black population in the United Kingdom, as well as dominant social attitudes and public discourse around race that incorporate a liberal multicultural reading of racial and cultural interaction that de-emphasizes racial difference.

13. For further discussions of pirate radio, see Hind and Mosco (1985).

14. While styles and images have become globalized, so too have critiques around issues that have an impact on the production of hip-hop music and culture on a global scale. At the Hip Hop and Social Change Conference at the Field Museum in Chicago, scholars, activists, and artists from the United States, South Africa, Chile, Tanzania, and Brazil addressed concerns such as the commodification of hip-hop and the need to create links between hip-hop's progressive factions. The discussions at this conference revealed the nuanced ways that hip-hop is being practiced, and the links that exist locally, nationally, and internationally.

15. The lack of public dialogue around racial issues was discussed in an article in the *Guardian* entitled "Gifted, Black, and Gone." The article stated that in England "there is no critical capacity to talk about race issues here; we have no such intellectual

tradition. We talk in very regressive ways; nineteenth century ideas about genes and blood are at the heart of a lot of 'commonsense' thinking, which is not challenged in schools" (May 30, 2000).

16. Ragga, sometimes called dancehall or bashment music, is a reggae derivative that features thick patois vocals rapped over a dominating bass. The lyrics are sometimes considered harsh due to their focus on Jamaican street life.

RACIALIZATION, GENDER, AND THE NEGOTIATION

OF POWER IN STOCKHOLM'S AFRICAN DANCE COURSES

LENA SAWYER

To just be, it is a way of being, that we Westerners many times lack but that in Africa is taken for granted.

—African dance course participant, as cited on www.djembenytt.se

The marketing and consumption of "African dance"[1] in Stockholm, Sweden are potent sites where gendered and racialized meanings are under fierce negotiation. This essay is an exploration of the micropolitics of globalization, that is, how abstract and generalizing descriptions of processes of globalization are also a part of the negotiation and production of identities in everyday encounters and spaces in the city of Stockholm.[2] I discuss the ways the travel of peoples, goods, and capital has also brought about new encounters and negotiations of meaning and power that occur in the "non-spectacular" aspects of everyday life (Essed 1991). African dance courses can be understood as specific "contact zones" where meanings of Africa are produced in global dialogues (Ebron 2002: 40) and used to negotiate power and identity. Modern meanings, and in particular those based on bound meanings of "race," geography, and culture, have also necessarily come under reformulation and rearticulation. Questions of who "legitimately" belongs and what criteria this belonging is based upon have become hot questions for not only nation-states but also individuals and their local understandings of community and self. These questions and debates frame the interactions and performances of identity even within microspaces such as dance courses.

In particular, this essay looks at how racial ideologies are enacted in constitutive yet shifting relation to class, gender, and other ideologies of power. I argue that while processes of globalization (mobility of individuals, ideas, goods) have contributed to the meeting of peoples once thought to be "far away," power asymmetries articulated through categories of "race," gender, and national belonging are not necessarily discarded in spaces of African cultural production and consumption in Sweden. Instead, in the dance courses where I have been interviewing, observing, and dancing over the last ten years debates about "authenticity" and the geographical space of Africa are used to refigure, disrupt, and affirm class, gender, and racialized ideologies of power.

As such these negotiations point to how meanings of "Africa" and "Africans" are not static but historically specific and under constant reformulation (Mudimbe 1988; Pratt 1992; Ebron 2002). For example, the criteria used to define concepts such as "Africa," "Africans," and "African cultural productions" have been given varied significance by different actors positioned in different locations and eras. These are meanings that are not only racialized but also gendered and sexualized. Perhaps most well known are the ways that the bodies of black African men and women have long been a foil onto which Western capitalist longings for a different self, culture, and nation have been projected (Gilman 1985b; Morrison 1992; Roediger 1991). At different historical periods, geographical locations, and cultural contexts, racialized understandings of "Europe" and normative "European men and women" have been created through opposition to an imagined "Africa" and "Africans." These historical imaginings of Africa as an "Other" have been used to legitimate colonialist exploitation as well as specific identities where privilege and subordination were legitimated through intersecting discourses of race, gender, sexuality, and culture.

Yet, as the work of Appiah (1992), Ebron (2000, 2002), and Stoller (2002) suggests, even counterarguments that seek to redeem Africa often unwittingly reproduce colonial categorizations and dichotomizations and reinscribe "Africa" and "Africans" as a unified place and people. As a potent global commodity Africa continues today to be imbued with specific meaning within specific contexts. This essay addresses one such space where Africa is invoked and enacted and discusses how these performances are linked to the cultural politics of race and gender in Stockholm, Sweden.

African Landscapes

In urban centers of Europe such as Stockholm processes associated with neoliberal economic and political globalization have gouged welfare-state benefits and contributed to the creation of an employment culture increasingly driven by policies of "flexible employment" and workplace "restructuring." These policies have produced negative social effects upon men and women in Stockholm, as the 1990s saw an increase in women's stress and employment "burn-out" as they tried to balance the pressures of careers in a gender-segregated employment market with the demands of family life. For those men and women categorized as "migrants" in Sweden, migration to Europe has not often brought the economic security and acceptance they sought; instead, many encounter not only a gender-segregated employment market but also one that is racialized (de los Reyes 2000). Migrants, especially those from non-European countries, face discrimination in the employment market (Sabuni and Sawyer 2001), and many migrants, in particular those carrying markers of a racial and religious "Other" in Europe (e.g., name, phenotype, and appearance), often use alternative employment, status, and advancement strategies. These strategies can include studying, finding employment in the informal economy, and/or migrating onward to other European countries, Canada, or the United States.

As a group, Africans[3] in Stockholm experience relatively high unemployment, and when they are employed they tend to find employment overwhelmingly in the low-paid service sector positions (in cleaning, public transportation, and elder care) (Sabuni and Sawyer 2001). However, compared to those of other "immigrant groups," such as the numerically larger groups of Iranians, Finns, and Greeks who live in Stockholm, African cultural productions are markedly visible in the public landscape of the city. In the last ten years shop signs have been observed in the Stockholm landscape that read: "Afro-Viking," "African Pearl Hair Salon," "Afro Art," "Tropicana," "Afro Exotic Center," and "African Bazaar." While many of these shops are geared toward servicing the African population in Stockholm with items important to maintaining diasporic community there (for example, hair products and styles, clothes, food products, telephone cards, music CDs and cassettes, and videos), dance courses are in comparison a commodification of Africa geared to a non-African, mostly ethnically Swedish population.[4] There have also developed in the last five to ten years more tertiary spaces whose emergence can be attributed to the growing popularity of "world music" in Sweden (and Europe), where, in addition to local musicians' participation, well-known artists such as Youssou N'Dour and Salif Keita have performed to sold-out concert halls.

There is a gendered labor division within the "African landscape" carved out in the city of Stockholm; for example, African men are the primary entrepreneurs in the African discotheque, dance, and drum businesses and courses, while African women are the primary entrepreneurs in the sale of food, hair products, and clothing. African men's interest in creating public spaces needs to be understood in relationship to the exclusion of migrant men, and African men in particular, from "Swedish" discotheques, bars, and restaurants. As one of the alternative economic niches carved out as a result of African (men's) migration, the African dance courses discussed in this essay are just *one* public African space in the Stockholm landscape.

Gambian men have a particular history as dance and drum instructors in Sweden, whose specificity according to the anthropologist Bawa Yamba can be traced to their specific pattern of migration to Sweden (Yamba 1983; Wagner and Yamba 1986). In comparison to the Swedish political and social climate that greeted East Africans who came with grants associated with Swedish development projects, African American war resisters and jazz musicians, South African and Namibian activists, and Liberian students who came in the 1960s and 1970s, the climate that greeted the Eritrean and Gambian migrants later in the 1980s differed significantly (Yamba 1983: 30–31). If the climate was, according to Yamba, "friendly" and the Africans "studious" in the 1970s, in the 1980s, when Eritreans came as political refugees (ibid.) and young Gambian boys migrated to Sweden mostly for adventure and economic reasons (Wagner and Yamba 1986: 202), Sweden was in recession. Moreover, the economic recession made for markedly different encounters with Swedish society for the two groups; Eritreans, who were classified as political refugees, received a variety of resources and economic support from the Swedish state, whereas Gambians, as holders of three-month visas, received no assistance (ibid.).

For Gambian men then, one of the few ways in which they could extend their visas was to quickly "get attached" to a Swedish woman (Wagner and Yamba 1986). It is likely that economic and social vulnerability explain why just this group has, since the 1980s, been central in the marketing of African dance (and drum) courses in Stockholm. Gabriel,[5] a Gambian man in his forties who was then unemployed, linked the economic vulnerability of Africans in Sweden with the dance courses they offered in Stockholm: "If you are an African, one way to survive is to teach African dance or drum; it doesn't matter if you have never danced professionally or trained at home under someone! Here you can teach them [Swedes] anything and even say you are a 'Masta'! . . . They [Swedes] will think it is African tradition just because a black is doing it" (August 3, 1995). Gabriel's description speaks of the difficult time that many Africans, in particular Gambians, have on the Swedish job market. In order to gain employment, Gabriel suggests that some African men remake themselves into musicians and dancers and benefit from racial stereotypes of musicality and sensuality associated with their bodies.

Barkary, a Gambian dance instructor in his late forties who had taught in Stockholm for over fifteen years, also described his involvement in African dance courses as being linked to Swedish cultural politics. Where Gabriel stressed economic marginalization and the unemployment of Africans, Barkary suggested that teaching African dance was not only about economic exchange (he worked as a subway driver) but also about the transformation of negative meanings of Africa. He invoked racialization, culture, and power inequalities when he said:

> I think you become a victim of discrimination and segregation if you don't have a strong self-confidence. I am proud of who I am. When someone looks at me as a black man I am proud. But when someone comes on the street and says "You are black!" you become irritated, because he is thinking black is something negative. And this is very serious and important. And this is one of the reasons I am not leaving African dance. You know I drive a subway, for twelve years, and that is how I live. But I won't leave African dance. One of the main reasons [I teach African dance] is to maintain my culture, to spread it out, so people can learn. "*Yes!* We [Africans] are here! And you should be proud!" (May 6, 1996)

Both Gabriel and Barkary's description of African dance is framed within a discourse of racialization and marginalization. African dance is used as a way to negotiate and challenge existing power inequalities through both strategically reproducing, as in Gabriel's case, and redefining, as in Barkary's case, historical meanings of Africa. For Barkary, the instruction of African dance in Stockholm contains the possibility of redeeming Africans and African culture from degrading Western and Swedish meanings.

Marketing "an Africa"

In the 1980s through the early 1990s black African men were the primary instructors of African dance courses, which were restricted to the large cities. By 2003 African dance had increased in such popularity that courses are now offered throughout the country, from the north to the south, in cities and in towns. There has been another shift as well, as today white Swedish women are at least half of those who market African dance courses and work as dance instructors. Collaboration between instructors exists in this "African scene"; for example, it is not uncommon to see web pages offering African dance and drum courses taught by a black African man and a white Swedish woman "team" who have a family business. As will be discussed later, white Swedish women's participation in dance courses can serve as an "entry port" into the African scene in Stockholm, which sometimes can lead to friendships, sexual contacts, marriages, children, and/or becoming what Ebron (2002) calls an "African enthusiast," a person who works to promote African culture (music, dance, art, literature).

On these web pages African dance is marketed similarly; brightly colored backgrounds frame texts that give information, dates, and prices for African dance courses in Sweden as well as offer dance performances for schools, companies, and parties.[6] More recently, tourism to specific African countries, in the form of two to three week dance, drum, and kora trips, has become available to those African culture enthusiasts with more money and time. Such web sites are evidence of how the commodification of culture has become an important "object of economic attraction" central to globalization (Ebron 2002: 164). In these web sites the desire to consume cultural diversity via tourism compresses geographical space and time—"Africa" is at the same time both "close" (via courses in Sweden) and "far away" (in African countries). Shared among advertisements is the concept of *personal transformation* through African dance. For example dance is described as giving "fun," "joy," "community," "energy," "life," and "harmony"; in addition, "dancers [will] regain contact with their natural selves." In these spaces, consumption of African culture promises not only to make available physical exercise but also an alteration in self.

Michel Foucault has written extensively about the ways that political and economic projects are intimately tied with the body, and in particular how understandings of Western bodies, as modern and controlled, were re-created by eighteenth-century Western discourses of self and sexuality (Foucault 1995). His insights have been taken up by scholars who have argued that one way modernity has been negotiated in Western industrialized centers is by contact with and the embodying of people and cultures *imagined* not as modern but as natural and premodern (Stacey 2000; Ebron 2002). This desire for contact with nature and the natural can be traced in the Swedish context to the industrialization of the late 1800s and the new bourgeoisie class's interest in nature. Yet twentieth-century Swedish modernization also focused on the individual body as a way to reshape the nation and its citizens into modern subjects, with body movement and comportment now indexing class and national belonging (Frykman and Löfgren 1987). As many scholars have pointed out, these processes of nation building and the development of new subjectivities have been tied to colonial discourses of gender, race, and sexuality (Stoler 1995; McClintock 1995; Anthias and Yuval-Davis 1993; Ware 1992). For instance, racialized and gendered discourses of Africans and African sexuality as both "natural" and "excessive" have been used to discipline and control white women and their sexuality (Ware 1992; Stoler 1995). Within this context, African dance course spaces can also be understood as "contact zones" of "safe" sexualized contact between white Swedish women and African men that enable women to explore the boundaries of their own racialized desire.

Yet at the same time, African culture and African dance in particular have long been important tools used by Westerners to question and critique Western society and life (Browning 1998). In particular, it is the embodied quality of sensuality attached to Africanness that is lauded by Western dancers of African dance, *just because* sensuality and sexuality are qualities rejected by Western societies. These qualities also invert contemporary Western stereotypic visions of Africa and Africans as "infectious" and in these moments, instead, it is Western society that is "sick." On the global stage, therefore, dystopic images of contemporary Africa are in dialogue with the strategic imagining of Africa as anticapitalist, a place of tradition, and "an idyllic un-stratified Africa, the Africa of 'African music'" (Ebron 2002: 34). This is an Africa that can be consumed in the contemporary context within what Jackie Stacey has called the "cultural supermarket" (2000), a space where especially Western women are presented with the possibility for *self-*

transformation through the consumption of commodified "global cultures" (i.e., Third World cultures). In this global marketplace, "an Africa" (Ebron 2002)—marked by the particular (and limited) constellation of music, dance, aesthetics—has been fashioned to meet Western desires, longings, and anxieties over modernization.

"Dance Talk" and Legitimation Strategies

In Stockholm, therefore, African dance emerges as a marketed, consumable product of leisure, a product that promises not only sensory and bodily pleasures but also a shift in the self. While the dance instructors in the early 1990s were generally West African men in their twenties through their early forties, a decade later white Swedish women in their thirties comprise at least half of those teaching African dance. However, the dance student population has remained the same—students are overwhelmingly female and white Swedish or Finnish women ranging in age from twenty to the early fifties. A few of the women I met had high-paying jobs as lawyers and journalists. However, the majority worked in lower-paid, female-dominated social service sectors such as child care, nursing, dental hygiene, the post office, and social work. These were women who had experienced some of the negative effects of globalization and economic restructuring during the 1990s. Some of them were on full- or part-time sick leave, with "burn-out" and stress symptoms making them unable (or unwilling) to participate in paid work.

For many white middle-class women the new gender contract that emerged in the 1960s, where the state sponsored a shift in the ideal of women and work to meet employment needs (Hirdman 1994), has not made good on promises to level men's and women's work activity. Today women in Sweden continue to work more than men and are often described as "working double" because they still have the main responsibility for reproductive work (Nyberg 2003). However, as the economic historian Paulina de los Reyes (2000) reminds us, the shift in gender contracts in the 1960s that supported "women's" entry into paid work occurred within a context where childless, working-class, white Swedish women as well as minority and migrant women had already been working outside of the home for a long time.[7] The Swedish employment market continues to be both gendered and racialized, and, as is the case elsewhere in Europe, migrant women are today continuing to "fill the gaps" for Swedish women and the problem of managing earning, caring, and domestic responsibilities (Gavanas and Williams 2004; Ehrenreich and Hochschild 2002; Nyberg 2003). However, while the increased demands of society surely affect all women in Sweden, it is important to point out that the women in the particular dance courses I attended were not only overwhelmingly white and nonmigrant Swedish, but they also had expendable income to spend on self-care. Hence, there are clearly class and ethnic dimensions to the strategies that women in Sweden employ to cope with the increased demands they face in the society.

In a society experienced by many dance students as stressful, exercise and a refocus on one's own body are perceived as ways to regain a sense of control. African dance can thus be placed into this larger frame of geopolitics and perceived social insecurity as courses are strategically marketed to speak back to middle-class anxieties and longing for peace of mind and calm. A 2003 brochure marketed a weekend African dance workshop that promised energy and happiness: "West African dance has its origins in everyday practices and traditional ceremonies and is danced today among other things at parties, weddings, and baptisms. The movements are natural and organic, the dances are performed barefoot and are accompanied by drums. You train your strength, feeling of the rhythm, and coordination. In communication with the drums you find energy and happiness."[8] In this brochure the main ingredients of "the Africa" created in African dance course spaces were revealed and weaved together a tantalizing image based on tradition, ceremony, and community. This advertisement specified dance to western Africa and provided more context than was usual. However, the Africa that was invoked was one where people were natural, organic, and sensual and where dance students would *find* something.

That the dance students in the African dance courses I attended sought a sensual transformation was evidenced in the special clothes the women changed into before the course began—armless shirts of light material and tight synthetic pants that cover the legs. Such tights, shorts, leotards, and tee-shirts were frequently brightly colored, multicolored, animal print, and/or batik-patterned, and women often accessorized their outfits with wooden-bead necklaces and earrings or with scarves that were tied around their hips and sometimes their heads. The emphasis on the hips, by tightly wrapping brightly colored scarves around the waist, was often even encouraged by dance teachers, who often stressed mobility and "looseness" in the hips. What is significant is that these were not clothes that would be worn outside of the African dance course space, either for work or for leisure. The dance clothes seemed to aid women in transforming their bodies into more natural, and thus more African, bodies. Sometimes women would also apply lipstick and eyeliner before class started, suggesting that for many of the women, sensuality and femininity were integral to their African dance.

In fact, the theme of *becoming a real woman* emerged in interviews as a potent frame for understanding oneself as a dancer of African dance. For example, one student, an unemployed postal worker in her forties, said that African dance allowed women dancers to "reconnect with our feminine and womanly sides. We can be real women again." This imagined reconnection with a more *natural womanly self* could be related to modern Swedish gender equality discourse that promised that a more equal division of reproductive labor in the home would accompany women's entry into paid work. Instead, many Swedish women now work double duty, and the effects of this "become part of the body in the form of tensions, seen in bunched shoulders and stiff hip movements" (Berg 2001: 168, translation my own). It is through consuming Oriental and African dance that some Swedish women envision their own gendered transformation and the possibility of revisiting a womanly self that has been worn out by working to meet multiple demands. This reconnection with womanhood is framed by understandings of "traditional gender identities" that existed in a premodern Swedish past, as well as imagined "traditional" gender relations of specific migrants in Sweden. White Swedish women's consumption of cultural products associated with the lifestyles and "cultures" of patriarchal "Others," as well as their talk about becoming "real women" again through this consumption, suggest the ambivalent, contradictory, and paradoxical gendered aspects of commodification and consumption.

Annika, a white Swedish instructor of African dance who was in her thirties, stressed the transformative aspects of dance when she explained why African dance was so popular among women in Sweden.

> There is a big sense of *community* in the [dance] courses. You can come and look like you want. The way you look, *any kind of body*. You don't need to come in and *conform* to a certain form, like in classical [dance]. Then there are those who go because it is a very good form of exercise, but then it also opens you up, it affects people . . . you move your body and in an organic way. Your body feels good and it influences your soul and everything. Your psyche. So that people keep at it year after year. People become so very changed. (May 10, 1996)

Here belonging in community and alternative criteria of the body are named as important reasons why women dance African dance. Dance is also described as producing an effect in the dancers—they become "open," "organic," and "feel good" in the body, in the soul, and in the psyche. It is through the body in movement that the soul and psyche are changed.

Of course, African dance in Stockholm also undergoes a considerable process of interpretation and translation that is related to the cultural politics of belonging in Stockholm. Two African teachers with whom I spoke noted that dance steps and music were tailored to (what they saw as) students' expectations and ideas about Africa in general and African dance in particular. This meant that they taught dance movements that were "easily broken into increments," those that "were less complicated." Further, they often described these dances as "traditional dances" and did not include those urban African dances popular on the dance floors in urban settings in both African and European countries. Both teachers spoke disdainfully about the ways that many of the (women) students regarded these courses not as spaces of complex cultural transmission but, as Barkary said, as "a place to exercise," to "sweat and go home." Here some of the power asymmetries within the commodification of African culture emerged—students' interest in physical exercise and reconnection with a "natural" self clashed with instructors' stakes in presenting African dance as a "real" dance form that requires years of training, studying, and deep specific knowledge.

Annika also complained about students' preconceived notions of African dance and their low expectations: "A lot of people think that African dance [is] oh it is only to hop around and be free and not do anything but that is in fact not African dance, that is your own dance to a drum. That is also cool because you . . . it is using a lot of improvisation. And there you feel yourself to be free, but later you get steps. To go into it and work . . . that is how I have been taught, and that is what I would like to pass on" (May 10, 1996). Here African dance was described as simple, as improvisational, as being "free" to move to drum music. This was in implicit comparison to the many years of dedicated study required of students of Western dance forms such as ballet. Annika responded to the characterization of African dance as just hopping around by asserting the importance of learning steps. Indeed, she suggested that like other dance forms, in African dance there are specific steps that must be taught and repeated, and that they would not necessarily be quickly validated as correct.

While both Annika and Barkary earlier attributed African dance's popularity to its *openness* as a dance form, distancing it from the "strict" controlled movements in more classical dance, they also asserted a similarity between dance forms by describing the boundaries of African dance. This contradiction mimics the "sedimented logics" that Ebron argues have been historically created in relation to "African music"—on the one hand, African cultural production is seen as "creating communal experience," but on the other hand, it remains in "a self-conscious dialogue with Western standards" (2002: 35).

Barkary drew parallels between the transgression of the boundaries of African dance to racialized inequalities in Swedish society. By positioning himself as a male "immigrant" in Swedish society, he challenged Swedish dance teachers' authenticity as instructors of African dance:

> People tell me "I dance *saba*," but it is their teacher who has taught them saba. And what kind [of saba] is it?! There is Wolof, Jolla [ethnic and language groups], many others play saba so differently. It feels a bit stupid but you don't say anything. I think it is very important—I am not criticizing anyone—what is most important is that our culture is spread. But it is important that it is not spread the wrong way, so that it can always continue. If you are going to teach *kokou* . . . it is about respect; you need to really go out and learn kokou. Many people go on a trip and then open a school—it is strange. What do they think? I have been living here [in Sweden] for nineteen years and have listened to Swedish music, but I am not going to try to teach Swedish music and say "This is what Swedish music is like!" It is about respect! But with African dance, it is a way to express feelings, it isn't just to write and . . . I am still trying to learn, and I can't understand how they take it up so quickly. The Swedes were able to dance as well as anyone else, but it takes patience and to really go in and learn. It takes more then to go down for two weeks or a month in Africa and learn; it is much more. It is very limited. You learn to dance as the teacher [dances]; every country and every culture has its own steps and tune. But the steps I teach [I say,] "It is important to recognize the step and what you are doing, how they [in an African culture or country] do it when they do it" (May 6, 1996).

Here, Barkary's comments spoke squarely back to Swedish cultural politics and brought the issue of power to bear on the dynamics of translating African dance into the Swedish context. In particular, he argued that African dance was decontextualized when taught by white Swedish women in Sweden and that dance steps which were formed in specific contexts (in Africa) have been lifted and reproduced in Sweden without recognition of their origins. He critiqued the white Swedish women who (like Annika) opened African dance schools in Stockholm and suggested that they lacked respect not only for African dance, but for Africans as well. He compared Swedes' relationship to African culture to his relationship to Swedish culture and asked rhetorically why Swedes who travel to African countries to study dance did not reciprocate his acknowledgment of the rich complexity of Swedish culture. The heavy weight of many centuries of unequal power relations between Africa and Europe frame his statement as Swedes' position of power and privilege in Africa contrast sharply with his position as a migrant in Sweden. Further, it should not be forgotten that the introduction of white Swedish women as dance instructors carves away from an economic niche created by West African men in Stockholm. Yet this is not part of Barkary's explicit challenge; instead, he introduces racialized understandings of space, place, and culture to critique white Swedish women's *legitimacy* as dance instructors.

Central to Barkary's challenge to Swedish instructors' legitimacy to teach African dance was the concept of a geographical Africa. Africa and physical proximity to Africa were important cultural currency for validation of one's positioning in relation to African dance. According to Barkary, Swedish teachers were brazen and disrespectful primarily because they had not spent much time in Africa and hence lacked a deep knowledge and respect for the complexity of African dance. This legitimating device emerged when Barkary discussed the difference between the Swedish and African contexts for transmitting African dance. He described how he had grown up with dance and referred to a specific context and community: "What happens is that the experiences I have are due to the fact that I learned to play [drums]. It was an old man [uncle] who taught us and people [were] watching while we were dancing. To mirror and to play [the drums]. Those are two different things— to mirror and to dance African dance. 'What is it that happens when you dance?' 'Why are you doing this?' [What happens is that] you come more and more into yourself. This is how you have to truly learn" (May 6, 1996).

Once again an African context is invoked as the more legitimate space for the transmission of African dance. Instead of the Swedish dance class settings, with their mirrored walls, fluorescent lights, and repetition of the same dance steps over and over, Barkary invoked a context of kinship and community, where an elder male taught and friends and family watched. "Africa" is an important conceptual referent and source of legitimation to both dance instructors and students alike; as contact with, birth in, and duration of time in African countries embellished people with cultural capital.

Where one learns African dance mattered also to Annika. As a white, Swedish, woman working as a teacher in a sector dominated by black African men, Annika had encountered questions as to her legitimacy as an instructor of African dance by both students and teachers. As for Barkary, geographical spaces *in* Africa were also significant legitimating sources. For example, she pointed out that she had taken "more than ten trips to Guinea Bissau and to Western countries to participate in dance classes," a fact also noted in her dance brochures, in which she is described as the "artistic leader and founder of [name of dance group]. With more than ten years of experience of African dance, and with recurring regular trips to Africa along with a burning love for dance as an expressive form for the desire for wholeness and a meeting-over-boundaries, Annika has been given respect and acknowledgment as an inspirational pedagogue and dancer within Sweden and outside of the country, not least in West Africa." Experiences outside of Sweden, frequent travels to Africa, and the respect (both inside of Sweden and "not least" in West Africa!) were used in the pamphlet to silence bound understandings of "race," geography, and African diasporic cultural production. In this way, Annika spoke back to the racialized economic imbalances between Europe and Africa that Barkary raised.

Annika also described how dance courses were sites where hegemonic historical understandings of African peripherality and European centrality were critiqued and even occasionally inverted. Annika invoked this inversion when she responded to my question about how she was received when she took students to Africa to study dance: "They appreciate it a lot when we go down [to Africa]. Most of them—there are exceptions—the majority were incredibly positive. We went down, for one time's sake the whites come down and we learn their culture, instead of going down to change and take away everything they have. Instead of going down to judge, we came as small thankful pupils, children" (May 10, 1996). In this configuration, "Africa" was the source for African dance, and Sweden was presented as peripheral to such cultural production. Whites went to the "source," a geographical Africa, to "learn" rather than to "change and take," and Africans were described as appreciative to be, for once, teachers rather than pupils. In both Annika and Barkary's descriptions bound racialized understandings of people, places, and cultures are meanings that can be strategically employed or discarded to meet individual dance instructors' desires for legitimacy.

Not surprisingly, bound understandings of bodies and their movements also framed student meaning making and performance within the African dance courses. I became aware of the salience of the usage of bound meanings of people, place, and culture early on in the dance courses. On the first day of Annika's class, while we were in the locker room changing into our dance clothes, some students asked each other whether the instructor was a "Swede" or an "African." One student would only take courses offered by Africans and said that Swedish teachers were "unable to really dance African dance. Africans have dance naturally." After hearing that Annika was "a Swede" this student packed up her clothes and decided to leave the course. These clusters of meaning also were invoked when some students compared their own (named as "Swedish") dance abilities to Barkary's (named as "African"). Finally, Annika also invoked African difference when she described the differences between Swedish and African bodies:

> Well, generally I think that Africans have an "earthy" feeling that we [Swedes] have to work to get. We have to really consciously work to go inward and try to find that feeling, work [ourselves] downward to the earth and find that about dance while they . . . yes, and they just have it. It is so incredibly wonderful to see the musicality in the body that isn't as obvious for us . . . in part also because we don't have it in our society in the same way. . . . Then the cold does its job, my God it is like, you can't bend steel! . . . One becomes softer when one is down there [in Africa]. I can feel it myself, one is softer. One becomes more relaxed. The climate also plays its part in many aspects. (May 10, 1996)

In this description, African and Swedish bodies were polar opposites. African bodies were "soft" when compared with "hard" Swedish bodies. If African bodies were more genuinely "earthy," "soft," and musical, Swedish bodies had to work hard to "soften," bend, and go inward and downward toward the earth and dance. These differences were, in Annika's estimation, due to society and climate. It was through African dance, work, and travel to geographic Africa in particular that Swedes "worked" to make their bodies like those of Africans. Africa was created as *the space* where bodies were "natural," "soft," and closer to earthy "instincts," qualities that Swedes were imagined to lack. Once again differences in culture and regional belonging were inscribed on the body.

However, bound notions of race, culture, and nationality presented a serious dilemma to those who sought to transmit African dance in Stockholm, as well as those white Swedish women who strove to consume African dance. For if African dance were "natural" to Africans, how then would it be possible for "stiff Swedes" to learn? Barkary addressed stereotypical notions of Africans having more "natural" dance abilities than Swedes by strategically reworking links between biology and culture: "Many of you think Africans are natural dancers and that Swedes cannot hear the rhythm of the drums, and thus you cannot dance. But this is not true, we all grow up hearing the beat of the drum, we originate from the same place and that is our mother's stomach. The first thing we hear as humans is the *boom boom boom* of our mother's heart" (February 26, 1996).

Barkary creatively invoked the same language of biology implied in people's characterizations of "African" and "Swedish" natures. Indeed, he later told me when I interviewed him that he was tired of hearing that "Africans have dance in their blood." Instead, Barkary, when referring to *dance students*, invoked the common language of maternity as he drew an analogy between African dance and music and the experience in the womb. Here, the sound of our mother's heart was a powerful equalizer to charges of biologically different "natures," and the boundaries of a community of African dance were opened to include white dancers.

Yet embellishing nationality with specific "natures" can also invest black Africans with cultural capital and authority as transmitters of African culture in ways that ultimately prove beneficial to African instructors. Some Africans employed these ideas to strategically present themselves as experts. Here "nature," an essence of racism, was reworked to create employment for at least a few of the many unemployed Africans in Stockholm and to challenge the "authenticity" of white Swedish women who have been marketing themselves as instructors of African dance.

This irritated white women instructors such as Annika because it challenged and delegitimated her abilities as a teacher of African dance:

> To be African, and that means drummers too, if only you are African, they [Swedes] think it's right, what you do is right just because you are . . . [African]. And that might not be right? You could hear a person playing in the subway and you just think "No!" But people think that it is correct just because it is a black who is doing it. That can also be translated to dance . . . someone doing it who really can't do much. But people come to that person anyway, just because, just because he is black. (May 10, 1996)

For Annika, linking culture, nationality, and race held little social meaning, and she criticized the ways male African bodies, as black bodies, were perceived to be more "natural" musicians and dancers than Swedes, and white Swedish women in particular. Yet whether she agreed or not with these meanings, it was clear from her responses that bound, racialized meanings of people, place, and culture required careful negotiation if she was to be taken as a legitimate teacher of African dance. She did this creatively later in the interview when she said, "I have asked myself very often 'Do I have a right to do this as a white?' [But] Mamadou has always supported me. He just says, 'There is no difference between black and white. The main thing is that you have respect and that you are an artist'" (May 10, 1996). While she strove to legitimate herself, she couldn't escape the discourse of European imperialism and cultural theft in Africa that haunted her efforts. Yet she chose instead to highlight those moments when such boundaries are transgressed and suggested that sincerity in learning was more important than geopolitical power inequalities between Africans and Swedes in Sweden.

Racialization and Cultural Politics of African Dance

African dance was not only an economic niche for black African men living in the periphery of the Swedish economy, and a cultural one for stressed out white Swedish women to, through an encounter with an imagined Africa, meet their natural womanly selves. It was also a space where people *performed* "Africa" to debate and negotiate racialized, gendered, and sexualized understandings of belonging and community in Stockholm. As such, dance classes were "contact zones" where peoples historically imagined as "far away" and distant from each other negotiated identities and power. In these particular spaces African dance was commodified and formed through the desires of middle-class white Swedish women and working-class black African men, desires that were at the same time rooted in Swedish particularities and broader historical and global relations. The cultural politics of belonging in Stockholm, and in particular hegemonic and static meanings of people, place, and culture, were reproduced but also strategically opposed. The huge pop music scene, modern and technologically sophisticated (Palmberg and Kirkegaard 2002), remained outside of these processes, even though they are perhaps more central to people's daily lives in urban African cities. The Africa created in dance spaces was neither urban nor modern, and instructors faced pressure to re-present an authentic Africa grounded within a "natural" premodernity as they at the same time struggled to draw in historical and contemporary power inequalities and geopolitical relations between Africa and Europe.

As such the Africa performed and debated in particular spaces such as dance courses in Stockholm must be understood as formed through, and negotiating, power relations embedded within the processes of commodification and Western demands for "authenticity," "premodernity," and understandings of naturalness. These are all potent ingredients for identity work as men and women in these spaces nationalize their bodies and movements to critique as well as to legitimate their own gendered and racialized belonging and that of others. While static, bound understandings of nation and racialization were a potent bundle of meanings to be reckoned with, Barkary, Annika, and the students I spoke with all portrayed the criteria of belonging and community as under fierce negotiation and constant change. Their performances of Africa within Stockholm's dance courses all pointed to the ways that power is constituted in multiple, contradictory, and conflicting intersections of ideologies of "race," gender, class, and geopolitics and how in the end mobilizing boundaries along lines of "race," gender, and class is always available to people because of the unequal power relationships among cultural producers and consumers in Sweden and, indeed, throughout the world.

Notes

1. "African dance" is a nonspecific term often used in Sweden to refer most broadly to body movements performed to (live) drum music.

2. Thanks to Isar Godreau and Diana Mulinari for our discussions about the politics of "ethnic" dance courses and to Deborah Thomas for constructive editorial feedback. The interviews cited in this essay were conducted as a portion of a larger Ph.D. research project on Swedishness, racism, and black diasporic identities in Stockholm (Sawyer 2000) conducted during 1995–96. During this period I participated in three different introductory and intermediate level "African dance" courses offered in Stockholm and conducted participant observation as well as structured tape-recorded interviews with instructors and dance students.

3. When I refer to Africa, I am referring to "black Africa," that is, sub-Saharan Africa. The reason for this distinction is that many Africans themselves often make a distinction between Arab northern Africa and "black Africa," and because I believe that the stereotyped racialized and sexualized images associated with black peoples, though overlapping with stereotypes of Arab Africans, are distinct.

4. From here onward the term "Swedish" will be used to refer to those people in Sweden who did not migrate there. However, in an effort to mark opposition to the

racialized aspects of the everyday usage of the term Swedish (as white), the term "*white* Swede" will be used to point out that not all Swedes are white.

5. All names of informants have been changed to protect their anonymity.

6. The sense of being a "community" has been strengthened via the web newspaper *www.djembenytt.se* (new djembe), which provides information on different African dance and drum courses, workshops, and trips to African countries being offered in Scandinavia.

7. For example, women were the *majority* of labor migrants to Sweden up until 1955 and worked mainly in the sector of "housework" as well as the textile industry (de los Reyes 2000: 36).

8. All translations from Swedish to English are my own.

MODERN BLACKNESS

Progress, "America," and the Politics of Popular Culture in Jamaica

DEBORAH A. THOMAS

This is a progressive tale, or rather a tale of progress redefined in Jamaica. Like most tales, it has its various twists and turns, but I am going to focus here on the beginning and end of a long "century"—1888 to 1998.[1] These two dates bookend a shift in the public power of the ideologies, practices, and aesthetics of lower-class black Jamaicans, a shift that provides insight into two different visions of the relationships between nationalism and racial formation. The first is drawn from a text published late in the nineteenth century, a text whose contributors formed part of the emergent postemancipation stratum of black middle-class Jamaicans. The teachers' and ministers' visions highlighted in the volume emphasize a locally rooted development model in which formerly enslaved black people, free from the physical and psychological bonds of the plantation, would continue to be transformed into a respectable peasantry and, eventually, a politically moderate citizenry, through diligent and "enlightened" middle-class leadership. The second vision is grounded in my own ethnographic research in a Jamaican community in rural St. Andrew at the end of the twentieth century. Here, what is emphasized is what I call "modern blackness"—a more racialized, individualist, autonomous, and consumerist vision of progress whereby a great many lower-class black Jamaican men and women are defining citizenship transnationally and therefore are increasingly bypassing local middle-class leadership to get what they need.

I argue that contemporary public invocations of blackness and black progress in Jamaica have become increasingly unmoored from the notions of communal morality and (multiple) territoriality expressed by the first published black nationalists during the late nineteenth century. As black Jamaicans have negotiated recent global transformations in order to chart new possibilities for their lives, their visions of progress and the media through which they express these visions have gained a new public prominence and even, to an extent, legitimacy. Central to this shift have been the intensification of transnational migration and the proliferation of media technologies, which have facilitated the amplification of a diasporic consciousness, and the increased political, economic, and social influence of the United States, which has allowed many black Jamaicans to evade the colonial class and race structures institutionalized by the British. These are, of course, not the only factors to consider, but I focus on them here in order to clarify where these two visions stand in relation to the creole multiracial nationalism that had become hegemonic in Jamaica by the time of independence in 1962, and what this implies regarding the power of the contemporary postcolonial state to control and structure public discourse. In doing so, I discuss the role of popular culture in generating, reflecting, and supporting recent transformations, and argue that dancehall music is neither merely a response nor a capitulation to hegemonic power. Instead, it marks the changing aesthetic and political space that serves new racial vindicationist projects.

Early Black Nationalism: Jamaica's Jubilee

The 1888 publication of *Jamaica's Jubilee; or, What We Are and What We Hope to Be* was the first published work by black Jamaicans that codified a critique of racism.[2] The book was geared toward demonstrating to a British audience the progress of ex-slaves in Jamaica during the fifty years since emancipation, and toward assuring them that blacks held no feelings of revenge. The five authors, all of whom had substantial connections to the nonconformist missionary churches, attempted to convince their readership that fifty years of freedom and missionary effort had benefited the people of Jamaica, who, with continued assistance, would progress even further. The book is divided into five essays, each of which tackles an aspect of Jamaica's past, present, and future, illuminating the meanings of freedom and progress for the authors at the end of the nineteenth century.

In their attempt to refute the widespread belief that black Jamaicans were incapable of possessing "those mental and moral qualities so indispensably necessary to his rise in the scale of true civilisation" (*JJ* 1888: 12), the authors outline several advances since emancipation. They cite the increase in elementary schools after the abolition of slavery as evidence of the ex-slaves' ability and desire to learn. The authors also place great emphasis upon the increased number of mutual improvement societies, reading clubs, and Christian associations, the proliferation of musical and social gatherings during Christmastime, and the increase of legal marriages. They argue that this type of progress was due to fifty years of "social liberty and equality, of religious privileges, of educational advantages, and of intercourse in various ways with civilized and Christian men" (75). The "Jubilee Five" also caution the readership against censuring Jamaicans for not having advanced further in the fifty years since emancipation, noting that *"no other people could, under similar circumstances, have reached a greater height on the ladder of social advancement within the same period of time"* (83, italics in original).

Significantly, the authors attribute the postemancipation developments in Jamaican society to the nonconformist missionaries, whom they view as having instilled in the slaves a desire for freedom and progress during slavery, and as having worked to counteract deleterious social phenomena such as laziness and apathy, which were, in their view, results of the slavery system. In contrast, the British colonial government is indicted for having abandoned the ex-slaves after emancipation and for having failed to initiate any policy that would counter the destabilizing influences of slavery. The authors' view that Britain left "Africa and her children" derailed on the path to civilization (*JJ* 1888: 13) reveals that while they accepted then current evolutionary paradigms, they also used social Darwinism to critique postemancipation British colonial policy. Further, their assertion that despite their African ancestry, black Jamaicans' positions as British subjects gave them the right to claim both a history and "the interest, sympathy, and protection of those who were instrumental in effecting the expatriation of [their] ancestors" (12) indicated that they expected some degree of reparations based on their legal equality as British subjects.

The writers' vision for future progress can be divided into two categories, with the first addressing the need to strengthen Jamaica's infrastructure. In this respect, they call for more effective management of the colony, greater access to training in scientific agriculture, a greater reliance on locally grown goods rather than imports, and the construction of more and better parochial roads. The second category of the authors' vision for the future concerns the need to strengthen Jamaicans' values. Progress, for them, rested on the pillars of industry (thoughtful and focused labor), economy (thrift and frugality), and godliness (Christian living). They located these values in the persona of the independent peasant based on their view that working on the sugar estates exerted a demoralizing influence that ultimately would hinder the development of respectable practices and values. Respectability, here, was defined as owning a small plot of land in the mountains, being able to support a family through small-scale agricultural production, having a quiet disposition, and living simply.[3] In their elaboration of these values, the authors consistently evoked the principle that individual effort was related to national development, arguing that the cultivation of respectability would give black Jamaicans entrance into "the brotherhood of nations" (JJ 1888: 48).

Finally, the authors make a plea for greater unity among Jamaicans. They argue that "internal jealousy" in the guise of racism and class prejudice "prevents steady advancement as a civilized people" (JJ 1888: 30), and that unless blacks in Jamaica united, the development of a national spirit would be inhibited. Here, it is notable that though their argument was general, they were also speaking on behalf of their race as it were: "We form the bulk by far of Jamaica's people" and therefore "Jamaica is emphatically ours" (111). The potential for the articulation of such a vision of ownership had terrified both the local elite and colonial administrators since the establishment of Jamaica as a plantation colony. Its appearance here allows us, I believe, to position *Jamaica's Jubilee* as the first published espousal of black nationalism in Jamaica.

Rebutting Racism

There are several reasons why the publication of *Jamaica's Jubilee* is critical to understanding the development of twentieth-century nationalist thought in Jamaica. The first is that despite the authors' reproduction of Social Darwinist premises regarding progress through imperial guidance, the book offers a counterpoint to the revival of the racist prejudices of the old planter histories. James Anthony Froude's *The English in the West Indies*, published in the same year as *Jamaica's Jubilee* (1888), became the most popular reading material for English visitors during the long passage by ship to the West

Indies. As a tract against both imperial absenteeism and self-government for the Caribbean colonies, Froude's text was ultimately a plea for a change in British imperial policy for the West Indies toward the model of the British Raj in India. He viewed West Indian blacks as innately inferior and as incapable of ruling themselves, let alone whites. While Froude's work is generally seen as an aberration within the growing liberalism of the late nineteenth century, at the same time his association of imperialism with all that was new, modern, and civilized, and his conviction that the emancipation of black West Indians began with their removal from Africa as slaves (Froude 1888: 236), reflected the growing ideology that Britain had an imperial responsibility, defined as both *right* and *duty*, to lead "weak nations" toward true freedom (207).

Froude's polemic did not go unanswered (see J. Thomas 1969 [1889]; Scholes 1899). Nevertheless, even Froude's detractors tended to accept the conventional paternalistic view that emancipation was an act of English benevolence (J. Thomas 1969 [1889]; see also Pullen-Berry 1903). This reveals the extent to which social Darwinism, as an ideology of racial progress, pervaded the analyses of even the most progressive or purportedly sympathetic observers, including the *Jubilee* authors. While this should underscore for us the difficulty of transcending context, it also points us toward consequences. By capitulating to the sectarian churches' view that the combination of religiously inspired behavioral and institutional change in conjunction with small (though significant) postemancipation reforms would lead to improved conditions for the mass of the population, the *Jubilee* authors relegated both systemic overhaul and explicitly racial mobilization to back burners. In this way, the vindicationist arguments put forth by the authors of *Jamaica's Jubilee* ultimately foreshadowed those advocated by mid-twentieth-century creole nationalist elites.

Privileging the Peasant

A second aspect of *Jamaica's Jubilee* that is critical to our understanding of twentieth-century creole nationalism in Jamaica is the authors' equation of progress in conditions of freedom with the development of an independent peasantry. Those improvements they delineated as necessary—more schools, more and better parochial roads, training in scientific agriculture, a stronger institutional infrastructure—were all policy matters that would facilitate the growth of a peasantry, rather than an estate-based wage-laboring population. The authors' privileging of a "respectable" peasant lifestyle over that of the sugar plantation worker directly countered the intentions of both Jamaican planters and British policy-makers at the moment of emancipation.

The historian Thomas Holt has argued that abolitionists and policy-makers sought to solve the "problem of freedom" by transforming slaves into reliable wage laborers by socializing former slaves to respond to the work incentives of free people and expanding their material aspirations (1992). Many of the apprentices and former slaves, however, had other aspirations, aspirations that often surprised observers from England and the United States traveling in the West Indies to assess the results of the "great experiment" of emancipation.[4] For example, during their sojourn in Jamaica, James Thome and J. Horace Kimball documented several instances of apprentices working on estates other than their own during their free time where wages were known to be higher, as well as refusing to work on the estates when they could make more money by selling the harvest from their own provision grounds. These trends led them to conclude that the former slaves' "notion of freedom was precisely the reverse of that which slaves are generally supposed to entertain; instead of associating it with a *release from labor*, they connected it with an *increase of labor*" (1838: 404, italics in original). John Bigelow, a West Indian planter, understood these trends as examples of the ex-slaves playing their options off each other since it was well known that Jamaican wages were below subsistence level (1970 [1851]). Bigelow also associated the desire among ex-slaves to own land with their growing participation in the political process, countering the view more generally held by planters that Jamaican small freeholders were politically apathetic. Because postemancipation legislation delineated property and literacy qualifications for voting in order to keep the former slaves tied to the estates, land ownership not only represented an alternative to working full time on the plantations and an opportunity to bargain with planters over the conditions of their labor but also their first chance to participate directly in the civic and political life of the colony as free subjects.

Among the former slaves, then, land rights emerged as the central theme of both freedom and community. The thwarted desire to own land would be among the principal factors leading to the Morant Bay Rebellion in 1865, the massive rural-to-urban, intraregional, and international labor migration from the 1880s throughout the early 1920s, and the labor rebellions of the late 1930s. As a result, by advocating reforms that would improve conditions for the peasantry, late-nineteenth-century intellectuals and nationalists like the authors of *Jamaica's Jubilee* continued to legitimize *both* the popular ideology that linked land rights to independence—culturally and socially, but also economically and politically—*and* the religious conviction that the figure of the independent peasant represented a more respectable type of human being. These ideologies have not waned. Land ownership and small-scale peasant production continued to signify a relative independence not only from the state but also from the more deleterious effects of increasing global capitalist integration throughout the second half of the twentieth century. On the issue of land reform in particular, then, the *Jubilee* five articulated an abiding concern with which twentieth-century nationalists would also have to continuously contend.

Subjects and Nationalists

Changes toward a more interventionist imperial policy by the late nineteenth century, despite the emergence of the free trade movement and laissez faire opinion, reflected the growing conviction within Britain that the state should play a greater role in the lives of its citizens. By the time the five *Jamaica's Jubilee* authors penned their essays the concept of empire as a mobilizing ideology designed to bridge racial and class-based divisions both in the colonies and in England was reaching its peak. This brings us to the third critical contribution of *Jamaica's Jubilee* to understanding the ideological and practical foundations of twentieth-century nationalism in Jamaica— the simultaneous proclamation of loyalty to Jamaica and to Great Britain within the context of an emergent diasporic sensibility.

The insistence that black people in Jamaica could claim a history based on their position as British subjects (*JJ* 1888: 12), the vision of Queen Victoria as the Great Ruler of the Universe and of emancipation as a great act of elevation (90), and the assertion that Britain—as "the most enlightened Christian nation on the face of the earth"—had a duty to assist the former slaves (14) all reflected an identification of the British Crown with benevolent and fair rule. The British government was viewed as protecting the interests of the former slaves both from direct persecution by local whites and from the planters' intermittent dalliances with the idea of annexation to the United States (Bakan 1990; Bryan 1991; Holt 1992; Robotham 1982). The former slaves' understanding of the relationship between the planters and the colonial government as antagonistic was long standing and would be long lasting.

It is important to note, however, that identification of the British Crown as protector among the former slaves and their descendants did not necessarily translate into loyalty to British imperialism or colonialism as an economic and political system, either on the part of the mass of the population or the emergent black intelligentsia. That the *Jamaica's Jubilee* authors ultimately regarded Jamaica as a nation, albeit an embryonic one, is incontrovertible. It is also apparent that their simultaneous loyalty to Britain and to Jamaica coexisted with their recognition that the position of blacks in Jamaica was part of a worldwide conception of blacks, Africa, and African civilization as having "as yet achieved nothing" (*JJ* 1888: 111). Indeed, this belief would lead many contemporary educated blacks to proselytize for the Christian church in Africa in an attempt to prove that blacks were capable of civilization, and that Africa, though currently wild and backward, could rise to prominence with the transference of Western civilization. The *Jamaica's Jubilee* authors' identification with Africa, then, was with its potential future rather than its present. Of course, this attitude that would alter with the emergence of Garveyism, which in its recognition of the significance of racism as a factor retarding black social, economic, and political progress presented a more radical challenge to hegemonic ideas regarding progress consolidated around the tenets of Christianity. What emerges as most significant here, however, is that the authors' self-assessments as British, as Jamaican, and as "children of Africa" were not presented as either/or propositions. Rather, they were able to express intense loyalty to all three aspects of their identity.

Here, it is critical to consider the role of Jamaicans' increased mobility during the second half of the nineteenth century, as well as technological developments and the growing economic penetration by the United States during this period. Following emancipation there was a rapid increase of communication within the island, complemented by extensive migration beyond Jamaica's shores. For the first time, an alternative to plantation wage labor or subsistence farming emerged, and after 1880 Jamaican laborers began to travel to Panama to construct the canal, to Costa Rica to work in the banana industry, and to Cuba for work on the sugar plantations after the World War I boom in production. As a result of these intraregional circulations, at any given moment at the end of the nineteenth century an average of one-quarter of the working-age male population was away from Jamaica. Later, Jamaicans were increasingly recruited for agricultural labor in the United States on Farm Work schemes. As a result, while mobility had become a taken-for-granted feature of life among Jamaica's laboring population by the fourth quarter of the nineteenth century, it has only been since the beginning of the twentieth century that the United States has become migrants' primary destination.

With the development of the banana industry under the auspices of American multinationals in the late 1800s, the United States displaced Great Britain as the dominant trading partner, and Jamaica became increasingly dependent upon American imports. Until the closing of immigration channels as a result of the U.S. Immigration Act of 1924—the act that extended, for the first time, a national origins quota system for immigrants from the Americas, including the Caribbean—greater economic interaction with the United States also provided thousands of Jamaicans with opportunities to increase their wages through both formal and informal emigration channels. Though aware of the potential social tensions that might arise as Jamaicans confronted postreconstruction racial relations and ideologies in America, many, including the *Jamaica's Jubilee* authors, celebrated the economic implications of an American-centered future: "[Here we are] just a stone's throw from America —America, whose prophets proclaim her a giant in embryo, and, what Jamaica is especially glad of, a giant whose increasingly capacious stomach will always be huge enough to demand all that little Jamaica can produce" (*JJ* 1888: 104).

These changes in Jamaica's political economy during the late nineteenth century exposed a greater proportion of the population more regularly to a wider range of ideas and experiences than those rooted in Jamaica. What emerged was an increasingly diasporic consciousness and experience that provided the potential for an organized *political* movement from multiple loyalties and locations. Indeed, while the five authors of *Jamaica's Jubilee* put forth their arguments primarily in economic and socioreligious terms, other late-nineteenth-century black nationalists agitated for increased participation in electoral politics as well as the establishment of alternative opportunities for political organization and involvement for black Jamaicans. Moreover, the debates in which these nationalists were integral participants were some of the first regarding the relevance of race to political identity and participation and to sociocultural and economic development.

While these early leaders struggled for postemancipation economic and political development for the masses of Jamaicans, they nevertheless distanced themselves from these same masses both socially and culturally. This was, in part, a result of their own position within Jamaica's late-nineteenth-century black middle class, a relatively unstable grouping of teachers, religious ministers, small-scale farmers, artisans, and constables (Bryan 1991). This grouping would ultimately produce the professional strata of black Jamaicans whose "respectability" and status were based on their education and their adherence to an idealized Victorian middle-class gender and family ideology rather than on the ownership of either land or other means of capitalist production. As black intellectuals, the *Jubilee* five insisted that they articulated important mass concerns on the basis of their shared blackness, but they distanced themselves from lower-class blacks and African-derived cultural expressions as a result of their own education and goals toward personal progress. The various ideological developments toward the end of the nineteenth century—the ascendance of social Darwinism as a new justification for stratified race relations, the privileging of the formation of an independent peasantry, and the simultaneous assertion of allegiance to Great Britain and Jamaica within the context of an emerging diasporic consciousness—reinforced these class and cultural cleavages. Early black nationalists, therefore, were in the precarious position of proving to local and international publics both their equality and their difference.

This was a trend that would continue among some sections of the nationalist movement. Indeed, the dual pillars upon which mid-twentieth-century creole multiracial nationalism rested echoed late-nineteenth-century emphases upon the moral economy of the peasant—specifically, the formation of relatively self-sufficient nuclear families organized internally according to a Victorian-gendered division of labor and the consolidation of moderate middle-class leadership. As Britain's empire was disintegrating, and as development policies pursued by successive Jamaican governments began to privilege the type of industrialization by invitation programs implemented in Puerto Rico, those liberal nationalists advocating creole multiracialism found themselves in the contradictory position of reproducing the colonial value system that had been strengthened during the period of Crown Colony rule in order to legitimize their leadership and provide for the population. To do so, they deflected active relationships to contemporary struggles in Africa, actively contained the development of other contemporary attempts to mobilize along class or racial lines, and emphasized social and economic reform instead of advocating either socioeconomic or political radicalism. This reformist tendency was consolidated during the period between the West Indies-wide labor rebellions in the late 1930s and the achievement of formal independence in 1962, despite the activism of sections of the Marxist movement (expelled from the People's National Party in 1952) and despite the emergence of alternative racialized perspectives and programs such as Bedwardism, Garveyism, Ethiopianism, and Rastafari. Indeed, these perspectives became marginalized within a public sphere dominated by the projection of territorially based multiracial harmony, and in this way creole multiracial nationalism became knotted to middle-class respectability and cultural hybridity.

At the same time, where late-nineteenth-century black nationalists were able to manipulate the racist ideology of imperialism as a civilizing mission to shame British imperial authorities into greater accountability toward their colonial subjects, mid-twentieth-century creole mobilizers also did so in order to argue for self-government. By proving their progress, both early black nationalists and later creole nationalists were able to demand equality either as human beings within the "brotherhood of Christians" or as citizens within the "brotherhood of nations." This is what has changed in the contemporary period. The context of globalization has facilitated the ascendance of a vision of progress that is unapologetically racialized and unrepentantly autonomous. This vision of progress is urban, migratory, based in youth-oriented popular culture, and influenced by African American popular style, and it eschews respectable citizenship as the bench mark of nationalist belonging.

Modern Blackness

Americanization, Capitalist Consumerism, and Cultural Imperialism
Where the *Jamaica's Jubilee* authors envisioned a future in which America would always be hungry enough to demand all that Jamaica *produced*, by the late 1990s it had become clear that what America had the ability to consume was Jamaican labor, male and female. But this intensification of migration during the late twentieth century also transformed local meanings of "America." In the rural hillside community where I conducted my research, villagers' view of America as a "land of opportunity" coexisted with the view of the United States as an "evil empire." The latter was, in large measure, due to its position in the global political economy and the impact this has had on economies like Jamaica's. In fact, when villagers identified the "global economy," they typically spoke of America (and very occasionally, Japan). America's appeal has clearly been ambivalent. For many of the poorer villagers, the "American dream" has not been without its nightmarish qualities, in part

due to their familiarity with American-style racism and their awareness that intensified global capitalism has widened the gap between rich and poor, not only between the United States and the rest of the developing world, but also within the United States itself. Moreover, "Americanization" has often been seen as the latest in a long line of oppressions, and Americans have been viewed as degenerate cultural influences. Indeed, villagers often attributed the perceived increases in consumerism, individualism, materialism, and a desire for instant gratification to American influence. America was perceived as the place to "make a living," but Jamaica was where you would "make life."

Nevertheless, many villagers also indicated that in the United States they experienced an ease of movement they didn't experience in Jamaica. This ease was both literal, as a result of more extensive infrastructural development, and social, due to what they believed was a greater potential for upward mobility and a less rigid system of social stratification. Whether or not the latter was actually true, the *belief* that social mobility was possible in America was, in itself, significant because it implied that increased access to the United States would open an avenue for Jamaicans to evade the colonial race and class structures that were institutionalized by the British. Notably, however, the America community members invoked was not the actual New York City neighborhoods where their families and friends lived in cramped apartments alongside African Americans, other West Indians, Puerto Ricans, Dominicans, and West Africans. Nor did it necessarily include Hartford, Miami, New Jersey, or anywhere else they knew Jamaicans lived or worked. Rather, the quotation-marked-off place "America,"[5] the "America" of the "dream," was upwardly mobile and phenotypically white, if not the green of the almighty dollar itself. Hip-hop and rhythm and blues were not really part of this America, though they formed a significant part not only of the immigration experience of (especially) younger community members but also of the media experience of Jamaicans of all ages. As a result, the America of immigrant dreams was bifurcated—a white America where they might work hard and earn enough money to "move forward in life," and a black America where they might live. Often, the images of these two Americas became more integrated once someone had actually migrated and confronted America's promises and prejudices for him- or herself.

Jamaicans' long-standing love-hate relationship with America, then, is an integral element of modern blackness. On one hand, lower-class black Jamaicans have adopted and adapted some of the trends offered by the popular African American sit-coms on television, through the collaborations between dancehall DJs and hip-hop artists, or on the streets of New York themselves. On the other hand, the difficulty of extracting personal and national development goals from the shadow of the United States has perpetuated an ongoing resentment.

Within this context, it is especially important to emphasize that many younger community members believed that as much as America had influenced Jamaican culture, Jamaica has also influenced American culture. As one younger man put it, "Jamaicans want American style, but Americans want to talk Jamaican, to walk Jamaican." He continued to argue for the elaboration of a critical distinction between learning from Americans and thinking like Americans:

> It's not like we're just taking information and they're just fooling us into thinking one way. They're changing because of us. It's a two-way thing. America right now is supreme, but not everybody is thinking like them. But we're learning from them. Everything has its good and bad and it's for us to decide what we want out of it. Some people might say we're picking up their culture, but if you look on some of the Americans, what they're doing is what we've been doing from long time, especially in terms of the music and the dancing. And I'm sure it's Jamaicans going to America that made it a big thing. It's a younger generation of people.

What is notable about this young man's statement is the extent to which he viewed cultural appropriation as a selective two-way process, albeit one that was implicitly uneven. This explains why some youth, in contrast to either the older generation of middle-class professionals or the generation of working-class Jamaicans politicized by the various movements during the 1970s, might not have seen America as an evil empire encroaching from the north. Contrary to the dominant image of the culturally bombarded and besieged Jamaican, powerless either to resist or to critique that which is imposed from "elsewhere"—the image often proliferated by those who disparaged the growing influence of the United States—youth asserted that David could not only challenge Goliath but could also influence what Goliath listened to, how he dressed, and what he liked. Indeed, this has been an important element of how Jamaicans view themselves and their importance on a global scale. That "likkle Jamaica" is known worldwide for its music and its elite athletes (even, or perhaps especially, its bobsledders), and that this recognition is completely out of proportion to the island's size, is noted in both public fora and private conversations over and over again. The frequency of this invocation also suggests a need among Jamaicans to carve out spaces in which Jamaicans feel, and indeed have, power and recognition within a global public sphere.

Even more importantly, the perspective offered by these youth reinforces the importance of a dialectical reading of the relationship between capitalist globalization and local cultural practices, and between consumerism and cultural imperialism. It also nuances the assertions of scholars who argue that global capitalism and its development models are destroying cultural diversity and creating a monoculture, and who identify "Americanization" as solely imperialist and nonnegotiable. What youth in the community argued instead marked an attempt to reinscribe and re-create their own agency within the process of consumption itself. In other words, while coveting American "name brands," they were also quick to point out the extent to which they defined consumer trends (in music selections, linguistic repertoires, clothing styles) within Jamaica and to extend this power to Jamaicans overseas. This is what I call "radical consumerism." It is not only an eschewal of creole middle-class models of progress through moderation and temperance but also an insistence that consumption is a creative and potentially liberatory process and that the ability both to influence and to reflect global style is, in fact, an important public power.

We need, therefore, to read capitalist consumption both dialectically and within the context of specific histories and political economies. This kind of analytic framework engages the possibility for alternative readings of "getting my share now, what's mine,"[6] readings that position what may look like crass (and perhaps imitative) materialism on the part of lower-class black Jamaicans as racially vindicating capitalist consumerism instead. Further, the basis of this consumerism—the ideology that positions progress as the result of amassing wealth—is not now limited to the Jamaican working classes. As David Scott has also pointed out, the new black middle class has been "less concerned with the virtues of taste, or the nationalist ideal of a cultural consensus, and more with markets and money" (2000: 295). In other words, this emphasis on capitalism and consumerism has, more recently, been linked to the elevation of a racial identity: "For the liberal and left brown middle classes of the 1970s, blackness was part of an abstract principle of social change. For the black middle class of the 1990s, by contrast, blackness is part of an individual (even individualistic) identity politics, part of an embodied identity whose marginalization is to be overcome by the politics of the new

PNP of P. J. Patterson, or the new consumer egalitarianism of the liberalized market" (296).

A dim view of these ideological shifts is often promulgated within both academic and popular fora. However, taking "radical consumerism" seriously may reveal that the lower-class black Jamaican man driving a "Bimma" has more on his mind than individualist conspicuous consumption. Instead, he is refashioning selfhood and reshaping stereotypical assumptions about racial possibilities through—rather than outside—capitalism. That is, black Jamaicans are simultaneously critiquing, selectively appropriating, and creatively redefining those aspects of the dominant capitalist ethos that they believe benefit themselves and their communities, both materially and psychologically. By making this argument, I do not mean to discount the effects of a globally hegemonic Americanism whereby the viability of global markets is secured for U.S. consumers and capitalists by any means necessary (including, or more accurately especially, military intervention) in ways that exploit and reproduce the relative weakness of states constrained by the IMF and the World Bank. What I am trying to stress is that within this context individuals do find ways to resignify dominant ideologies and practices in order to resituate themselves as powerful actors within their own transnational spheres.

The Politics of Modern Blackness and Hegemonic Reordering in Jamaica

In rereading the meanings of rationality, autonomy, reflection, subjectivity, and power from the slaves' point of view, Paul Gilroy has argued that black intellectual and expressive cultural production elaborates a "counterculture of modernity" (1993: 1). Gilroy considers black music, in particular, to constitute an "alternative public sphere" (1987: 215). This is because among Black Atlantic populations, the production and consumption of music has blurred modern Euro-American boundaries between ethics and aesthetics, life and art, and performer and crowd. For Gilroy, public expressions of blackness are correlated with the values of egalitarianism, community, and reciprocity. Insofar as these values represent challenges to dominant norms associated with the effects of slavery and capitalist development—hierarchy, individualism, and greed—they have been held up as evidence of resistance (with a capital "R"). However, the popular cultural forms associated with modern blackness represent and reproduce aspects of contemporary dominant systems of belief—such as "making it" in the marketplace—and these aspects also embody particular political visions. This raises thorny questions for academics, policy makers, and activists concerned with the transformative potential of popular cultural production and representation. If modern blackness is supposed to be countercultural, where is dancehall's counter-hegemonic politics? If it marks a new kind of representation holding a new public power, does it embody a new mode of articulating protest? Does it carry a particular vision for the future?

While black expressive cultural forms reflect an alternative historical consciousness and provide the means to articulate and maintain oppositional identities and values, they have also always existed "partly inside and not always against the grand narrative of Enlightenment and its operational principles" (Gilroy 1993: 48). Within this context, we are usually quick to recognize that compliance has not always indicated consent. However, it is also true that noncompliance does not always translate into resistance. Inheritors of the contradictory legacies of the Enlightenment and slavery, democracy and imperialism, scientific rationalism and racism, the descendants of Africans throughout the Atlantic world have been forced to develop a world view that enables them to negotiate Western tenets of civilization while at the same time creatively critiquing them. This inherently double-sided structural formation has meant that for black people, *at least* dual visions, lifestyles, consciousnesses are not only possible but also necessary. I emphasize the "at least" in this sentence to suggest that neither the Du Boisian "double consciousness" framework nor the various iterations of cultural duality can account for the complexity of the material and ideological cultural formulations I have described in these pages. Like other anthropologists, I am interested here in moving beyond structuralism's legacy, in insisting that we contemplate the relatedness of binary terms instead of considering them only as oppositional. From this perspective, modernity and tradition, global and local, secular and sacred, state and nation, and yes, hegemony and resistance are fluid *relationships*, mutually constituting conceptual tools rather than oppositional, categorizational poles.

Intellectuals and activists alike have been concerned to assess the transformative potential of popular cultural practices and representations in Jamaica because of their power to reveal the ways nonelites have negotiated the systems and opportunities institutionalized by local leaderships and multilateral financial agencies while at the same time maintaining their own ways of living and values, even as these are modified with time, technology, and experience. In attempting to pinpoint key aspects of popular political consciousness that have provided a foundation for counterhegemonic material and ideological strategies among Jamaicans over time, several scholars have identified black lower-class politico-religious ideology as embodying transformative spiritual, cultural, and political agendas simultaneously (Bakan 1990; Bogues 2002; Carnegie 2002; Chevannes 1998). Within other spheres, late-twentieth-century, lower-class, urban black Jamaican cultural production and sociopolitical practices have been seen as embodying an increased "cultural confidence," a confidence that has occasioned an "expansion of their social autonomy, and a meteoric rise in their social power" (Gray 1994: 177). While these formulations help us to discern some of the ways people marginalized from the formal institutions of power create sociocultural, economic, and political openings for themselves, they can only tell us part of the story. This is, in part, because even when considering transterritorial or diasporic formations they tend to situate counterhegemonic cultural production within narratives of national or racial progress that are ultimately territorially based, and therefore beholden, in one way or another, to the narrative of progress espoused by creole nationalists.

But the profound restructuring of the link between territory and nationalism throughout the Caribbean by the end of the twentieth century has had ramifications that are not mitigated by governments' attempts to police the cultural boundaries of citizenship and belonging. If Jamaica is now wherever Jamaicans are, then the processes of Jamaican racial, class, and gender formation—both in Jamaica and in diaspora—are always negotiated in relation to those processes occurring elsewhere. The emergent politics of modern blackness is therefore neither univocal nor univalent but nevertheless has the potential to alter Jamaicans' political and social possibilities in the twenty-first century as significantly as the explicit conceptualization of the African Diaspora as a common community did in the late nineteenth century and the early twentieth. This is because it is a politics that is rooted in the changing ways people define community, restructure their lives in order to survive, and reorganize racialized, classed, and gendered identities within the public sphere. The narratives of duality and double consciousness can only ever partially capture the complexity and dynamism of these imaginative and material worlds that are sometimes created through surprising collaborations.

If we approached a more complex understanding of the politics of popular culture, we would, for example, reveal the emphasis on consumerism as something more than false consciousness and a capitulation to Americanized commodifications of desire. Instead, we might apprehend it as a desire for a particular kind of modernity that in specific social realms is "coproduced" with other diasporic communities. Here, I am borrowing the idea of coproduction from Elizabeth McAlister, whose discussion of Haitian Rara in New York City marks a tension between the concepts of diaspora and transnationalism. Noting that Rara in New York is in dialogue with the Haitian branches of dancehall and African American hip-hop culture, and explicating the complex and changing relationships forged among Haitian and Jamaican migrants in Florida and Brooklyn, McAlister arrives at the important insight that "the process of identity building is coproduced with other minority communities, and not just against hegemonic groups" (2002: 198). In other words, there is a complex historical political economy that surrounds the respatializations and resignifications of Rara, and its meanings are generated not only among Haitians in relation to elites (in Haiti) or whites (in the United States) but also laterally among other diasporic populations (see also Gilroy 1987). In Jamaica, modern blackness is coproduced with urban and primarily working-class African Americans who live in Jamaicans' social worlds—both real and imagined—as media producers and neighbors, in relation to middle- and upper-class Jamaicans in Jamaica as well as West Indians and Euro-Americans in the United States and elsewhere.

On one hand modern blackness provides visions for upward mobility within today's globalized economy that are alternative to those professed by professional middle-class Jamaicans. On the other hand, these visions don't necessarily open the door to long-term transformations in social, political, and economic hierarchies. For example, while the entrepreneurial zeal with which people in the community where I conducted research seek to take advantage of migratory possibilities has facilitated their relative success within a global labor market, it has also drained the community of young people with skills, presented serious challenges to the development of leadership locally, further disadvantaged those community members who are not able to migrate, and perpetuated an outward outlook whereby local ambitions require foreign realization. At the same time, migration is a critical opportunity within a context where, in spite of increased access to education, Jamaicans cannot find remunerative work locally that is related to their specific skills. The "two-sidedness" of modern blackness is also expressed within its popular representations, such as dancehall music and its associated culture. By this, I mean that the textual dimensions of popular cultural production often both celebrate the culture of dancehall and recuperate aspects of the culture of respectability.

Because modern blackness is both a part of, and itself embodies, the cultural plurality that frames the range of ideological and political possibilities for contemporary Jamaicans, it is less a stable and coherent ideological framework for action than a way of seeing, organizing, and imagining a changed world. It embodies a public power previously unattained, one that encompasses a framework for facing a global political economy in which Jamaica is never as powerful as it exists in the imaginations of Jamaicans. Popular cultural production in contemporary Jamaica must be positioned neither as a kind of contradictory false consciousness nor as inherently or hopefully resistant or revolutionary. Instead, we must take seriously the cultural dimensions of intensified globalization in Jamaica to more clearly apprehend the political implications of a shift not only in the balance of power between the respectable state and popular culture but also in the composition of these dimensions at specific moments in time.

Notes

1. This essay is the product of fieldwork supported by the Wenner-Gren Foundation for Anthropological Research (#6063). As with any writing, it is also the result of dialogue and debate. I am particularly thankful for the comments of Kamari Clarke, Faye Harrison, Maureen Mahon, John Jackson, Tina Campt, and the anonymous readers for *small axe* who provided insightful suggestions on an earlier version (and the journal for permitting republication in revised form here).

2. "Colored" people—meaning mixed "brown" folk—were not invited to contribute to this volume in the view that black Jamaicans would more forcefully reflect the impact of emancipation and missionary activity on the population of ex-slaves. In the preface, the authors insisted that they should not be seen as exceptions within the race. Rather, they wanted the British public to know that there were many others like them who also would have been able to write the book. Biographical information for the contributors can be found in C. Wilson 1929.

3. Elsewhere, I discuss more fully the dynamic articulations of gender, color, and class that undergirded this definition of respectability, and the ways the concept and practice of respectability has been implicated within diverse sectors of the nationalist project (D. Thomas 2004). See also Austin-Broos 1997; Ford-Smith 1997; and Reddock 1994.

4. See, for example, Thome and Kimball 1838; Phillippo 1969 (1843); Bigelow 1970 (1851); and Gardner 1873.

5. John L. Jackson Jr. uses this term—a "quotation-marked-off place"—to describe the ways Harlem residents and media moguls evoke the mythical Harlemworld of second "renaissances" and souped-up Range Rovers as against their own Harlem realities (2001).

6. These are lyrics to Jimmy Cliff's "The Harder They Come."

BIBLIOGRAPHY

Abraham, Linus. 2002. "The Black Woman as a Marker of Hypersexuality in Western Mythology: A Contemporary Manifestation in the Film *The Scarlet Letter.*" *Journal of Communication Inquiry* 26 (2): 193–214.

Abu-Lughod, Lila. 1989. "Bedouins, Cassettes and Technologies of Public Culture." *Middle East Report* (July-August): 7–11.

——. 1993. *Writing Women's Worlds: Bedoin Stories.* Berkeley: University of California Press.

——. 2005. *Dramas of Nationhood: The Politics of Television in Egypt.* Chicago: University of Chicago Press.

Adams, David W. 1995. *Education for Extinction: American Indians and the Boarding School Experience, 1875–1928.* Lawrence: University Press of Kansas.

Adams, Henley C. 2004. "Fighting an Uphill Battle: Race, Politics, Power, and Institutionalization in Cuba." *Latin American Research Review* 39 (1): 168–82.

Adi, Hakim. 2000. "Pan-Africanism and West African Nationalism in Britain." *African Studies Review* 43 (1): 69–82.

Advocacy Project. 2003. "Girls for Sale: Building a Coalition to Fight Trafficking in Nigeria." http://www.advocacynet.org/cpage_view/nigtraffick_girlsforsale_g_25.html.

Aghatise, Esohe. 2002. "Trafficking for Prostitution in Italy." Paper presented at the Expert Group Meeting on Trafficking in Women and Girls, Glen Cove, N.Y., November 18–22.

Akyeampong, Emmanuel. 2003. "Diaspora and Drug Trafficking in West Africa: A Case Study of Ghana." Paper presented at the Association for the Study of the Worldwide African Diaspora's conference titled "Affirmations and Contestations:

Interpreting the Connections between Africa and the African Diaspora," Northwestern University, Evanston, Ill., October 2–4.

Albuquerque, Luís de and Maria Emíla Madeira Santos. 1991. *História de Cabo Verde.* Vol. 1. Lisbon: Tropical Institute.

Alexander, M. Jacqui, and Mohanty, Chandra, eds. 1997. *Feminist Genealogies, Colonial Legacies, Democratic Futures.* London: Routledge.

Allen, Lillian. 1986. "I Fight Back." In *The Penguin Anthology of Caribbean Verse*, ed. Paula Burnett. Harmondsworth: Penguin.

Alonso, Manuel A. 1974. *El gíbaro: Cuadro de costumbres de la Isla de Puerto Rico.* San Juan: Instituto de Cultura Puertorriqueña.

Amadiume, Ifi. 1987. *Male Daughters, Female Husbands: Gender and Sex in an African Society.* London: Zed.

———. 2000. *Daughters of the Goddess, Daughters of Imperialism.* London: Zed.

Amaral, Ilidio do. 1964. *Santiago de Cabo Verde: A terra e os homes.* Lisbon: Junta de Investigaçao do Ultramar.

Anarfi, John. 1998. "Ghanaian Women and Prostitution in Cote d'Ivoire." In *Global Sex Workers,* ed. Kamala Kempadoo and Jo Doezema, 104–13. London: Routledge.

Andrade, Elisa. 1998. "Do Mito a Historia." In *Cabo Verde: Insulariedade e literatura,* ed. Manuel Veiga. Paris: Editions Karthala.

Andrijasevic, Rutvica. 2003. "The Difference Borders Make: (Il)legality, Migration and Trafficking in Italy Among Eastern European Women in Prostitution." In *Uprootings/Regroundings: Questions of Home and Migration,* ed. Sara Ahmed et al., 251–71. Oxford: Berg.

Anthias, Floya. 1998. "Evaluating 'Diaspora': Beyond Ethnicity." *Sociology* 32 (3): 557–80.

———.2001. "New Hybridities, Old Concepts: The Limits of 'Culture.'" *Ethnic and Racial Studies* 24 (4): 619–41.

Anthias, Flora, and Nira Yuval-Davis. 1993. *Racialized Boundaries: Race, Nation, Gender, Colour and Class and the Anti-Racist Struggle.* London: Routledge.

Appadurai, Arjun. 1989. "On Moving Targets." *Public Culture* 2 (1): i–iv.

———. 1990. "Disjuncture and Difference in the Global Cultural Economy." *Public Culture* 2 (2): 1–24.

———. 1994. "Disjuncture and Difference in the Global Cultural Economy." In *Colonial Discourse and Post-Colonial Theory: A Reader,* ed. Patrick Williams and Laura Chrisman. New York: Columbia University Press.

———. 1996. *Modernity at Large: Cultural Dimensions of Globalization.* Minneapolis: University of Minnesota Press.

———. 2001. "Grassroots Globalization and the Research Imagination." In *Globalization,* ed. Arjun Appadurai, 1–21. Durham, N.C.: Duke University Press.

———, ed. 1986. *The Social Life of Things: Commodities in Cultural Perspective.* Cambridge: Cambridge University Press.

Appiah, Anthony. 1992. *In My Father's House: Africa in the Philosophy of Culture*. New York: Oxford University Press.

Armstrong, Mary F. M. 1887. *Richard Armstrong: America, Hawaii*. Hampton, VA: Normal School Press.

Armstrong, Richard. Papers. Manuscript Division, Library of Congress.

Armstrong, Samuel C. 1878. "Editorials about Papers on Conjuring." *Southern Workman* 7 (4): 26–35.

———. 1909. "From the Beginning." In *Memories of Old Hampton*. 1–15. Hampton, VA: The Armstrong League of Hampton Workers, The Institute Press.

———. Personal Memoirs and Letters. Compiled by Helen Ludlow. Williams College Archives and Special Collections, Williamstown, Mass.

Atkinson, Rowland. 2000. "Measuring Displacement and Gentrification in Greater London." *Urban Studies* 37 (1): 149–65.

Austin-Broos, Diane. 1997. *Jamaica Genesis*. Chicago: University of Chicago Press.

Aymer, Paula. 1997. *Uprooted Women: Migrant Domestics in the Caribbean*. Westport, CT: Praeger.

Axel, Brian Keith. 2002. "The Diasporic Imaginary." *Public Culture* 14 (2): 411–28.

Back, Les. 1996. *New Ethnicities and Urban Culture: Racisms and Multiculture in Young Lives*. London: University College London Press.

Bacon, Alice M. 1890. "Silhouettes." *Southern Workman* 19 (11): 124–25.

———. 1893. "Folk-Lore and Ethnology." *Southern Workman* 22 (12): 180–81.

———. 1898. "Work and Methods of the Hampton Folk-Lore Society." *Journal of American Folk-Lore* 11:17–21.

Bacon, Alice M., and Leonora Herron. 1896. "Conjuring and Conjure Doctors in the Southern United States." *Journal of American Folk-Lore* 9: 143–47, 224–26.

Bakan, Abigail. 1990. *Ideology and Class Conflict in Jamaica*. Montreal: McGill-Queens University Press.

Baker, Lee D. 1998. *From Savage to Negro: Anthropology and the Construction of Race, 1896–1954*. Berkeley: University of California Press.

Bakhtin, M. M. 1986. "Toward a Methodology for the Human Sciences." In *Speech Genres and Other Late Essays*, trans. Verne W. McGee, 159–72. Austin: University of Texas Press.

Bales, Kevin. 2000. *Disposable People*. London: University of California.

Ballonoff, Paul. 1976. *Mathematical Foundations of Social Anthropology*. The Hague: Mouton.

Banco Popular de Puerto Rico. 2001. *Raíces*. Documentary directed by Paloma Suau. Color. 90 min. Videocassette.

Banks, F. D. 1894. "Plantation Courtship." *Journal of American Folk-Lore* 7: 147–49.

———. 1895. "Plantation Courtship." *Journal of American Folk-Lore* 8: 106.

Barcellos, Christiano José de Senna. 1899–1900. *Subsídios para a historia de Cabo Verde e Guiné, I–II*. Lisbon: Tipografia da Academia Real das Ciências.

Barton, Halbert. 1995. "The Drum-Dance Challenge: An Anthropological Study of Gender, Race, and Class Marginalization of Bomba in Puerto Rico." Ph.D. diss., Cornell University.

Basch, Linda. 2001. "Transnational Social Relations and the Politics of National Identity: An Eastern Caribbean Case Study." In *Islands in the City: West Indian Migration to New York*, ed. Nancy Foner. Berkeley: University of California Press.

Basch, Linda, Nina Glick Schiller and Cristina Szanton-Blanc. 1994. *Nations Unbound: Transnational Projects, Postcolonial Predicaments, and Deterritorialized Nation-States*. Langhorne, PA: Gordon and Breach.

Baud, Michiel. 1987. "The Origins of Capitalist Agriculture in the Dominican Republic." *LARR* 22 (3): 135–53.

——. 1993. "Una frontera-refugio: Dominicanos y Haitianos contra el estado (1870–1930)." *Estudios Sociales* 26 (92): 5–28.

Behar, Ruth. 1995. "Introduction: Out of Exile." In *Women Writing Culture*, ed. Ruth Behar and Deborah Gordon, 1–32. Berkeley: University of California Press.

Bell, Michael J. 1973. "William W. Newell and American Folklore Scholarship." *Journal of the Folklore Institute* 10: 7–21.

Bendix, Regina. 1997. *In Search of Authenticity: The Formation of Folklore Studies*. Wisconsin: University of Wisconsin Press.

Benjamin, Walter. 1978. *Reflections*. New York: Schocken.

——.2003a [1939]. "Central Park." Translated by Edmund Jephcott et al. In *Walter Benjamin: Selected Writings, Volume 4—1983–1940*, ed. Howard Eiland and Michael W. Jennings, 161–99. Cambridge: Harvard University Press, Belknap Press.

——. 2003b [1940]. "On the Concept of History." Trans. Edmund Jephcott et al. In *Walter Benjamin: Selected Writings, Volume 4—1983–1940*, ed. Howard Eiland and Michael W. Jennings, 389–400. Cambridge: Harvard University Press, Belknap Press.

Berg, Lasse. 2001. *Där hemma här borta: Moten med Orienten I Sverige och Norge*. Stockholm: Carlssons.

Berman, Jacqueline. 2003. "(Un)Popular Strangers and Crises (Un)Bounded: Discourses of Sex-Trafficking, the European Political Community and the Panicked State of the Modern State." *European Journal of International Relations* 9 (1): 37–86.

Berman, Marshall. 1988. *All That Is Solid Melts into Air: The Experience of Modernity*. New York: Penguin.

Besson, Jean. 1984. "Family Land and Caribbean Society: Toward an Ethnography of Afro-Caribbean Peasantries." In *Perspectives on Caribbean Regional Identity*, ed. Elizabeth M. Thomas-Hope. Liverpool: Liverpool University Press.

Best, Amy L. 2000. *Prom Night: Youth, Schools, and Popular Culture*. New York: Routledge.

Bhattacharyya, Gargi, John Gabriel, and Stephen Small. 2002. *Race and Power: Global Racism in the Twenty-First Century*. New York: Routledge.

Bianchini, Franco. 1997. "GLC R.I.P.: Cultural Policies in London 1981–1986." *New Formations* (1): 103–15.

Bigelow, John. 1970 [1851]. *Jamaica in 1850, or the Effects of Sixteen Years of Freedom on a Slave Colony*. Westport, CT: Negro Universities Press.

Billen, Andrew. 2002. "Television-Devilish Pursuits." *New Statesman*, January 21.

Bindman, Jo. 1998. "An International Perspective on Slavery in the Sex Industry." In *Global Sex Workers*, ed. Kamala Kempadoo and Jo Doezema, 65–68. London: Routledge.

Bird, William. 2001. *Paint By Number*. Princeton, N.J.: Princeton Architectural Press.

Blanco, Tomás. 1953. "El elogio de la plena (1934)." In *Antología de ensayos*, ed. Tomás Blanco. México: Editorial Orión.

Bliss, Peggy Ann. 1995. "Black, White, Puerto Rican All Over." *The San Juan Star*, March, 22.

Blum, Jack. 2002. "Under the Radar Screen: Corruption, the Hidden Market, and Inequities." Panel presentation at the EPIIC Symposium on Global Inequities, Tufts University, Boston, February 28–March 3.

Bobo, Jacqueline, ed. 2001. *Black Feminist Cultural Criticism*. Malden, MA: Blackwell.

Bogues, Anthony. 2002. "Politics, Nation, and PostColony: Caribbean Inflections." *Small Axe* 6 (1): 1–30.

Boletim Official do Governo Geral de Cabo-Verde, 1862–1910. Praia, Cabo Verde.

Bolles, A. Lynn. 1983. "Kitchens Hit by Priorities: Employed Working-Class Jamaican Women Confront the IMF." In *Women, Men, and the International Divisions of Labor*, ed. June Nash and Maria Patricia Fernandez-Kelly, 138–60. Albany, NY: State University of New York Press.

——. 1996. *Sister Jamaica: A Study of Women, Work, and Households in Kingston*. New York: University Press of America.

——. 2003. " 'The Caribbean Is on Sale': Globalization and Women Tourist Workers in Jamaica." Paper presented at the American Anthropological Association meetings, Chicago, November 21.

Bordo, Susan. 1993. *Unbearable Weight: Feminism, Western Culture and the Body*. Berkeley: University of California Press.

Bourdieu, Pierre. 1990. *The Logic of Practice*. Stanford, Calif.: Stanford University Press.

Bousquet, Ben, and Colin Douglas. 1991. *West Indian Women at War*. London: Lawrence and Wishart.

Brah, Avtar. 1996. *Cartographies of Diaspora: Contesting Identities*. New York: Routledge.

Braziel, Jana Evans, and Anita Mannur. 2003. "Nation, Migration and Globalization: Points of Contention in Diaspora Studies." In *Theorizing Diaspora*, ed. Jana Evans Braziel and Anita Mannur, 1–22. Oxford: Blackwell.

Briggs, Adam, and Adam Cobley. 1999. " 'I like my Shit Sagged': Fashion, 'Black Musics' and Subcultures." *Journal of Youth Studies* 2 (3): 337–52.

Brinton, Daniel G. 1890. *Races and Peoples: Lectures on the Science of Ethnography*. New York: Hodges.

Brodkin, Karen. 2000. "Global Capitalism: What's Race Got to Do with It?" *American Ethnologist* 27 (2): 237–256.

Brown, Bill. 2003. *A Sense of Things*. Chicago: University of Chicago Press.

Brown, Jacqueline Nassy. 1998. "Black Liverpool, Black America, and the Gendering of Diasporic Space." *Cultural Anthropology* 13 (3): 291–325.

———. 2005. *Dropping Anchor, Setting Sail: Geographies of Race in Black Liverpool*. Princeton, NJ: Princeton University Press.

Browning, Barbara. 1998. *Infectious Rhythm: Metaphors of Contagion and the Spread of African Culture*. London: Routledge.

Brumble, H. D. 1988. *American Indian Autobiography*. Berkeley: University of California Press.

Brussa, Licia. 1998. "The TAMPEP Project in Western Europe." In *Global Sex Workers*, ed. Kamala Kempadoo and Jo Doezema, pp. 231–40. London: Routledge.

Bryan, Patrick. 1991. *The Jamaican People, 1880–1902: Race, Class, and Social Control*. London: Macmillan Education.

Burdick, John 1992. "The Myth of Racial Democracy." *Report on the Americas* 25 (4): 40–44.

Busia, Abena. 2000. "Plenary Comments" at the inaugural conference of ASWAD (Association for the Study of the Worldwide African Diaspora), entitled "Crossing the Boundaries: The African Diaspora in the New Millennium," New York University, September 20–23.

Butchart, Alexander. 1998. *The Anatomy of Power: European Constructions of the African Body*. London: Zed.

Butler, Judith. 1993. *Bodies that Matter: On the Discursive Limits of Sex*. New York: Routledge.

Butler, Kim. 2001. "Defining Diaspora, Refining a Discourse." *Diaspora* 10 (2): 189–219.

Campbell, Colin. 1995. "The Sociology of Consumption." In *Acknowledging Consumption: A Review of New Studies*, ed. Daniel Miller, 96–124. London: Routledge.

Campbell, Horace. 1985. *Rasta and Resistance*. London: Hansib.

Campt, Tina M. 2004. *Other Germans: Black Germans and the Politics of Race, Gender, and Memory in the Third Reich*. Ann Arbor: University of Michigan Press.

Canon, Margaret. 1995. *The Invisible Empire: Racism in Canada*. Toronto: Random House.

Carby, Hazel, ed. 1999. *Cultures in Babylon: Black Britain and African America*. London: Verso.

Carnegie, Charles. 2002. *Postnationalism Prefigured: Caribbean Borderlands*. New Brunswick, N.J.: Rutgers University Press.

Carreira, António. 1977. *Migracões nas Ilhas de Cabo Verde*. Praia, Cape Verde: Instituto Caboverdiano do Livro.

———. 2000. *Cabo Verde: Formação e extinção de uma sociedade escravoata (1460–1878)*. Praia, Cape Verde: Instituto Caboverdiano do Livro e do Disco.

Carter, Bob, Clive Harris, Marci Green, and Rick Halpern. 1996. "Immigration Policy and the Racialization of Migrant Labour: The Construction of National Identities in the USA and Britain." *Ethnic and Racial Studies* 19 (1): 135–57.

Carter, Bob, Clive Harris, and Shirley Joshi. 1993. "The 1951–55 Conservative Government and the Racialization of Black Immigration." In *Inside Babylon: The Caribbean Diaspora in Britain*, ed. Winston James and Clive Harris 55–72. London: Verso.

Carter, Donald. 2003. Preface to *New African Diasporas*, ed. Khalid Koser, ix–xix. London: Routledge.

Centner, Ryan. 2002. "Neoliberalism and Third World Cities: Structurally Adjusted Urbanism as a Way of Life, from Buenos Aires to Istanbul to Kuala Lumpur." EPIIC Symposium on Global Inequities, Tufts University, Boston, February 28–March 3.

Chabal, Patrick. 1996. "The African Crisis: Context and Interpretation." In *Postcolonial Identities in Africa*, ed. Richard Werbner and Terence Ranger, 29–54. London: Zed.

Chamberlain, Mary. 1997. *Narratives of Exile and Return*. NY: St. Martin's Press.

Chambers, Iain. 1988. *Popular Culture: The Metropolitan Experience*. London: Methuen.

Channel Four. 2002. "Tuscany: Foreign Bodies." January 13.

Chapkis, Wendy. 2000. "Power and Control in the Commercial Sex Trade." In *Sex for Sale*, ed. Ronald Weitzer, 181–202. London: Routledge.

(charles), Helen. 1997. "The Language of Womanism: Rethinking Difference." In *Black British Feminism*, ed. Heidi Mirza, 278–97. London: Routledge.

Chauncey, George. 1994. *Gay New York: Gender, Urban Culture, and the Makings of the Gay Male World, 1890–1940*. New York: Basic Books.

———. 1995. *Why Marriage? The History Shaping Today's Debate Over Gay Equality*. New York: Basic Books.

Chevannes, Barry, ed. 1998. *Rastafari and Other Afro-Caribbean Worldviews*. New Brunswick, N.J.: Rutgers University Press.

Chin, Elizabeth M. 2001. *Purchasing Power: Black Kids and American Consumer Culture*. Minneapolis: University of Minnesota Press.

Chuck D. 1997. *Fight the Power: Rap, Race and Reality*. Edinburgh: Payback Press.

Clarke, Edith. 1957. *My Mother Who Fathered Me: A Study of the Family in Three Selected Communities in Jamaica*. London: G. Allen and Unwin.

Clarke, George Elliot, ed. 1997. *Eyeing the North Star: Directions in African-Canadian Literature*. Toronto: McLelland and Stewart Inc.

Clarke, Kamari Maxine. 2004. *Mapping Yoruba Networks: Power and Agency in the Making of Transnational Communities*. Durham, N.C.: Duke University Press.

Clifford, James. 1988. *The Predicament of Culture: Twentieth-Century Ethnography, Literature, and Art*. Cambridge, Mass.: Harvard University Press.

——. 1997. *Routes: Travel and Translation in the Late Twentieth Century*. Cambridge, Mass.: Harvard University Press.

Clift, Stephen, and Simon Carter, eds. 2000. *Tourism and Sex*. London: Pinter.

Codrington, Raymond. 2001. "Sessions from the Big Smoke: Rap, Race and Class in London." Ph.D. diss., City University of New York Graduate Center.

Cohen, Robin. 1997. *Global Diasporas: An Introduction*. London: UCL Press.

Colen, Shellee. 1989. " 'Just a Little Respect': West Indian Domestic Workers in New York City." In *Muchchas No More: Household Workers in Latin America and the Carribbean*, eds. Elsa Chaney and Mary Gracia Castro, 171–194. Philadelphia: Temple University Press.

Colen, Shellee and Roger Sanjek, eds. 1990. *At Work in Homes: Household Workers in World Perspective*. American Ethnological Society Monograph Series, no. 3.

Collins, Patricia Hill. 1990. *Black Feminist Thought*. Boston: Unwin Hyman.

——. 2004. *Black Sexual Politics: African Americans, Gender and the New Racism*. New York: Routledge.

Comaroff, Jean, and John Comaroff. 1993. Introduction to *Modernity and Its Malcontents: Ritual and Power in Post-Colonial Africa*, ed. Jean Comaroff and John Comaroff, xi–xxxvi. Chicago: University of Chicago Press.

——. 1997. *Of Revelation and Revolution: The Dialectics of Modernity on a South African Frontier*. Vol. 2. Chicago: University of Chicago Press.

——.2001. "Millennial Capitalism: First Thoughts on a Second Coming." In *Millennial Capitalism and the Culture of Neoliberalism*, ed. Jean Comaroff and John L. Comaroff, 1–56. Durham, N.C.: Duke University Press.

Cooper, Anna J. 1894. Letter to the Editor. *Southern Workman* 23 (1): 5.

Cooper, Frederick. 2001. "What Is the Concept of Globalization Good For?: An African Historian's Perspective." *African Affairs* 100: 189–213.

Coronil, Fernando. 1996. "Beyond Occidentalism: Toward Nonimperial Geohistorical Categories." *Cultural Anthropology* 11 (1): 51–87.

Corrêa, Mendes. 1943. *Raças do império*. Lisbon: Junta de Investigações do Ultramar.

Crane, Kristine. 2001. "Italian Haven Offers Hope to Trafficked Women." *Christian Science Monitor* 93 (237): 7.

Crummell, Alexander. 1894. Letter to the Editor. *Southern Workman* 23 (1): 5.

Current, Winifred. 2002. "Evicting Memory: Displacing Work and Home in a Gentrifying Neighborhood." Paper presented at Upward Neighborhood Trajectories conference, University of Glasgow, Sept. 26–27.

Daniel, E. Valentine. 2002. "The Refugee: A Discourse on Displacement." In *Exotic No More: Anthropology on the Frontlines*, ed. Jeremy MacClancy, 270–86. Chicago: University of Chicago Press.

Darnell, Regna. 1973. "American Anthropology and the Development of Folklore Scholarship." *Journal of the Folklore Institute* (10): 23–39.

David-West, Tonye. 2002. "In Search of a Virgin in Nigeria." March 5, http://nigeria world.com/feature/publication/david-west/030502.html.

Dávila, Arlene M. 1997. *Sponsored Identities: Cultural Politics in Puerto Rico*. Philadelphia: Temple University Press.

Davis, Kathy. 1997. "Embody-ing Theory: Beyond Modernist and Postmodernist Readings of the Body." In *Embodied Practices*, ed. Kathy Davis, 1–26. London: Sage.

D'Cunha, Jean. 2002. "Trafficking in Persons: A Gender and Rights Perspective." Paper presented at the Expert Group Meeting on Trafficking in Women and Girls, Glen Cove, N.Y., November 18–22.

"Dear Teacher." 1876. *Southern Workman* 5 (6): 46.

"Death of Rev. Richard Armstrong." 1860. *The Friend* 9 (10 N.S.): 76–77.

de Certeau, Michel, Luce Giard, and Pierre Mayol. 1998. *The Practice of Everyday Life*. Vol. 2, *Living and Cooking*. Minneapolis: University of Minnesota Press.

Deere, Carmen D., Peggy Antrobus, and Lynn Bolles. 1990. In *The Shadows of the Sun*. Boulder, Colo.: Westview Press.

de la Fuente, Alejandro 2001. *A Nation for All: Race, Inequality, and Politics in Twentieth-Century Cuba*. Chapel Hill: University of North Carolina Press.

Delaney, Martin. 1968. *Condition, Elevation, Emigration and Destiny of the Colored People of the United States*. New York: Arno Press and the *New York Times*.

de los Reyes, Paulina. 2000. Folkhemmets Paradoxer: Genus och Etnicitet i den Svenska Modellen. *KUT* (2): 27–47.

DeMott, Benj. 1988. *The Future Is Unwritten: Working-Class Youth Cultures in England and America*. *Critical Texts* 5 (1): 42–58.

Derby, Lauren. 1994. "Haitians, Magic, and Money: *Raza* and Society in the Haitian-Dominican Borderlands, 1900 to 1937." *Comparative Studies in History and Society* 36 (3): 488–526.

Desai, Ashwin. 2003. *The Poors of Chatsworth: Race, Class, and Social Movements in Post-Apartheid South Africa*. Durban: Madiba.

di Cortemiglia, Vittoria Luda. 2003. Desk review for the Programme of Action against Trafficking in Minors and Young Women from Nigeria into Italy for the Purpose of Sexual Exploitation. Turin, Italy: United Nations Interregional Crime and Justice Research Institute.

Doezema, Jo. 1998. "Forced to Choose: Beyond the Voluntary v. Forced Prostitution. Dichotomy." In *Global Sex Workers*, ed. Kamala Kempadoo and Jo Doezema, 34–50. London: Routledge.

Domínguez, Virginia. 1986. The Marketing of Heritage. *American Ethnologist* 13 (3): 546–55.

——. 1989. *People as Object, People as Subject: Selfhood and Peoplehood in Contemporary Israel*. Madison: University of Wisconsin Press.

Donham, Donald. 1999. *Marxist Modern: An Ethnographic History of the Ethiopian Revolution*. Berkeley: University of California Press.

——. 2002. "On Being Modern in a Capitalist World: Some Conceptual and Comparative Issues." In *Critically Modern: Alternatives, Alterities, Anthropologies*, ed. Bruce Knauft, 241–57. Indianapolis: Indiana University Press.

Dopico, Ana María. 2002. "Picturing Havana: History, Vision, and the Scramble for Cuba." Nepantla 3 (3): 451–93.

Douglass, Frederick. 2000 [1893]. Speech at Colored American Day (August 25, 1893). In *All the World Is Here: The Black Presence at White City*, ed. Christopher R. Reed, 193–94. Bloomington: Indiana University Press.

Doy, Gen. 1998. "More than Meets the Eye: Representations of Black Women in Mid-19th Century French Photography." *Women's Studies International Forum* 21 (3): 305–19.

Drachler, Jacob, Ed. 1975. *Black Homeland/Black Diaspora*. Port Washington, N.Y.: Kennikat Press.

Drake, St. Clair. 1987. *Black Folk Here and There.*, Vol. 1. Los Angeles: University of California Press.

———. 1990. *Black Folk Here and There*. Vol. 2. Los Angeles: University of California Press.

Duany, Jorge. 1997. From the Bohío to the Caserío: Urban Housing Conditions in Puerto Rico. In *Self-Help Housing, the Poor, and the State in the Caribbean*, ed. Robert B. Potter. Knoxville: The University of Tennessee Press.

———. 2000. "Nation on the Move: The Construction of Cultural Identities in Puerto Rico and the Diaspora." *American Ethnologist* 27 (1): 25–31.

Duany, Jorge, Luisa Hernández Angueira, and César Rey. 1995. *El Barrio Gandul: Economía subterránea y migración indocumentada en Puerto Rico*. Caracas: Nueva Sociedad.

Du Bois, W. E. B. 1935. *Black Reconstruction: An Essay toward the History of the Part Which Black Folk Played in the Attempt to Reconstruct Democracy in America, 1860–1880*. New York: Harcourt, Brace, and Company.

———. 1989 [1903]. *The Souls of Black Folk*. New York: Bantam.

Du Bois, W. E. B., and Augustus G. Dill. 1968 [1910]. "The College-Bred Negro American: Report of a Social Study Made by Atlanta University under the Patronage of the Trustees of the John F. Slater Fund; with Proceedings of the 15th Annual Conference for the Study of Negro Problems, held at Atlanta University, on Tuesday, May 24, 1910." In *The Atlanta University Publications*, ed. William L. Katz, 1–136. New York: Arno Press and the *New York Times*.

duCille, Ann. 1996a. *Skin Trade*. Cambridge, Mass.: Harvard University Press.

———. 1996b. "Toy Theory: Black Barbie and the Deep Play of Difference." In *Skin Trade*. Cambridge, Mass.: Harvard University Press.

Dussel, Enrique. 1998. "Beyond Eurocentrism: The World and the Limits of Modernity." In *The Cultures of Globalization*, ed. Fredric Jameson and Masao Miyoshi. Durham, N.C.: Duke University Press.

Eastman, Elaine. 1896. Address of Mrs. Eastman. Proceedings of the Thirteenth Annual Meeting of the Lake Mohonk Conference of the Friends of the Indian, 1895, pp. 92–94.

Ebron, Paulla. 2000. "Tourists as Pilgrims: Commercial Fashioning of Transatlantic Politics." *American Ethnologist* 26 (4): 910–32.

———. 2002. *Performing Africa*. Princeton, N.J.: Princeton University Press.

Edwards, Brent Hayes. 2001. "The Uses of Diaspora." *Social Text* 66: 44–73.

———. 2003. *The Practice of Diaspora: Literature, Translation, and the Rise of Black Internationalism*. Cambridge, Mass.: Harvard University Press.

Edwards, Elizabeth. 2001. *Raw Histories: Photography, Anthropology and Museums*. Oxford: Berg.

Ehrenreich, Barbara, and Arlie Russell Hochschild. 2002. *Global Woman: Nannies, Maids and Sex Workers in the New Economy*. New York: Metropolitan Books.

Elliott, Michael. 2002. *The Culture Concept: Writing and Difference in the Age of Realism*. Minneapolis: University of Minnesota Press.

Ellison, Ralph. 1987. *Invisible Man*. London: Penguin.

"Ending the Global Sex Trade." 2000. *Christian Science Monitor* 92 (21): 5.

Enloe, Cynthia. 1990. *Bananas, Beaches, and Bases: Making Feminist Sense of International Politics*. Berkeley: University of California Press.

Escobar, Arturo. 1995. *Encountering Development*. Princeton, N.J.: Princeton University Press.

Eshun, Kodwo. 1999. *More Brilliant Than the Sun: Adventures in Sonic Fiction*. London: Quarter Books.

Essed, Philomena. 1991. *Understanding Everyday Racism: An Interdisciplinary Theory*. Sage Publications: California.

Esteban Deive, Carlos. 1978. *El Indio, el negro, y la vida tradicional dominicana*. Santo Domingo: Museo del Hombre Dominicano.

———. 1992. *Vodú y magia en Santo Domingo*. 3d ed. Santo Domingo: Fundación Cultural Dominicana.

Esteves, Maria do Céu. 1991. *Portugal, país de imigração*. Lisbon: Instituto de Estudos para o Desenvolvimento.

Evbayiro, Hilary. 2000. "Nigerian Women's Involvement in International Prostitution: A Case for Edo Bashing." June 13, 2000. http://nigeriaworld.com/feature/publication/evbayiro/0613100.html.

Fanon, Frantz. 1967. *Black Skin, White Masks*. New York: Grove Press.

Farmer, Paul, Margaret Connors, and Jane Simmons. 1996a. "Rereading Social Science." In *Women, Poverty and AIDS: Sex, Drugs and Structural Violence*, ed. Paul Farmer, Margaret Connors, and Jane Simmons. 147–206. Monroe, Maine: Common Courage Press.

———, eds. 1996b. *Women, Poverty and AIDS: Sex, Drugs and Structural Violence*. Monroe, Maine: Common Courage Press.

Farred, Grant. 2003. *The Repressions of the Modernist Unconscious: A Critique of the "African Renaissance": Postmodernism, Postcoloniality, and African Studies,* ed. Zine Magubane. Trenton, N.J..: Africa World Press.

Featherstone, Mike, ed. 1990. *Global Culture: Nationalism, Globalization, and Modernity*. London: Sage.

Ferguson, James. 1990. *The Anti-Politics Machine: 'Development,' Depoliticization, and Bureaucratic Power in Lesotho*. New York: Cambridge University Press.

——. 1999. *Expectations of Modernity: Myths and Meanings of Urban Life on the Zambian Copperbelt*. Berkeley: University of California Press.

——. 2002. "Of Mimicry and Membership: Africans and the 'New World Society.' " *Cultural Anthropology* 17 (4): 551–69.

Fernandes, Gabriel. 2002. *A diluição da África: Uma interpretação da saga identitária cabo-verdiana no panorama político (pós)colonia*. Florianopolis, Brasil: Ed. Da UFSC.

Fernandes, Sujatha. 2003. "Fear of a Black Nation: Local Rappers, Transnational Crossings, and State Power in Contemporary Cuba." *Anthropological Quarterly* 76 (4): 575–608.

Fernandez, Nadine. 1996. "The Color of Love: Young Interracial Couples in Cuba." *Latin American Perspectives* 23 (1): 99–117.

——. 2001. "The Changing Discourse on Race in Contemporary Cuba." *Qualitative Studies in Education* 14 (2): 117–32.

Fernandez-Kelly, Maria Patricia. 1983. *For We Are Sold, I and My People: Women and Industry in Mexico's Frontier*. Albany: State University of New York Press.

Fernandez Robaina, Tomás. 1990. *El Negro en Cuba, 1902–1958*. Havana: Ciencias Sociales.

Ferrao, Luis Á. 1993. "Nacionalismo, hispanismo y élite intelectual en el Puerto Rico de los años treinta." In *Del nacionalismo al populismo: Cultura y política en Puerto Rico*, ed. Silvia Álvarez-Curbelo and María E. Rodríguez-Castro. Río Piedras, P.R.: Ediciones Huracán.

Ferreras, Ramon Alberto. 1983. *Negros: Media Isla 4*. Santo Domingo: Editorial del Nordeste.

Fikes, Kesha. n.d. "Managing African Portugal." Manuscript on Cape Verdean Migrant Labor in Portugal.

——. 2000. "Santiaguense Women's Transnationality in Portugal: Labor Rights, Diasporic Transformation and Citizenship." Ph.D. diss., University of California at Los Angeles.

Fiske, John. 1987. *Television Culture*. New York: Methuen.

Foner, Nancy. 2001. "Introduction: West Indian Migration to New York City: An Overview." In *Islands in the City: West Indian Migration to New York City*, ed. Nancy Foner Berkeley: University of California Press.

Ford, Clyde. 1999. *The Hero with an African Face*. London: Bantam.

Ford-Smith, Honor. 1997. "Ring Ding in a Tight Corner." In *Feminist Genealogies, Colonial Legacies, Democratic Futures*, ed. Chandra T. Mohanty and M. Jacqui Alexander, 213–58. New York: Routledge.

Foreman, Murray. 2002. *The Hood Comes First: Race, Space, and Place in Rap and Hip Hop*. Middletown, Conn.: Wesleyan University Press.

Foucault, Michel. 1978. *The History of Sexuality*. 1st American ed. Translated from the French by Robert Hurley. New York: Pantheon.

———. 1995. *Discipline and Punish: The Birth of the Prison*. Translated by Alan Sheridan. Reprint, New York: Vintage.

Fraser, Nancy, 1992. "Rethinking the Public Sphere: A Contribution to the Critique of Actually Existing Democracy." In *Habermas and the Public Sphere*, ed. Craig Calhoun, 109–42. Cambridge, Mass: MIT Press.

Frederik, Laurie A. 2001. "The Contestation of Cuba's Public Sphere in National Theater and the Transformation from *Teatro Bufo* to *Teatro Nuevo*." *Gestos* 31: 65–97.

Fredrickson, George M. 1971. *The Black Image in the White Mind*. Hanover, N.H.: Wesleyan University Press.

Freeman, Lance, and Frank Braconi. 2002. "Gentrification and Displacement: New York City in the 1990s." *The Urban Prospect* 8 (1) (January/February): 1–4.

Friedman, Jonathan. 1993. "Order and Disorder in Global Systems: A Sketch." *Social Research* 60 (2): 205–34.

———. 1994. *Cultural Identity and Global Process*. London: Sage.

———. 2003. "Globalizing Languages: Ideologies and Realities of the Contemporary Global System." *American Anthropologist* 105 (4): 744–52.

Friedman, Susan. 1999. *Mappings*. Princeton, N.J.: Princeton University Press.

Froude, James Anthony. 1888. *The English in the West Indies, or The Bow of Ulysses*. London: Longmans, Green, and Co.

Fryer, Peter. 1988. *Staying Power: The History of Black People in Britain*. London: Pluto Press.

Frykman, Jonas, and Orvar Löfgren. 1987. *Culture Builders: A Historical Anthropology of Middle Class Life*. Translated by Alan Crozier. New Brunswick, N.J.: Rutgers University Press.

Fukuyama, Francis. 1992. *The End of History and the Last Man*. New York: Free Press.

Furtado, Cláudio Alves. 1993. *A transformação das estruturas agrarias numa Sociedade de Mudança—Santiago, Cabo Verde*. Praia, Cape Verde: Instituto Caboverdiano do Livro e do Disco.

———. 1997. *Génese e (re)produção da classe dirigente em Cabo Verde*. Praia, Cape Verde: Instituto Caboverdiano do Livro e do Disco.

Gaines, Kevin K. 1996. *Uplifting the Race: Black Leadership, Politics, and Culture in the Twentieth Century*. Chapel Hill: University of North Carolina Press.

Gaonkar, Dilip Parameshorar. 2001. "On Alternative Modernities." In *Alternative Modernities*, ed. D. P. Gaonkar, 1–23. Durham, N.C.: Duke University Press.

García Canclini, Néstor. 1989. *Culturas híbridas: Estrategias para entrar y salir de la modernidad*. México City: Grijalbo.

———. 1999. *La globalizacion imaginada*. Barcelona: Paidos.

Gardner, W. J. 1873. *A History of Jamaica*. London: Frank Cass and Co., Ltd.

Gates, Henry Louis. 1999. *Wonders of the African World*. 1st American ed. New York: Knopf.

Gates, Merrill E. 1900. President's Address. Proceedings of the Seventeenth Annual Meeting of the Lake Mohonk Conference of Friends of the Indian, 1899, pp. 8–13.

Gavanas, Anna, and Fiona Williams. 2004. "New Masters/New Servants? The Relations of Gender, Migration and the Commodification of Care." In *Wohlfahrstaat und Geschlechterverhältnis im Umbruch: Was kommt nach dem Ernährermodell?*, 130–52. Jahrbuch für Europa und Nordamerika-Studien 2003, ed. S. Leitner, I. Osner, and M. Schratzenstaller. Opladen: Leske and Budrich.

Geertz, Clifford, 1988. *Works and Lives: The Anthropologist as Author*. Stanford, Calif.: Stanford University Press.

———. 2000 [1973]. *The Interpretation of Cultures: Selected Essays*. New York: Basic Books.

Geschiere, Peter. 1997. *The Modernity of Witchcraft: Politics and the Occult in Postcolonial Africa*. Translated by Peter Geschiere and Janet Roitman. Charlottesville: University of Virginia Press.

Geyer-Ryan, Helga. 1994. *Fables of Desire: Studies in the Ethics of Art and Gender*. London: Polity Press.

Giammarinaro, Maria Grazia. 2002. "Trafficking in Women and Girls." Paper presented at the Expert Group Meeting on Trafficking in Women and Girls, Glen Cove, N.Y., November 18–22.

"Gifted, Black, and Gone." 2000. *Guardian*, May 30.

Gilder, George. 1981. *Wealth and Power*. New York: Basic Books.

Gilliam, Angela M. 2001. "A Black Feminist Perspective on the Sexual Commodification of Women in the New Global Culture." In *Black Feminist Anthropology*, ed. Irma McClaurin, 150–86. London: Rutgers University Press.

Gilman, Sander. 1985a. "Black Bodies, White Bodies: Toward an Iconography of Female Sexuality in Late Nineteenth-Century Art, Medicine, and Literature." *Critical Inquiry* 12 (1): 204–42.

———. 1985b. *Difference and Pathology*. Ithaca: Cornell University Press.

Gilroy, Paul. 1987. *There Ain't No Black in the Union Jack: The Cultural Politics of Race and Nation*. Chicago: University of Chicago Press.

———. 1991. "Sounds Authentic—Black Music, Ethnicity and the Challenge of a Changing Same." *Journal of Black Music Research* 11 (2): 111–132.

———. 1993. *The Black Atlantic: Modernity and Double Consciousness*. Cambridge, Mass.: Harvard University Press.

———. 2000. *Against Race: Imagining Political Culture Beyond the Color Line*. Cambridge, Mass.: Harvard University Press.

Ginsburg, Faye. 2002. "Fieldwork at the Movies: Anthropology and Media." In *Exotic*

No More: Anthropology on the Frontlines, ed. Jeremy MacClancy, 356–76. Berkeley: University of California Press.

Giusti Cordero, Juan A. 1996. "Afro–Puerto Rican Cultural Studies: Beyond Cultura Negroide and Antillanismo." *Centro* 3 (1-2): 56–77.

Glass, Ruth. 1964. "Introduction: Aspects of Change." In *London: Aspects of Change*, ed. Centre for Urban Studies. London: MacGibbon and Kee.

Gleeson, Brendan, and Nicholas Low. 2001. *Governing for the Environment: Global Problems, Ethics, and Democracy.* New York: Palgrave.

Glick Schiller, Nina, and Georges Fouron. 2001. *Georges Woke Up Laughing: Long Distance Nationalism and the Search for Home.* Durham, N.C.: Duke University Press.

Glick Schiller, Nina, Linda Basch, and Cristina Szanton-Blanc, eds. 1992. *Towards a Transnational Perspective on Migration: Race, Class, Ethnicity and Nationalism Reconsidered.* New York: New York Academy of Sciences.

Goddard, Victoria Ana, ed. 2000. *Gender, Agency and Change.* London: Routledge.

Godreau, Isar. 1998. "Missing the Mix: San Antón and the Racial Dynamics of 'Nationalism' in Puerto Rico." Ph.D. diss., University of California, Santa Cruz.

——. 2000. La semántica fugitiva: Raza, color y vida cotidiana en Puerto Rico. *Revista de Ciencias Sociales* 9: 52–71.

Gold, Peter. 2000. *Europe or Africa?: A Contemporary Study of the Spanish North African Enclaves of Ceuta and Melilla.* Liverpool: Liverpool University Press.

Gomes dos Anjos, José Carlos. 2002. *Intelectuais, literatura e poder em Cabo Verde.* Praia, Cape Verde: INIPC.

González, Mireza. 1995. "De cara a San Antón." *El Vocero*, May 8, S4–5.

Gordon, Edmond T. 1999. "The African Diaspora: Toward an Ethnography of Diasporic Identification." *Journal of American Folklore* 112 (445): 282–96.

Gottfried, Stockinger. 1990. *Crónicas de Campo II: Ilha de Santiago.* Praia, Cape Verde: Instituto Caboverdiano do Livro e do Disco.

Graeber, David. 2002. "For a New Anarchism." *New Left Review* 13 (1-2): 61–79.

Gray, Obika. 1994. "Discovering the Social Power of the Poor." *Social and Economic Studies* 43 (3): 169–89.

Green, Charles, ed. 1997. *Globalization and Survival in the Black Diaspora.* Albany: State University of New York Press.

Greenleaves, Jennifer. 2000. "Divided in Unity: The Nigerian Diaspora in Italy." Paper presented at the Colloquium on New African Diasporas at the School of Oriental and African Studies, University of London, May 5.

Grewall, Inderpal and Caren Kaplan, eds. 1994. *Scattered Hegemonies: Postmodernity and Transnational Feminist Practices.* Minneapolis: University of Minnesota Press.

Grier, George, and Eunice Grier. 1980. "Urban Displacement: A Reconnaissance." In *Back to the City: Issues in Neighborhood Renovations*, ed. Shirley Bradway Laska and Daphne Spain, 252–69. New York: Pergamon Press.

Gupta, Akhil, and James Ferguson. 1992. "Beyond 'Culture': Space, Identity, and the Politics of Difference." *Cultural Anthropology* 7 (1): 6–23.

———, eds. 1997. *Anthropological Locations: Boundaries and Grounds of a Field Science.* Berkeley: University of California Press.

Gutiérrez, Pedro Juan. 1998. *Trilogia sucia de La Habana.* Barcelona: Anagrama.

Gysels, Marjolein, Robert Pool, and Betty Nnalusiba. 2002. "Women Who Sell Sex in a Ugandan Trading Town: Life Histories, Survival Strategies and Risk." *Social Science and Medicine* 54(2): 179–92.

Hagedorn, Katherine J. 2001. *Divine Utterances: The Performance of Afro-Cuban Santeria.* Washington: Smithsonian Institution Press.

Hale, Charles. 1999. "Travel Warning: Elite Appropriations of Hybridity, Mestizaje, Antiracism, Equality, and Other Progressive-Sounding Discourses in Highland Guatemala." *Journal of American Folklore* 112 (445): 297–315.

Haley, Alex. 1976. *Roots: The Saga of an American Family.* New York: Dell.

Hall, Catherine. 2002. *Civilising Subjects: Metropole and Colony in the English Imagination 1830–1867.* Cambridge: Polity.

———. 2004. "Discussion on Empire and Globalisation." Today Programme, BBC Radio 4, January 12.

Hall, Stuart. 1978. *Policing the Crisis: 'Mugging,' the State, and Law and Order.* New York: Holmes and Meier.

———. 1987. "Minimal Selves." In *ICA Documents: Black Film, British Cinema,* ed. Kobena Mercer. London: Institute of Contemporary Arts.

———. 1991. "The Local and the Global: Globalization and Ethnicity." In *Culture, Globalization, and the World-System: Contemporary Conditions for the Representation of Identity,* ed. Anthony King, 19–39. Minneapolis: University of Minnesota Press.

———. 1993. "What Is This 'Black' in Black Popular Culture." In *Black Popular Culture,* ed. Gina Dent. Seattle: Bay Press.

———. 1994. "Cultural Identity and Diaspora." In *Colonial Discourse and Postcolonial Theory: A Reader,* ed. Patrick Williams and Laura Chrisman. New York: Columbia University Press.

———. 1996. "The After-life of Frantz Fanon: Why Fanon? Why Now? Why Black Skin, White Masks?" In *The Fact of Blackness: Frantz Fanon and Visual Representation,* ed. Alan Read, 12–37. London: Institute of Contemporary Arts.

———. 2000. "Frontlines and Backyards: The Terms of Change." In *Black British Culture and Society: A Text Reader,* ed. Kwesi Owusu, 127–29. London: Routledge.

Halter, Marilyn. 1993. *Between Race and Ethnicity: Cape Verdean American Immigrants, 1860–1965.* Urbana: University of Illinois Press.

Hammonds, Evelynn. 1997. "Toward a Genealogy of Black Female Sexuality: The Problematic of Silence." In *Feminist Genealogies, Colonial Legacies, Democratic Futures,* ed. M. Jacqui Alexander and Chandra Mohanty, 170–82. London: Routledge.

Hampton Normal and Agricultural Institute. 1893. *Twenty-two Years' Work of the*

Hampton Normal and Agricultural Institute at Hampton, Virginia: Records of Negro and Indian Graduates and Ex-students. Hampton, Va.: Normal School Press.

Hanchard, Michael G. 1994. *Orpheus and Power: The Movimento Negro of Rio de Janeiro and Sao Paulo, Brazil*. Princeton, N.J.: Princeton University Press.

——. 2001. "Afro–Modernity: Temporality, Politics, and the African Diaspora." In *Alternative Modernities*, ed. D. P. Gaonkar, 272–298. Durham, N.C.: Duke University Press.

Handler, Richard. 1988. *Nationalism and the Politics of Culture in Quebec*. Madison: University of Wisconsin Press.

Handler, Richard, and Eric Gable. 1997. *The New History in an Old Museum*. Durham, N.C.: Duke University Press.

Hannerz, Ulf. 1996. *Transnational Connections: Culture, People, Places*. New York: Routledge.

Harding, Jeremy. 2000. *The Uninvited: Refugees at the Rich Man's Gate*. London: Profile Books with the *London Review of Books*.

Hardt, Michael, and Antonio Negri. 2000. *Empire*. Cambridge, Mass.: Harvard University Press.

——. 2004. *Multitude: War and Democracy in the Age of Empire*. New York: Penguin.

Harris, Clive. 1993. Post-war Migration and the Industrial Reserve Army. In *Inside Babylon: The Caribbean Diaspora in Britain*, ed. Winston James and Clive Harris, 9–54. London: Verso.

Harrison, Faye, ed. 1991. *Decolonizing Anthropology*. 2d ed. Arlington, Va.: Association of Black Anthropologists.

——. 1995. "Writing Against the Grain: Cultural Politics of Difference in the Work of Alice Walker." In *Women Writing Culture*, ed. Ruth Behar and D. Gordon, 233–48. Berkeley: University of California Press.

Harvey, David. 1989. *The Condition of Postmodernity: An Enquiry into the Origins of Cultural Change*. Oxford: Basil Blackwell.

——. 2001. *Spaces of Capital: Towards a Critical Geography*. New York: Routledge.

——. 2003. *The New Imperialism*. New York: Oxford University Press.

Hayes, Rutherford B. 1966 [1879]. "Third Annual Message (State of the Union Address to the 46th Congress)." In *The State of the Union Messages of the Presidents*, ed. Fred L. Israel, 1371–95. New York: Chelsea House.

Helg, Aline. 1995. *Our Rightful Share: The Afro-Cuban Struggle for Equality*. Chapel Hill: University of North Carolina Press.

Hennessy, Rosemary. 2000. *Profit and Pleasure: Sexual Identities in Late Capitalism*. London: Routledge.

Henriques, Fernando. 1962. *Prostitution and Society: Primitive, Classical and Oriental*. New York: Citadel.

Hernandez-Reguant, Ariana. 1999. "Kwanzaa and the U.S. Ethnic Mosaic." In *Representations of Blackness and the Performance of Identities*, ed. J. Muteba Rahier. Wesport, Conn.: Bergin and Garvey.

——. 2002. "Radio Taino and the Globalization of the Cuban Culture Industries." Ph.D. diss., University of Chicago, Department of Anthropology.

Herskovits, Melville. 1941. *The Myth of the Negro Past*. New York: Harper.

Herskovits, Melville, and Frances S. Herskovits. 1947. *Trinidad Village*. New York: Knopf.

Hesmondhalgh, David, and Caspar Melville. 2001. "Urban Breakbeat Culture: Repercussions of Hip Hop in the United Kingdom." In *Global Noise: Rap and Music Outside of the USA*. Hanover, N.H.: Wesleyan University Press.

Hesse, Barnor. 2000. *Unsettled Multiculturalisms: Diaspora, Entanglements, Transruptions*. New York: Zed.

Hind, John, and Stephen Mosco. 1985. *Rebel Radio: The Full Story of British Pirate Radio*. London: Pluto Press.

Hirdman, Yvonne. 1994. "Kvinnorna I välfärdstaten." In *Den Svenska Modellen*, ed. Per Thullberg and Kjell Östberg. Stockholm: Studentlitteratur.

Hobsbawm, Eric, and Terrence Ranger. 1983. *The Invention of Tradition*. New York: Cambridge University Press.

Holt, Thomas. 1992. *The Problem of Freedom: Race, Labor, and Politics in Jamaica and Britain, 1832–1938*. Baltimore: Johns Hopkins University Press.

——. 2000. *The Problem of Race in the 21st Century*. Cambridge, Mass.: Harvard University Press.

hooks, bell. 1991. *Yearning: Race, Gender and Cultural Politics*. London: Turnaround.

——. 1992. *Black Looks: Race and Representation*. Boston: South End Press.

Horowitz, Craig. 1998. "The Anti–Sharpton." *New York Magazine*, January 26, 28–31, 90–91.

Hoxie, Frederick E. 1984. *A Final Promise: The Campaign to Assimilate the Indians, 1880–1920*. Lincoln: University of Nebraska Press.

Hull, Gloria, Patricia Bell Scott, and Barbara Smith, eds. 1982. *All the Women Are White, All the Blacks Are Men, But Some of Us Are Brave: Black Women's Studies*. Old Westbury, N.Y.: Feminist Press.

Hunter, Tera W. 1997. *To "Joy My Freedom": Southern Black Women's Lives and Labors after the Civil War*. Cambridge, Mass.: Harvard University Press.

Hutchison, William R. 1987. *Errand to the World: American Protestant Thought and Foreign Missions*. Chicago: University of Chicago Press.

Inda, Jonathan Xavier, and Renato Rosaldo. 2002. "Introduction: A World in Motion." In *The Anthropology of Globalization*, ed. Jonathan Xavier Inda and Renato Rosaldo, 1–34. Oxford: Blackwell.

International Organization for Migration. 1996. *Trafficking in Women to Italy for Sexual Exploitation*. Geneva: International Organization for Migration.

Jackson, John L. Jr. 2001. *Harlemworld: Doing Race and Class in Contemporary Black America*. Chicago: University of Chicago Press.

Jackson, Kenneth. 1985. *Crabgrass Frontier: The Suburbanization of the United States*. Oxford: Oxford University Press.

Jamaica's Jubilee; or, What We Are and What We Hope to Be. 1888. By Five of Themselves. London: S. W. Partridge and Co.

James, C. L. R. 1989 [1963]. *The Black Jacobins: Toussaint L'Ouverture and the San Domingo Revolution.* New York: Vintage.

James, Winston. 1998. *Holding Aloft the Banner of Ethiopia: Caribbean Radicalism in Early Twentieth Century.* New York: Verso.

James, Winston and Clive Harris, eds. 1993. *Inside Babylon: The Caribbean Diaspora in Britain.* London: Verso.

Jameson, Fredric. 1998. "Notes on Globalization as a Philosophical Issue." In *The Cultures of Globalization,* ed. Fredric Jameson and Masao Miyoshi. Durham, N.C.: Duke University Press.

——. 2003. "Utopia and Actually Existing Being." Paper presented at The Future of Utopia conference, Durham, N.C., April 24–27.

Jones, Simon. 1988. *Black Culture, White Youth: The Reggae Tradition From JA to UK.* London: Macmillan Education.

Joyce, Joyce Ann. 1999. "African-Centered Womanism: Connecting Africa to the Diaspora." In *The African Diaspora,* ed. Isidore Okpewho, Carole Boyce Davies, and Ali Mazrui, 538–54. Bloomington: Indiana University Press.

Julien, Isaac. 1995. *The Darker Side of Black* (videorecording). New York: Drift Distributors.

Kaplan, Amy. 1993. "Left Alone with America: The Absence of Empire in the Study of American Culture." In *Cultures of United States Imperialism,* ed. Amy Kaplan and Donald E. Pease, 3–20. Durham, N.C.: Duke University Press.

Karim, Imam Benjamin, ed. 1971. *The End of White World Supremacy: Four Speeches by Malcolm X.* New York: Seaver.

Kasinitz, Philip. 1992. *Caribbean New York: Black Immigrants and the Politics of Race.* Ithaca: Cornell University Press.

Kearney, Michael. 1991. Borders and Boundaries of State and Self at the End of Empire." *Journal of Historical Sociology* 4 (1): 52–74.

Kempadoo, Kamala. 1998. "Introduction: Globalizing Sex Workers' Rights." In *Global Sex Workers,* ed. Kamala Kempadoo and Jo Doezema, 1–28. London: Routledge.

——. 1999. "Continuities and Change: Five Centuries of Prostitution in the Caribbean." In *Sun, Sex, and Gold: Tourism and Sex Work in the Caribbean,* ed. Kamala Kempadoo, 3–33. Lanham, Md.: Rowman and Littlefield.

Kingsnorth, Paul. 2003. *One No, Many Yeses: A Journey to the Heart of the Global Resistance Movement.* London: Free Press.

Kleinfield, N. R. 2000. "Guarding the Borders of the Hip-hop Nation." *New York Times,* July 6.

Knauft, Bruce, ed. 2002. *Critically modern. Alternatives, Alterities, Anthropologies.* Bloomington: Indiana University Press.

Kofman, Eleonore, Annie Phizucklea, Parvati Raghuran, and Rosemary Sales. 2000.

Gender and International Migration in Europe: Employment, Welfare, and Politics. London: Routledge.

Kolawole, Mary E. Modupe. 1997. *Womanism and African Consciousness.* Trenton, N.J.: Africa World Press.

Koser, Khalid, ed. 2003. *New African Diasporas.* London: Routledge.

Kutzinski, Vera. 1993. *Sugar's Secrets: Race and the Erotics of Cuban Nationalism.* Charlottesville: University of Virginia Press.

Laferrière, Dany. 1987. *How to Make Love to a Negro Without Getting Tired.* Toronto: Coach House Press.

——. 1994. *Why Must a Black Writer Write about Sex?* Toronto: Coach House Press.

Larkin, Brian. 1997. "Indian Films and Nigerian Lovers: Media and the Creation of Parallel Modernities." *Africa* 67 (3): 406–40.

Lawrence, Errol. 1982. "Just Plain Common Sense: The 'Roots' of Racism." In *The Empire Strikes Back: Race and Racism in 70s Britain.* London: Routledge.

Lederer, Laura. 2001. *Commercial Sexual Exploitation of Women and Children: A Human Rights Report.* Washington: The Protection Project.

Lee, Barrett A., and David C. Hodge. 1984. "Spatial Differentials in Residential Displacement." *Urban Studies* 21: 219–31.

Lefebvre, Henri. 1991. *The Production of Space.* Translated by D. Nicholson-Smith. Cambridge, Mass.: Blackwell.

Lentin, Ronit. 2003. "Strangers and Strollers: (Re)searching Ireland's Gendered Migratory Spaces." Paper presented at the international conference titled "Women's Movement: Migrant Women Transforming Ireland," Trinity College, Dublin, March 20–21.

Lerner, Gerda, ed. 1972. *Black Women in White America: A Documentary History.* New York: Random House.

Lessa, Almerindo, and Jacques Ruffié, eds. 1960. *Seroantropologia das Ilhas de Cabo Verde: Mesa redonda sobre o homen cabo-verdiano.* Lisbon: Junta de Investigações do Ultramar.

Lewis, Laura 2000. "Blacks, Black Indians, Afromexicans: The Dynamics of Race, Nation, and Identity in a Mexican Moreno Community (Guerrero)." *American Ethnologist* 27 (4): 898–926.

Ley, David. 1993. "Gentrification in Recession: Social Change in Six Canadian Inner Cities, 1981–1986." *Urban Geography* 13 (3): 230–56.

Lindsey, Donald. 1995. *Indians at Hampton Institute, 1877–1923.* Urbana: University of Illinois Press.

Lipsitz, George. 1994. *Dangerous Crossroads: Popular Music, Postmodernism and the Poetics of Place.* London: Verso.

Little, Kenneth. 1973. *African Women in Towns.* Cambridge: Cambridge University Press.

Lodge, Tom. 1983. *Black Politics in South Africa since 1945.* New York: Longman.

Lomnitz, Claudio. 1994. "Decadence in Times of Globalization." *Cultural Anthropology* 9 (2): 257–67.

Lopes, Baltasar. 1956. *Cabo Verde visto por Gilberto Freyre*. Boletim Cabo Verde, no. 84–86. Praia: Cabo Verde.

Lorde, Audre. 1984. *Sister, Outsider*. Trumansburg, N.Y.: Crossing Press.

Lott, Eric. 1993. *Love and Theft: Blackface Minstrelsy and the American Working Class*. New York: Oxford University Press.

Loude, Jean-Yves. 1999. *Cabo Verde: Notas Atlânticas*. Mem Martins, Portugal: Publicações Europa-América.

Ludwig, Sämi. 1994. "Dialogic Possession in Ishmael Reed's Mumbo Jumbo: Bakhtin, Voodoo, and the Materiality of Multicultural Discourse." In *The Black Columbiad: Defining Moments in African American Literature and Culture*. Cambridge, Mass.: Harvard University Press.

Lundahl, Mats, and Jan Lundius. 1990. "Socioeconomic Foundations of a Messianic Cult: Olivorismo in the Dominican Republic." In *Agrarian Society in History: Essays in Honour of Magnus Morner*, ed. Mats Lundahl and Thommy Svensson, 201–38. London: Routledge.

Lundius, Jan. 1995. *The Great Power of God in San Juan Valley: Syncretism and Messianism in the Dominican Republic*. Lund: Lunds Universitet.

Lundius, Jan, and Mats Lundahl. 1989. "Olivorio Mateo: Vida y muerte de un dios campesino." *Estudios Sociales* 22 (76): 3–87.

———. *Peasants and Religion: A Socioeconomic Study of Dios Olivorio and the Palma Sola Movement in the Dominican Republic*. London: Routledge.

Mackey, Eva. 1999. *The House of Difference: Cultural Politics and National Identity in Canada*. New York: Routledge.

Magubane, Zine. 2001. "Which Bodies Matter?: Feminism, Poststructuralism, Race and the Curious Odyssey of the 'Hottentot Venus.'" *Gender and Society* 15 (6): 816–34.

Maier, Karl. 2000. *This House Has Fallen: Nigeria in Crisis*. London: Penguin.

Makofsky, Abraham. 1989. "Experience of Native Americans at a Black College: Indian Students at Hampton Institute, 1878–1912." *Ethnic Studies* 17 (3): 31–46.

Mama, Amina. 1997. "Sheroes and Villains: Conceptualizing Colonial and Contemporary Violence against Women in Africa." In *Feminist Genealogies, Colonial Legacies, Democratic Futures*, ed. M. Jacqui Alexander and Chandra Mohanty, 46–63. London: Routledge.

Mandela, Nelson. 1997. "Presidential Report—50th National Conference of the African National Congress," December 16.

Mankekar, Purnima. 1999. *Screening Culture, Viewing Politics: An Ethnography of Television, Womanhood, and Nation in Postcolonial India*. Durham: Duke University Press.

Marable, Manning. 2004. "Globalization and Racialization," August 13, www.zmag.org/content/showarticle.cfm?SectionID=30&ItemID=6034.

Marble, Michelle. 1996. "Europe Urged to Curb Sexual Exploitation of Women." *Women's Health Weekly,* June 24.

Marcus, George. 1995. "Ethnography In/Of the World System: The Emergence of Multi-Sited Ethnography." *Annual Review of Anthropology.* 24: 95–117.

Mariano, Gabriel. 1959. "Do Funco ao Sobrado ou o Mundo que o Mulatto Criou," in *Coloquios Cabo-Verdianos,* ed. Jorge Dias. Lisbon: Junta de Investigaçães do Ultramar.

Marshall, Annecka. 1996. "From Sexual Denigration to Self-Respect: Resisting Images of Black Female Sexuality." In *Reconstructing Womanhood, Reconstructing Feminism,* ed. Delia Jarrett-Macauley, 5–35. London: Routledge.

Martin Shaw, Carolyn, and Kamari Clarke. 1995. "Rethinking African American Cultural Politics." Paper presented at the meeting of the American Anthropological Association, Washington, D.C., November 30–December 4.

Martinez, Lusitania. 1991. *Palma Sola: Opresión y esperanza (su geografía mítica y social).* Santo Domingo: Ediciones CEDEE.

Martínez-San Miguel, Yolanda. 1998. "De ilegales e indocumentados: Representaciones culturales de la migración dominicana en Puerto Rico." *Revista de Ciencias Sociales* 4: 147–72.

Matory, James Lorand. 1994. *Sex and the Empire That Is No More: Gender and the Politics of Metaphor in Oyo Yoruba Religion.* Minneapolis: University of Minnesota Press.

Maurer, Bill. 2000. "A Fish Story: Rethinking Globalization on Virgin Gorda, British Virgin Islands." *American Ethnologist* 27 (3): 670–701.

Mazrui, Ali. 1986. *The Africans: A Reader.* New York: Praeger.

Mbeki, Thabo. 2000. Speech given at the Youth Conference on Nation Building, Centurion City Hall, South Africa, June 16.

Mbembe, Achille. 2001a. *On the Postcolony.* Berkeley: University of California Press.

——. 2001b. "Ways of Seeing: Beyond the New Nativism: Introduction." *African Studies Review* 44 (2): 1–14.

McAlister, Elizabeth. 2002. *Rara!: Vodou, Power, and Performance in Haiti and Its Diaspora.* Berkeley: University of California Press.

McClintock, Anne. 1995. *Imperial Leather: Race, Gender, and Sexuality in the Colonial Contest.* London: Routledge.

McRobbie, Angela. 1994. "Different, Youthful, Subjectivities: Towards a Cultural Sociology of Youth." In *Postmodernism and Popular Culture.* London: Routledge.

——. 1999. *In the Culture Society: Art, Fashion and Popular Music.* London: Routledge.

Mead, Lawrence. 1992. *The New Politics of Poverty: The Non-working Poor in America.* New York: HarperCollins.

Meeks, Brian. 2000. *Narratives of Resistance.* Kingston: University Press of the West Indies.

Meintel, Dierdre. 1984. *Race, Culture and Portuguese Colonialism in Cabo Verde.* Syracuse, N.Y.: Syracuse University Press.

Menand, Louis, 2001. *The Metaphysical Club: The Story of Ideas in America*. New York: Farrar Straus and Giroux.

Mercer, Kobena. 1992. *Welcome to the Jungle: New Positions in Black Cultural Studies*. London: Routledge.

Mies, Maria. 1986. Patriarchy and Accumulation on a World Scale: Women in the International Division of Labor. London: Zed.

Mignolo, Walter D. 2000. *Local Histories/Global Designs: Coloniality, Subaltern Knowledges, and Border Thinking*. Princeton, N.J.: Princeton University Press.

Millán-Pabón, Carmen. 1995. "Sagradas las raíces." *El Nuevo Día*, June 16, 5.

Miller, Daniel. 1994. *Modernity: An Ethnographic Approach (Dualism and Mass Consumption in Trinidad)*. Oxford: Berg.

———. 2001. *The Dialectics of Shopping*. Chicago: University of Chicago Press.

Mintz, Sidney. 1977. "North American Anthropological Contributions to Caribbean Studies." *Boletín de Estudios Latinoamericanos y del Caribe* 22: 66–82.

———. 1985. *Sweetness and Power: The Place of Sugar in Modern History*. New York: Peguin.

———. 1996. "Enduring Substances, Trying Theories: The Caribbean Region as Oi Koumene." *Journal of the Royal Anthropological Institute* 2 (2): 289–312.

Mirza, Heidi Safia, ed. *Black British Feminism: A Reader*. New York: Routledge.

Modood, Tariq. 1994. "Political Blackness and British Asians." *Sociology* 28 (4): 859–76.

Modood, Tariq, and Pnina Werbner, eds. 1997. *The Politics of Multiculturalism in the New Europe*. London: Zed.

Mohanty, Chandra Talpade. 1991."Cartographies of Struggle: Third World Hopes and the Politics of Feminism." In *Third World Hopes and the Politics of Feminism*, ed. Chandra Mohanty, Ann Russo, and Lourdes Torres, 1–47. Bloomington: University of Indiana Press.

———. 1997. "Women Workers and Capitalist Scripts: Ideologies of Domination, Common Interests, and the Politics of Solidarity." In *Feminist Genealogies, Colonial Legacies, Democratic Futures*, ed. M. Jacqui Alexander and Chandra Mohanty, 3–29. New York: Routledge.

Mooney, Bel. 1999. "Editorial." *The Daily Mail*, July 21, p. A10.

Moore, Robin D. 1997. *Nationalizing Blackness: Afrocubanismo and Artistic Revolution in Havana, 1920–1940*. Pittsburgh: University of Pittsburgh Press.

Morris, Lydia. 2002. *Managing Migration: Civic Stratification and Migrants' Rights*. London: Routledge.

Morrison, Toni. 1992. *Playing in the Dark: Whiteness in the Literary Imagination*. Cambridge, Mass.: Harvard University Press.

———. 1998. *Paradise*. New York: Knopf.

Moser, Caroline. 1993. *Gender Planning and Development*. London: Routledge.

Moutinho, Mario. 2000. *O indígena no pensamento colonial Português: 1895–1961*. Lisbon: Edições Universitárias Lusófonas.

Moya Pons, Frank. 1981. "Dominican National Identity and Return Migration." *Center for Latin American Studies Occasional Papers* 1: 23–33.

———. 1990. "Import-Substitution Industrialization Policies in the Dominican Republic, 1925–61." *Hispanic American Historical Review* 70 (4): 539–77.

———. 1995. *The Dominican Republic: A National History*. New Rochelle, N.Y.: Hispaniola Books.

Mudimbe, Valentin. 1988. *The Invention of Africa*. Bloomington: Indiana University Press.

———. 1994. *The Invention of Africa*. London: James Currey.

Mullard, Chris. 1982. "Multiracial Education in Britain: From Assimilation to Cultural Pluralism." In *Race, Migration, and Schooling*, ed. John Tierney. London: Holt, Rinehart and Winston.

Mullings, Leith. 2005. "Anthropology and Antiracism: An Agenda." Keynote address presented at the annual meeting of the Society for the Anthropology of North America (SANA), Autonomous University of the Yucatan, Mérida, Mexico, May 5.

Muñoz, José Esteban. 1999. *Disidentifications: Queers of Color and the Performance of Politics*. Minneapolis: University of Minnesota Press.

Murnane, Richard J., and Frank Levy. 1996. *Teaching the New Basic Skills: Principles for Educating Children to Thrive in a Changing Economy*. New York: Free Press.

Murray, Alison. 1998. "Debt-Bondage and Trafficking: Don't Believe the Hype." In *Global Sex Workers*, ed. Kamala Kempadoo and Jo Doezema, 51–64. London: Routledge.

Murray, Charles. 1984. *Losing Ground: American Social Policy, 1950 to 1980*. New York: Basic Books.

Mustapha, A. R. 1985. "On Combating Women's Exploitation and Oppression in Nigeria." In *Women in Nigeria*, ed. S. Bappa and the Women in Nigeria Editorial Committee, 241–46. London: Zed.

Narayan, Uma. 1997. *Dislocating Cultures: Identities, Traditions, and Third World Feminism*. London: Routledge.

Nash, June and Maria Patricia Fernandez-Kelly, eds. 1983. *Women, Men, and the International Division of Labor*. Albany: State University of New York Press.

National Center for Education Statistics. 1989. *Digest of Educational Statistics*. Washington, D.C.: NCES.

Newell, William W. 1983 [1894]. "The Importance and Utility of the Collection of Negro Folklore." In *Strange Ways and Sweet Dreams: Afro-American Folklore from the Hampton Institute*, ed. Donald Waters, 186–90. Boston: G. K. Hall.

Nielsen, Kai. 2003. *Globalization and Justice*. Amherst, N.Y.: Humanity Books.

Niger-Thomas, Margaret. 2001. "Women and the Arts of Smuggling." *African Studies Review* 44 (2): 43–70.

Nyberg, Anita. 2003. "Tillväxt i obalans: Om kvinnors och mäns sysselsättning, loner och hushållsarbete." In *Arbetsliv i omvandling*, ed. Casten Von Otter, 123–40. Stockholm: Arbetslivsinstitutet.

Obichere, Boniface. 1975. "Afro-Americans in Africa: Recent Experiences." In *Black Homeland/Black Diaspora*, ed. Jacob Drachler, 15–42. Port Washington, N.Y.: Kennikat Press.

Ogden, Jessica. 1996. "Producing Respect: The 'Proper Woman' in Postcolonial Kampala." In *Postcolonial Identities in Africa*, ed. Richard Werbner and Terence Ranger, 165–92. London: Zed.

Oguntoye, Katharina, May Opitz, and Dagmar Schultz, eds. 1991. *Showing Our Colors: Afro–German Women Speak Out*. Amherst: University of Massachusetts Press.

Okojie, Christiana, O. Okojie, K. Eghafona, G. Vincent-Osaghae, and V. Kalu. 2003. "Report of Field Survey in Edo State, Nigeria." Report to the Programme of Action against Trafficking in Minors and Young Women from Nigeria into Italy for the Purpose of Sexual Exploitation. Turin, Italy: United Nations Interregional Crime and Justice Research Institute.

Oliver, Paul. 1990. Young, Black, and Gifted: Afro-American and Afro-Caribbean Music in Britain 1963–88. In *Black Music in Britain: Essays on the Afro-Asian Contribution to Popular Music*, ed. Anthony Marks Milton Keynes: Open University Press.

Olwig, Karen. 1998. Caribbean Family Land: A Modern Commons. *Plantation Society in the Americas* 4 (2 and 3): 135–58.

Omi, Michael, and Howard Winant. 1986. *Racial Formation in the United States from the 1960s to the 1980s*. New York: Routledge and Kegan Paul.

Ong, Aihwa. 1987. *Spirits of Resistance and Capitalist Discipline: Factory Women in Malaysia*. Albany: State University of New York Press.

——.1995. "Women out of China: Travelling Tales and Travelling Theories in Postcolonial Feminism." In *Women Writing Culture*, ed. Ruth Behar and Deborah Gordon, 350–72. Berkeley: University of California Press.

——. 1999. *Flexible Citizenship: The Cultural Logic of Transnationality*. Durham, N.C.: Duke University Press.

Ong, Aihwa, and Donald M. Nonini, eds. 1997. "Chinese Transnationalism as an Alternative Modernity." In *Ungrounded Empires: The Cultural Politics of Modern Chinese Nationalism*, ed. Aihwa Ong and Donald M. Nonini, 3–33. New York: Routledge.

Orovio, Helio. 1999. "La timba brava." Paper presented at the Cubadisco Coloquio de Música Cubana I, Havana, May 10–15.

Ortiz, Fernando. 1995. *Cuban Counterpoint: Tobacco and Sugar*. Durham, N.C.: Duke University Press.

Orubuloye, I. O., Pat Caldwell, and John C. Caldwell. 1994. " Commercial Sex Workers in Nigeria in the Shadow of AIDS." In *Sexual Networking and AIDS in Sub-Saharan Africa: Behavioural Research and the Social Context*, ed. I. O. Orubuloye, John C. Caldwell, Pat Caldwell, and Gigi Santow, 101–116. Canberra: Health Transition Centre, Australia National University.

Osgerby, Bill. 1998. *Youth in Britain since 1945*. Oxford: Blackwell.

Osofsky, Gilbert. 1966. *Harlem: The Making of a Ghetto*. New York: Harper and Row.

Oyewumi, Oyeronke. 1997. *The Invention of Women: Making an African Sense of Western Gender Discourses*. Minneapolis: University of Minnesota Press.

Pacini Hernandez, Deborah, and Reebee Garofalo. 1999/2000. "Hip Hop in Havana: Rap, Race and National Identity in Contemporary Cuba." *Journal of Popular Music Studies* 11/12: 18–47.

Paley, Julia. 1999. *Marketing Democracy: Power and Social Movements in Post-Dictatorship Chile*. Berkeley: University of California Press.

Palmberg, Mai, and Kirkegaard, Annemette, eds. 2002. *Playing with Identities in Contemporary Music in Africa*. Uppsala: Nordic Africa Institute.

Palmié, Stephan. 2002. *Wizards and Scientists: Explorations in Afro-Cuban Modernity and Tradition*. Durham, N.C.: Duke University Press.

Parreñas, Rhacel. 2001. *Servants of Globalization: Women, Migration, and Domestic Work*. Stanford, Calif.: Stanford University Press.

Pattanaik, Bandana. 2002. "Conclusion: Where Do We Go from Here?" In *Transnational Prostitution*, ed. Susanne Thorbek and Bandana Pattanaik, 217–30. London: Zed.

Patterson, Tiffany, and Kelley, Robin. 2000. "Unfinished Migrations: Reflections on the African Diaspora and the Making of the Modern World." *African Studies Review* 43 (1): 11–46.

Patullo, Polly. 1996. "Reclaiming the Heritage Trail: Culture and Identity." In *Last Resorts: The Cost of Tourism in the Caribbean*, ed. Polly Patullo. Kingston: Ian Randle.

Pedreira, Antonio S. 1935. *La actualidad del jíbaro*. Río Piedras, P.R.: Universidad de Puerto Rico.

Pereira, Daniel. 1984. *A situação da Ilha de Santiago no primeiro quartel do século XVIII*. São Vicente, Cape Verde: Edição do Instituto Caboverdiano do Livro.

Petras, James. 1990. "The World Market: Battleground for the 1990s." *Journal of Contemporary Asia*. 20 (2): 145–176.

Petryna, Adriana. 2002. *Life Exposed: Biological Citizenship after Chernobyl*. Princeton, N.J.: Princeton University Press.

Phillippo, James. 1969 [1843]. *Jamaica: Its Past and Present State*. London: Davisons of Pall Mall.

Piot, Charles. 1999. *Remotely Global: Village Modernity in West Africa*. Chicago: University of Chicago Press.

Pipher, Mary. 1994. *Reviving Ophelia: Saving the Selves of Adolescent Girls*. New York: Ballantine.

Povinelli, Elizabeth A. 2002. *The Cunning of Recognition: Indigenous Alterities and the Making of Australian Multiculturalism*. Durham, N.C.: Duke University Press.

Povinelli, Elizabeth, and George Chauncey. 1999. "Thinking Sexuality Transnationally." *Gay and Lesbian Quarterly* 5 (4): 439–50.

Pratt, Mary Louise. 1992. *Imperial Eyes: Travel Writing and Transculturation*. London: Routledge.

Pred, Allan and Michael J. Watts. 1993. *Reworking Modernity: Capitalisms and Symbolic Discontent*. New Brunswick, N.J.: Rutgers University Press.

Price, Richard. 1998. *The Convict and the Colonel*. Boston: Beacon Press.

Price, Richard, and Sally Price. 2003. *The Root of Roots or, How Afro-American Anthropology Got Its Start*. Chicago: Prickly Paradigm Press.

Prina, Franco. 2003. "Trade and Exploitation of Minors and Young Nigerian Women for Prostitution in Italy." Report to the Programme of Action against Trafficking in Minors and Young Women from Nigeria into Italy for the Purpose of Sexual Exploitation. Turin, Italy: United Nations Interregional Crime and Justice Research Institute.

Pullen-Berry, Elizabeth. 1903. *Jamaica as It Is, 1903*. London: T. Fisher Unwin.

Pusich, António. 1860–61. *Memória ou descrição fisico-politico das Ilhas de Cabo Verde (1810)*. Parte não oficial, serie 2. Lisbon: Anais do Conselho Ultramarino.

Reddock, Rhoda. 1994. *Women, Labour and Politics in Trinidad and Tobago*. London: Zed.

Reed, Adolph. 1999. *Stirrings in the Jar: Black Politics in the Post Civil Rights Era*. Minneapolis: University of Minnesota Press.

Riggs, Marlon. 1994. *Black Is . . . Black Ain't*. California newsreel.

Roach, Jacqui, and Petal Felix. 1989. "Black Looks." In *The Female Gaze*, ed. Lorraine Gamman and Margaret Marshment, 130–42. Seattle: Real Comet Press.

Robertson, Roland. 1995. "Glocalization: Time-Space and Homogeneity-Heterogeneity." In *Global Modernities*, ed. Mike Featherstone, Scott Lash, and Roland Robertson, 25–44. London: Sage.

Robinson, William H. 1977. "Indian Education at Hampton Institute." In *Stony the Road: Chapters in the History of Hampton Institute*, ed. Keith L. Schall, pp. 1–33. Charlottesville: University Press of Virginia.

Robotham, Don. 1982. "The Notorious Riot." ISER Working Paper, no. 28. Mona: University of the West Indies Press.

——. 1997. "Postcolonialities: The Challenge of New Modernities." *International Social Science Journal* 153: 357–371.

Rodgers-Rose. 1980. *The Black Woman*. Beverly Hills: Sage.

Rodríguez-Vázquez, Juan. 2004. *El sueño que no cesa: La nación deseada en el debate intellectual y politico puertorriqueño, 1920–1940*. San Juan: Ediciones Callejón.

Rodríguez Velez, Wendalina. 1982. *El turbante blanco: Muertos, santos, y vivos en lucha politica*. Santo Domingo: Museo del Hombre Dominicano.

Roediger, David. 1991. *The Wages of Whiteness: Race and the Making of the American Working Class*. London: Verso.

Rofel, Lisa. 1999a. *Other Modernities: Gendered Yearnings in China after Socialism*. Berkeley: University of California Press.

———. 1999b. "Qualities of Desire: Imagining Gay Identities in China." *Gay and Lesbian Quarterly* 5 (4): 451–74.

Rogers, Reuel. 2001. "'Black Like Who?' Afro-Caribbean Immigrants, African Americans, and the Politics of Group Identity." In *Islands in the City: West Indian Migration to New York*, ed. Nancy Foner. Berkeley: University of California Press.

Rose, Tricia. 1994. *Black Noise*. Hanover, N.H.: Wesleyan University Press.

Rouse, Roger. 1995. "Questions of Identity: Personhood and Collectivity in Transnational Migrations to the United States." *Critique of Anthropology*. 15 (4): 351–380.

Ryan, Chris, and C. Michael Hall. 2001. *Sex Tourism*. London: Routledge.

"Saartjie's Journey Comes Full Circle." 2002. *South African Times*, May 1.

Sabuni, Kitti, and Lena Sawyer. 2001. *Afrikaner och arbete i Stockholm: En förstudie*. Stockholm: Afrosvenskarnas Riksförbundet Rapport Serie.

Safa, Helen. 1981. "Runaway Shops and Female Employment: The Search for Cheap Labor." *Signs* 7: 418–434.

———. 1995. *The Myth of the Male Breadwinner: Women and Industrialization in the Caribbean*. Boulder, Colo.: Westview Press.

Sanchez Taylor, Jacqueline. 2000. "Tourism and 'Embodied' Commodities: Sex Tourism in the Caribbean." In *Tourism and Sex*, ed. Stephen Clift and Simon Carter, 41–53. London: Pinter.

San Miguel, Pedro L. 1994. "Un libro para romper el silencio: Estado y campesinos al inicio de la era de Trujillo, de Orlando Inoa." *Estudios Sociales* 27 (98): 83–92.

———. 1997. *La isla imaginada: Historia, identitidad, y utopía en la Española*. Santo Domingo: La Isla Negra and Ediciones La Trinitaria.

Santos, Maria Emília Madeira and Luís de Albuquerque. 2003. *História de Cabo Verde*, vol. 3. Lisbon: Tropical Institute.

Sassen, Saskia. 1994. *Cities in a World Economy*. Thousand Oaks, Calif.: Pine Forge Press.

———. 1999. *Guests and Aliens*. New York: New Press.

———. 2000a. *Globalization and Its Discontents: Essays on the New Mobility of People and Money*. New York: The New Press.

———. 2000b. "Women's Burden: Counter-Geographies of Globalization and the Feminization of Survival." *Journal of International Affairs* 53 (2): 503–24.

Sawyer, Lena. 2000. "Black and Swedish: Racialization and the Cultural Politics of Belonging in Stockholm." Ph.D. diss., University of California, Santa Cruz.

Scarano, Francisco A. 1992. *Haciendas y barrracones: Azúcar y esclavitud en Ponce Puerto Rico, 1800–1850*. Río Piedras, P.R.: Ediciones Huracán.

Schein, Louisa. 2000. "Introduction: East Asian Sexualities." *East Asia* 18 (4): 5–12.

Schill, Michael H., and Richard P. Nathan. 1983. *Revitalizing America's Cities: Neighborhood Reinvestment and Displacement*. Albany: State University New York Press.

Schipper, Mineke. 1999. *Imagining Insiders: Africa and the Question of Belonging*. London: Cassell.

Schmitt, Carl. 1985. *Political Theology: Four Chapters on the Concept of Sovereignty.* Cambridge, Mass.: MIT Press.

——, ed. 1996. *The Concept of the Political.* Chicago: University of Chicago Press.

Scholes, T. E. S. 1899. *The British Empire and Alliances, or Britain's Duty to Her Colonies and Subject Races.* London: Elliot Stock.

Scott, David. 1991. "That Event, This Memory: Notes on the Anthropology of African Diasporas in the New World." *Diaspora* 1 (3): 261–84.

——. 1999. *Refashioning Futures: Criticism after Postcoloniality.* Princeton, N.J.: Princeton University Press.

——. 2000. "The Permanence of Pluralism." In *Without Guarantees: In Honour of Stuart Hall,* ed. Paul Gilroy, Lawrence Grossberg, and Angela McRobbie, 282–301. New York: Verso.

Scott, James C. 1990. *Domination and the Arts of Resistance: Hidden Transcripts.* New Haven, Conn.: Yale University Press.

Sen, Amartya. 1999. *Development as Freedom.* Oxford: Oxford University Press.

Sen, Gita and Caren Grown. 1987. *Development, Crises, and Alternative Visions: Third World Women's Perspectives.* New York: Monthly Review Press.

Senna Barcellos, Cristiano Jose de. 1904. *Alguns apontamentos sobre as fomes de Cabe, desde 1719 a 1904.* Lisbon: Tipografia da Academia Real das Ciências.

Sennah, Kalefa. 2003. "Britain's Great Black Hip Hop Hope." *New York Times,* December 14.

Sharma, Sanjay, John Hutnyk, Aswani Sharma. 1996. *Dis-Orienting Rhythms: The Politics of the New Asian Dance Music.* Atlantic Highlands, N.J.: Zed.

Sharpley-Whiting, T. Denean. 1999. *Black Venus: Sexualized Savages, Primal Fears, and Primitive Narratives in French.* Durham, N.C.: Duke University Press.

Sharps, Ronald L. 1991. *Happy Days and Sorrow Songs: Interpretations of Negro Folklore by Black Intellectuals, 1893–1928.* Washington: George Washington University Press.

Shaw, Carolyn Martin. 2001. "Disciplining the Black Female Body: Learning Feminism in Africa and the United States." In *Black Feminist Anthropology,* ed. Irma McClaurin, 102–25. New Brunswick, N.J.: Rutgers University Press.

Sheriff, Robin. 2000. "Exposing Silence as Cultural Censorship: A Brazilian Case." *American Anthropologist* 102 (1): 114–32.

Shyllon, Folarin. 1982. *Black People in Britain: A Historical and Analytical Overview.* In *Global Dimensions of the African Diaspora,* ed. Joseph Harris. Washington: Howard University Press.

Silva, J. M. da. 1953. *O sistema português de política indígena.* Coimbra: Coimbra Editora Lda.

——. 1955. *O trabalho indígena.* 2d ed. Lisbon: Agência Geral do Ultramar.

Silveira, Onesimo. 1996. "Cabo Verde: Una Experiência Políticanos Trópicas." *Política Internacional* 1 (13): 87–108.

Silverblatt, Irene. 2004. *Modern Inquisitions: Peru and the Origins of the Civilized World*. Durham, N.C.: Duke University Press.

Simmons, Janie, Paul Farmer, and Brooke G. Schoepf. 1996. "A Global Perspective." In *Women, Poverty and AIDS: Sex, Drugs and Structural Violence*, ed. Paul Farmer, et al., 39–90. Monroe, Maine: Common Courage Press.

Sivanandan, A. 1981. From Resistance to Rebellion: Asian and Afro-Caribbean Struggles in Britain. *Race and Class* 23 (2–3): 111–51.

Skidmore, Thomas E. 1974. *Black into White: Race and Nationality in Brazilian Thought*. New York: Oxford University Press.

"Slay Anything," *Hollywood Reporter*, May 21, 2001.

Small, Stephen. 1994. *Racialised Barriers: The Black Experience in the United States and England in the 1980s*. New York: Routledge.

Smith, Barbara, ed. 1983. *Homegirls: A Black Feminist Anthology*. New York: Kitchen Table Women of Color Press.

Smith, Michael Peter and Luis Guarnizo, eds. 1998. *Transnationalism from Below*. New Brunswick, N.J.: Transaction Books.

Smith, Neil. 1996. *The New Urban Frontier: Gentrification and the Revanchist City*. London: Routledge.

Smith, R. T. 1956. *The Negro Family in British Guyana*. London: Routledge and Kegan Paul.

Smith, Valerie. 1998. *Not Just Gender: Black Feminist Readings*. New York: Routledge.

Soja, Edward. 1989. *Postmodern Geographies: The Reassertion of Space in Critical Social Theory*. New York: Verso.

Solomos, John. 1989. *Race and Racism in Britain*. Hampshire: Macmillan.

Spanger, Marlene. 2002. "Black Prostitutes in Denmark." In *Transnational Prostitution: Changing Global Patterns*, ed. Susanne Thorbek and Bandana Pattanaik, 121–36. London: Zed.

Spivak, Gayatri. 1988. "Can the Subaltern Speak?" In *Marxism and the Interpretation of Culture*, ed. Cary Nelson and Lawrence Grossberg, 271–313. Urbana: University of Illinois.

Spivey, Donald. 1978. *Schooling for the New Slavery: Black Industrial Education, 1868–1915*. Westport, Conn.: Greenwood Press.

Stacey, Jackie. 2000. "Global Culture, Global Nature." In *Global Culture, Global Nature*, ed. Sarah Franklin, Celia Lury, and Jackie Stacey. London: Routledge.

Stepan, Nancy L. 1991. *The Hour of Eugenics: Race, Gender and Nation in Latin America*. Ithaca, N.Y.: Cornell University Press.

Stoler, Ann Laura. 1995. *Race and the Education of Desire: Foucault's History of Sexuality and the Colonial Order of Things*. Durham, N.C.: Duke University Press.

Stoller, Paul. 2002. *Money Has No Smell: The Africanization of New York City*. Chicago: University of Chicago Press.

Stolzoff, Norman. 2000. *Wake the Town and Tell the People: Dancehall Culture in Jamaica*. Durham, N.C.: Duke University Press.

Striffler, Steve and Mark Moberg. 2003. *Banana Wars: Power, Production, and History in the Americas*. Durham, N.C.: Duke University Press.

Strong, Tracy B. 1996. Foreword to *The Concept of the Political*, ed. Carl Schmitt. Chicago: University of Chicago Press.

Sudbury, Julia. 2004. "From the Point of No Return to the Women's Prison: Writing Spaces of Confinement into Diaspora Studies." *Canadian Woman Studies* 23 (2): 154–63.

Sutton, Constance and Elsa Chaney, eds. 1987. *Caribbean Life in New York City: Sociocultural Dimensions*. Staten Island: Center for Migration Studies.

Swarns, Rachel L. 2002. "Disillusion Rises Among South Africa's Poor." *New York Times*, December 28, A: 4.

Talbot, Edith A. 1969 [1904]. *Samuel Chapman Armstrong*. New York: Negro Universities Press.

Tamagnini, Eusebio. 1934. "Os problemas da mesticagem." Plenary speech given at the Congresso Nacional de Anthropologia Colonial I. Ediçães da I Exposição Colonial Portuguesa. Porto, Portugal.

Tandia, Oumar. 1998. "Prostitution in Senegal." In *Global Sex Workers*, ed. Kamala Kempadoo and Jo Doezema, 240–45. London: Routledge.

Taylor, Ernest Kweku. 2002. "Trafficking in Women and Girls." Paper presented at the Expert Group Meeting on Trafficking in Women and Girls, Glen Cove, N.Y., November 18–22.

Taylor, Monique. 2002. *Harlem: Between Heaven and Hell*. Minneapolis: University of Minnesota Press.

Terborg-Penn, Rosalyn, and Andrea Benton Rushing, eds. 1996. *Women in Africa and the African Diaspora*. 2d ed. Washington: Howard University Press.

Thomas, Deborah A. 2004. *Modern Blackness: Nationalism, Globalization, and the Politics of Culture in Jamaica*. Durham, N.C.: Duke University Press.

Thomas, John Jacob. 1969 [1889]. *Froudacity*. London: New Beacon Books.

Thome, Jas, and J. Horace Kimball. 1838. *Emancipation in the West Indies: A Six Month's Tour in Antigua, Barbadoes, and Jamaica*. New York: The American Anti-Slavery Society.

Thorbek, Susanne. 2002. "Introduction: Prostitution in a Global Context: Changing Patterns." In *Transnational Prostitution*, ed. Susanne Thorbek and Bandana Pattanaik, 1–11. London: Zed.

Tomazinho, Maria José Clemente. 1996. Uma Perspectiva das Relaçães Entre Senhores e Escraros nallha Santiago na Primeira Metade do Século XIX. MA Thesis. Universidade Nova de Lisboa. Lisbon, Portugal.

Toure. 1998. "Foxy Brown: The Sexy MC Weighs in on the State of Hip Hop." *Rolling Stone.com*, December 2.

Trinh T. Minh-ha. 1988. "Not You/Like You." In *Making Face, Making Soul*, ed. Gloria Anzaldua. San Francisco: Aunt Lute.

———. 1989. *Woman, Native, Other*. Bloomington: Indiana University Press.

———. 1991. *When the Moon Waxes Red: Representation, Gender and Cultural Politics*. New York: Routledge.

Trouillot, Michel Rolph. 1992. "The Caribbean Region: An Open Frontier in Anthropological Theory." *Annual Review of Anthropology* 21: 19–42.

———. 1995. *Silencing the Past: Power and Production of History*. Boston: Beacon.

———. 2001. "The Anthropology of the State in the Age of Globalization." *Current Anthropology* 42 (1): 125–38.

———. 2002. "The Otherwise Modern: Caribbean Lessons from the Savage Slot." In *Critically Modern: Alternatives, Alterities, Anthropologies*, ed. Bruce Knauft, 220–37. Indianapolis: Indiana University Press.

———. 2003. *Global Transformations: Anthropology and the Modern World*. New York: Palgrave Macmillan.

Tsing, Anna Lowenhaupt. 1993. *In the Realm of the Diamond Queen: Marginality in an Out-of-the-Way Place*. Princeton, N.J.: Princeton University Press.

———. 2000. "The Global Situation." *Cultural Anthropology* 15 (3): 327–60.

Turits, Richard. 1998. "The Foundations of Despotism: Agrarian Reform, Rural Transformation, and Present-State Compromise in Trujillo's Dominican Republic." In *Identity and Struggle at the Margins of the Nation-State: The Laboring Peoples of Central America and the Hispanic Caribbean*, ed. Avira Chomsky and Aldo Lauria-Santiago, 292–333. Durham, N.C.: Duke University Press.

Turner, Victor W. 1969. *The Ritual Process: Structure and Anti-structure*. Chicago: Aldine.

Ume-Ezeoke, Juliet. 2003. Desk review for the Programme of Action against Trafficking in Minors and Young Women from Nigeria into Italy for the Purpose of Sexual Exploitation. Turin, Italy: United Nations Interregional Crime and Justice Research Institute.

Urbain, Patrick. 1997. "Datos sobre San Antón solicitados durante entrevista con el Arq. Javier Bonnin-Orozco." Ponce, P.R.: Gobierno Autónomo de Ponce, Oficina de Ordenación Territorial.

Van Deburg, W. L. 1992. *New Day in Babylon: The Black Power Movement and American Culture, 1965–1975*. Chicago: University of Chicago Press.

Veiga, Manuel. 1998. *Cabo Verde: Insularidade e literatura*. Paris: Editions Karthala.

Verdery, Katherine. 1993a. "Ethnic Relations, Economies of Shortage, and the Transition in Eastern Europe." In *Socialism: Ideals, Ideologies, and Local Practice*, ed. Chris Hann. New York: Routledge.

———. 1993b. "Nationalism and National Sentiments in Post-Socialist Romania." *Slavic Review* 52: 179–203.

———. 1996. *What Was Socialism, and What Comes Next?* Princeton, N.J.: Princeton University Press.

Vicent, Mauricio. 2001. "Pasaporte conyugal." *El País*, July 22.

Vigdor, Jacob. 2001. "Does Gentrification Harm the Poor?" Unpublished paper, Duke University.

Visweswaran, Kamala. 1998. "Race and the Culture of Anthropology." *American Anthropolgist* 100 (1): 70–83.

Wade, Peter. 1997. *Race and Ethnicity in Latin America*. London: Pluto Press.

Wagner, Ulla, and Bawa Yamba. 1986. "Going North and Getting Attached: The Case of the Gambians." *Ethnos* 51 (3–4): 199–222.

Walcott, Rinaldo. 1997. *Black Like Who: Writing Black Canada*. Toronto: Insomniac Press.

Walker, Alice. 1971. *You Can't Keep a Good Woman Down*. New York: Harcourt Brace Jovanovich.

——. 1983. *In Search of Our Mother's Gardens: Womanist Prose*. New York: Harcourt Brace Jovanovich.

Wallace, Michele. 1990a. *Invisibility Blues: From Pop to Theory*. London: Verso.

——. 1990b. "Modernism, Postmodernism and the Problem of the Visual in Afro-American Culture." In *Out There: Marginalization and Contemporary Cultures*, ed. R. Ferguson, M. Gever, T. T. Minh-ha, and C. West. Cambridge, Mass.: MIT Press.

Walvin, James. 2000. *Making the Black Atlantic: Britain and the African Diaspora*. New York: Cassel.

Ward, Kathryn, ed. 1990. *Women Workers and Global Restructuring*. Ithaca, N.Y.: Cornell University Press.

Ware, Vron. 1992. *Beyond the Pale: White Women, Racism and History*. London: Verso.

Warner, Michael. 2002. "Publics and Counterpublics." *Public Culture* 14 (1): 49–90.

Waters, Donald J., ed. 1983. *Strange Ways and Sweet Dreams: Afro-American Folklore from the Hampton Institute*. Boston: G. K. Hall.

Waters, Malcom. 1995. *Globalization*. New York: Routledge.

Waters, Mary C. 1994a. "Ethnic and Racial Identities of Second-Generation Black Immigrants in New York City." *International Migration Review* 28: 795–820.

——. 1994b. "West Indian Immigrants, African-Americans and Whites in the Workplace: Different Perspectives on American Race Relations." Paper presented at the American Sociological Association, Los Angeles, August 5–9.

——. 1996a. "Ethnic and Racial Groups in the USA: Conflict and Cooperation." In *Ethnicity and Power in the Contemporary World*, ed. Kumar Rupensinghe and V. Tishkov. London: U.N. University.

——. 1996b. "Ethnic and Racial Identities of Second-Generation Black Immigrants in New York City." In *The New Second Generation*, ed. Alejandro Portes. New York: Russell Sage Foundation.

——. 1999. *Black Identities: West Indian Immigrant Dreams and American Realities*. Cambridge, Mass.: Harvard University Press.

Watkins-Owens, Irma. 1996. *Blood Relations: Caribbean Immigrants and the Harlem Community 1900–1930*. Bloomington: Indiana University Press.

——. 2001. "Early Twentieth-Century Caribbean Women: Migration and Social Networks in New York City." In *Islands in the City: West Indian Migration to New York*, ed. Nancy Foner. Berkeley: University of California Press.

Wattie, Chris. 2000. National Post Online News. "Ex-NBA Player's Custody Case Reaches High Court." http://nationalpost.com/news/story.html?f=/stories/20000630/331979. html. June 30.

Weitzer, Ronald. 2000. "Why We Need More Research on Sex Work." In *Sex for Sale*, ed. Ronald Weitzer, 1–17. London: Routledge.

West-Duran, Alan. 2004. "Rap's Diasporic Dialogues: Cuba's Redefinition of Blackness." *Journal of Popular Music Studies* 16 (1): 4–39.

Westwood, Sallie, and Phizacklea, Annie. 2000. *Trans-Nationalism and the Politics of Belonging*. London: Routledge.

White, Ackrel E. 1878. "To the Hampton Alumni Association." *Southern Workman* 7 (7): 54.

White, E. Frances. 2001. *Dark Continent of Our Bodies: Black Feminism and the Politics of Respectability*. Philadelphia: Temple University Press.

White, Elisa Joy. 2002. "The New Irish Storytelling: Media, Representations and Racialised Identities." In *Racism and Anti-Racism in Ireland*, ed. Ronit Lentin and Robbie McVeigh, 102–28. Belfast: Beyond the Pale.

Whitfield, Esther. 2002. "Autobiografía sucia: The Body Impolitic of *Trilogía sucia de la Habana*." *Revista de Estudios Hispánicos* 36 (2): 329–53.

Whitten, Norman E. Jr., and Arlene Torres. 1998. "To Forge the Future in the Fires of the Past: An Interpretive Essay on Racism, Domination, Resistance, and Liberation." In *Blackness in Latin America and the Caribbean*, vol. 1, ed. Norman E. Whitten, Jr. and Arlene Torres, 3–33. Bloomington: Indiana University Press.

Whitten, Norman E. Jr., and Arlene Torres, eds. 1998. *Blackness in Latin America and the Caribbean*, vols. 1 and 2. Bloomington: Indiana University Press.

Wijers, Marjan. 1998. "Women, Labor and Migration: The Position of Trafficked Women and Strategies for Support." In *Global Sex Workers*, ed. Kamala Kempadoo and Jo Doezema, 69–78. London: Routledge.

Wilk, Richard. 2002. "Television, Time, and the National Imaginary in Belize." In *Media Worlds*, ed. Faye Ginsburg, Lila Abu-Lughod, and Brian Larkin, 171–86. Berkeley: University of California Press.

Williams, Brackette. 1996. "Introduction: Mannish Women and Gender after the Act." In *Women Out of Place*. London: Routledge.

Williams, Eric. 1993 [1944]. *Capitalism and Slavery*. London: André Deutsch.

Wilson, C. A. 1929. *Men of Vision: A Series of Biographical Sketches of Men Who Have Made Their Mark Upon Time*. Kingston, Jamaica: The Gleaner Co., Ltd.

Wilson, James, and George Kelling. 1982. "Broken Windows: The Police and Public Safety." *Atlantic Monthly* 249 (3): 1–11.

Wilson, William Julius. 1978. *The Declining Significance of Race: Blacks and Changing American Institutions*. Chicago: University of Chicago Press.

——. 1987. *The Truly Disadvantaged: The Inner City, The Underclass, and Public Policy*. Chicago: University of Chicago Press.

Winant, Howard. 2000. "Race and Race Theory." *Annual Review of Sociology* 26: 169–85.

———. 2001. *The World Is a Ghetto: Race and Democracy since World War II*. New York: Basic Books.

Winks, Robin. 1997. *The Blacks in Canada: A History*. 2d ed. Montreal: McGill-Queen's University Press.

Wolf, Eric. 1982. *Europe and the People without History*. Berkeley: University of California Press.

Wood, Joe. 1989. "Sex and the Single Negro: Dany Laferrière's Penile Code." *Village Voice* 28 (February): 47–48.

X, Malcolm. 1965. *Malcolm X Speaks: Selected Speeches and Statements*. New York: Grove Press.

Yamba, Bawa. 1983. "En afrikans möte med Sverige." In *Afrikaner i Sverige*, ed. Statens Invandrarverk, 24–51. Linköping: Linköpings Tryckeri.

Yelvington, Kevin A. 2002. "History, Memory, and Identity: A Programmatic Prolegomenon." *Critique of Anthropology* 22 (3): 227–56.

Zavala, Iris M. 1992. *Colonialism and Culture: Hispanic Modernisms and the Social Imaginary*. Bloomington: Indiana University Press.

Zuberi, Tukufu. 2001. *Thicker than Blood: How Racial Statistics Lie*. Minneapolis: University of Minnesota Press.

Zukin, Sharon. 1995. *The Cultures of Cities*. Cambridge: Blackwell.

CONTRIBUTORS

ROBERT ADAMS JR. is the associate director of the Institute of African American Research at the University of North Carolina, Chapel Hill. An anthropologist by training, he is currently completing a book on Dominican Vodú. His research interests include the African Diaspora, Afro-Caribbean religions, critical race theory, education policy, poetics, and social theory. He has conducted field research in Brazil, the Dominican Republic, Haiti, Mexico, and South Africa.

LEE D. BAKER is an associate professor of cultural anthropology and African and African American Studies at Duke University. He is the author of *From Savage to Negro: Anthropology and the Construction of Race, 1896–1954* and editor of *Life in America: Identity and Everyday Experience.* He has recently completed a manuscript entitled *Performers, Reformers, and Racists: Anthropology and the Racial Politics of Culture.*

JACQUELINE NASSY BROWN is an assistant professor of anthropology at Hunter College of the City University of New York. Focusing on the mutual construction of race and place in Britain, her work examines the role of localization processes in the formation of racial categories, communities, and identities, including those that cross national boundaries and might be called diasporic. Her goal of lending ethnographic depth to the study of black Atlantic cultures is evident in her book, *Dropping Anchor, Setting Sail: Geographies of Race in Black Liverpool.*

TINA M. CAMPT is associate professor of women's studies at Duke University. As a historian of modern Germany and as a feminist oral historian, Campt theorizes processes of racialization, gendering, and subjecthood in the history of black Germans during the Third Reich. She is the author of *Other Germans: Black Germans and the*

Politics of Race, Gender, and Memory in the Third Reich. She is currently working on a project on memory and the African Diaspora in Europe.

KAMARI M. CLARKE is an associate professor at Yale University and a research scientist at the Yale Law School. Over the years, Clarke's research has ranged from studies of social and religious movements in the United States and West Africa to related transnational legal movements to inquiries into the cultural politics of power and justice. She is the author of *Mapping Yoruba Networks: Power and Agency in the Making of Transnational Networks* and is completing a book on the human rights movements of nongovernmental organizations (NGOs) and the cultural politics of international treaties and tribunals.

RAYMOND CODRINGTON is the founding director of the Julian C. Dixon Institute for Cultural Studies and the assistant curator of anthropology at the Natural History Museum of Los Angeles County. Earlier, he was an assistant professor of anthropology at the State University of New York, Purchase. His research interests include rap music, popular culture, race, and museum studies. He has conducted fieldwork in London, Chicago, and New York.

GRANT FARRED is an associate professor in the literature program at Duke University. He is author of *What's My Name? Black Vernacular Intellectuals* and *Midfielders Moment: Coloured Literature and Culture in Contemporary South Africa*. He is also the editor of *Rethinking C. L. R. James* (Basil Blackwell Publishers, 1996). His forthcoming work includes the coedited volume (with C. L. Cole), *Exercising Power: The Athletic Body in Public Space* and *Long Distance Love: A Passion for Football*. He is the general editor of the journal *South Atlantic Quarterly*.

KESHA FIKES is an assistant professor of anthropology at the University of Chicago. She is completing a manuscript entitled *Managing African Portugal*; it observes the Portuguese state's regulation of Cape Verdean migrant labor practices within an EU-oriented Portugal. Fikes's primary research focus is the paradoxical relationship between the territorial process of decolonization and the legal possibilities of emigration from Africa to the West. She examines the realities of African sovereignty within the context of restrictions that transnationally curtail and monitor African emigrations.

ISAR P. GODREAU is the director of the Institute of Interdisciplinary Research at the University of Puerto Rico at Cayey. She is also an adjunct professor of anthropology at the University of Texas at Austin. Her work examines how dynamics of race, racism, and national identity in Puerto Rico develop in the context of the island's neocolonial relationship to the United States. Her current research interests are focused on developing antiracist pedagogical strategies and census racial categories that are relevant for and respond to the Puerto Rican context.

ARIANA HERNANDEZ-REGUANT is a cultural anthropologist and a music critic. She is currently an assistant professor of media studies at the University of California, San Diego. She has conducted research in both the United States and Cuba and has published articles on Afrocentricity and Kwanzaa, Cuban cultural identity and the Cuban culture industries, late socialism and cultural production, and the globalization of intellectual property. She is currently working on a book manuscript on the commercialization of Cuban popular culture during the 1990s, editing a volume on Cuba's late socialism, and editing another one on Latin Americanism, alternative geographies, and Cuban intellectual production.

JAYNE O. IFEKWUNIGWE is formerly a reader in anthropology at the University of East London and currently a visiting scholar in the Cultural Anthropology Department at Duke University. Her research interests include comparative mixed-race theories and identity politics; feminist, (post)colonial, and transnational geneologies of the African Diaspora; and the discrepant management of public memories in cultural and heritage tourism. She has published widely on these issues. Among her most recent publications are *Scattered Belongings: Cultural Paradoxes of "Race," Nation and Gender* and the edited collection *"Mixed Race" Studies: A Reader*. She is currently working on a new book project entitled *Out of Africa ("By Any Means Necessary"): Recent Clandestine West African Migrants and the Gendered Politics of Survival.*

JOHN L. JACKSON JR., a filmmaker and urban anthropologist, is an associate professor of cultural anthropology at Duke University. His first book, *Harlemworld: Doing Race and Class in Contemporary Black America*, received an honorable mention in 2002 from the American Studies Association for the John Hope Franklin Prize, awarded to "the best-published book in American Studies." His second book, *Real Black: Adventures in Racial Sincerity* was published by the University of Chicago Press in 2005.

ONEKA LABENNETT is an assistant professor in the Department of Sociology and Anthropology at the College of the Holy Cross. She received her Ph.D. in social anthropology from Harvard University in 2002. A native of Guyana, her research focuses on adolescent immigrant girls from the Anglophone Caribbean living in Brooklyn, New York. She is the author of "West Indian Americans," in *Encyclopedia of Sex and Gender: Men and Women in the World's Cultures* (Kluwer Academic Plenum Publishers, 2004). At Holy Cross LaBennett teaches courses such as Youth Culture and Consumption, Constructing Race, and Television and the Family.

NAOMI PABST is an assistant professor of African American studies and American studies at Yale University. Her research interests include black diasporic literature and cultural studies, travel theory, feminist theory, critical race theory, and critical mixed race studies.

LENA SAWYER received her Ph.D. in cultural anthropology from the University of California, Santa Cruz, in 2000. Her dissertation is entitled "Black and Swedish:

Racialization and the Cultural Production of Belonging in Stockholm." She is currently an assistant professor in international and intercultural social work at Mid-Sweden University in Sweden. During the fall of 2002 she was a guest researcher at the Nordic Africa Institute in Uppsala, Sweden, and during the spring and fall of 2003 she worked as a researcher at Uppsala University, Sweden, on the EU research project "The European Dilemma: Institutional Patterns of Racial Discrimination" led by Professor Masoud Kamali. In the spring of 2004 she was on sabbatical in West Africa where she conducted preliminary research on transnational welfare in and between the Gambia and Sweden.

DEBORAH A. THOMAS is an associate professor in Duke University's Department of Cultural Anthropology. A former professional dancer, her work focuses on the changing relationships among the political and cultural dimensions of nationalism, globalization, and popular culture. Her book *Modern Blackness: Nationalism, Globalization, and the Politics of Culture in Jamaica* was published in 2004. She is currently working on a new research project focusing on a contract labor program, developed by the Jamaican Ministry of Labour, that sponsors the seasonal migration of Jamaican women for work in hotels throughout the United States.

Index

Adams, Robert, 15

African Americans: African identity of, 80–81, 84–85, 134; African nobility-redemption narrative and, 133, 134, 140–41; blackness constructed by, 106–7, 120–23; black studies and, 135, 147, 152 n.9; heritage tourism and, 135–38, 146, 150, 152 n.5; intercultural address and, 94–95, 99, 102–4, 108–11; racial uplift discourse and, 38–39, 44–47, 51–52; rap culture and, 306–7; representations of, in mass culture, 140–43, 282–83; use of term, 147–48; West Indians' relations with, 28, 282, 287–88, 290–94, 297 n.4. *See also* Canadian blacks; Hampton Normal and Agricultural Institute; Harlem

African dance: advertisements for, 321, 324; authenticity of Swedish dance teachers and, 327–28; clothing, 324–25; as cultural transmission, 326; geographical Africa and, 328, 329; as natural, 325, 330–31; self-transformation expected from, 322–25; white Swedish women as instructors of, 321, 325, 327–28, 329–32; women as students of, 323

African diaspora, 100–104, 109, 117, 122, 135, 151 n.4, 206–7, 222 n.1

African National Congress (ANC), 231, 235, 238, 241–42, 244–45

Africanness: Africa diasporic and, 100–104, 109, 117, 122, 135, 151 n.4, 206–7, 222; black power movement and, 86, 144–46, 152 n.7; clothing and, 137, 234–35; knowledge of, 148–49, 152 nn.9, 11, 12; Ôyïtúnji African Village (South Carolina) and, 135–39, 146, 152 n.5; of Santiago (Cape Verde), 160, 162–63, 169 n.9; slave narratives and, 133–36, 140–42, 152 n.5; tourism and, 135–38, 146, 150, 152 n.5; Yoruba, 135, 136, 146, 257. *See also* African Americans; African dance; Black identity; Post-apartheid South Africa; South Africa

African nobility-redemption narrative, 133, 134, 140–42

Afrikaner National Party (NP), 235

Canadian blacks: American origins of, 115–22; Elijah Edwards case and, 122–23; exclusion of, from Niagara Conference, 115–16; misconceptions of, 113; police brutality and, 124

Canclini, Garcia, 262

Cannon, Margaret, 114, 115, 127

Cape Verde, 156; African identity of, 160, 162–63; colonial history of, 158; creolization in, 158–59, 169 n.3; immigration and, 164–65; Portugal's relations with, 21, 157, 164–65; racial identification in, 154–55, 160, 166, 169 n.1; slavery in, 159, 161

Capitalism: America and, 346–52; difference and, 8; modernization and, 58; opportunities of, 7–8; post-apartheid South Africa and, 232, 238–39; racial belonging and, 135; racialized labor and, 11–12; sex work as wage labor, 214–15; timba broadcasts and, 263. *See also* Consumerism

Carlisle Indian Industrial School, 43, 48, 54 n.4

Carmichael, Stokely, 145

Carreira, António, 159

Cary, Mary Ann Shadd, 113–14

Catholic Church, 211–12, 224 n.4

Christianity. *See* Hampton Folk-Lore Society; Hampton Normal and Agricultural Institute; Missionaries

Ciudad Santa, 65, 66, 69–70

Civil rights movement, 19, 80–81, 82, 84–85, 104, 117, 144, 283

Clark, Kenneth and Mamie, 283

Clarke, George Elliot, 121–22, 124

Clarke, Kamari Maxine, 19, 20–21

Codrington, Raymond, 29

Collins, Patricia Hill, 119

Colusso, Enrica, 210

Consumerism: adolescents as thoughtful consumers and, 28, 282, 297 n.3; of

African American–influenced rap, 307; African goods in Stockholm and, 318–19; American influences on, 7, 346; cultural imperialism and, 348; cultural products and, 143, 149–50, 280–81, 282–83, 285; identity formation and, 26; positive images of black culture and, 283; radical, 346–49; self-transformation and, 323; sex work and, 214–15; timba and, 261. *See also* Tourism

Cooper, Anna Julia, 49

Cordero, Rafael, 174

Corrêa, Mendes, 163

Cortés, Jose Luis, 254

Crenshaw, Kimberlé, 119

Creoles, 158–59, 166–67, 169 n.3, 339–40, 341, 342, 344

Crummell, Alexander, 49

Cuba: CubaDisco, 264, 276 n.36; pre-revolutionary popular culture of, 256; race in, 179, 180, 250, 255, 259–60, 273 nn.3, 4, 5; Radio Taino, 263, 276 n.35; religion in, 256–57; Special Period, 28, 250, 252, 260–61, 263, 271, 272; tourism in, 27–28, 249–50, 261. *See also* Afro-Cubans; Timba

Cuban Music Institute, 264

Cuevas, Nicolas, 68–69

Cultural production, 16, 139, 302–3, 318–19, 349–53

Dancehall, 26, 290, 347, 350, 352–53

David-West, Tonye, 216

De Klerk, W. B., 231

Delaney, Martin, 113–14

Delgado, Issac, 259

De los Reyes, Paulina, 323

Dizzie Rascal, 310, 311

Dominguez, Virginia, 178

Dominican Republic: Afro-Dominicans, 57–58, 62, 63, 64–70, 72; immigration to Puerto Rico and, 180, 187 n.6; modernist desire in, 57–59, 71; nationalism (*Dominicanidad*) and, 56; privatization of communal lands in, 61, 68; sugar plantations in, 59, 60, 61, 64; tax collection in, 60–61; Trujillo dictatorship in, 68–70; United States and, 59, 61, 66–68; Vodú and, 57–58, 64–70, 72. *See also* Liborismo/Liboristas; San Juan Valley

Donham, Donald, 11, 34 n.5

Douglass, Frederick, 38, 52

Du Bois, W. E. B., 17, 33, 115, 121, 350

Du Cille, Ann, 121

Ebron, Paulla, 317, 321, 327

Edo State, Nigeria, 217–18, 219

Education: black studies departments, 135, 147, 152 n.9; cultural assimilation and, 42; the Hampton idea and, 42, 43; heritage agenda in, 147–49, 152 nn.9, 11, 12; multiculturalism and, 147; racial accommodation in, 42

Edwards, Elijah, 122–23

Elijah Edwards case, 122–23

Elijah Muhammad, 146

Ellison, Ralph, 228

English in the West Indies, The (Froude), 338–39

Essentialism, 115–16, 241

Fanon, Frantz, 124, 163

Farred, Grant, 23

Feminism, 86, 89, 112, 113, 119–21

Fernandes, Gabriel, 163

Fernandez Robaina, Tomás, 274 n.20

Fikes, Kesha, 21

"Foreign Bodies" (Channel Four series), 210–12

Foucault, Michel, 151 n.3, 227, 234, 322

Freyre, G., 155, 169 n.2, 186 n.2

Friedman, Susan, 124

From Five to Seven, 263, 270, 276 n.35

Froude, James Anthony, 338–39

Garveyism, 18, 114, 342, 345

Gates, Henry Louis, 141–42, 143, 252

Gates, Merrill E., 38

Geller, Sarah Michelle, 283

Gentrification: African Americans and, 197–98; displacement and, 195, 205 n.4; eviction of tenants and, 201, 204; of Harlem, 190, 192; privatization and, 193, 195–96, 201–4; profiteering and, 201; public spaces and, 195–96, 201–4; real estate prices and, 197–98; suburbanization and, 194

German blacks: African Americans and, 109; black America used by, 94–95, 109; black identity of, 95–96, 103, 109; blackness constructed by, 100–101, 106–7; communal memory of, 95–96, 109; diasporic relations of, 95–96, 108, 109; isolation of, 104–5

Gilman, Sander, 211, 213

Gilroy, Paul: Black Atlantic and, 13, 14, 25; on black communities, 74–75, 108; on black music, 349; on conceptualizations of race, 226–27; counterculture of modernity and, 349; on dance performance, 267; on defining diaspora, 13, 14; on media images of race, 296–97; on post-apartheid racial identities, 240, 241, 243; public expressions of blackness and, 349; as against race, 229, 234, 235, 237; on the racialized body, 23, 226–27; on syncretism of black expressive cultures, 105; on timba, 252

Godreau, Isar, 21–22

Gomes dos Anjos, José Carlos, 163

Great Britain: antiblack discourse and, 301, 313 n.6; black Jamaicans and, 337, 342; Caribbean immigration to, 300–

McAlister, Elizabeth, 352

Media: African Americans' heritage in, 140–43; antiblack discourse in, 301; black power movement in, 144, 145; black youth attraction to white characters in, 282, 283; *Buffy the Vampire Slayer*, 28–29, 280–85, 287; diasporic consciousness and, 336; *From Five to Seven*, 263, 270, 276 n.35; ghettoization of, 286–87, 297 n.6; images of Africa in, 211–12; Palma Sola movement opposed in, 69–70; pan-Africanism and, 144; race and racism in, 238; rap music, 305–6; residents of San Antón housing project and, 177. *See also music headings*

Meintel, Dierdre, 164

Men: black machismo, 27–28, 266–70, 277 n.45; Cuban male as "other," 266; homosexuality and, 120, 285; privileging of black male oppression, 119–20; timba dancing and, 254

Middle class, 21, 195, 201–4, 324, 343–44, 348–49

Migration: black America, 16, 29, 83; of black Liverpudlian women to United States, 73, 85–86, 88–90; to Canada, 114, 116; of Cape Verdeans, 157, 161–62, 164–65; Caribbean immigration to United Kingdom, 300–301, 313 nn.5, 6; displacement and, 195, 205 n.4; economic stability and, 24–25; forced exile of San Juan Valley peasants and, 64, 68; of Jamaicans, 342–43, 345–47, 352; marriage and, 85–86, 89; of middle class to Harlem, 195, 201–4; of modern blackness, 352; of political refugees, 318, 319; of Puerto Ricans to America, 173; racial identity and, 18–19, 73–74, 159–60; of sex workers, 22–23, 207–8, 214–17, 222; West Africa and, 123, 207–8. *See also* Sex work

Missionaries: American Missionary Association, 42, 43; anthropology and, 47; educational initiatives of, 40–41; in Hawaii, 40–41; in Jamaica, 336, 337, 342; modernity and, 14–15; racial uplift discourse and, 38–39, 44–45, 46–47, 51–52; slaves and, 336, 337; in West Africa, 43

Modern blackness: defined, 345, 352

Modernism: in Dominican Republic, 58–60; elites, 58–59, 62, 65–66, 69–70, 71; Liborismo as threat to, 65; popular, 64; progress and, 61; as sign of desire, 71

Modernity: Atlantic Ocean and, 11–12; black expressive cultural production and, 349–52; blackness and, 62–64, 349–52; defined, 11; modernist project, 58; multivocal history of, 56; national imagination and, 62; progress and, 58; tradition of, 183; whitening and, 173. *See also* Missionaries; Post-apartheid South Africa

Modernization: the body and, 322; borders as defining, 59–61; cattle ranching and, 60–61; Dominican, campaign, 57; economic transformations of, 64; national imagination and, 62

Modood, Tariq, 313 n.2

Morant Bay Rebellion, 340

Morrison, Toni, 228, 232–34, 238

Moton, Robert R., 49–50

Mudimbe, Valentin, 133

Mulatta/mulattoes, 63, 155, 160, 266, 269–70

Mullard, Chris, 118

Mullings, Leith, 3

Multiculturalism, 29, 114, 118, 119, 123–24, 147–48

Muñoz, José Esteban, 186 n.2, 252, 262

Muñoz Martin, Luis, 183

Music: *bomba* , 173, 178, 179, 180–81, 183;

Racial identity (*continued*)
olina) and, 135–39, 146, 152 n.5; in
post-apartheid South Africa, 240–41;
publications by black presses, 148–49,
152 nn.11, 12; in Puerto Rico, 22, 171,
179, 180–81, 182, 187 nn.8, 9; racial
ambiguity, 155, 157–61, 169 n.1; skin
color and, 63, 155, 160, 187 nn.8, 9, 266,
269–70, 272 n.1, 273 n.3, 296. *See also*
Youth
Racial uplift discourse, 38–39, 44–45,
46–47, 51–52
Racism: Afro-Dominicans, 62–63; of
American GIS, 79, 84; black female
sexuality and, 208, 210–13, 223 n.3; in
Canadian multiculturalism, 29, 114,
118–19, 123–24; Caribbean immigrants
in Great Britain and, 300–301, 313
nn.5, 6; Garveyism and, 18, 345;
homophobia and, 120; imperialism
and, 345; *Jamaica's Jubilee* and, 336–
37, 338–39, 343; media representations
of Nigerian women sex workers and,
210–12; neo-Nazism and, 97; racialized body, 23, 184, 210–15, 226–28,
234–35, 241, 322, 324. *See also* Post-
apartheid South Africa; South Africa
Radio Taino, 263, 276 n.35
Randolph, A. Philip, 114
Rangel, Charles, 195, 200
Ranger, Terrance, 143
Rap music: African Americans and, 306,
308; American influence on, 306, 308,
310; celebrity and social mobility of
U.S. rappers, 309; emergence of, 302–
3; globalization and, 308, 314 n.14; language of, 307, 309–11; mainstreamers
of, 306–7; Mastermind Crew, 303;
radio programming and, 305–6; violent images in, 235, 307–9, 314 n.15. *See
also* Timba
Rap videos, 309, 310, 312

Reggae, 26, 303, 304, 309–11, 315 n.16
Riggs, Marlon, 120
Robinson, Jackie, 114
Rolando, Gloria, 274 n.20
Roots: Saga of an American Family
(Haley), 140–42
Roots Manuva, 309–10
Roth, Philip, 228

San Juan Valley: cattle ranching in, 61;
Dominican modernism challenged
by, 59–60; fencing of, 60, 63; Haitian
nationalists aided by residents of, 66;
staple crops cultivation in, 60, 61; Tru-
jillo dictatorship and, 68. *See also*
Liborismo/Liboristas
Santeria, 256–57, 277 n.45
Sawyer, Lena, 29–30
Schill, Michael, 205 n.4
Schmitt, Carl, 230, 246 nn.1, 3
Scott, David, 168, 348
Scott, James, 57
Scott, Patricia Bell, 120
Sen, Amartya, 221
Sexuality: of adolescents, 284–85, 290,
291; Afro-Cuban men and, 266–70;
black machismo and, 27–28, 266–70,
277 n.45; blackness and, 266; clothing
styles and, 292–93; dance moves (*el
tembleque*) and, 254, 267, 270; deviant
black female, 208–13, 223 n.3; graphic
images of, 268, 277 n.50; homosexuality, 120, 285; mulatta, 266, 269–70;
nation building and, 322
Sex work: agency in, 208, 213, 215, 217,
220, 224 n.6; deviant female sexuality
as marketing strategies, 213; as economic strategy, 219, 220; from Edo
State, 217–18, 219; empowerment of,
221; HIV/AIDS, 225 n.8; initiatives for,
211–12, 221, 224 n.4, 225 n.9; madams
and, 213, 217, 224 n.6; media represen-

tations of, 210–12; migration and, 22–23, 207–8, 214–17, 222; poverty and, 214, 215, 216, 224 n.7

Sharpley-Whiting, T. Denean, 208, 211

Silveira, Onesimo, 163

Sivanandan, A., 313 n.2

Slavery: African complicity in, 141, 142; apprenticeships and, 340; asylum in Canada, 113, 114–15, 119, 122; Atlantic slave trade, 11; British government and, 341–342; Cape Verde and, 159, 161, 162; debt bondage and, 214, 215, 216, 224 n.7; *Jamaica's Jubilee* and, 336–37, 338–39, 343; missionaries and, 336, 337; narratives, 133–36, 140–42, 152 n.5; Negro associated with, 144; as wage labor, 340; West Indian blacks and, 339

Small, Stephen, 124

Smith, Barbara, 119–20

Smith, Valerie, 119–20

Social Darwinism, 59, 337, 338, 339, 344

South Africa: African National Congress (ANC), 231, 235, 238, 241–42, 244–45; Afrikaner National Party (ANC), 235; Baartman, Saartjie, 211, 212, 213, 223 n.3; black opposition in, 229–30; black youth violence in, 230; Nelson Mandela, 230, 231–32, 236–37, 243; Thabo Mbeki, 230, 231, 232, 238–39, 242–45; migration to Sweden from, 319; Non-European Unity Movement (NEUM), 235; Truth and Reconciliation Commission, 231; unemployment in, 238, 239, 243

Southern Workman, 43, 44–45, 46

Spivak, Gayatri Chakravorty, 115–16

Stacey, Jackie, 322

Stoller, Paul, 317

Student Nonviolent Coordinating Committee (SNCC), 145

Sudbury, Julia, 92n2

Sugar plantations, 59, 60, 61, 64, 65

Thatcher, Margaret, 302

Thomas, Deborah, 30–31

Thome, James, 340

Thompson, Robert Farris, 13

Timba, 27–28, 249; black machismo and, 27–28, 266–70, 277 n.45; celebrity culture of, 261, 263, 271; criticism of, 267–68; Cuban identity and, 251, 260–62, 272; dance moves (*el tembleque*), 254, 267, 270; *From Five to Seven*, 263, 270, 276 n.35; government support for, 262; La Tropical club, 264–65, 276 n.38; love as theme in, 265, 266; lyrics of, 249, 252–54, 255, 260, 266, 272 n.1; marketing of, 263, 271; moña and, 275 n.29; NG La Banda, 254, 255, 258, 259, 264, 274 n.15, 276 n.33; racial prejudice addressed by, 255; as resistance, 271; Santeria, 256–67, 277 n.45; sexualized performances of, 252–53; *solar* (inner-city tenement) and, 258–59

Tourism: aesthetic of local poverty and, 256; for African culture enthusiasts, 321; in Cuba, 27–28, 249–50, 256, 261; heritage, 135–38, 146, 150, 152 n.5; homeland visits and, 136–38, 141–42; in Puerto Rico, 174, 179, 183, 187 n.3

Toussaint, François Dominique, 228, 231

Trinh Minh-ha, 125

Trouillot, Michel Rolph, 58, 120

Trujillo, Rafael Leonidas, 68–70

Tubman, Harriet, 114

Turnley, David, 264

Tuskegee Institute, 42

Tutu, Desmond, 231

United States: black subjectivity in, 117, 125–29, 146–48; civil rights movement in, 19, 80–81, 82, 84–85, 104, 117, 144–

United States (*continued*)
45, 283; Dominican Republic and, 59, 61, 66–69; government support for buisness in, 195–96; hip-hop in, 303; imperialism and, 59; institutional racism in, 123–24; Jamaican immigration to, 342–43, 345–46; multiculturalism in, 147–48; Puerto Rico and, 173, 178, 182, 187 n.4; rap culture in, 235, 307–9, 314 n.15; representations of black history in, 140–43

Ventura, Manuel, 69
Ventura Rodriguez, Leon and Plinio, 68–69
Vicent, Mauricio, 266
Vigdor, Jacob, 205 n.5
Vodú, 57–58, 64–70, 72, 146

Walcott, Rinaldo, 115, 120–21, 124
Walker, Alice, 112, 113
Wallace, Michelle, 283, 295
Washington, Booker T., 42
Waters, Mary, 118, 289
West Africa, 43, 135–39, 146, 152 n.5
West-Duran, Alan, 252
West Indian adolescent girls: *Buffy the Vampire Slayer* and, 28–29, 280–85; clothing of, 292–93; consumption and leisure evaluated by, 291–92; on gender roles, 289; mobility of, 289; multiple identities negotiated by, 289–90; negative/positive frameworks for interpretation, 291–92, 294–96; parents involvement with, 289–90, 298 n.7; television show preferences, 286–87, 297 n.6
West Indians: African Americans' relations with, 28, 282, 287–88, 290–94, 297 n.4; *The English in the West Indies* (Froude), 338–39; immigration of, to United Kingdom, 300–301, 313 nn.5, 6;

London sound influenced by, 309–11, 315 n.16; racialization of, 300–301, 313 nn.5, 6
Westwood, Tim, 306, 307
Whiteness: black identity, 144–45, 152 n.7; black youth attraction to, 282, 283; *blanqueamiento* (whiteness), 22, 171–73, 182; consumer products and, 287; displacements of blackness, 180; national symbols and, 184; in *Paradise* (Morrison), 232–35, 238; in post-apartheid South Africa, 232–38; privilege of, 63; racial discourse and, 235; social mobility in America and, 346
Williams, Brackette, 269
Williams, Rhonda, 119–20
Winks, Robin, 115
Wolf, Eric, 56
Women: Africa as common heritage, 86, 99–104; black identity of, 73, 104–7; on black machismo, 268–70; dance and, 254, 321, 325, 327–28, 329–32; employment of, 207, 318, 321, 323–25, 327–28, 329–32, 334 n.7; feminism and, 86, 89, 112, 113, 119–21; as heads of households, 180–81, 187 n.7, 282; as hip-hop artists, 292–93, 295; HIV/AIDS infection and, 225 n.8; interracial marriages and, 75–76, 265–66, 269–70, 319–20; labor migrations of, 164; on liberating spaces of America, 86, 87, 89, 91; as mothers of West Indian adolescent girls, 290–91, 298 n.7; mulatta, 266, 269–70, 273 n.3; Nigerian women sex workers (*see* Sex work); political activism of, 98, 103–4; sexualized images of, 210–13, 223 n.3. *See also* West Indian adolescent girls
Wright, Richard, 114

Yamba, Bawa, 319
Yoruba, 135, 136, 146, 257

Youth: on America, 81–83, 303, 347; *Buffy the Vampire Slayer* and, 28–29, 280–85, 287; clothing of, 292–94, 295, 307; as consumers, 7, 28, 282, 283, 297 n.3, 348; in Cuba, 250, 254; Jamaican, on America, 347–48; migration of, 352; multiple identities negotiated by, 289–90, 310–11; music and, 280, 304–5, 307–9, 346; positive representations of African Americans and, 282–83; racial identity of, 82–85, 121–22, 287, 308; sexuality of, 284–85, 290, 291; social class status and, 281–82; social space for, 281, 287, 290; violence and, 230, 301, 307–9; visibility of, 285–86, 294; West Indian–African American relations and, 28, 282, 287–88, 290–94, 297 n.4; whiteness as attractive to, 181, 283. *See also* Hip-hop cultural production; Rap music

Zamora, Oreste, 66
Zimbabwe, 244–45

LIBRARY OF CONGRESS CATALOGING-IN-PUBLICATION DATA

Globalization and race : transformations in the cultural

production of blackness / edited by Kamari Maxine Clarke

and Deborah A. Thomas.

p. cm.

Includes bibliographical references and index.

ISBN 0-8223-3759-2 (cloth : alk. paper)

ISBN 0-8223-3772-x (pbk. : alk. paper)

1. Black race. 2. Blacks—Race identity. 3. Blacks—

Folklore. 4. African Americans in poular culture.

5. Globalization and culture. 6. Globalization—Political

aspects. 7. African diaspora. I. Clarke, Kamari Maxine

II. Thomas, Deborah A.

GN645.G54 2006

305.896—dc22   2005031754